Further praise for HUMAN GIVENS:

"In *Human Givens* Griffin and Tyrrell offer innovative perspectives on promoting effective living. They have synthesized brain and social research in such a way that they provide new templates for understanding how to unlock the best in human nature."
Dr Jeffrey K. Zeig, Director of the Milton H. Erickson Foundation

"[This] approach offers a refreshing alternative to reams of expensive psychobabble." *The Big Issue*

"Real breakthroughs in the behavioural sciences are rare, and it's smart to beware of hype. But not all scientific progress is incremental. Sometimes, as in the germ theory of disease, it's exponential. Griffin and Tyrrell's contribution advances psychology as much as the introduction of the Arabic numeric system with its zero digit advanced mathematics." *Washington Times*

"While books are never a cure for what ails us in life, they are often a catalyst, a trigger that fires off those rare and profound 'aha!' moments that lead to deeper insights and understanding. *Human Givens* is such a catalyst." *Jack Davies*

"Important original work ... both aesthetically pleasing and of immense practical use... has great relevance to all areas of life... could save (tax payers) millions of pounds. A remarkable achievement, which should attract the attention of any truly curious human being."
Dr Farouk Okhai, Consultant Psychiatrist in Psychotherapy

"*Human Givens* is the most practical and intuitive book I've read in years. People have been speculating about the utility of dreams for decades, but I think you guys have it hammered."
Charles Hayes, Autodidactic Press, USA

"Psychology doesn't have to be difficult and mystique has no part especially when the writers cross boundaries to take from all quarters and from there synthesize with such clarity. Some purists may not like it [*Human Givens*] but broken fences facilitate a wider view and allow one to see further." *Leo Kingdon*

HUMAN GIVENS

ALSO BY THE AUTHORS

Godhead: The brain's big bang
Joe Griffin and Ivan Tyrrell

Why We Dream
(updated version of *Dreaming Reality:
How dreaming keeps us sane or can drive us mad*)
Joe Griffin and Ivan Tyrrell

How to lift depression ... fast
Joe Griffin and Ivan Tyrrell

How to Master Anxiety
Joe Griffin and Ivan Tyrrell

*Freedom from Addiction: The secret
behind successful addiction busting*
Joe Griffin and Ivan Tyrrell

*Release from Anger: Practical help
for controlling unreasonable rage*
Joe Griffin and Ivan Tyrrell

*An Idea in Practice: Using the
human givens approach*
Joe Griffin and Ivan Tyrrell (Eds)

A Universe that Dreams
Joe Griffin

Listening to Idries Shah
Ivan Tyrrell

The Origin of Dreams
Joe Griffin

The Survival Option
Ivan Tyrrell

HUMAN GIVENS

An empowering approach to emotional
health and clear thinking

Joe Griffin and Ivan Tyrrell

PUBLISHING

PUBLISHING

PRINTING HISTORY:
New, updated paperback edition: 2024

Hardback edition first published in Great Britain 2003
Reprinted 2003

Paperback edition first published in Great Britain 2004
Reprinted 2006, 2007, 2011

2nd edition 2013
Reprinted 2015, 2018, 2020

Copyright © Joe Griffin and Ivan Tyrrell 2003, 2013, 2015, 2018, 2023

The right of Joe Griffin and Ivan Tyrrell to be identified as the authors of this work has been asserted in accordance with sections 77 and 78 of the Copyright Designs and Patents Act 1988. Some of the material, expanded in this book, has been published previously in the form of monographs.

Published by HG Publishing an imprint of
Human Givens Publishing Ltd, Chalvington,
East Sussex, BN27 3TD, United Kingdom.
www.humangivens.com

A catalogue record for this book is available from the British Library.

1-899398-92-9
ISBN-13 978-1-899398-92-8

All rights reserved. No part of this publication may be reproduced, stored in a retrieval system, or transmitted in any form or by any means electronic, mechanical, photocopying, recording, or otherwise, without the prior written permission of the publishers.

Typeset in Sabon and Franklin Gothic.
Printed and bound by Short Run Press Limited, Exeter, EX2 7LW.

CONTENTS

Acknowledgments v
Foreword by Dr Farouk Okhai vi

PART I: NEW DISCOVERIES ABOUT HUMAN NATURE
    Prologue 3

Chapter 1   Seeking completion 5
    The need for meaning
    The postmodernist fallacy
    The science of human nature
    Adapting to now

Chapter 2   Where does human nature come from? 17
    The risk and the prize
    Why the brain is a metaphorical pattern-matching organ
    Without sleep, we warm blooded creatures die

Chapter 3   The dreaming brain 30
    Modern dream theories
    The all-important PGO spikes
    Recording dreams
    To dream, and let off steam
    Why we dream in metaphor – and then forget our dreams
    The richness of the REM state
    Anticipating reality
    Is dreaming connected to learning?
    Why we evolved to dream
    A dream ship
    Some bitter juice
    Using dreams intelligently

| Chapter 4 | The mind entranced: sane and insane | 62 |

          First things first – directing attention
          The trance state of dreaming
          Posthypnotic suggestions and the REM state
          Hypnosis and expectation
          Scientific study of hypnosis
          Focusing attention – inwards and outwards
          Uses and abuses of hypnosis
          Dreams, hypnosis and psychosis
          The observing self
          Hypnotic ability

PART II: **APPRECIATING OUR BIOLOGICAL INHERITANCE**

| Chapter 5 | The human givens | 97 |

The need for security
  The need for autonomy and control
    Coping with change
    Taking responsibility
  Attention: the need to give and receive it
  The need for intimacy
    Love and resilience
  Need for community: the search for social support
    The threats to community life
    The too many tribes problem
    The law of 150
    By helping ourselves we help others
  The need for status
  The need for privacy
  The need to become competent and achieve
  The need for meaning
  Needs can be met unhealthily, too
  Keeping greed in check

| Chapter 6 | Mind, brain, body | 164 |

        The stress factor
        All the rage
        Why depression is linked to disease
        The great addiction mystery
        Functional disorders
        Stress can even be contagious
        Using the mind to help the body

| Chapter 7 | Understanding difference: gender, identity and neurodivergence | 181 |

        Not so gendered brain
        Identifying as…
        Water babies and our distant aquatic past
        Fishy features
        Autistic fishlike behaviours
        Oceanic feelings of transcendence
        Help for the 'water babies'
        When context is missing
        How does a brain become aware of context?
        Context blindness
        Other theories
        Examples of context blindness
        Struggling to cope
        Dancing with horses
        Chaotic emotions
        Left- and right-brained context blindness
        More women than men
        Sense of self
        The observing self
        Context blindness as an organizing idea

PART III: EMOTIONAL HEALTH AND CLEAR THINKING

Chapter 8   APET model: the key to effective psychotherapy   225
     The birth of the APET model
     The importance of perception
     Emotions before thought
     Three vital principles
     The power of thought
     Using the APET model
     Panic attacks
     Obsessions
     Negative ruminations
     Anger disorders
     Addictions
     Molar memories
     Placebo – nocebo
     Nocebo counselling
     Metaphor, storytelling and learning
     The bigger pattern
     The RIGAAR model
     Why human givens therapy should be more widely available

Chapter 9   A very human vulnerability – depression (and how to lift it)   287
     Depression is not a genetic illness
     Dreaming and depression
     Some important provisos
     Why some people get depressed and others don't
     Bipolar disorder
     Effective psychotherapy for depression
     Blueprint for an effective therapy session
     Taking the wrong road
     An avoidable death
     More casebook examples

| Chapter 10 | Terror in the brain: overcoming trauma | 328 |

        Freeze, fight or flight
        Creating calm
        How to cure post-traumatic stress disorder
        Why EMDR and EFT may also work
        Fast, non-voyeuristic and safe treatment for trauma
        Curing phobias
        Panic attacks and agoraphobia
        Obsessive compulsive disorder (OCD)
        The chair's problem

References and notes   365
Index   402

Acknowledgments

IN THE writing of this book, and evolving the ideas and teaching material that stem from it, we have relied greatly on the voluntary and involuntary, witting and unwitting, contributions from far too many people to individually acknowledge: wives, families, friends, colleagues and patients. We thank you all.

We have also had very direct help from Denise Winn and Jane Tyrrell with the organizing, presentation and editing of the material. We thank Denise Winn for her considerable work in bringing the material up to date for our newest edition, and Ezra Hewing and Ian Thomson for their invaluable help in this. We also wish to give thanks to the other members of the Human Givens Integrity Group, Gareth Hughes and Andrew Morrice, for their helpful input.

Our thanks are also due to Elizabeth Abbott whose letter greatly illuminated the section on psychosis. And to Farouk Okhai for reading the original manuscript and contributing such an encouraging foreword.

Grateful thanks are also due to the estate of Idries Shah for allowing us to quote from his work, particularly the long passage on attention from his book, *Learning How to Learn*. He, more than anyone else, understood and appreciated the real significance of the givens of human nature.

Foreword

IT IS A general rule in medicine that, when there are a number of different theories purporting to explain a condition, one can be certain that all of them are wrong, though each may have certain facts right. There are over four hundred different models of psychotherapy in the West today, with the proponents of each model competing with the others and laying claim to primacy. How is it possible to have so many different models when there is general agreement about how the brain works? Can you imagine having four hundred different schools of physics or mathematics? By dint of clear thinking, Joe Griffin and Ivan Tyrrell lead us out of this muddle. They have assembled verifiable scientific information on how the brain works, including important original work of their own, and created a new organizing idea – the human givens approach – that has the potential to transform the practice of psychiatry, psychotherapy and counselling. Although my interest is in psychiatry and psychotherapy, it is obvious to me that this big idea also has great relevance to other important areas of life, such as education, social work and personal relationships. Some of the information in this book will be new and startling to many, some, at first glance, will appear familiar. But Griffin and Tyrrell's assembly of it is unique in that the bits and pieces that stick out in other therapy models now fit together, and this fit is both aesthetically pleasing and of immense practical use.

For example, they succeed in making reading about depression exciting! This common, rapidly rising condition is costing Western society enormous pain, emotional and financial. It is also a major cause of premature death through suicide. Depressed mood, loss of interest and enjoyment, fatigue, poor concentration, guilt, suicidal thoughts, and disturbed sleep and appetite, are generally agreed criteria used to diagnose depression. Often a person with depression will complain of early morning wakening, with depressed mood and tiredness worst at that time. To overcome the fatigue he or she may try to sleep longer than usual but the tiredness persists. We also know that very many depressed people spend a greater proportion of sleep time in the REM (rapid eye movement) state, that artificially shortening the REM periods leads to a temporary lifting of the depression, and that anti-depressants, when effective, shorten the REM sleep time.

Griffin and Tyrrell link these findings in a way that makes sense of the facts and provides the basis for rational treatment which could save millions of pounds (the APET model). The story begins with Griffin's findings from his research into dreams and REM sleep and makes a convincing case for the central importance of REM sleep in depression. A trigger or Activating stimulus (which may be a divorce, death, unemployment and so on) sends the brain on a search for similar Patterns (previous negative events) setting off a train of introspection which gives rise to the Emotion of depression with resultant Thoughts (such as "I am useless", "nothing ever goes right for me") that the depressed person gets locked into seeing as absolute truth. The prolonged REM sleep periods are attempts to deactivate this highly arousing chain of introspection, explaining the early morning wakening (in the more severely depressed) as a mechanism to limit the exhaustion caused by the intense REM activity.

If, when depressed, we are locked into ruminating on all that has gone wrong in our lives, it makes sense that treatment should aim at reversing this deepening spiral. Griffin and Tyrrell explain how the REM state can be accessed to lift the trance of depression quickly using inborn biological mechanisms. Their insight into depression makes sense of the unfortunate, but not uncommon, occurrence that will be familiar to many psychiatrists. Often a patient with depression is admitted to hospital or seen in a clinic, and put on antidepressant medicine, but found to be even more depressed a few days or weeks later. Many such patients are often encouraged, by well-meaning staff, including counsellors and therapists, to "talk about their problems". In the light of the findings presented in this book, however, talking about problems and past failures can be seen to simply grind in a guilt-ridden, worthless, useless and unlovable self-narrative as 'the truth' from the patient's locked-in perspective.

In contrast to insight and 'getting to the root' therapies, cognitive and behavioural methods have been shown to be effective for depression. We can now see that this is because they engage the cognitive or motor circuits of the brain, thus allowing the locked-in, highly aroused emotional brain to calm down, so enabling the patient to see alternative truths, possibilities and stories for his or her predicament. In addition to pointing out the erroneous assumption that thought precedes emotion, which formed the basis of the cognitive behaviour therapy model, the APET frame, which they introduce here, provides a much broader perspective – just as significant, perhaps, as the introduction of the Arabic numerical system with its zero digit was to mathematics, providing as it did a much wider vista than the Roman number system (I–X).

People love stories and this book is illuminated with a number of these, including those known as case histories. Case histories, stories, metaphors, pictures and jokes make things much clearer than a linear argument. Imagine describing a rose to someone who has never seen one and then asking him to identify one at a florist's. But show him even a sketch (i.e. a pattern) of a rose and from then on he will recognize one regardless of the variety. Griffin and Tyrrell explain that we 'see' the world through such patterns, and run into problems when we use the wrong pattern to make sense of our predicaments.

Perception through pattern matching is of crucial importance in the development of post traumatic stress disorder (PTSD) and phobias. In both, the Activating stimulus (the trauma or phobia) is of such moment that it establishes as a Pattern, both conscious (things we are aware of) and non-conscious inputs registered by the brain as belonging together, so that future experiences with even a fragment of that pattern evoke the terror (Emotion) of the original encounter. Again Griffin and Tyrrell explain how this can be reversed by accessing the REM state, with resolution of symptoms often in one or two sessions. Another fascinating topic covered, and one of the human givens, is the attention factor. 'Attention-seeking' and 'manipulative' are often-used pejorative descriptions of patients and clients, but if the importance of both giving and receiving attention as a normal human need were more widely recognized, the health systems of the world would be freed of an enormous burden. The 'thick notes (or thick chart) syndrome' is no doubt familiar to many hospital doctors: a patient is passed from one specialist to another with each doctor doing a set of investigations and often surgery to remove various organs, but the patient keeps coming back again and again! If their attention needs were met effectively in other ways these particular patients would not need to fulfil them through the ritual of history, examination, investigation, medication and surgery. On the flip side, if doctors and therapists were more aware of the attention factor, they would be better prepared for avoiding the trap of prolonging treatment in order to have their own attention needs met through their patients. As Griffin and Tyrrell relate, the evidence for the importance of the attention factor includes a shocking, ancient, but relatively unknown, experiment carried out by a European emperor.

And there are yet more treasures in this remarkable book including: why trance (focused attention) is a normal frequent everyday occurrence, during which suggestibility is heightened, and its role both in helping (the placebo effect, the transmission of culture and its morals) and harming (the nocebo effect, indoctrination); the conceptualization of schizophrenia as waking reality processed through the dreaming brain; why unbridled anger makes you stupid and shortens your life; the therapeutic usefulness of seeing addictions as attempts to meet basic human needs; and why avoiding greed and helping others is good for your health.

The authors have put in a lot of work to show how knowledge of the way the brain works (gathered from a panorama of psychology, psychiatry, sociology, anthropology and neuroscience), can be used to help the distressed humanely. This book should be essential reading for all psychiatrists, psychologists, therapists and counsellors. For the general public, this knowledge is vital if they are to protect themselves, friends and relatives from the chicanery, often unwitting, which passes for much that is called counselling and psychotherapy.

This book is a remarkable achievement that should attract the attention of any truly curious human being.

Farouk Okhai
Consultant psychiatrist (now retired)

PART ONE

New Discoveries About Human Nature

PROLOGUE

Why we need to understand healthy minds

IT TOOK millions of years for the human mind to evolve to the point where we have the knowledge to direct our own development. We have reached a watershed. Exciting discoveries about how the mind/body system works show how human nature can unfold to create effective and fulfilled individuals. What will we do with this knowledge?

Science has discovered that nature endows each healthy human conception with a wonderful array of living 'templates' – an infinitely rich treasure-house of incomplete patterns that instinctively seek completion in the environment from the moment of birth, and that continue to do so as we grow and evolve throughout our lives. These patterns are expressed as physical and emotional needs and are in a state of continuous ebb and flow. If we are fortunate, and are born into a culture and environment that provides us with the means to get those needs met, we develop well. It is precisely the way needs are met, by the impact life has on them, that determines the individual nature, character and mental health of each person. Studying these innate patterns, and charting their unfolding, is the new science of human nature, which is what this book is about.

Only by co-operating with these natural processes – the human givens – can children be educated and matured into independent, fully integrated and fulfilled adults. And, when things go wrong and people lose their way, only by working in alignment with the human givens can other people help them overcome emotional problems such as depression, anxiety, addictions, anger disorders and psychotic breakdowns.

And perhaps it is only by understanding these natural processes and overcoming the disadvantages we are also heir to – such as greed, vanity and the ease with which we can be conditioned – that we will evolve further.

CHAPTER ONE

Seeking completion

WE SHARE in common with all living organisms – including plants and the most humble, single-celled, protozoan creature – the fact that we have an 'inner nature', which we have biologically inherited, that is always seeking the right environmental stimuli to unfold properly. This truth is easily seen when we study other living things but is harder to grasp in ourselves because we are so wrapped up in the process every moment of our lives.

Every microclimate supports plants that cannot live elsewhere. The warmth and humidity of tropical South American jungles, for example, support over 8,200 orchid species, each with its own special requirements: the right soil conditions, nutriment, temperature, light and pollinating potential. The more unusual the microclimate, the more rare and exotic the plant.[1] The more common the plant, the less complex its environmental needs and the more resilient it is. Any gardener who sees that a plant is not flourishing will recognize immediately that a deficiency in the environment – too little or too much water, for example – is preventing healthy growth, or that the plant has a disease compromising its biological integrity.

At a basic level, all organisms seek nourishment to renew themselves and then give waste material back to the environment to be recycled again and again. Oxygen, the waste gas of plant life, for example, becomes an energy source for animal life.

If we look at human beings in the same way as a gardener studies plants, we can ask: what physical, psychological and social nutriment does this creature need for the successful bringing to fruition of its innate nature? We can also look for what might be preventing these inner templates from connecting to the greater world. But a person is not a plant and we need not just material but also mental, emotional and, some would say, spiritual nourishment if we are to flourish. And, while plants 'know' how to grow, children and adults need structured guidance to optimise their own self development.

The need for meaning

An important human given, the need for meaning, is driving us to write this book. This ancient natural human desire, the quest to understand, originally grew out of primitive creatures' evolving ability to move independently. Indeed, movement is fundamental to the very existence of brains, which developed primarily to control movement, to predict the outcome of movement and remember the result of past movements. Plants, by contrast, never evolved brains since they did not need to do this. (There is a tiny marine creature called the sea squirt, which, in the earlier part of its life, swims around like a tadpole. It has a brain and a nerve cord to control its movements. But, when it matures, it attaches itself to a rock and stays in one place like a plant. Thereupon it digests its own brain and nerve cord because it no longer has a use for them.[2])

The mental faculty for controlling movement is crucial to daily life. It is involved in conceiving an idea about what to do, planning a response and then carrying it out. (Literally, when we think about getting a book down from a shelf, our brains mentally simulate the movement.) So important is it that the primary motor cortex and the premotor cortex are both located in the frontal lobes, the part of the brain which manages higher-level executive functioning and which determines not only where we direct our attention but also the relationship between short-term working memory and long-term memory.

It also appears to direct consciousness itself, which is why the frontal lobes have been termed the 'executive' function of the brain.[3] Movement and meaning are inextricably linked.

The contemporary search for meaning is infinitely more sophisticated than that of our primitive ancestors like the sea squirt. It now extends multi-dimensionally to the edge of the known universe and down to the sub-atomic level – even beyond space and time. For more than 40,000 years, since the beginning of cave art in the cultural explosion of the Upper Palaeolithic period, the search for meaning beyond day-to-day survival was spearheaded by remarkable individuals and groups who passed their knowledge on down through the ages.

Initially, through pre-gnostic ('pre-knowing') shamanistic traditions where sticks, stones and animals were worshipped, they explored both human nature and the reality around them, and they expressed and taught their findings through a framework that today is often called 'spiritual': a fluid mix of excitatory practices, beliefs, rituals and experiences all involved in achieving and using altered states of consciousness.[4] Freed as we are from the historical and ideological framework of those times, it is clear that these 'spiritual' researchers were on an evolutionary quest, investigating how to unfold our inner nature more effectively and, in the process, unlock the secrets of outer nature. This effort eventually resulted in the evolution of gnostic ('knowing') traditions. In essence, their *spiritual* quest was a *scientific* quest to understand more of reality by refining their perceptual apparatus in order to see more clearly into the heart of nature. The gnostic teachers among them, who always stood outside the ideologies of their time, always contended that within each human being there is the potential for a far richer personality, or perception. If this inner perception is to develop, it must first be conceived of as a possibility.[5] Its basis, therefore, must rest, in part, on refined imagination.

A person needs preparation (in other words, appropriate environmental input) in order to attain more intelligent perception. And an essential part of the preparation involves a calming down or diminishing of aspects of personality which hinder, or even destroy, the possibilities of refined perception. These include traits such as vanity, greed, self-obsession, etc. People driven by obsessions, for example, are unable to stand back and see beyond them. Likewise, people who are ruled by emotions cannot make progress, because strong emotions overwhelm finer perceptions, just as raucous shouting drowns out a gentle whisper.[6]

History shows that 'spiritual' knowledge, wherever it has appeared publicly, is quickly polluted by the greed in the world; the teachings of wiser people inevitably degenerate into dogma-driven cults, fossilize and become self-perpetuating power structures. Wars are fought, people are indoctrinated and ignorance is entrenched, causing terrible havoc around the world.[7] (Cult formation is not limited to extreme religious groups. It can be found in political parties, within academia, the arts, scientific laboratories, and business – in fact in any situation where people meet regularly, emotions are raised and charismatic personalities exert influence for their own ends.[8])

But the essential pattern of this ancient knowledge about human development is perfectly echoed by, and in tune with, the findings of modern science about not only the physical universe but human development at all levels. Neurobiology, psychology and sociology all show that there are inner patterns of perception that seek to connect with the greater world and, when they do, allow for greater refinement and progress as human beings. And it is clear that, when these developmental processes are blocked, we cannot move on.

For example, we cannot be mentally healthy if we are isolated. In her article, "What it feels like to be a child with no friends", Celia Brayfield wrote in the *Sunday Times*[9] about the effect of being brought up by a reclusive mother: "Friend was a word I didn't know when I went to primary school. We didn't do friends in our family. An old, dark leylandii hedge ended our garden and behind it we lived in complete isolation. My mother was content but I was suffocating with loneliness. When I got to school nobody wanted to play with me and quite a lot of children wanted to beat me up."

Little Celia drifted unhappily around, thinking, "I want to be your friend but I don't know how," and "… wondering why the other children were being so horrible. When people pick on you, you feel you must deserve it. I didn't know the rules and I certainly didn't know any of the songs or rhymes or skipping games a girl needs if she's going to be a social success in the playground.

"With no friends, I was also an easy victim for the bullies," she said. "On top of the normal day-to-day punching and kicking, the ringleader once threw me face first down a flight of stairs."

The article was inspired by a report that had just been published on social skills teaching in British primary schools. The report estimated that one primary school child in five had problems related to lack of social skills and poor mental health. It also highlighted the considerable body of research showing that, when small children have emotional difficulties, they can't learn anything.[10]

That was in 2001 and it isn't a problem that has gone away. Over 20 years later, in April 2022, Amanda Spielman, then Ofsted's chief inspector, reported that the covid-19 pandemic had significantly delayed development of social skills in children, with increasing numbers unable to understand facial expressions, as a result of having fewer opportunities to develop their social and emotional skills during the restrictions of lockdowns and because of mask wearing.[11]

Celia Brayfield wrote, "I was acting that [2001 finding] out wonderfully [at school]. Although my mother made sure that I knew my letters and numbers before I started school, I lost them instantly and was soon lagging behind the rest of my class. The teachers thought I might never learn to read.

"I was saved by a teacher who took me aside in the playground and asked why I wasn't playing with my friends. Miss Potter was few people's favourite, a strict lady with fierce red lipstick, but her heart was surely in the right place. When I answered that I hadn't got any friends, she gave me a lecture on basic social skills. It began, 'To have a friend you must be a friend,' and, although I couldn't have been more than six, I've never forgotten it. Take the initiative, talk to people, smile, be nice and kind, do as you would be done by. It was probably the most useful thing I ever learnt in school.

"I went right out and did what Miss Potter had recommended and very soon had excellent friends."

Despite a successful career, missing the natural window of opportunity to learn essential social skills in the vital first years still left a shadow over her life. "I'm still not sure I'm doing life right," she said. "Often, I feel I'm lurching through relationships like young Frankenstein's monster trying to tap dance. I hear myself talking and my conversation sounds as appropriate as Eliza Doolittle on her outing to Ascot. I envy the dazzling creatures who draw a vast circle of friends around them like moths to a flame and I know I'll never be one of them. But I get by and I hate to think how my life would have worked out if Miss Potter hadn't intervened in it."

This example of what happens when just one need is not adequately met perfectly illustrates the principle behind the human givens approach. Here we see that, if the need to connect with others is not supported in the important first few years of life, it affects development and our lives as adults. Without meaningful connections to family, friends or colleagues, it's not easy to move our lives forward. In such circumstances anyone, however intelligent, can become emotionally overwrought, begin to worry excessively and become stuck in the cycle of depression, unless such a lack is resolved.

With this modern needs-focused view of human nature, the old questions about the meaning of life can be put into sharper focus and we can develop a contemporary understanding about them. Just as one human given is that we are social creatures and need connection to a group of people who accept us, so too is it a given that we need meaning. But, just as its roots are in movement, meaning cannot be a static thing. It must, as in ancient times, be a 'stretching' process that continues to reveal new meanings by refining our perceptions and thus increasing our knowledge. There is always more to learn and understand. It is this stretching process, as our brains continually resculpt through new learning, that makes us such an adaptable species.

We can all feel a sense of flow, meaning and purpose when we challenge ourselves in some way: advancing a project, or developing a sport, skill, craft or art. As we stretch ourselves, something within us is seeking to fulfil an inner need through finding its completion in the environment[12] – a process that might be termed spiritual. Obviously, the challenges people face will vary from person to person. It might be, for a businessman, the process of developing a new business or, for a musician, mastering difficult new music, and, as such, the process will be a spiritual one, because it serves to refine perceptions. And yet an activity that is initially stretching will soon become mechanical if, for instance, the business isn't developed once it is up and running or if the mastered music is simply repeated. To be stretched further, we need to seek new challenges. The brain always needs new challenges to keep it stretched, otherwise neurons (brain cells) start to atrophy. A busy brain is a healthy brain.[13]

Mountaineers, for example, can spend years preparing to do something that to others might seem inherently pointless: to climb the sheer face of a huge mountain, at the top of which the rarefied air is difficult to breathe. Why would they want to do something as uncomfortable and dangerous as that? Well, for them, it is an intensely meaningful experience. They have more bliss in their hearts as a consequence of doing it. That is what draws them to climbing. Life *always* seems more significant when we stretch ourselves, in whatever way, because we are then more connected to reality. Many human drives, such as those for goal seeking, for physical agility, for endurance, for visual accuracy, for teamwork and for status, would find fulfilment in mountaineering, but this would satisfy climbers only for a limited duration. If mountaineering becomes too routine, and the climbers are no longer stretched, it ceases to be a spiritual activity for them because they no longer have to make a conscious effort to achieve mastery of it.

If we feel lonely, anxious, greedy, depressed or angry, there are clearly aspects of ourselves that are not being stretched. Parts of our nature have not developed properly, preventing the refinement and unfolding of other aspects of ourselves. We cannot develop more refined perceptions without fulfilling more basic human needs and appetites first and in a balanced way – just as alcoholics cannot develop and stretch their capacity for human relationships because of their drunken behaviour.

Nature gives each of us the potential to develop, but we have to be continually challenged to find proper fulfilment. There is a continuum. Getting our basic needs met is at one end, and the unadulterated search for truth, the most profound and difficult form of stretching for us, is at the other. So we can view the ongoing stretching of our capacities (as our inner templates try to find a match to relate to in the environment) as a developmental process. If this is what the spiritual quest is really about – connecting the inner to the outer – we can see it on a natural continuum, a scale built into the way matter and life has evolved.

The postmodernist fallacy

This idea is, of course, the opposite of the ubiquitous, some would say anarchic, postmodernist views that originated in modern art and design, took root and spread through all aspects of our culture like a virulent infection, and are still rampant today. Postmodernists believe that there are no absolute truths and therefore, because everybody's point of view can be deconstructed, all opinions are of equal value. They promote this with totalitarian ruthlessness, institutionalizing and imposing political correctness on the rest of us.[14] This may often seem harmless, as when someone can lie in bed all day claiming that this is a work of art simply because they say it is, and financially profit from their 'work'. Such behaviour gives people something silly to talk about. But some postmodernists do much more than exploit the gullible. They go so far as to say that all thought is equally relevant (that there are no boundaries, no rules, no hierarchies, no objective reality and all facts just 'social constructs') and elevate 'feelings' above reason; furthermore, all species are of equal value, and a human being is no more important than an ant. This 'deconstructionalism', as it is termed, is a pseudo-scientific quest for negation and is even taught in schools and universities.

But the postmodern concept is made redundant because we, *and nature*, can measure. The scaling question to ask is, to what degree does a plant or creature connect up its innate genetic templates to the environment and how complex are those templates, in terms of refinement of its perceptions? Clearly, a bat has access to an echo-sound location template that we do not possess. But, in overall complexity, its templates must be scaled lower than ours. In humans, for example, moral behaviour results from the ability to perceive and act on our shared interdependence and respect for other people's needs. To look at herding for a moment, we can see the herding instinct in a cloud of midges, birds, cows, and other animals; and we can see it, in human beings, in any large gathering such as in football stadiums or churches. While getting together and singing from the same hymn sheet is clearly a low-grade activity, it is at a higher level than the swarming of midges because a human grouping contains more possibilities for learning, development and change.

There cannot *but* be measurable differences between human beings: some can run faster than others; some are less mathematically ignorant; some have more mechanical aptitude; some have more musical aptitude, etc. Clearly, different templates are differently refined in different people. It is the degree to which a species evolves more refined templates that determines how advanced it is. And, just as there are more highly evolved – adaptable – species, so will there be more highly evolved, adaptable, individual members of a species.

The growing knowledge that there is such a natural scale for gauging not only the development of a species but how individual members are flourishing will, it is to be hoped, consign destructive post-modernist beliefs to curious footnotes of history.

The science of human nature

The ultimate aim of education (the word comes from the Latin *educare*, meaning to draw forth, bring out, develop from a latent condition) is to unfold and refine what is within. In real education (as opposed to conditioning people or training them to pass exams), the way we know that a young person or pupil is progressing is by observing how well they are learning to discern subtle distinctions in the meaning of observable phenomena as their perceptions become more refined. The process of successfully matching up inner patterns to the outer world is not experienced as a vague subjective feeling that could just as easily be generated by drugs. It is revealed objectively, in the ability of a person to perceive more of the richness of the patterns by which the world operates and therefore be more effectively engaged in it. This is why it is often said that a truly spiritual person is not a hermit sitting on a mountain contemplating his navel, but someone involved in the world, working, serving others and opposing tyranny of all kinds.

Such an understanding removes the so-called conflict between science and spirituality – which is, in fact, only a conflict between fundamentalism in science and fundamentalism in religion. If spirituality is the search for meaning, the ultimate stretching of human potential, this must be the science of human nature and its unfolding.

Science and spirituality are therefore compatible, something the wisdom traditions down the millennia have always maintained. Once we realize that spirituality is about getting needs met, the complexity of relationships and connecting up patterns of understanding about how the world operates, we can see that it cannot be separated from the search for knowledge. Moreover, when a real understanding is present, it enables the possessor to be more effective in the world.

We know that at least 45,000 years ago in Europe, when it was initially colonised by modern humans, and seemingly much, much earlier in many other parts of the world, which are only now being better studied, human beings became more than intelligent animals just instinctively reacting to promptings from the natural world all around.[15] A great leap forward in human evolution occurred, sometimes called "the brain's big bang"[16]: we discovered how to access the dreaming brain, our own reality generator, so we could consciously daydream and use our imaginations, drawing on memories of the past, to visualize possible futures. The most talented individuals and groups who took this step and developed their imaginations quickly learned how to plan more successful hunting trips, solve problems, develop more specialized new tools, empathize and ask abstract questions (complex language, with a past and future tense, cannot develop without imagination), make music and entertain, decorate and clothe themselves, and educate children more efficiently. Some remarkable individuals seem to have elected to teach others, including children (as we know, from preserved footprints), how to access their imaginations by taking them deep into mountain tunnels and caves, sometimes two or three miles underground.

Here, far away from the constant noisy distractions of the natural world, they taught them to use their brains in a novel way, to conjure up new thoughts and images. In such quiet subterranean centres, what we can only term 'psychological research' took place, and cave art began. Here were schools[17] for developing outward focused imagination and speeding our ability to learn, directly connect with and understand, in greater depth, the natural world and a sense of invisible powers beyond it. People studied and thought about animal behaviour in new ways until eventually it was possible to domesticate, use and breed many formerly wild creatures. Fellow man also became infinitely more interesting to our ancestors, as, once possessed of imagination, they could not help but be aware that their lives were precarious and difficult, and began to realize that individual survival would be much better assured within social groupings. They could imagine how they might change their situation and stretch themselves in non-selfish ways for the long-term benefit of all.

About 12,000 years ago, in many regions of the world, we changed from being hunter-gatherers to farmers. Early farmers needed the ability to observe seasonal changes closely over long periods. They had to analyze information, perceive what was needed for a crop to develop its potential as food or medicine, learn how to plan long term and to find solutions to problems that arose, such as how to irrigate dry land and organize the manpower to harvest crops. They also needed a certain philosophical attitude towards the unpredictability of weather, blight and so on, and had to take account of the fact that skills were unevenly distributed in the tribe. Without access to imagination, none of these capacities could have come into being, and the development of farming, and the civilizations that arose as a result of it, would never have taken place.

Adapting to now

We nomadic hunters, farmers, villagers and small-town dwellers have reached the 21st century where most of us now live in urban conglomerations of great complexity. The wonderful boon of imagination we were given all those thousands of years ago, as well as creating what is great in our culture, has also created an environment that seems out of control. We have the means to magnify our greeds and have made a world that whirls around us so fast, and in such disturbing ways, that we can no longer trust our culture to reliably provide the psychological nourishment for us to develop fully as human beings. When things go wrong and there are power cuts, transport system failures, wars, financial market crashes etc. – individuals feel helpless. The speed of change, and the carelessness with which governments instigate change, explains much of the massive increase in many forms of mental illness. Statistics published in 2020 by the mental health charity Mind indicate that one in four people will experience a mental health problem each year in England, and one in six experience a common mental health problem in any given week.[18] A report from the former Children's Commissioner, published in 2021, showed that one in six children aged between five and 19 "had a probable mental health condition" the previous year, up from one in nine in 2017.[19] During the covid-19 pandemic, abuse and child neglect increased dramatically, with a staggering one million referrals made for help from children's mental health services in the UK.[20]

To make another leap forward in our evolution, one every bit as significant as the great leap forward of 65,000 years ago, we urgently need to understand the inner processes that must be properly nourished for psychologically healthy human beings to mature, and nurture our children accordingly.[21] That will involve a huge shift in perceptions for much of our species. Without such a shift, however, we can see that we are heading towards massive and unsustainable levels of mental illness, leading, perhaps, to our destruction. But human development grows out of necessity, and the pressure this puts on us generates fertile seeds of hope, waiting, hiding in strange places, for the right conditions to bring on the next phase in what will, we hope, be our continuing story.

CHAPTER TWO

Where does human nature come from?

IT IS A TRUISM that we come, as all matter must, from the stars. The basic elements, vast energies and great distances of deepest space that we measure with our sophisticated instruments and try to understand with our science and struggle to grasp in our imaginations are where our consciousness originally came from. These fundamental physical elements and material processes in the universe may be our evolutionary parent, but to understand human nature we need first to pick up the story closer to home.

The unfolding growth of any living thing – plant or animal – can seem to the unsophisticated mind as if it is powered by some magical unearthly force. It is certainly an infinitely complex process. But we know that it relies on information transcribed from the genes, passed down through the ages. Genes provide the factual basis for the existence of any living thing. They are hereditary blueprints encapsulated in deoxyribonucleic acid (DNA), the complex double-helix molecular structure of which was discovered by James Watson and Francis Crick in 1953, building on the work of scientists before them.

But how do the genes insert their programmes, particularly for instinctive behaviour, into the brain? The answer, it seems, is that it happens in what is known as the rapid eye movement (REM) state of brain activity and, if you wish to understand how your mind works, there is perhaps no better place to start than by looking at the REM state, an enormously important human given. In the early days of sleep research, various terms were employed to designate this active stage of sleep. Michel Jouvet, for example, called it paradoxical sleep; other researchers called it dream sleep. But the term REM sleep, although unsatisfactory in that it is only descriptive of one physical phenomenon associated with the state, is the one widely used throughout the scientific community to designate it. So we use this term in this book. However, we broaden it out to include other states in which brain activity is akin to that experienced during REM sleep, terming them all the REM state.

Curiously, it was also in 1953 that the REM state discovery was first published, by the American researchers Aserinsky and Kleitman.[1] They noticed that, for a considerable amount of our sleep time, the brain was in a state of comparative rest. This state became known as slow-wave sleep, the most recuperative part of any 24-hour period for any mammal. This is when the body is at its most efficient in fighting off infection and when tissue damage is repaired. But Aserinsky and Kleitman also observed that, for nearly a quarter of all sleep periods, the sleeping person exhibited darting, rapid eye movements behind the closed eye-lids. They then soon established that the brain was highly active at this time, using as much energy as when awake. But it was several years before the connection between this state and programming instincts was made.

As we illustrate in this book, many mysteries of human psychology and mental health have been solved through studying the implications of the information that scientists painstakingly gathered as a result of Aserinsky and Kleitman's discovery. We now know, for example, why we evolved to dream; what dreaming is doing for us each night; why depressed people so commonly wake up exhausted (and how they get depressed in the first place); how the brain can become traumatized; how the brain learns; why we are so easy to condition, brainwash and manipulate; what psychosis is; how and why exchanging attention is so important; what hypnosis is – and much more.

The risk and the prize

To begin our exploration, we must ask some fundamental questions about the role of sleep. Why do mammals sleep? Day and night, in forests and fields, desert and tundra, caves and houses, creatures find the safest places in which to curl up and fall asleep. And, whilst asleep, why do they spend the majority of the time in slow-wave sleep – the state in which the body and brain recuperate from the previous day's wear and tear – and some of the time in the REM state, completely paralysed, cut off from sensory contact with the world and all its dangers? What possible evolutionary advantage could there be for creatures to be so vulnerable for so much of the day – literally paralysed and at risk from hungry predators?

It was the French scientist Michel Jouvet who discovered that REM sleep was accompanied by muscle paralysis – specifically, the inhibition of antigravity muscles.[2] (The internationally agreed system for recording sleep phases includes recording the signals coming from the muscles, as well as eye movements and brain waves.) And he was also the first to suggest that REM sleep may have evolved to permit more freedom in the expression of instinctive behaviours, pointing out that REM sleep, homeothermia (being warm-blooded) and the flexibility of instinctive behaviours are linked; being warm-blooded allowed the higher vertebrates more freedom of behaviour and was inevitably accompanied, as mammals continued to evolve, by increased complexity in brain development.[3] In other words, once mammals and birds could keep a constant internal temperature, instead of their behaviour being governed, as in cold-blooded creatures, by simple set responses to changes in the environment, they became far more mobile with more options available to them.

There was a downside to achieving this increased mobility, however, and that was that the fivefold increase in the energy they needed to expend to achieve it had to be matched by a fivefold increase in energy intake.[4] It made no evolutionary sense for the increase in flexibility to be expended purely in increased time spent searching for food. Animals could save some energy by sleeping when they weren't hungry or when no food sources were available (and perhaps this is when slow-wave sleep developed) but this alone wouldn't help generate the required extra energy.

What was also needed was a more highly developed and intelligent brain that would enable mammals to inhibit instinctive drives when they weren't required and to stimulate those actions that were likely to be more productive. And, indeed, scientists have now identified the neurons in the medial prefrontal cortex (part of the cerebral cortex, which is much more highly developed in mammals than in reptiles), which act on the brainstem to stop social animals from acting on impulsive instincts when inappropriate to do so.[5] To enable this new intelligent input, a new type of programming had to be developed. A type of programming that would make instinctive responses much more flexible and capable of being modified in their expression by this ongoing stream of information being processed by the cortex. The

REM state appears to have developed for this purpose. The recognition of the importance of REM sleep as a programming state grew out of a crucial set of findings about when REM sleep occurs, gathered from information collected in sleep laboratories around the world. It soon became clear to scientists that REM sleep occurs most frequently when we are very young and less often when we get older. Also, it starts long before we are born. At between 27 and 40 weeks, human foetuses spend up to 80 per cent of their time in REM sleep. When they are born, 67 per cent of sleep time is REM sleep, a proportion that gradually reduces to 25 per cent by middle childhood. As healthy adults we spend about a quarter of our sleep in the REM state, until we reach old age, when the amount lessens. This clearly supports the idea that REM sleep is a programming state.

So too does the fascinating finding of William Dement and his colleagues in America. They noted that the amount of REM sleep an animal has depends upon how mature it is at birth.[6] Those species whose young are born capable of living almost fully independently, in terms of both mental and physical functions, have very little REM sleep at birth. Those that are highly immature when born, however, show high levels of REM sleep. A baby guinea pig, for example, is born fully developed – a perfect miniature of its parents. At birth it needs to spend just 15 per cent of its sleep in the REM state. By contrast, the newborn rat is totally immature. It is born blind, naked and immobile, and spends 95 per cent of its sleep time in the REM state. But it doesn't stay immature for long and, within a month, REM sleep accounts for under a third of its sleep time.

The conclusion that Dement and his colleagues reached is that REM sleep is most important for the very young and clearly has something to do with the developing brain. Maybe, they thought, it provides stimulation for the developing cerebrum in an environment (the womb) where not a lot that is new and stimulating occurs. But meanwhile, back in France, Professor Michel Jouvet was suggesting a more plausible reason for the variations in length of REM sleep, one that fitted with the findings of Dement and his colleagues but improved upon their conclusions.

Jouvet suggested that REM sleep is concerned with programming the central nervous system to carry out instinctive behaviours.[7] He showed experimentally that REM sleep is controlled by a primitive part of the brain and that, when a particular area of the midbrain is removed (the part which controls the inhibition of the antigravity muscles), cats seem to act out their dreams, which take the form of instinctive behaviours such as chasing or attacking (invisible aggressors), mating, drinking or grooming motions and fear reactions.[8]

Other scientists' research findings supported his conclusions. It was observed, for example, that human babies also act out what appear to be sophisticated expressions of emotion during REM sleep – showing apparent perplexity, disdain, scepticism and amusement, etc. – and that they don't do this while awake.[9] Moreover, some of these emotions, scepticism and disdain for example, don't come into use until later in life. Another researcher noted that young babies smile in REM sleep, yet they don't do so when awake till they are several weeks old.[10] And yet another suggested that, because newborns can breathe, suckle and swallow as soon as they are born, none of which behaviours is required in the womb, they may learn this instinctive ability during REM sleep. (Observation of foetal lambs has shown breathing movements of the chest wall in REM sleep, regardless of the lack of air to breathe.[11]) In a much more recent finding, third-trimester foetuses turned to track red dots shone into the womb more often when the dots formed the shape of a face than when they were random. Babies look for human faces as soon as they are born and it appears they learn to do this while in the womb.[12] Furthermore, babies born prematurely are seen to spend as much time in the REM state as they would have if they had remained in the womb for the normal 40-week term.

All this adds up to compelling evidence that the REM state serves to programme instinctive behaviours which the young of the species will need as they go through life. This endogenous source of stimulation sculpts the development of the brain. After an animal is born, the stimuli it encounters as it grows continually prompt the unfolding of more layers of this instinctive knowledge. Ever more complex neuronal connections are created in each stage of its life. When, as we reach sexual maturity, we set out to find a mate, fall in 'love' and produce children of our own, we are acting out the instincts laid down from our genes whilst asleep in the REM state many years before.

Now we come to another important question. If we just had straightforward, set, instinctive responses to everything we ever encountered in life we would be nothing more than mechanical robots. So, how exactly do these instinctive templates laid down in REM sleep make mammals more adaptable, flexible and intelligent?

Why the brain is a metaphorical pattern-matching organ

Clearly, animals we share the world with have instinctive responses that are the same throughout a species. Horses, for example, have their own way of communicating with one another, which has been studied in depth by many people. Monty Roberts, the original 'horse whisperer', is quite clear that this language is an ancient pattern of behaviour that *all* horses share. "The language of horses is universal. It has not even so much as an accent. So, if I go to Japan or Australia or Canada or Germany, wherever, it is exactly the same."[13] But we also know that horses and all other mammals have greater flexibility to adapt to changes in the environment than cold-blooded creatures, such as fish and reptiles, do.

This flexibility gives great advantages. Birds, for instance, which also exhibit REM sleep for short periods, instinctively set about building nests. But the diversity of shape, size, composition and location of nests built by birds, even of the same species, shows how great the variation can be in the execution of this seemingly simple piece of instinctive behaviour.[14] In effect, birds are programmed with an instinct to look for 'twig-like' things with which to build the nest and 'soft' materials with which to line it. This flexibility allows them to use straw, wire, plastic, etc., as well as twigs, to build a nest, and feathers, paper, foam, moss, scraps of cloth, etc., to line it. Similarly, many parent and baby mammals use the uniqueness of their voices to identify where the other is when they are out of sight. Humans might not be able to tell the sounds of baby animals apart but the parents clearly can. The instinct to respond to another's voice pattern is flexible enough to include the whole range of voice patterns that may be found within a species, from among which the individual can select the right voice as being 'like' the kind it is programmed to look for.

The more unspecified the parameters of genetically anticipated stimuli (and responses as well), the greater will be the flexibility in the animal's behaviour, and the greater the environmental learning component of the instinctive behaviour can be. In other words, the more patterns to match to that a creature has, the greater its metaphorical ability and the more flexibly it can operate and evolve. An example from studies of tool making by chimpanzees illustrates this. When they discover that their fingers are not long enough to get into the nests of the tasty (to them) ants and termites, chimpanzees will select a twig, strip it of leaves and push the thin end of the twig deep into the nest. They then wait patiently for the food to walk out along the twig, whereupon they gently pick it off and eat it.[15]

The more complex the life form, the more varied and rich are the instinctive patterns, or templates, laid down in it. Human beings are the most flexible of all mammals; therefore, our instinctive programming has the largest capacity for environmental input. By the time they are born, as already mentioned, babies are already primed to look for human faces and build rapport. As leading child development specialists say in *How Babies Think*, "[As babies] we know, quite directly, that we are like other people and they are like us."[16] This can only be as a result of instinctive programming.

To achieve this intelligence, instinctive programmes need to be sufficiently flexible to allow for a wide range of environmental variation. No baby can know in advance the exact shape or colour of its mother's face, nor the language that she speaks. Babies, like all mammals, need to know how to act in whatever environment they find themselves. This, it seems, is why instinctive *but incomplete* patterns of behaviour are programmed into the developing young of a species. The more incomplete or unspecified the 'programme' is, the greater the flexibility in a creature's behaviour, and the greater the opportunity to learn from the environment.

So we have partially answered why it is we need to sleep and go into the REM state. It has to do with the risky enterprise of evolving warm-bloodedness. That was the prize. For mobile life forms to become more flexible in their relationship with other creatures and inanimate matter – the plant kingdom and ever-changing weather and food supplies – they needed to develop the ability to exercise more choices. And the metaphorical abilities we evolved – to look for something important for our survival that is 'like' something we have been programmed to recognize (e.g., in the case of a baby, a nipple or the teat of a bottle or even, for a time, a finger tip) allow us to do that. It is these same metaphorical abilities that we use to learn language, build rapport, use imagination, question and analyze our own emotional responses and so on. And they are all programmed into us during REM sleep as metaphorical patterns. Since the patterns are never exact, they have to be held in an incomplete metaphorical form.

So, the brain is essentially a metaphorical pattern-matching organ, constantly seeking environmental stimuli to match up to the instinctive and learned responses amassed since conception. Not only does this give us the ability to recognize something we need (such as a nipple or teat) but it is the means by which we recognize something when we come across it again (we see a chair and can identify it by pattern matching, at the speed of light, to our knowledge of what chairs tend to look like). We use pattern-matching and metaphor to communicate with others ("it's like this" or "it's like that") and to build on our understandings about the world (inventors often devise new ways of doing things by enlarging on or adapting the way something is achieved in nature). Our brains are constantly pattern matching, relating what is new to what we already know.

Metaphorical communication is an intrinsic part of the way all human beings understand and communicate experience. This is particularly important for therapists and teachers to understand because, just as we have the potential to identify appropriate metaphors, we may also make inappropriate metaphorical matches between two patterns. In fact, error is inevitable on some occasions because the capacity for analogy or metaphor *derives biologically from the programming of instinctive behaviour*. Instinctive templates for behaviour can only specify patterns to be identified in an approximate way. Many people have seen films of the ethologist Konrad Lorenz being followed around everywhere by a family of young goslings. Goslings are pre-programmed to attach themselves to the first large moving object they encounter after hatching because, normally, this would be their mother. Now, if that large moving object happens to be Konrad Lorenz's wellington boots and they attach to him and not the mother goose, clearly the wrong metaphorical patterns have been identified. The birds bonded with Lorenz: they followed him persistently; they became distressed when he left them and ran to him for support when they felt frightened.[17] Clearly this was a situation where the matching of an instinctive template to its environmental counterpart had gone awry. Human beings have a far more sophisticated, creative capacity for identifying metaphor than do animals, but it stems directly from the metaphorical processes found throughout the animal kingdom. We have the ability to think analogically, that is, to think holistically, and to recognize how a pattern metaphorically matches another pattern. But we also have the ability to think logically, to break problems down and analyze them. Our conscious mind's preferred mode of operation is logical thought while that of our unconscious mind is analogical or 'association of ideas', as it is sometimes called. Unconscious thinking, therefore, represents by far the largest part of brain activity because everything of which we are not immediately conscious is, by definition, unconscious.

A great many mental problems are caused by these thinking processes going awry. When someone who has been sexually abused in a past relationship, for example, finds that they cannot bring themselves to have sex with a present partner whom they love, they are making a false analogical connection between the old abusive relationship and the new healthy one. It is a form of learned helplessness that logical, conscious faculties seem powerless to overcome. Another example of false analogy matching is when a person is highly aroused early in their sexual life and makes associations between that arousal and particular objects, activities or situations. They then continue to be sexually 'turned on' by such connections (fetishism), which can seem inexplicably perverse to others. From this perspective, the goslings following Lorenz's wellington boots are 'perverts'.

When people unconsciously match present events to patterns established in the past that are inappropriate to the current situation, they need help to unhook those patterns. Such faulty conditioned responses get in the way of a normal response, preventing them from being fully in the present. (There are well-established techniques for doing this, which we explain in Chapter 10.) By contrast, the type of counselling that encourages the emotional re-experience of past problematic situations has the undesired effect of enhancing the mismatch – engraining the inappropriate patterns deeper – and thereby raising the emotional pitch, harming the patient and preventing them from overcoming their difficulties. Of course some counsellors who encourage patients to review their pasts emotionally do quickly progress to encouraging their patients to take a more empowering view of their history, reframing it so as not to see themselves as victims. This can be highly beneficial.

Without sleep, we warm-blooded creatures die

We know that REM sleep remains essential throughout life. The dramatic results from the first known experiments on sleep deprivation, conducted over a hundred years ago, found that it took between seven and ten days for puppies to die if they had no sleep. Why they died was unknown to the researchers at the time. Postmortem examinations showed no obvious changes in brain tissue or other vital organs.[18]

One of the great veterans of sleep research was Allan Rechtschaffen who, with enormous ingenuity, devised experiments with rats that enabled scientists to study the effects of 'net' sleep deprivation on test animals without other variables getting in the way. His control animals slept normally but in every other way were treated the same as those deprived of sleep. He found that there was no doubt sleep deprivation alone was responsible for the death of the test animals.[19]

Rechtschaffen and his colleagues searched and searched for explanations. At first they suspected a drop in body temperature might be the cause because all the test rats showed a decline in body temperature. But, when the experimental rats were kept warm with heaters, they still died. Breakdown in bodily tissues caused by accelerated metabolism or systemic infections was also ruled out in a series of elaborate experiments.[20]

Even though Rechtschaffen's studies failed to find out the direct cause of death in his sleep-deprived rats, they did provide us with new information. One consistent observation was that the test rats ate increased amounts of food while, at the same time, losing weight. These changes suggested that sleep-deprived animals have an increased metabolic rate, as though they have an increased need of energy. In fact, near death, the sleep-deprived animals showed an energy expenditure two to three times above normal. This could be caused only by excessive heat loss or by a dramatic change in the set point of the brain thermostat.

Rechtschaffen thought hard about this and went on to devise more ingenious experiments which showed that, indeed, the set point of the brain mechanism that keeps internal heat at a constant level was increased by sleep deprivation. Rats who had been deprived of sleep for two weeks preferred to remain in a 'heat corridor' where the ambient temperature was 50°C (122°F). The control rats found that unbearably hot and fled as fast as their legs could carry them to the part of the corridor where the ambient temperature was 30°C (86°F). Clearly, if the test rats preferred to be in a much hotter environment, their internal thermostats had been altered. Sleep deprivation disrupted the activity of the brain cells responsible for temperature regulation.

In further experiments, Rechtschaffen found that rats prevented from having REM sleep were unable to keep their body temperature stable. It became clear to him that REM sleep deprivation did not cause a change in the brain thermostat but did cause the disruption in heat conservation. The link between the evolution of warm-bloodedness and the REM state in the brain could not be more clear.

Interestingly, when sleep-deprived animals were near death and then allowed to sleep, all of these changes could be reversed. Most remarkable was that the animals showed large amounts of REM sleep rebound. They had to catch up on what they had missed. On the first day that they were allowed to sleep without interruption, overall length of REM sleep was five to ten times greater than normal. Rechtschaffen's conclusion was that "the need for paradoxical (REM) sleep may exceed the need for other sleep stages".

Other eminent researchers have gone much further. "REM, it seems, is some sort of supersleep," said J. Allan Hobson.[21] He gives three reasons to support this. The first is that, "although it normally occupies only about 20 per cent of the total time we sleep each night, it takes only six weeks of deprivation of REM sleep alone to kill rats, compared with four weeks for complete sleep deprivation. Based on its relative duration of only 20 per cent of sleep time, we would predict that five times as long a deprivation period would be required if both states were equally life-enhancing." On these terms, one minute of REM sleep is worth five minutes of non-REM sleep.

The second reason he gives to support the idea of REM supersleep is one that will please catnappers around the world. Short naps are surprisingly beneficial "if they occur at times in the day when REM sleep probability is high. Daytime naps are different from night sleep in that we may fall directly into a REM period and stay there for the duration of the nap. Since the time of peak REM probability is greatest in the late morning, the tendency of naps to be composed of REM sleep is highest then and falls thereafter till the onset of night sleep (about 12 hours later)." The implication is that a little bit of sleep, at the right time of day, may be more useful than the same amount later on.

The third reason is that "following the deprivation of even small amounts of REM sleep, there is a prompt and complete repayment. The subject who has been denied REM sleep launches into extended REM periods as soon as he is allowed to sleep normally. In recent drug studies, when REM sleep was prevented, the payback seemed to be made with interest. More REM sleep was paid back than was lost."

He then goes on to propose "a link between brain-mind states and genetics" which makes sense, given the evidence that our instincts are laid down from our genes in the REM state.

We would go further and suggest, from these findings, that, since babies show REM from about 10 weeks, it is the primary state of consciousness. As the sense organs start to receive inputs from the environment, the brain pattern matches to the instinctive templates programmed in during the REM state. Every time a new pattern match is made, it is preceded by a spark of consciousness, an alertness about what might be, followed by that 'ah ha!' moment as the pattern is recognized. After a baby's birth, this happens at an ever-accelerating rate, as templates for breathing, swallowing, seeing and connecting with human faces, responding to human touch, drawing milk from a mother's breasts, etc., are matched up to reality. As children grow and come across situations and things that they don't instinctively know how to deal with, the more conscious they become.

Waking consciousness is clearly a modification of the REM state. When the outside universe first gives feedback to the brain that it can pattern match to, it is the templates programmed in during the REM state that generate a model of reality in us from which we operate. As we experience more, adding more memories, the reality we generate becomes ever more complex. Just as waking reality is a modification of the REM state, derived from input through our senses from the outside world, so our dream reality – when information from the outside world is cut off – also depends on the REM state, as we shall see.

But why, once we are programmed in early life with all of the instinctive behaviour patterns we require, do we need to continue to go into the REM state every night of our lives and, in a state of body paralysis, dream our dreams? To penetrate the secrets of nature requires great concentration and application. In the next chapter we will look at how the result of such effort, piecing together the implications of existing scientific knowledge about the REM state, and building upon it, has yielded the answer. This answer is having many surprising consequences and has enabled the development of key insights, not only into dreaming but also into how we learn, depression, post-traumatic stress disorder (PTSD), psychosis and autism, as well as giving us a richer understanding of consciousness itself. And all of these insights have huge practical applications.

CHAPTER THREE

The dreaming brain

WHEN WE wake up and remember our dreams, we are aware of a vivid quality that we totally believed in while dreaming. Sometimes we recall them as feeling more intensely real than waking reality. It is as if, while dreaming, we are 'locked' in our dream, removed from the outside world, engaged in something important. And that is exactly the case – as we will see.

Studying and interpreting dreams has a long history. The intensity and ubiquity of the dreaming experience made mankind certain that dreams were significant in some mysterious way. From ancient Sumeria we have written records from over 4,000 years ago that recount the oldest known heroic tale, *The Epic of Gilgamesh*. It is about the search for immortality and is full of dream accounts. In one dramatic dream, for example, Enkidu, the travelling companion of Gilgamesh, sees what the afterlife is like and this gives him a sense of certainty about the relationship between life and death that influences his whole view of the world.

To the ancient Greeks, dream interpretation was almost an industry. At one time there were about 420 sleep temples; these were dedicated to Asclepius, an acclaimed healer of 11th century BC, and were where dream interpretation was practised to seek answers to problems and cures for illnesses. People would lie down on a *kline* (the Greek word for the bed used in these temples), whilst incubating dreams in which medicaments or other means to restore health in a sick person were said to be revealed to the dreamer. The influence of Asclepius continues to this day: from the names of his daughters, Panacea and Hygieia, we have the terms 'panacea' and 'hygiene', and the word *kline* is the root of the modern word 'clinic'.

So important were dreams to the Greeks in the ancient world that they had a god of dreams, Oneiros, whose name was given to the *Oneirocritica* (the interpretation of dreams), a series of five books by the Greek Artemidorus, who lived in Italy in the second century. He held a sophisticated view of dream interpretation, believing that the same type of dream could have a different meaning depending on the character and circumstances of the individual dreamer. The *Oneirocritica* was the second book to be printed in Europe on the Gutenberg Press and was still being used as a dream manual up until the 19th century.

Many Greeks believed that remembered dreams could influence waking action and that they were also channels of communication between man and his gods. They even had a means of accounting for why some dreams were based on reality and came true, while others didn't – true dreams came from the 'Gate of Horn' while false dreams came from the 'Gate of Ivory'. But some Greeks took what is regarded today as a more modern view. For example, Petronius wrote: "It is neither the gods nor divine commandments that send the dreams down from the heavens, but each one of us makes them for himself." Plato noted that our higher reasoning faculties were absent in dreams, leaving the way open to the expression of unbridled passion. He asserted that in all people there was a lawless wild beast whose presence is glimpsed in dreams of passion and anger. But he also thought it possible to have morally superior dreams, when reasoning is appropriately stimulated, and for knowledge, which we didn't know we had access to, to come into us in dreams.

Aristotle argued that so-called 'prophetic' dreams were simply coincidences, not heavenly messages, declaring that the most skilful interpreter of dreams is "he who has the faculty for absorbing resemblances", in other words, someone who can make metaphorical connections between waking events in the dreamer's life and the dream content. He also believed that dreams could in some way reflect the physical state of the dreamer and could therefore be used as a diagnostic tool, an idea also proposed by Asclepius and Hippocrates.

The Bible is full of significant dreams in which God imparts advice to individuals specially chosen to receive it. Early Christians adopted wholesale the beliefs about dreams and their significance from other religions, just as readily as they incorporated existing sacred sites, rituals and beliefs from earlier belief systems. This changed in the fifth century after the time of Saint Jerome, a Christian monk and celebrated 'Father of the Church'. We know from his writings that he was obsessed with sex. Consequently, he had frequent sexually explicit dreams (which, predictably, he denounced as the work of the devil). His view that dreams were from the devil spread throughout the Christian world, was actively promoted by the Inquisition, and didn't begin to fade until after the Renaissance. After Jerome, any revelation given to an individual in a dream was seen as satanic because only the Church had the right to interpret God's word and those interested in studying dreams, or pronouncing on the basis of them, were associated with the devil. Later, Martin Luther, the founder of Protestantism, endorsed this view. In his eyes, sin was "the confederate and father of foul dreams".

The learning and insights of the ancient cultures of Greece and Rome, as well as middle and central Asia, were collected, translated and preserved by Muslim scholars after the rise of Islam. Dreams and dream interpretation played a major role in Islamic cultures – the Koran itself is said to have been revealed to Mohammed largely in a series of dream visions – and dream 'interpreters' were once widespread.[1] But it wasn't until the 19th century that European scientists started to take an interest in the role of dreaming and made hypotheses about the connection of dreams with events experienced while awake and emotions insufficiently suppressed during sleep. It was Sigmund Freud who merged all this together with his theory of the unconscious, to create the first modern theory of dreaming.[2] In 1900, he published his mammoth work, *The Interpretation of Dreams*, a title borrowed from Artemidorus, the Greek scholar who had published five books on the subject over 1,700 years earlier.

Freud believed that dreams represented "the royal road to understanding the unconscious". His theory was crucially informed by his understanding of neurosis, which he saw as an individual's unwitting expression of the inevitable conflict between conscious wishes and unconscious repressed ones. Dreams, he concluded, were the product of repressed wishes in the unconscious mind breaking through briefly into consciousness. (When an individual was awake, he reasoned, these wishes were 'censored' by some part of the conscious mind, whereas, during sleep, they could slip past if they were disguised in the form of a dream.) Freud thought that dreams were protective, enabling unconscious wishes to be expressed but without disturbing sleep. If the repressed wishes were not disguised sufficiently well in a dream, however, the 'censor' would be alerted and the dreamer would awaken, aware of having experienced what we call a nightmare.

Freud had many complex explanations for why dreams take the forms they do, seeing these as necessary distortions enabling repressed infantile wishes to be linked to an individual's active store of waking concerns and worries, or even insignificant thoughts and images, to get past the 'censor'. The deep meaning of the dream could only be reached, he believed, by means of free association to each of the elements recalled from the dreams – i.e. letting the mind roam freely, having taken as a starting point a dream element such as a fall or an erotic encounter with a dark-haired stranger. Freud was convinced that all dreams had a sexual concern at source.

Carl Gustav Jung, Freud's one time colleague, felt that, although free association might reveal a client's deep psychological concerns, it couldn't reveal the meaning of a dream. Nor did he feel happy with Freud's idea that dreams were disguised to slip past a 'censor'. He thought that dream symbols must be the unconscious mind's natural 'language'. He developed the idea of the 'collective unconscious', his term for an archaic consciousness of primitive people from which, he said, modern consciousness evolved. These archaic elements, he suggested, were sometimes expressed in dreams as archetypes, which could only be deciphered through a broad knowledge of myth and legend.[3] Jung's theory, though never as popular or well known as that of Freud, informed the widely held modern view that dreams can help the conscious mind handle emotional problems more effectively. (This, however, is only indirectly the case, as will be explained shortly.)

Modern dream theories

In 1953, the researcher Calvin Hall put forward a cognitive theory of dreaming, with dreams being a continuation of normal thinking processes about daily personal concerns.[4] He concluded this on the basis of findings from research that he was carrying out when the first atomic bomb was dropped in Japan. None of the content of his subjects' dreams reflected this momentous event in any way. Hall thought that dreams were like works of art, through which ideas and concerns were transmuted into pictures. These images, once perceived by the conscious mind in a dream, would enable dreamers to develop a true sense of their self-conceptions, unadulterated by conscious distortions. He collected an impressive amount of evidence for his theory by recording other people's dreams, making careful content analyses and showing how often the content of the dreams correlated with the dreamers' known waking concerns. However, his basic tenet that dreams are personal communications does not really stand up. Why, after all, would nature devise such an intricate biological system to generate 'works of art' that – far from reliably communicating our preoccupations – are largely forgotten on waking?

This is where thinking about dreaming remained, until the uncovering of new and irrefutable scientific information made it possible to develop a whole new understanding. As we have seen, around the time that Hall was developing his cognitive theory, biological knowledge about the nature of sleep was progressing rapidly. Exciting new findings emerged from sleep research laboratories, following on from the discovery by Aserinsky and Kleitman that sleep occurs in different phases, including the phase of sleep that occurs every 90 minutes throughout sleep and is accompanied by rapid eye movements (REM).[5] It was quickly established that REM accounts for between one and a half and two hours of sleep time per night.[6] Moreover, people who volunteered their services to sleep research laboratories and who were awoken during REM sleep were found to remember their dreams 80 per cent of the time. Whereas, when they were awoken from what came to be called slow-wave sleep, and from other stages of sleep, they could recall their dreams only seven per cent of the time. It was then found that not only humans experienced REM sleep. Nearly all mammals go into REM sleep, as we described in the last chapter. Even birds exhibit the REM state for short periods. For scientists, this finding alone put paid to the highly speculative Freudian and Jungian theories about dreaming because it was inconceivable that anyone could ascribe neuroses to cows, unresolved Oedipal complexes to kangaroos and archetypal myths to the parrot family.

Mental activity akin to dreaming, but usually of a more prosaic, recursive nature, has also been detected in about 60 per cent of non-REM awakenings. The mind is not by any means completely switched off during non-REM sleep. Mental activity, such as thinking, occurs at least some of the time, as do dreamlike processes. However, these are qualitatively different and can be separated out by sleep researchers. These non-REM dreams tend to be shorter, less complex, less visually and emotionally intense and less surreal: in short, less dreamlike. Their production involves very different parts of the brain. The dreamlike fragments that are most like REM are collected from Stage I onset sleep, which has a similar cortical arousal pattern to REM sleep.[7] An explanation of why dreams can occur at this stage will be particularly revealing, as we shall see later. For now though, we are noting that a partial engagement of the dream production system can be observed outside of the REM state proper.

The all-important PGO spikes

New information piled up. Michel Jouvet's discovery that REM sleep was accompanied by muscle paralysis – specifically, the inhibition of antigravity muscles – was also crucial, when linked to a different finding by Giuseppe Moruzzi. Moruzzi found that the REM state could be divided into 'tonic' and 'phasic' components. In the tonic phase, which lasts throughout REM sleep, the muscles are immobilized. However, periodically, bursts of sudden brief activity are imposed upon this underlying immobility, explaining not only the rapid eye movements but also the fine twitching of the muscles that also occurs.[8] This is the phasic stage. In this stage, changes in breathing and heart rate were also detected.[9]

All of these bursts of activity happen when electrical signals, called PGO spikes, occur in the brain. These signals arise at the bottom of the brain (in an area of the brainstem called the pons), move upwards into the midbrain (to a part called the geniculate body) and then to the occipital cortex, part of the cerebral cortex. The signal gets its name PGO from its course – from pons (P) to geniculate body (G) to occipital cortex (O).

It soon became clear that the neurological system that generates the PGO spikes and the resultant phasic component of REM sleep is completely distinct from the system that causes the muscle immobility,[10] and can also be detected in other phases of sleep.[11] This would indicate that PGO spike activity may be linked to dreams, as these too occur outside of REM sleep. It may even explain why dreams occur in sleep phases other than REM and why the dreams are not so complete – because, as previously suggested, there is only partial rather than total engagement of the dream production system in hypnagogic dreaming (the twilight zone between wakefulness and sleep).[12]

We need, therefore, to think about the PGO spikes as a discrete but important aspect of REM sleep and dreaming. Studies into the effects of depriving humans of REM sleep for a night or more have shown that, on the first night that REM sleep is allowed again, there is an increase both in the amount of REM sleep experienced and in the amount of eye darting and muscle twitching that goes on – the PGO spike-generated phasic activity.[13,14] In an experiment in which a cat was aroused very gently at the point of entering REM sleep, the researcher, William Dement, found that, although the cat didn't re-enter the REM state when it went back to sleep, there was still a lot of PGO spike activity. Even when REM deprivation had occurred for a couple of days, the cat attempted no increase in REM sleep to compensate for all it had lost. But it did continue to show plenty of PGO spike activity. Importantly, this revealed that it is the phasic element that accompanies REM sleep which we can't do without, not the REM sleep stage itself, even though REM sleep is the most usual form in which we make up for the phasic deprivation. Clearly, something important is going on in the brain at these times of sudden PGO spike activity.

Dement also found that, when he deprived cats of REM sleep for any appreciable period, they started to show highly increased arousal patterns, becoming easily sexually aroused or easily tipped into aggression and rage. A few days after he gave them a drug which inhibits the synthesis of the brain chemical serotonin they started to produce PGO spike brain activity when awake. (It wasn't at that time known that PGO spikes could also ordinarily be produced when awake.) The cats showed hallucinatory behaviour and underwent dramatic personality changes – they were hypersexual, aggressive and constantly wanted to eat. Then, as time passed, and the PGO spike activity spread evenly throughout waking and sleeping, the cats became lethargic as if exhausted.

What was going on? Dement concluded that there are two systems via which animals, including humans, carry out, or discharge, instinctive impulses, and that we only have so much energy available to us with which to do so, after which our stores become depleted. Our instinctive behaviour is partly governed by the basic drives to drink, eat, reproduce, etc. The rest of it is governed by the PGO spikes, which do not operate when basic drives (for instance, to eat) are in operation. But what is the second drive system, governed by the PGO spikes during REM sleep, discharging? Although Dement came up with a suggestion, he was never really happy with it. As he put it himself, it seemed implausible to imagine that REM sleep exists to stop the nervous system from becoming overexcited. We can show, however, that the PGO spikes do indeed govern an important drive discharge system, a highly sophisticated one with vital consequences for our emotional and physical health.

Dement and others had been paying attention to the role of PGO spikes during sleep. In the 1980s, another team of researchers made the discovery, referred to above, that PGO spikes also show in the brain during normal waking behaviour. PGO spikes, it appears, are part of the alerting system or 'orientation response' that draws our attention towards anything new and potentially threatening that is happening in our environment.[15,16] So the spikes are activated when there is a loud noise, and we turn towards it to see what caused it, or when a smell of burning leads us to the kitchen or when a sudden movement draws our eye. At the same time as the spikes are generated, we freeze momentarily (paralysis); signals start stimulating the cortex to let it know that something needs our attention, and other physiological reactions occur that are also characteristic of the REM state. In other words, the REM state is, effectively, one prolonged orientation response. The significance of this will be shown shortly.

The compelling evidence that REM sleep serves to programme instinctive behaviours which the young of the species will need to activate as they go through life might lead one to argue that, once the programming is done, the need for REM sleep should cease. Jouvet attempts an explanation for this. He suggests that programming instinctive behaviours on a continual basis enables more flexibility. Thus, according to an animal or human's individual experience in life, REM sleep might enable either the original programming to be reasserted (nature over nurture) or allow the effects of experience to modify the programming (nurture over nature). However, no analysis of dreams from REM sleep showed any consistent pattern of interaction between waking behaviour and the rehearsal of instinctive drives. Thus, although their discoveries added enormously to our understanding of REM sleep's early purpose, neither Dement,

Jouvet or any of the other great researchers in the field were able to put a finger on why REM sleep is essential right through life for our survival. They had not answered the most fundamental question: why do we spend about a twelfth of our entire lives dreaming?

To answer this question it was necessary to look once more at the content of dreams, but in a light informed by the new biological discoveries. This is exactly what was done by one of the writers of this book, Joe Griffin, in research carried out during the 1980s and 1990s. The full story of how he reached his findings and arrived at what is now known as the expectation fulfilment theory of dreaming is told in the book *Why We Dream*.[17] The following is a short account, taken from an interview with him about his work.

Recording dreams

"My interest in studying why we dream began when I was a young psychologist. I woke up one morning and then drifted back to sleep and dreamed I was climbing a castle wall, which was starting to crumble, much to my alarm. When I awoke, with this image still vivid in my mind, I realized that just before I had gone back to sleep again, I had been thinking about a childhood experience when I had pulled myself up on a wall to retrieve a ball which had fallen on the other side. As I climbed the wall I grasped a stone, which loosened and fell away. I fell backwards on to the grass verge and the stone hit me on the forehead, making a gash large enough to require stitches. I still have the scar.

"I was already extremely interested in dreams and had read as much of the relevant scientific literature as I could find. So I knew about Calvin Hall's theory that dreams were 'works of art' which reflected the unvarnished personal concerns of the dreamer. It seemed clear to me that my dream was a graphic version of my earlier thoughts but with some significant changes. The roadside wall had become a castle wall and the single stone which came loose was replaced by an entire crumbling wall. Also, the dream seemed to reflect what just happened to have been in my mind after waking and before I dozed off again, which could hardly be considered to be a personal 'concern' of momentous proportions. So that was the moment I decided I would collect my dreams on a systematic basis and see whether I could link them with waking concerns or not.

"The problem I then faced was that I only rarely recalled my dreams. I knew from research findings that we all dream several times a night, even if we only rarely recall a dream. I also knew from personal experience that, when we do recall a dream, it is essential to tell somebody else about it immediately, or to write it down, otherwise we automatically seem to forget them. Certainly, whenever I go back to sleep again following recall of a vivid dream, I rarely remember it when I wake up. The solution, I decided, was to do as many before me had done and keep a pen and paper beside my bed so that, when I did remember a dream, I could commit it to paper straight away and not risk forgetting it.

"Over a period of time I became more and more proficient at recalling my dreams. I reached a point where I could automatically wake up after a dream sequence and record it there and then. What was more difficult was to recall and reflect on my thoughts and experiences of the previous day, which I hypothesized would be the subject of the dreams. Because of the metaphorical richness of the dream content, it was almost impossible for me to detach myself sufficiently, straight away, to identify what the elements of the dream might be standing for. I found it more fruitful to put the dream to one side and come back to it some time later, with a fresher mind. When I became more adept at doing this, I would almost invariably find myself recalling an experience or concern that showed a striking structural and symbolic similarity to the dream sequence. As I continued to collect and study my own and other people's dreams over the next nine months, I became convinced that dreams were representations of the most emotionally arousing experiences of the previous waking period. What's more, these experiences were *always* expressed in symbolic or metaphorical imagery.

"I recorded any dream, however insignificant it seemed, and was struck to notice that still all the dream elements were metaphorical.(It is accepted that dreams use metaphor but had not been known that *all* are cloaked in it.) I found that no one except the dreamer ever 'played' themselves in any ordinary way. If husbands, mothers or other relatives or friends featured in a dream as themselves, they were either out of 'shot' or were symbolically disguised in some way. Often relatives, friends or colleagues, even celebrities, appeared not as themselves but as relevant aspects of the dreamer's personality.

"This can be clearly demonstrated in a dream reported to me by Michael, an Irishman who came to see me for help with a personal problem. He had been a hospital porter but had recently begun training to become a psychiatric nurse, and was worried because he badly kept wanting to laugh at inappropriate moments when in the company of his fellow students. To relieve this need to laugh, he had developed the habit of making a jocular remark and then laughing heartily at it himself. This worked well enough with hospital porters but was not going down too well among his new student colleagues who, due to their training in psychology, had become more hypersensitive to odd traits in one another. I had suggested that his need to laugh was due not so much to his seeing humour in any given situation but more to his need to relieve the embarrassment he was experiencing in it.

"A few days later Michael reported a dream to me in which he was in a church which had a waist-high wall dividing the altar from the area where the congregation was sitting. In the dream he was on the other side of this wall from the congregation, and was urinating up against it. Standing on the altar was the chat show host Terry Wogan; he was the only one who could see what Michael was doing and was laughing. Everyone else started laughing too, assuming Michael had cracked a joke.

"In this dream, it seems clear that Terry Wogan (whom Michael had recently seen in person) stands for an aspect of Michael himself – the public image he thinks other people have of him: a witty and intelligent Irishman. People in the dream assume he has made a joke but in fact he is laughing at his own embarrassment. Even the urination is an interesting metaphor for his tension ('pissing' himself) and the uncontrollable need to laugh ('pissing himself' laughing). The wall dividing the altar from the congregation represents the barrier between his hidden self – the part that is anxious and embarrassed in company – and his public self, whom people see laughing.

"However, although the metaphorical pattern of this dream is extremely clear, I did not yet have an explanation for why dreams should so reliably take this form.

"At the end of nine months I felt confident that dreams were metaphorical expressions of waking concerns and presumed that the most important waking concerns were what the brain chose as the subjects for dreams. At this point, why we needed to dream, and why we dream in metaphor, still remained a mystery, but at least I could put the hypothesis that dreams were metaphorical translations of our most important waking concerns to a scientific test. If this theory was right, it should be possible to set up an experiment to predict the theme of dreams in advance. All one would have to do is to make a list of one's most important waking concerns in the day before dreaming, then compare this list of predicted dream themes to the actual dream themes recorded from the dream material collected during the night. If the theory was correct, the predicted dream themes should match those recorded.

"So as to have access to as many of my dreams as possible during the period of the experiment, I decided to set my alarm clock at two hourly intervals every night for a week. Each evening I prepared my list of dream theme predictions, based on my most important emotional concerns of the day. To my utter dismay, the experimental results quickly showed that the theory could only be partly correct. Some of the predicted themes did appear in dreams but some of my most confident predictions failed to materialize. More disturbing still was the fact that often the dream themes reflected relatively trivial waking concerns whilst ignoring major ones. Clearly, some additional criteria besides emotional importance were being used by my brain to select the themes from waking experience to feature in my dreams. I decided to carry on collecting my dreams for another 12 months to see if I could identify what these criteria could be, but they continued to elude me.

"The breakthrough came when I had a row with my wife, Liz. She, a hard-working nurse, was, unsurprisingly, getting extremely fed up with being woken several times every night by my alarm, as I single-mindedly pursued my research. I was also suffering from tiredness and the stress of constant reflection on each previous day's happenings in order to explain dreams. This pressure resulted in an enormous row between us one night at bedtime. We both vented our feelings fully and turned away to sleep back to back, in a huff. As I was lying there it crossed my mind, before we eventually fell asleep, that this row was very likely to form the basis of a dream. So, I did what any self respecting experimenter would do: I risked further complaints from

Liz, switched the light back on, and noted it.

"Yet, although I recorded five dreams that night, and my worries about the success of the experiment featured symbolically in a few of them, none contained anything that could be related to the row. It was while puzzling over this that the missing piece of the jigsaw suddenly fell into place: during the row with my wife I had *fully expressed* my anger, therefore completing the pattern of arousal, whereas my on-going worries about the experiment were *not discharged*. What becomes the subject of dreams, I suddenly realized, is not any emotionally arousing events but *unexpressed* emotionally arousing concerns from the previous day that had not completed the arousal/discharge cycle. Far from supporting Freud's theory that dreams reflect subconscious infantile wishes, I confirmed, as I continued for several more years to collect and study dream content, that anything emotionally arousing, even television programmes, can become the subject matter of dreams if the arousal pattern is not completed – acted out – in the daytime.

"I concluded from this that dreaming is the acting out of uncompleted emotionally arousing introspections, all elements of which appear in the guise of sensory analogues – metaphorical representations. And this process would serve to free up the brain to deal with the emotionally arousing events of the following day, instead of having to maintain a readiness to continue responding to the emotionally arousing introspections of the day before.

"It follows that an important benefit of this REM process is that it serves to preserve the integrity of our instinctive personality – our underlying instinctive templates. This is because inhibitions placed upon the expression of an instinctive reaction pattern whilst we are awake are removed by acting out the completion of the pattern in the dream process.

"This does not, of course, mean that we can't learn to modify the expression of our instincts. On the contrary, because of our highly evolved prefrontal cortex, we can, with practice over time, learn to control, for example, our anger and the expression of it, just as we can learn to postpone immediate satisfaction of our lusts and appetites. But dreaming maintains the original instinctive impulses at their original strength, as given to us by our genes. This is necessary because, although, thanks to the prefrontal cortex, we can learn to control the expression of instinctive impulses, we may also need access to them in different circumstances. For example, anger is mostly not an appropriate reaction for normal minor irritations; the smooth running of social intercourse is more often better served when it is inhibited. But there are times when anger could be vital to our survival, to defend ourselves from physical attack, and we need access to it. Fortunately, the cortex is infinitely malleable and we can do that. It is a wonderfully flexible system whereby the instinctive core personality is kept intact but its expression can continually readapt to different circumstances. Our instincts are never closed down permanently in a specific direction. We can always go back to the original template.

"Just think what a disaster it would be if nature allowed us to be able to turn our instincts down permanently, with ease. We would be infinitely less flexible creatures. A child could quickly learn, say, that it is better to stay quiet and be non-assertive in threatening situations. But later on, in situations where it is absolutely essential to survival to be assertive (call "Fire!" for instance), he or she would effectively be crippled.

"So, one of the big advantages of dreaming is that it stops us becoming completely conditioned creatures. It is no accident that most totalitarian leaders sooner or later hit upon the effectiveness of sleep deprivation in order to torture and brainwash prisoners.[18] This is effective because, without REM sleep to re-mint the core templates and keep them in order, people quickly become unstable and more easily brainwashed and reprogrammed.

"If I was right about all this, I thought, this would be a very different matter from dreaming serving to solve problems or deal with concerns or even just to throw light on our worries, as others had suggested. It would mean that the dreaming process is, instead, a method of making 'space' in the brain. Without it we would need the most gigantic brains to contain all our unexpressed drives and concerns. Indeed, support for this idea came from research findings about one of the most primitive mammals: the duck-billed platypus.

"It has a huge cerebral cortex, compared with what might be expected, and spends more time in REM sleep than any other creature – up to eight hours a day. This suggests that it is reprogramming entire instinctive programmes on a daily basis. Not only that, the evidence shows that the REM sleep of the platypus is the kind we see in the programming stage of the foetus.* The cortex is not stimulated and so dreaming cannot be taking place.[19]

"I further found that, if an issue is an ongoing concern, it will very likely be thought about again the next day and reappear in some form in next night's dream, hence repetitive dreams. This is all backed up by my experimental findings over 12 years of collecting dreams and by evolutionary explanations for the role of REM sleep, which help explain not only why the discharge of emotionally arousing events is needed, but also why dreams are metaphorical."

To dream, and let off steam

So, to summarize the expectation fulfilment theory of dreaming, REM sleep continues into adulthood so that we can dream and thereby maintain the integrity of the instinctive templates that themselves were laid down in the REM state. It deactivates, once it has been stimulated, any undischarged emotional arousal that would be unproductive and consume unnecessarily high amounts of energy. We wouldn't survive very long if we all lashed out every time we got irritated or if we attempted to engage in sex every time a sexual thought crossed our minds. Bottling up such arousals and storing them would require much too much brain space. (Alas, we don't have a 'pensieve', the wonderful invention into which Albus Dumbledore, Harry Potter's headmaster at the Hogwarts School for Wizards, would siphon off all the thoughts and memories he didn't want to crowd his head with.[20]) So we have to have another way to deal with them. Not only would storing patterns of arousal take up too much capacity in our brain, it would also cause another major problem. The repeated inhibition

---

* Mammals, such as whales and dolphins, also have disproportionately large cortices. For a long time it was believed that they did not have REM sleep because they suffered the Ondine curse: they could only let one hemisphere sleep at a time because they might drown if they spent time paralysed in REM sleep. Hence the extra-large cortex. However, later observations showed that this genus seemed to have evolved a highly specialized form of sleep that had the characteristic jerks of the head, neck and sometimes the whole body and the rapid eye movements typical of REM sleep in terrestrial animals. But these periods only last a very short time: the animal is paralysed, rolls over and begins to sink but then comes out of this sleep state to swim and breathe again. [Lyamain, O. I. et al (2000) Rest and activity states in a gray whale. *Journal of Sleep Research*, 9, 3, 261–267.]

by the cortex of instinctive impulses would weaken or deactivate the instinctive impulses themselves. This would be a disaster for all mammals. To give another example of what might happen in such circumstances, if we were to punish children every time they got angry at home, they would soon learn never to get angry. We would have *conditioned* away their instinctive impulse towards anger as a defence mechanism. This might not cause problems at home, but what if they are bullied at school? They would be powerless victims. (Of course, not defending themselves against bullying could become a conditioned response, in such circumstances, but can be reversed with effective therapy at any time later.)

Now we can see the brilliance of the REM state. By allowing, for example, a restrained anger impulse to be expressed in a dream, but not to be recorded by the cerebral cortex (we only recall a dream if it is immediately processed by the brain on waking), the aggressive instinct is maintained, and the cortex can restrain its expression in unsuitable contexts. This makes for maximum flexibility, allowing us to modify instinctive impulses in certain circumstances and express them in others, when warranted.

In the years since Joe Griffin developed his theory, more and more scientific evidence has emerged to support it. It has now clearly been shown, for instance, that there is a match between the content of dreams and waking concerns and that it is the most emotionally significant waking events which feature in our dreams.[21,22,23,24] Dissipation of emotional arousal relies on the reactivation of emotional memory during sleep.[25] Further, when we have experienced highly emotionally arousing events, we need REM sleep to calm down the agitated networks in the brain.[26,27,28] When deprived of REM sleep, negative emotions from the previous day persist into the next one,[29,30] as might be expected if these have not been able to be discharged in the normal fashion overnight.

Why we dream in metaphor – and then forget our dreams

Once all the findings from biological studies, scientific research into sleep patterns and Joe Griffin's experiments on dreams are pieced together, we can see that REM sleep remains concerned with instinctive drives throughout life but its later role is to deactivate them, leaving the prefrontal cortex free to deal with the emotionally arousing events of the following day. And, just as programming instincts involves creating a pattern or template for which an analogue can be found in the environment (twig-like materials, a friendly human face, etc.), so it makes sense that deactivation also uses sensory analogues or metaphors, enabling the brain to draw on images which *represent* the unexpressed emotional arousals of the day.

Because the right hemisphere is specialized for using metaphor (and the left more usually is dominant for detail, using logic and language[31]), we would expect that dreaming would primarily be a right hemisphere function. And this is so. REM sleep, as has been confirmed many times, is associated with brainstem arousal, right hemisphere activation, and low-level left hemisphere arousal.[32] (This means that, while the right hemisphere dreams the dream, there can still be some left brain 'interior dialogue', puzzling over the dream sequence. However, such left hemisphere musings still accept the reality of the dream.)

But there is another, much more important reason for why we dream in metaphor. We do so to prevent our memory stores from becoming either corrupt or incomplete.

To illustrate how this works, let's take the scenario of an office party, where, perhaps disinhibited by alcohol, Amy, the operations manager, discovers a hitherto hidden sexual attraction to the managing director, which appears to be reciprocated. As she is a responsible married woman with three children under the age of four, she doesn't act upon it. But that night, in line with the expectation fulfilment theory of dreaming, she will need to complete the expectation aroused, both to discharge the still 'live' emotional expectation that is taking up brain space and also to preserve the integrity of her emotional instincts. But there is a problem. If Amy dreams that, as a result of her attraction at the party, her boss whisks her away on a romantic holiday, she will be creating a memory that is partially false. It might be argued that we are perfectly well able to distinguish dreams from reality – we do so whenever we happen to remember our dreams. But, during dreaming, lines of connection to the brain networks that govern critical thinking are largely closed and it is only afterwards, if the dream is remembered, that it can be rationalized.

If, on the other hand, as is usual for us all, Amy forgets her dream, she will have gaps in her memory of what actually happened, since the dream involves both real (the attraction at the party) and fantasy (the romantic holiday) experiences. We use our memory of experiences to help us predict how to react in similar circumstances in the future: a memory system with significant memories missing would be next to useless for this purpose.

Using an analogous experience as a means of completing the arousal provides a perfect solution. It enables the arousal to be discharged and the metaphorical dream material can be safely forgotten, but the original record of what happened (the attraction at the party) can still be remembered. So Amy may dream that she has been whisked away on her romantic assignation not with her boss but with some celebrity whom she also finds attractive. The dream can be forgotten (or enjoyed, if remembered) but the original arousal that inspired the dream is safely stored in memory, reminding Amy not to be alone in potentially compromising circumstances with her boss. What has been discharged is the *arousal* associated with the instinctive urge but, importantly, the instinctive urge itself in the context it was experienced is remembered. (Neuroscientists Julia Keeler, Douglas Pretsell and Trevor Robbins proposed something similar in their paper describing experiments showing the key role of memory of adverse experiences in learning. They stated that imagined adverse consequences, when we weigh up whether or not to follow a certain course, are encoded as analogues, not literal memories, in order to keep them separate from memories of actual experiences.[33])

All this also explains why it is actually *important* that we usually forget our dreams. When we are awake, the hippocampus puts together our experience (visual, textural, auditory, etc) of recent events to form long-term memories which can become integrated into the cerebral cortex. It does that to facilitate efficient pattern matching. But, as discussed above, if the dream is allowed to be stored as a real memory, it will corrupt the memory store and greatly diminish our ability reliably to predict the outcome of similar experiences in the future. PET scans and other types of research have shown that, in dreaming, the prefrontal cortex is largely inactive. This effectively prevents the hippocampus from sending the metaphorical dream information to the cortex for long-term storage – which in itself strongly indicates that dreams are not intended to be remembered.[34] Sleep researchers have now positively been able to show that melanin-concentrating hormones active during REM sleep produce neurons in the brain region termed the hypothalamus that actively contribute to forgetting in the hippocampus.[35]

But sometimes we do recall our dreams. Might this not undo all our good dream work? The answer is no, because the arousal is switched off once the expectation is acted out. And, once we are awake, the cortex is switched back on, enabling us to compare dream content to what is really happening around us and, thus, to distinguish between dream and reality.

The richness of the REM state

The REM state does not so much *simulate* a kind of reality in dreams as *generate* reality. What we experience in dreaming is an intensely real construction that we totally believe in at the time. It is a reality that in many ways can seem emotionally much richer than the reality of the waking state. We can illustrate this with a dream that was quoted in *Why We Dream*. This is how the dreamer described it:

"We are going to a party. My family is there. I am walking along the road with my cousin and all our aunts and uncles. We call into a shop for sweets. My cousin gets served but the girl behind the counter does not seem to understand my instructions. She keeps getting the wrong bar of chocolate and seems very rude. We go into another shop and I get an old fashioned bag of Maltesers and we eat these small balls of honeycomb covered in milk chocolate. We then see my aunts, and my mother, walking up the road. All my aunts look as though they have been put through a chocolate machine; they all appear as different types of chocolate. I notice that my mother appears as my favourite chocolate, a packet of Maltesers. But she is falling some distance behind my aunts. I am annoyed that they are not waiting for her. My family are talking about a skirt that had been given to them by Granny. It is decided to give it to me try on. I do so and it fits me perfectly."

The dream was based on the following waking experiences:

1. The previous day a member of the dreamer's family had invited her to a party. The anticipated party provides the setting for the dream.

2. The dreamer was a senior nurse and, on her ward round the previous day, she had been accompanied by an inexperienced junior nurse who seemed unable to carry out correctly the instructions she gave her and had been rather insolent. This analogy is represented in the dream by her difficulty in getting served by the rude shop assistant.
3. The old fashioned bag of chocolates relates to her weakness for eating chocolate (she had bought some on the way home from work the previous evening). The 'old fashioned' relates to her strongly held view that this weakness is handed down through the generations in her family.
4. The image of her aunts and mother as bars of chocolate relates to a conversation she had had a couple of days earlier with her boyfriend concerning her weight. He had said that, unless she was careful, she would continue to put on weight, just like the rest of her family, who were all overweight. These worries were re-stimulated by her guilty feelings at buying chocolate on her way home.
5. Another dream theme is the annoyance she feels when she sees her mother falling behind her aunts and her aunts not waiting for her.
6. This reflects her concern for her mother, who had recently had heart trouble. She felt annoyed when she learned that her aunts were rushing to their doctors to have their hearts checked without waiting to see how her mother got on. Thinking about weight led her to recall her annoyance at her aunts' recent behaviour.
7. The final theme is that of the skirt, given by her grandmother, which fits her perfectly. Her aunts and her mother inherit their figure from her grandmother. The 'perfectly fitting' skirt is an analogy for inheriting the family 'figure', caused by a liking of sweet things, that she thinks she has inherited.

Every element in dreams is an analogical representation of something else connected with a waking event. So it is that, in this dream, the dreamer's mother and her aunts don't appear as themselves but analogically manifest as different types of chocolate bar.

Clearly, this little dream vignette contains multiple levels of meaning. At the same time as expressing the dreamer's concern that her aunts were more bothered about their own health than her mother's, it also expresses her naturally greater affection for her mother than for her aunts, through the representation of her mother as her favourite chocolate. Further, the image of the aunts all being made out of chocolate succinctly conveys their having a common genetic pool, as does the skirt that fits. It also incorporates the dreamer's worries about eating too much chocolate and putting on weight herself, and about whether her mother's liking for chocolate was a contributory factor to her mother's heart disease.

All these sources of emotional arousal are represented in one brief dream and thereby deactivated. But in waking reality we can't handle images with multiple relationships *simultaneously* because it is too confusing and would keep us in a state where we could not make discriminations and choices about how to act. The meanings of images in waking reality have to be selected from 'boxes' of separate meanings. We could all list a number of things that a chair could represent and be used for, for example, but we can only see a chair from a single point of view at a time – will we bump into it? Do we need to sit down in it? Is it comfortable? Is it an antique? Is it damaged? When functioning day to day, the brain has to cut down on the metaphorical richness available to us in the REM state that dreaming employs. We would be overwhelmed otherwise.

Anticipating reality

When we are awake, the brain is always trying to anticipate reality. Moment by moment, it is constructing a model of what it expects reality to be, by matching information it receives through the senses to pre-existing patterns already stored. So a tree is recognized to be a tree and a particular smell is recognized to signify a roast dinner cooking in the oven. It is only when what is expected *fails* to materialize that we get a sudden jolt of awareness, such as when we realize that a stick we see on the path ahead is not a stick, because it is starting to move, or when, as we start down a flight of steps in the dark, there isn't another step where we expect it to be. In such circumstances, the brain immediately fires the orientation response, focusing our attention on the discrepancy between the expected pattern (a stick, another step) and the new pattern that has been identified or matched (snake! no step!), so as to anticipate how important a survival issue it might be and set in train the appropriate reaction. In that split second of fear and unknowing, we draw on the REM state, with its huge library of metaphorical information, to attempt to make sense of what is happening: the moving stick is a snake (we get it right); we are falling to our deaths (we get it wrong – the distance between the steps is just a little deeper than we had expected).

Very many neuroscientists now talk in terms of the 'predictions' (which we call pattern matching) which the brain uses to make sense of our environment.[36] Neuroscientist and psychologist Lisa Feldman Barrett explains this concept succinctly in her book *How Emotions Are Made*: "Your brain has learned that a single sensory cue, such as a loud bang, can have many different causes – a door being slammed, a bursting balloon, a hand clap, a gunshot. It distinguishes which of these different causes is most relevant only by their probability in different contexts. It asks, which combination of my past experiences provides the closest match to this sound, given this *particular situation* with its accompanying sights, smells and other sensations?

"So, trapped within the skull, with only past experiences as a guide, your brain makes *predictions*. ... Here I'm focusing on predictions at a microscopic scale as millions of neurons talk to one another. These neural conversations try to anticipate every fragment of sight, sound, smell, taste and touch that you will experience and every action that you will take. These predictions are your brain's best guesses of what's going on in the world around you, and how to deal with it to keep you alive and well."[37]

So a prime function of the brain is always to anticipate the next moment of reality, second-guessing what the experience will be, so as to be ready to react appropriately. If you are walking down an unfamiliar, creepy lane one moonlit night and become aware of a strange lump ahead by the side of the road, your imagination might decide it looks like a dead body, filling you with apprehension. This emotionally arousing anticipated scenario is released to be pattern matched to incoming sensory patterns. But, when you draw up close, you find it is only a discarded bag of old clothes. The expected dead man 'reality' is disconfirmed.

In dreaming, of course, there are no incoming sensory patterns to match to. And, since we can only focus our attention if there is a pattern to focus on, real or imagined, the dreaming brain pattern matches to uncompleted expectations from waking (worries or concerns of the day that weren't resolved before bedtime), expressed metaphorically. This pattern match will always be to an emotionally arousing but as yet unmanifested concern from when we were previously awake. In effect, even when dreaming, the brain is still trying to generate a model of reality. Dreams have to be about expectations because that is the way that the brain works 24 hours a day.

We can see the power of expectation in conversations. When somebody is trying to get their meaning across word by word, a listener who is paying attention seems to receive the information in a holistic way and is often able to predict the speaker's next point. This is because, using the incoming information and previous patterns of memory, the listener is anticipating what is being said and modelling it in their mind. That is why so many conversations can almost appear telepathic. You know what the other person is about to say, or understand what they are getting at, so you can add to it. Indeed, it has recently been verified by scientific research involving brain scanning that the brain is constantly trying to guess the next word when we are reading or listening to someone speaking.[38]

Is dreaming connected to learning?

A popular theory to explain the function of REM sleep is that it is primarily involved in the consolidation of new learnings. The evidence used to support this comes from animal and human learning experiments.[39] When learning involves emotional arousal, it has been observed that REM sleep increases in the hours afterwards and recordings from individual brain cells in the hippocampus during REM sleep show that the nerve cells that were involved in the arousing experience fire again.[40] The conclusion drawn is that the learning is being rehearsed and embedded in REM sleep.

However, it is not surprising if, after REM sleep, animals and people have an improvement in memory. This is because REM sleep is designed to reduce emotional interference in the brain from the previous day's uncompleted patterns of arousal arising from all the activation of anticipations that didn't work out. This would have the effect of improving performance anyway. The fact that the same nerve cells fire is also predicted by our theory, which holds that the *structure* of the waking experience that caused the autonomic (involuntary) arousal is maintained in the dream state. All that is different is that the content has changed into metaphors.

Of course, most learning situations cause autonomic arousal – even in experiments with rats, where much of the 'consolidation of new learning theory' originates. (Exploration of mazes is, for a rat, a highly autonomically arousing experience.) Whilst learning, we don't know what is going to happen; we are anticipating. Some of the time we get it right, some of the time we get it wrong. Some of the things we are anticipating may be dangerous, such as what might be round the corner in a maze for a rat; or distressing, such as the possibility of our failing an important exam. So the very essence of any learning situation is that we are generating expectations, some of which are confirmed and some of which are not confirmed. We would therefore anticipate that they would be manifested in REM sleep and that the same nerve cells that fired during that learning experience would be re-fired in REM sleep. Indeed, as said above that the more emotionally arousing the learning experience, the more REM sleep follows and that learning material that is not emotionally arousing produces no increase in REM sleep.[41]

Clearly, too many facts are not accommodated by the 'REM sleep is memory consolidation' theory. It does not answer why patients who are depressed commonly have excessive REM sleep and their ability to concentrate, learn and memorize is impaired whilst depressed.[42] On the other hand, patients suffering from depression who are put on monoamine oxidase inhibitors, antidepressants which totally block REM sleep, show a significant improvement in their ability to recall new information.[43] So, far from REM sleep consolidating learning and the recall of information, the elimination of REM sleep actually seems to facilitate the acquisition of learning and the recall of information in some situations. Jouvet has reported several cases that confound the 'REM sleep consolidates learning' theory. He describes, for example, the case of a patient with syringomyelia, a painful disease of the spinal cord that, for more than three months, prevented him from sleeping, as verified by a continuous polygraph recording. This patient had no problems with learning or memory.[44]

Another famous case commented on by Jouvet concerned a lawyer in Israel who was a victim of a shrapnel lesion in his brainstem and had no REM sleep for several years. In spite of this, he maintained his professional activity as a lawyer, which involved him in constant new learning as he prepared his cases. He would have been unable to carry out his job if he had had impaired memory.[45]

So, at best, the improvement in memory following REM sleep is a secondary consequence and the hypothesis that REM sleep evolved for consolidation of memory does not hold up. When the emotionally aroused expectations which failed to manifest in the learning situation are deactivated by the dream, it then becomes possible for the correct manifestations to be consolidated into long-term memory, without interference from the emotional arousal caused by the failed expectations. To return to the scenario of a rat exploring a maze: the rat may be anticipating the possibility of danger around every corner. In dream form that night, it will explore the maze again, but this time actually see the anticipated danger. This completes the activated circuit and switches it off, allowing the original memory trace to be consolidated and recalled without interference. In the case of the lawyer referred to above, the shrapnel wound in the brainstem that prevented REM sleep also prevented activation of the flight-or-fight impulse. Although clearly that would have brought problems of its own, one effect was lack of emotional arousal around learning, meaning that no arousals needed deactivating.

Why we evolved to dream

Dreaming is nature's solution to the problem that, once an instinct-driven pattern is activated, usually the only way to deactivate it is by carrying it out – which clearly does not give animals the flexibility they need to survive. Animals needed to evolve the ability to inhibit, when necessary, arousals such as anger or sexual urges, and deactivate them later, in a different way. Otherwise the arousal is unhealthily retained in the autonomic nervous system. That's why we evolved to dream. During REM sleep the activated instinct patterns 'left over' from waking are vicariously run out, thus deactivating them and releasing the data processing potential of the cerebral cortex to deal with the emotionally arousing contingencies of the next day.

Thus we can see the beautiful economy of nature. The same process that programmes instinctive behaviour – the genetically anticipated patterns of stimulation – are also used to deactivate 'left over' anticipated patterns of stimulation from waking – the activated instinctive drive patterns. The instinctive frames of reference programmed in REM sleep don't have sensory content until they are matched up with their environmental counterparts. The anticipated or introspected stimulation which gives rise to dreaming, on the other hand, does have sensory content, hence its analogical processing in REM sleep – dreaming. Thus nature accomplishes two essential functions with the same process.

A dream collected by Ivan illustrates the metaphorical translation that occurs and gives a clear example of this process at work.

A dream ship

Ivan woke up one Monday morning, having dreamed that he was on a Norwegian cruise ship, which was odd because he had never been on a cruise. The ship had two decks, both of which were divided into a number of compartments, and had rails. The ship was extremely crowded and the passengers were moving very slowly, shuffling from one compartment to the next. Ivan, somewhat against his will, felt himself going with the flow. Every time he left a compartment he felt a sense of relief wash over him. There were several strange things about the ship. For one thing, he couldn't see the sea. For another, to his surprise and indignation, the crew of the ship seemed dirty and their manners inconsiderate: he had always thought of the Scandinavians as clean and polite people. In one compartment, he came upon the late Harry Worth, a comedian whose heyday was several decades ago and whom Ivan had never found very amusing. Harry Worth was trying to make the passengers laugh, but no one was taking any notice of him. He struck Ivan as a rather sad character.

This is how Ivan explained why he came to have this peculiar dream: "As I reflected on the dream after waking, I couldn't at first see what it was about. Then I asked myself what I had done the previous day that had got me aroused but which I had not expressed my feelings about and immediately the parallels with what had happened to me became clear. It was possible to read off the metaphorical translations my mind had made in the REM state.

"Sunday is normally a day I use to wind down after a busy week, which regularly involves a fair amount of travelling. But on this particular Sunday I had promised to go with my wife to IKEA, the large Swedish (not Norwegian) 'warehouse' company that specializes in reasonably priced household items and self-assembly furniture. We had just moved to a new house and she wanted to buy some items for it. Since I often feel a bit guilty about being away so much, I had not only agreed to go to IKEA but actually pretended that I wanted to go! The feelings I didn't express were that, in fact, shopping on a Sunday is the last thing I ever want to do and I felt we couldn't afford to spend any money since we had just taken on a large mortgage.

"We drove 40 miles, from our home in Sussex, up the motorway to the IKEA in Croydon, South London. It turned out to be a warehouse decked out on two floors with rails everywhere (like a ship). It was heaving with people, even though it was a Sunday. The staff (crew) all seemed to have dreadful, streaming colds and were coughing and sneezing. I clearly remember thinking it was disgusting that they were spreading their germs over so many people, crammed together in such a tight space. IKEA is set out in separate 'compartments', one for kitchen furniture, another for dining room furniture, another for living room furniture, and so on, through bathroom, bedroom, home office and garden furniture. We slowly moved with the crowd from compartment to compartment, with me pretending to be interested as my wife examined everything.

"In one 'compartment' a clown (represented in the dream by Harry Worth) was trying to entertain people with balloon tricks but nobody was taking any notice of him. I remember watching him for a while, thinking what a rotten job he had and feeling rather sorry for him. Although my wife looked at everything, she didn't in the end buy anything, so, every time we left a section, I felt relieved that she hadn't spent any money! (This was represented in the dream as relief on leaving each compartment.)"

This dream enacted Ivan's frustrating experience, but with even the most minor details changed (such as the ship being Norwegian instead of Swedish). The ease with which every aspect of it can be related to an observation he made or a feeling he experienced makes it a perfect illustration of how the deactivation process works during dream sleep. Metaphors used in dreams are not necessarily very sophisticated. The brain tends to draw on whatever images are closest at hand or are most familiar, which is why some images recur again and again. (Also the dream may be deactivating the same concerns which are worried about day after day, and therefore uses the same repeat images.) Often a person seen on television the night before may appear in a dream, standing in for someone in real life because an aspect of their personality or story resonates with something of emotional significance in the dreamer's life. Completely banal images feature quite often. For instance, a woman who had been struggling with an essay she was writing for a college exam, uncertain she was getting the level right, had a dream in which she was a teacher. When she came to the front of the class to sit at the teacher's desk, she found two chairs side by side, one far too high for her and the other far too low. Although she pretty quickly saw the parallel with her concerns, she wondered why she had come up with the image of a chair, until she recalled her husband casually mentioning the evening before that the adjustable chair at their son's computer seemed too low for him, so he had raised it.

Some bitter juice

Any number of dreams demonstrate the validity of this explanation for the surreal content and vital function of dreams. Here are two examples from work in therapeutic settings.

Joe was demonstrating counselling skills to trainee addiction counsellors, working with a volunteer client who had been attending an addiction treatment centre. The client, a 60-year-old man called Kenneth, reported the following dream. He dreamed that he was squeezing juice from a grapefruit into his father's mouth as his father sat relaxing in a chair. While he was doing this, his father was complaining vociferously to his wife about her faults. Eventually Kenneth lost his temper and started shouting at his father for behaving in that way towards his mother.

In the counselling session, by enquiring about Kenneth's concerns of the previous day, Joe was able to help him sort out what the dream referred to.

Kenneth had been attending an addiction centre in an effort to control his drinking. He felt he had been getting on well with the senior therapist whom he had been seeing, and with whom he had shared a lot of painful material about his life. Then, on the day before the dream, he arrived for his session with his therapist, only to be told that he was going to be seeing someone new, an extremely young and, he assumed, inexperienced woman. Ill at ease because of her youth, he decided he didn't want to work with her, and walked out of the session. His previous therapist was then called, and she proceeded to tell him off for treating a member of staff in that way. Kenneth thought to himself, "I have co-operated fully with the senior therapist by telling her the bitter experiences of my life and she really shouldn't be telling me off." But he held back on the impulse to defend himself, and said nothing.

In the dream, the senior therapist was represented by his father, who was always a dominant character and regularly bawled at his wife. Kenneth felt that he had given the therapist what she wanted (the bitter juice of the grapefruit he was giving his father representing the painful events in his life that he had shared with her). Yet here she was yelling at him (this, in the dream, taking the form of his father yelling at his mother). At the end of the dream, however, he finally stood up for himself, although he hadn't in real life. Joe was able to congratulate Kenneth for the assertive way he reacted in his dream; this raised Kenneth's self-esteem and gave him a strong sense of empowerment, which he took with him from the session.

In another instance, a psychiatric nurse used her knowledge of Joe's theory to help a Bosnian refugee who had come to England and begun to suffer terrible recurring nightmares about grenades going off in his mouth. As he had witnessed appalling atrocities in Bosnia, his psychiatrist was planning to treat him for post-traumatic stress disorder. The nurse, however, mindful of the dream theory, decided to ask the man if he had anything on his mind in this country. It turned out that, because his English was so poor, he was very anxious that he would unintentionally say something wrong, which would set the authorities against him and he and his family would be forced to return to Bosnia. It was instantly clear – to him and to the nurse and the psychiatrist – that the grenades in his mouth symbolized his fear of destroying his and his family's chances with his inability to communicate clearly in English. Once he was reassured that he would not be sent back, whatever he said, the nightmares stopped entirely.

Using dreams intelligently

Dream metaphors that clients bring to counselling sessions can often have therapeutic value in this way. They may help clients to see more objectively what is troubling them, and may help the therapist realize how the client is feeling about the therapeutic relationship. Studying the content of one's dreams can also have the benefit of enabling us to stand back from our emotional concerns and look at them more dispassionately.

The finding that dream content always relates to waking concerns of the previous day is a crucially important understanding for any therapist tempted to act on the basis of a client's dream. It is never safe, for instance, to assume that dream content corresponds to something that has happened in a person's life, because the content is always a metaphorical representation of something else. Clinical experience has long indicated, for instance, that very many children are taken to see psychiatrists and psychotherapists because of nightmares and flashbacks and other typical symptoms of post-traumatic stress caused by frightening films seen on television and videos.[46] If they start to worry, "Could something like this be real/happen to me?" they are likely to have a dream relating to such anticipations.

Even an arousing thought is sufficient to generate a dream. For example, there are therapists who work on the (ill-advised) assumption that a client with an eating disorder almost certainly has a history of sexual abuse, recognized or not. Such a therapist may gently try to probe whether any such event did indeed occur at any stage in childhood, in the belief that memories of abuse are often pushed to the back of the mind and repressed, because they are so devastating. Having been asked a question of this nature about abuse, which may seem an extremely unexpected and shocking possibility to them, the patient is likely to introspect about their childhood after the session, trying to remember any ambiguous or suspicious events and feelings. This inevitably creates unresolved emotional arousals which would then translate into a dream, metaphorically involving abuse of some kind. When the dream is reported at the next therapy session, the therapist is likely to leap on it, seeing the dream as evidence confirming that abuse did occur and was repressed, and has now been triggered into consciousness. In such a way are uneasy spirals of misunderstandings begun. This has been a factor in cases of false memory syndrome, where parents protest that they are innocent of the 'abuse' apparently dredged up in therapy.[47]

It is quite possible that genuine, distressing events from long ago can be the subject of a dream – but *only* if the event was consciously thought about the previous day. If, for some reason, indignant emotions were aroused whilst reminiscing about the unjust bullying by a teacher long ago when you were at school, you could not act out and resolve the situation now because nothing can change the fact that it happened – so you would have to complete the pattern in a dream, when you could supply a different outcome and deactivate the emotion. Likewise, if someone is currently being bullied at work, their dreams might draw upon childhood bullying memories as a metaphor for the present experience, but the dreams would be about the *current* bullying which evokes patterns from the past that are being used metaphorically.

It is important to emphasize that we use the terms 'conscious' and 'unconscious' differently from the way used by Freud, and the psychoanalytical and psychodynamic movement that followed in his powerful wake. The conscious mind we talk about can only hold on to relatively few pieces of information at any one time as it tries to puzzle out something. Everything else is unconscious. Freud, of course, saw conscious activity as being censored, sanitised thoughts, and the unconscious as the repository of everything that was repressed. (And, whereas Freud considered dreams the cesspit of the unconscious, the dreaming that occurs in REM sleep can now be seen as nature's version of the flushed toilet!) One of Freud's notions that infected the 20th century world was that therapy should endlessly dredge up the emotional history of patients and was, necessarily, a painful process. The effect of this was that for decades psychoanalytical therapists routinely undid the highly effective stress control work nature carried out for us each night, as it lowered emotional arousal in the dreaming process and preserved the integrity of our endowment of instincts.

This is why it has often been observed by ordinary folk that people having long-term psychoanalysis may seem to become ever more self-absorbed and *less* mentally healthy. The fact is that we don't even remember most of our dreams. Nature doesn't need us to. Dreaming is an automatic process that is performing a vital function outside of waking consciousness.

Alas, even without the interference of misguided therapists, we can regularly undo all the good work of the dream state just by thinking about the same worrying things day after day. This has an especial effect upon the REM sleep mechanism, which we will explain in the chapter on depression.

One of the most important implications of the expectation fulfilment theory of dreaming is that we can now see that the REM state is itself separate from the dream. Dreaming takes place in the REM state, which functions as a reality generator. The power and importance of the REM state in many key areas of mammalian life is only now just starting to be appreciated.

CHAPTER FOUR

The mind entranced: sane and insane

THE MYSTERY of why we evolved to dream, and the puzzle about what dreaming does for us every night, is, we contend, largely solved. If this insight – that the brain evolved to dream to deal with unresolved emotional arousals – is true, it should, as is often the case with a new discovery, throw more light on other mysteries, just as when one climbs a mountain and can see much further than from lower down. The view we are going to explore now has many exotic and bizarre aspects but they all cohere and make sense in the light of this knowledge.

Human beings in trance states clearly exhibit strange behaviours that have fascinated people since the dawn of self-awareness. It is these that we are going to examine first. Trance behaviours include: a massive increase in susceptibility to suggestion, great tolerance of painful procedures (skin piercing, burning), religious conversions, hallucinations, indoctrination, age regression, profound stillness, and the opposite – super physical performance. In trance, amnesia can be induced, creativity stimulated, blood flow altered, the immune system boosted, major operations – including amputations – undergone without pain, skin conditions (including ichthyosis, a deforming skin disease which causes the epidermis to become dry and horny like thick fish scales) cured and stigmata made to appear. Moods can be changed; depressed people can laugh again and overwhelming fears be faced and overcome. Also, in trance, strange transformations of character can occur: shy people may behave confidently, inhibited people turn into sexual exhibitionists and cowards discover bravery.

Trance can be induced by drugs, music, rhythmic dancing, rituals, shock, hypnotic language, touch, sexual activity, reflection, staring, recalling particular memories, stories, changing breathing patterns, any stimulus that arouses strong emotion and, paradoxically, any form of deep relaxation that lowers emotional arousal. It is, therefore, a common everyday experience. Yet it is still mysterious and unrecognized by most people, who react just like the fish in the old story: these fish, as they swam in the ocean, kept puzzling over this thing they kept hearing about, called 'water', and what it could possibly be! The history of hypnosis shows its rocky ride over thousands of years – accepted in some cultures, feared and banned in others. Down the ages its use has been associated with great therapeutic benefits (which it undoubtedly can confer), but also severe warnings about dangers that can arise from using hypnosis – for the hypnotic subject *and* the hypnotist – which we think are real. The enormous amount of literature the subject has generated, and still generates, is full of techniques, case histories, examples of strange phenomena associated with trance and hypnosis, and endless speculation, but no clear explanation for what it is that happens in trance.

With the advent of more sophisticated imaging techniques – such as electroencephalography (EEG), functional magnetic resonance imaging, near-infrared spectroscopy, positron emission tomography (PET scans) and computer tomography – it has become possible for scientists to glean information about what appears to be happening in the brain when someone is hypnotized. However, as researchers who carried out a meta-analysis of the most reliable studies pointed out, the different methodologies used have made it difficult to generalize from findings – which also, because of focusing on different things, often even contradict each other. Not only do methods for investigating hypnosis differ, including how it is induced, but "the tendency for researchers to home in on specific brain regions, rather than look at activity across the whole brain, narrows possible comparisons across studies."[1]

Still, as the authors of a systematic review of 40 studies, published in 2022, were able to conclude, "Despite a broad heterogenicity of included studies, evidence of functional changes in brain activity using hypnosis was identified. ... Suggestions during hypnosis can cause dynamic changes in brain activity."[2] Specifically, the areas in the brain responsible for processing cognition and emotion show greater activity during hypnosis.

How can a state so easy to induce in so many, often apparently contradictory, ways, and so easy to observe be so little understood? On the one hand, there is increasing evidence that hypnosis is an altered state of consciousness. It was shown decades ago that, when people responded to suggestions under hypnosis (for instance that they could feel pain), the appropriate parts of the brain were activated but that they were not activated in people who only pretended to be hypnotized.[3] On the other side of the debate, some deny that such studies provide evidence of a trance state because all they show is that people are responding to suggestions, which people do out of trance just as easily. What is being measured is suggestibility, not an altered state of consciousness, they may say.

So, what criteria would satisfy such people that hypnosis actually exists? The answer is, none. This is because they are looking for a state of consciousness that cannot be accessed by any means other than by hypnosis. And, if the brain is not behaving in an abnormal fashion specific only to hypnosis when someone is hypnotized, they will never bring themselves to agree that hypnosis is happening.

It seems very clear to us that not only do hypnotic states exist but also that they are naturally occurring states of mind that people dip in and out of, to varying extents, all the time. In that sense, it is not an altered state of consciousness, which is why its detractors have such difficulty identifying it, but a state which, whether we are aware of it or not, is utterly familiar to us all – just like the water that the fish were so oblivious of living in. To unwrap and explore the implications of this – which extend even to our understanding of the evolution of consciousness – we need to start with a definition.

First things first – directing attention

We define a trance state, as do many others, as a focused state of attention during which wider environmental stimuli are ignored. The greatest innovative 20th century influence on the clinical use of hypnosis was American psychiatrist Milton H. Erickson. "There are many ways of inducing a trance," he said. "What you do is ask patients primarily to give their attention to one particular idea. You get them to centre their attention on their own experiential learning ... to direct their attention to processes which are taking place within them. Thus you can induce a trance by directing patients' attention to experiences, to memories, to ideas, to concepts that belong to them. All you do is direct the patients' attention to those processes within themselves."[4]

It really is as simple as that. Anyone who can focus their attention, who has a good imagination or who can become emotionally aroused can be hypnotized (hypnosis is simply the art of getting people into the trance state). So it follows that a focused state of attention can be generated in thousands of ways, each with a direct bearing on the type and/or quality of trance state induced.

The most basic trance state (which we share with animals[5]) occurs when we become highly emotional. When emotion takes over, it locks our attention on what has aroused us, to the increasing exclusion of other information from the environment. This focus means we are seeing reality from only one particular perspective because there is less connectivity with the brain networks concerned with reality checking.[6] You can see this clearly when someone gets angry and you cannot reason with them. In anger a person is totally focused on their own view, incapable of seeing other points of view, and will appear stupid. We see this narrowed-down focus in all instinct-driven emotional states, including anxiety, fear, disgust, greed, aggression, lust and elation.

Another way we enter trance is when we *voluntarily* choose to focus our attention on something that interests us. If we are intensely interested in football, for example, and choose to watch a game, we become absorbed. Again, although voluntarily entered into, this state involves emotional arousal as the fortunes of the teams fluctuate. So this could also be described as an emotionally induced trance state – but deliberately engendered by oneself. Indeed, any good observer of their own and other people's behaviour will recognize that *any* form of absorbing activity entered into voluntarily is trance inducing: reading, music, drawing, enjoying a film or TV programme, athletic activity, sexual behaviour, dancing, work, concentration on ideas, watching something closely and so on.

But there is yet another trance state fundamental to our daily lives and behaviour – one produced when somebody *else* focuses our attention. This, too, is one of nature's amazing solutions to a primary survival need we all share. Without it, we could not absorb family and cultural norms, relate to other people or live in interconnected groups. (Why this is so will become clear later.) Mentally healthy mothers are instinctively expert at focusing young children's attention. Good teachers focus the attention of children; the friendly raconteur in the pub focuses our attention, as does a good salesman and the leaders who arise in society. When this happens, we can be deemed to be in a trance state. This is because, when our attention is guided, certain aspects of reality are left out, as has now been scientifically shown,[7] and certain courses of action are made more compelling to us by the person organizing the presentation of the evidence, story or plan of action that we are hearing. To the extent that they succeed in focusing our attention in a way that we accept, we are suggestible. So trance states can be created in us simply by another person focusing our attention.

Then there is the type of trance state that the hypnotist or hypnotherapist supposedly creates. Some people claim that there is something unusual about this kind of trance state, while others say that it is no different from the state of suggestibility that occurs in everyday life – such as we have described above – or merely results from anxiety to please the hypnotist and so comply with whatever suggestions are made.

To some extent both parties are right. Whilst dreaming at night, for example, we might vividly experience ourselves in a field of snow, even though we are actually tucked up in our warm beds. There is nothing abnormal about dreaming. We all do it. But when we dream we are experiencing the creation of an alternative reality *in our imagination* – which can be thought of as the brain's own 'reality generator'. So going into a hypnotic trance is not really so extraordinary because every night, in our dream state, we unquestioningly believe in the alternative reality our brain presents to us – we can actually *feel* we are in a field of snow. Even when not in a dream state some people are quite good at sensing what it would be like to be in a field of snow – the whiteness, intense cold and so on.

It may be helpful to think in terms of two major types of trance states: posthypnotic trance states and programming trance states, both of which are seen in the REM state in animals and humans. We have earlier discussed at length how the foetus in the womb and the child in early life are pre-programmed in the REM state with the instinctive behaviours appropriate for different circumstances and stages of life.[8]

However, the brain does not just rely on pre-programmed patterns; it can also learn new ones. New learning is always the result of existing patterns being added to or changed. In short, old patterns are enriched. Every new thing we learn is also learned in a programming trance state – we are absorbed, our attention locked.

However, whenever we act without thought or conscious effort – when we are on automatic, going about our routine daily affairs – we are pattern matching to an earlier time when we first learned such responses in the REM (trance) state. So whenever we repeat those actions or responses, we are, in effect, acting out posthypnotic suggestions. We have been programmed to act in whatever way it is that we have learned.

We most commonly associate posthypnotic suggestion with what occurs at public demonstrations by hypnotists to provide the audience with amusement. What happens is, however, no more mysterious than what we have just described. Suppose the hypnotist puts someone into trance (stage hypnotists always choose people who go into trance easily) and, before bringing them out of it, tells them that, whenever afterwards they hear a clock strike three, they will feel an itch on their forehead and scratch it. Whenever the clock strikes three, it activates that programming and they scratch. They are not aware of it when they are doing it but, nonetheless, their behaviour is being controlled by a posthypnotic programme.

Similarly, when you get angry because you have a strong feeling that somebody is trespassing on your rights, you may suddenly strike out or hit them or say something aggressive in an involuntary way. When you calm down, you will say, "Why the hell did I do that …? What made me say that! What came over me …?" But, nonetheless, at the time you felt compelled to act as you did, just as a person is compelled to act from a posthypnotic suggestion given by a hypnotist. This is an important similarity. Indeed, you would be acting from a posthypnotic suggestion. At some time in your past you would have learned to react with that behaviour when your fight-or-flight response was switched on under extreme provocation. As we have written elsewhere in more detail, all learning is essentially post-hypnotic.*

---

* Griffin, J. and Tyrrell, I. (2011) *Godhead, The brain's big bang: the explosive origin of creativity, mysticism and mental illness.* HG Publishing.

A considerable amount of human behaviour is the result of exposure to these kinds of posthypnotic suggestions, programmed during interactions with the family, peer groups and the wider culture. Some may be harmless in effect, as when suddenly feeling compelled to use a catch phrase from a popular TV programme. Others, we think, are not so benign. But the point we are making is that hypnotic phenomena are a given. And when we *deliberately* put a person who is a good hypnotic subject into a hypnotic state, we are activating the very processes that the brain itself activates during dream sleep, including the brain's astonishing and powerful reality generator.

The trance state of dreaming

Now we come to the connection between dreaming and hypnosis. Hypnosis can be defined as *any artificial way of accessing the REM state*, the same brain state in which dreaming occurs. When the ramifications of this are understood, many of the mysteries and controversies surrounding hypnosis are resolved.

In dreaming we have an example of the trance state par excellence. It is the deepest trance state we know. When we dream, not only is our attention being directed in an involuntary fashion but an alternative visionary reality is created that, 99 per cent of the time, we totally accept whilst in the dream. This is so every night for all of us. (It can occasionally happen, of course, that a person becomes aware that they are having a dream – so called lucid dreaming.)

Even those who believe that trance states don't exist will agree that we all dream and that dreaming is a separate state from waking consciousness. It has also repeatedly been demonstrated in sleep laboratories that, in the dream state, emotional networks in the brain are firing off on all cylinders and generating the dreams.[9] That gives us a strong clue as to how and why trance states evolved in the first place. They are connected to emotions. Another vital clue comes from the research we have already described which shows that the REM state during which dreaming takes place is involved with programming instinctive frames of reference into our brain – instinctive activities that are based in our emotions.[10]

It is often observed that a deeply hypnotized person can hallucinate all kinds of realities, depending on their hypnotic ability and the skill of the hypnotist.[11] They hallucinate with the same intensity that occurs in the dream state and, whilst in the trance, have the same belief in its being real. It is only with the breakthrough in our understanding of the origin of dreams that we now understand why this is so.[12] We now know that the dream is like a script that is processed in metaphorical imagery by the reality generator in the REM state. In hypnosis we are directly accessing this reality generator and the hypnotist is providing the script. Even light trance, because it is a focusing of attention, taps into the same mechanism that salesmen, teachers, entertainers and others *inadvertently* use all the time to stimulate the imaginations of the people who are listening. Any close observer of people will have noticed rapid eye movements in those who are absorbed – the same movements that we see in dreaming. Clearly there is a connection.

But there is more to it than that. When the dream state naturally occurs, the dreamer's body is normally paralysed, all muscle tone disappearing as they switch off outside perceptions of reality in order to focus on the inward reality. So there are physiological similarities between the dream state and what can be activated in the hypnotic state – and that *is* different from being absorbed by the salesman's hypnotic patter. Trance is clearly a matter of degree. Its characteristics change, just as water can change – solidify into ice or evaporate. What you can do with ice is quite different from what you can do with steam, but it is water all the same and retains its fundamental quality.

So, when a person has been put into a hypnotic state and they are imagining fields of snow or whatever, the skilled hypnotist can, in a good subject, evoke other physiological aspects of the REM state, such as paralysis of the body. These may even occur in some people spontaneously. And, because the body in the REM state naturally shuts out sensory information, it is easy, for example, to block out pain, alter sensory perceptions or, as some stage hypnotists do, convince people that parts of their body are missing.

The trance state that the good salesman creates is hypnotic; the trance state in which someone is asked to imagine something, an alternative reality, is also hypnotic. But, with a good trance subject, you can alter their perceptions through changing their physiological state. In all these cases, what is happening is that the latent abilities that are naturally present in the REM state are being invoked: namely, shutting out certain physiological sensations and changing a person's perception so that one part of the brain takes in information while another part of the brain blocks it. This also occurs spontaneously during the dream state: a person can call or shout to you when you're dreaming, yet your brain may ignore it – though, sometimes, certain information does filter through and can affect the content of dreams. So there is a block, or partial block, against outside information getting into the dream state, just as there is in hypnosis. In hypnosis, subjects can be made to alter their blood pressure, stimulate their immune systems and other remarkable and well-documented things.[13] But even this has parallels with dreaming in the REM state. Who has not woken up, heart pounding, sweating and flushed from an arousing dream or a nightmare that has had strong physiological effects? And the immune system's healing response is known to be more highly active during periods of right hemispherical dominance during the day and night[14] and it is the right hemisphere of the brain that is dominant in dreaming and trance.[15]

So now we can see that many of the strange and seemingly bizarre phenomena evoked during hypnosis are quite normal when viewed as REM state activity. Once it is understood that all we are doing in hypnosis is evoking the latent capacities of the REM state, the strange mystery of hypnosis – pain control, dissociation, hallucination, being absorbed, alterations of perception, paralysis etc. – no longer baffles. It's a puzzle solved.

Even the fact that we mostly forget our dreams, unless we make a conscious effort to fix them in our consciousness by telling them back to ourselves immediately on waking, is paralleled with the common experience of amnesia for hypnotic experiences.

Posthypnotic suggestions and the REM state

It's curious that we forget our dreams so easily when we wake up but that, later in the day, something can trigger a memory of a dream. The dream template comes back to us only when a pattern is recognized in the environment that relates closely to it. This may be connected to post-hypnotic functions, because, as we have shown, sleep is not the exclusive medium for the REM state. As we have seen, the REM state can be accessed in other ways, such as during the directing of attention in a hypnotic induction, or when having attention directed to emotionally disturbing memories. As earlier explained, in dreaming the REM state is activated spontaneously to deal with unresolved emotional arousals from the previous waking period.

Research by Erickson,[16] for example, showed that, if a person who has been given a posthypnotic suggestion is interrupted while carrying it out and given another suggestion, they respond to the new suggestion too. In other words, it is because they go back into the trance state whilst carrying out the first suggestion that they are in the state to be programmed to carry out the second one as well.

So, any time we become emotional or are acting through instinct, we are in a trance state where we are more easily programmed. At such times our attention can be diverted and somebody can take control over aspects of our behaviour. That is what all dictators, evangelists and salesmen do; they have learned how to raise the emotional pitch so as to focus and lock people's attention, making it easy to influence them to their own ends.

In charismatic 'religious' healing services, for example, the emotional temperature is raised at the outset, automatically putting people into trance states. They are then more suggestible and it is quite an easy matter to invoke, for example, the blocking of pain through dissociation. Members of the congregation can feel their pain diminish and believe that cures are effected (as indeed can occur in the case of psychosomatic problems) and, if the leaders are unscrupulous, experience a compelling urge to part with lots of money.

Dr Graham Wagstaff, who researched and wrote extensively on hypnosis, became interested in it in 1970 when, as a university student, he was hypnotized by the magician Kreskin and made to perform typical stage hypnosis activities, as people do on such occasions. After the show, he decided that he had done what he did by simulating trance and that hypnosis wasn't real. He afterwards devoted his academic career to proving that hypnosis as a separate state does not exist and is best explained as a form of social compliance.[17]

This brings to mind the story of the young man who went to a hypnotist and, when he was in a trance, the hypnotist talked to him about whales, for no reason that he could fathom. He then went off to university and studied whales, even earning a PhD for his work in this area, and continued to spend his whole career studying whales, without realizing that he was responding to a posthypnotic suggestion. Equally, Wagstaff spent much of his professional life studying hypnosis, so profound was its effect on him!

The compliance theory doesn't hold up. Other people's research gives a perfectly adequate explanation for Wagstaff's reaction. In one experiment, for example, Erickson gave a person a posthypnotic suggestion to open a window on a freezing cold day. His instructions were specific. When the clock struck at a certain time, he was to open the window. And when, indeed, the subject did so in response to the hypnotic suggestion, he was asked, "Why did you do that?" And he replied, "I am just so hot in here." This was despite the fact that everyone else was freezing. In other words, he made up his own reasons to justify his odd behaviour.

In another experiment, a woman was given the suggestion that she would take off her shoe and fill it with alcohol at a very posh dinner party. At the dinner she filled her shoe with champagne. Again, when asked why she did this odd thing, she came up with a bizarre explanation, totally unaware that she was responding to a post-hypnotic suggestion.

So, when Wagstaff, a highly intelligent man, found himself doing bizarre things at a hypnosis show he had to create his own rationalization for his behaviour, thereby creating the delusion that he was doing it through free choice.

This rationalizing behaviour has been shown time and time again to occur: the left hemisphere of the brain, which wants to dig into the detail and find rational explanations for things, is unaware that the right hemisphere of the brain is responding to a posthypnotic suggestion, so it performs true to form and casts around to find a cause that sounds reasonable. This was shown vividly in the case of 'split-brain' patients – people in whom the connection between the two hemispheres had been surgically severed, usually as a treatment for very severe epilepsy. When a patient responded non-verbally (perhaps by laughing or blushing) when something was presented only to their left visual field (the right hemisphere controls the left side of the body, while the left hemisphere controls the right side), the person, asked to account for their reaction, would make up a likely reason, as it was the task of the left hemisphere to find the words but the left hemisphere would not have known the true reason for the response.

Quite often, very rational people are good hypnotic subjects. Joe is, to most people who know him, a very rational sort of person. He remembered once responding to a posthypnotic suggestion to go and look for a certain book. After doing so, he remembered saying to himself, "I'm not really responding to a posthypnotic suggestion; I *know* that I'm doing this. It's my own free choice." Of course, if he really had free choice, he wouldn't have done it!

Hypnotherapists have even learned to exploit the intellectual, analytical thinking mode of sceptical patients by using a hypnotic confusional language technique. In a quiet, firm voice they might say something like, "*And sometimes a child makes the right mistakes for the wrong reasons, and sometimes a child makes the wrong mistakes for the right reasons, and some of those mistakes that are right now can be wrong at a later time, and some of the wrong mistakes now can be made right at a later time, and some of the understandings now that can be misunderstood at a later time can only be understood at a far later time ... and it all belongs to you ...*" and so on for some minutes. After listening to a confusing monologue like this for a while, even the most intellectually resistant client invariably gives up trying to figure out all the meanings and just 'escapes' into trance.

Wagstaff's rationalization took over much of his life because his mind was clearly unhappy with the rationalization. He had the compulsion to spend his academic life trying to prove his rationalization was correct. People who have been controlled by hypnotic experiences can have the course of their whole lives dictated by it, which is one of the dangers inherent in 'playing around' with hypnosis.

It is because of confusion between the idea of trance states, which are essentially posthypnotic emotional states, and the physiological correlates of the trance state which can be activated in hypnosis, namely dissociation, amnesia, anaesthesia etc., that some people have the impression that hypnosis is an *unusual* altered state of consciousness. It is not. It is an essential, *everyday* part of our natural genetic inheritance of mind/body functioning.

When carrying out a posthypnotic suggestion, we are, effectively, in the dream state. Because we look perfectly normal, however, this may not be obvious to scientific observers. But we all know, from when we recall being in the dream state ourselves, that we experience an alternate reality in dreams and, *de facto*, are in an altered state of consciousness for the duration of the dream. If very few people *ever* remembered their dreams, it would have been difficult to prove that the dream state existed. But, as it is, we can be quite certain that dreaming is a separate state of consciousness, even though the patterns of brain activity whilst dreaming are almost identical to those when we are wide awake.

Hypnosis and expectation

It is, of course, important for people to know that trances are states of focused attention that we all go in and out of all of the time. Psychotherapists and counsellors who know how to make positive use of this to help people are generally more effective. But its use extends beyond psychology. In good subjects we can trigger physiological features of the REM state, namely shutting out pain, altering other physiological perceptions and enabling dissociation from unhelpful preoccupations. Some people still doubt that it is possible but, once experienced – e.g. having a pain-free major operation with hypnosis as the only anaesthesia, as Ivan has done – it is impossible to deny.

To the degree that we have expectations about anything, our consciousness is shaped by those expectations. This means that in everyday life we are continually going in and out of trance but to varying depths because our expectation is selectively focusing our attention, thus always preventing us from seeing the bigger picture – what's really there. We may see just what we expect to see, or what we are interested in seeing. And the more involved we are in our expectations, the more emotionally aroused we are. This is easy to observe when members of the public meet a famous person whom they admire or are in thrall to: they are in a trance; their attention is completely focused. This is why bizarre behaviour such as sycophancy so often occurs at such meetings.

It has long been observed that expectation can play an important role in hypnotic induction (although it is not an essential element, since people can unwittingly be hypnotized). When we observe the effect of expectation on what trance actually is, we can see highlighted the nature of the trance state itself. This is because the REM state is a reality generator and will tend to fulfil the expectations that a person has about trance. If the person associates trance with relaxation, for example, then the REM state has the capacity to produce relaxation. In contrast, children don't tend to associate hypnosis with relaxation (or anything else), so they can be more active when in a trance.

Ernest Rossi, who did much to publicize the work of Milton H. Erickson, once said at a seminar that one of the best ways to get people into a trance state is to have them observe someone else go into one first. By the process of observation, their expectations about going into trance are heightened and it is then much easier to work with them. This is as one would expect because, when attention is being focused and emotion is aroused, people are already highly suggestible. By the time they sit in the therapist's chair to be hypnotized, they are already in a trance.

In Ireland there is an interesting phrase used to describe people who have had a lot to drink. They say, "He was really 'locked' last night!" What it means is that the drinker's consciousness was locked into a certain perspective. Once he started, all he wanted was to drink and drink and that (trance state) was the only reality that existed for him all evening. The outside world and outside responsibility did not exist at all.

The words 'your conscious mind is locked' are descriptive of what a trance state is. In trance, consciousness *is* locked because it is focused. An unexpected sudden bang or noise that makes another person jump has no effect on the person in trance.

We have no doubt that, as physiological monitoring instruments continue to develop and are capable of even more subtle observations of brain activity, there will be even more physiological indices of the trance state of hypnosis

Scientific study of hypnosis

It is clear that an understanding of how emotions work, how genetic programming takes place and how the imaginative mind can be focused by other people are prerequisites for understanding hypnosis. In other words, the trance state is a human given and can be understood in terms of other important human givens – our emotional responses, our imaginations and the REM state. It is an intrinsic part of daily life: a reality that can quite easily be understood with the right organizing idea.

Of course, many scientists researching hypnosis naturally want to follow the traditional protocols that scientists working in other areas usually use. But these fixed and mechanistic tools of investigation are not always suitable for studying human consciousness and attention – as shown by what happened in the early days of clinical research into the subject. Absurd conclusions were reached about hypnosis because experimenters were using scripts to hypnotize people. Those who did not respond were described as unhypnotizable or bad hypnotic subjects. (Unfortunately many hypnotherapy training courses still encourage people to use scripts, which inhibits rapport building and is a limiting, inflexible way to offer suggestions in hypnosis.)

One of the mistakes made by some of those who denied the reality of hypnosis was that they defined hypnosis as the state induced by a specific type of induction process. Then they found that people who are good hypnotic subjects could be put into a similar state of consciousness without that induction and so concluded that induction was not necessary, therefore hypnosis didn't exist, and thus the terms 'hypnosis' and 'trance' were redundant.[18]

We believe that the words 'hypnosis' and 'trance' are useful. Nevertheless, as therapists, we find that so many people have been conditioned into a pejorative view of the word 'hypnosis' that we prefer to use the term 'guided imagery' instead, which evokes less negative reaction. Although some people can be hypnotized by a mechanically read hypnotic script, as commonly used in laboratory conditions, more subtlety is usually required, as Erickson and others showed. An effective practitioner will take a flexible approach and use their subjects' own interests, creative imagination and behavioural traits to induce trance. Hypnotic ability varies enormously from individual to individual but, sooner or later, with enough time, *anyone* with normal brain functioning can be induced into a trance.

Lay people are perfectly capable of accurately identifying trance states in themselves and other people, and we know that hypnotic inductions and trance phenomena have been the subject of serious experiment for thousands of years in various cultures, resulting in highly sophisticated therapeutic effects.[19]

Focusing attention – inwards and outwards

We have a need for trance, as can be seen by our seeking out experiences that put us into it. For example, golfers will say, "I find it just so relaxing; that's why I play. I come out here and I can switch off everything else. Nothing exists for me then but the game." We feel more alive when focused on a task in a trance state.

It is as if, for all of us, our consciousness – the constant switching of attention that enables us to see reality in multi-dimensions as much as possible – is a real burden we carry around. Every time we switch attention we arouse, to some degree, the fight-or-flight response and activate a corresponding amount of stress hormones.[20] That creates tremendous wear and tear.[21] But, when we can go into a relaxed, absorbing trance state and our attention is kept focused, the fight-or-flight response is subdued.[22] Perhaps, without realizing it, we are all looking for experiences where we can put the burden down and thereby avoid using energy for the emotionally arousing activity of constantly switching attention.

It is impossible to be anxious and relaxed at the same time. Relaxation is a lovely state to be in. It's entrancing! It's what a lot of people derive from many forms of alternative therapy or from drinking alcohol – their attention and consciousness get 'locked', so they don't need to make much effort. This temporarily filters out certain stress reactions that would otherwise affect their mind/body system. It's a temporary relief of course. You cannot escape reality for long.

Playing football or badminton will have the same effect. No matter what problems or what deadlines we have, once we start playing the game we are totally released – everything else just disappears for an hour. We become unconscious of our concerns for a while. The only thing that matters is the game, nothing else. When the wider reality is temporarily forgotten, it is a refreshing release from day-to-day pressures. Whilst playing sport does involve physiological activation of the fight-or-flight response, there is an instinctive follow-through, when one can play well, that switches off the arousal of the conscious decision making usually associated with it. That's why it seems so effortless – going into a state of 'flow' involves very little conscious decision making.

Depressed people stop doing things they used to enjoy, so they no longer have that release. Once trapped in a negative (unhelpful) trance state they lose the energy required to focus themselves on a wider horizon, one that has meaning and purpose.

The trance of depression[23] is quite unlike the trance of playing badminton, for example, which, by contrast, is an exhilarating state. That's because, when playing, we are totally focused *outwards*, not *inwards*. And what we are not doing, when in that outward-focused trance, is carrying the burden of decisions to be made, deadlines to be met – all the things in life that require conscious choices and reality checking. We may also *try* to escape the burden through negative trance states. We become lazy, dreamy, depressed, anxious or angry. We abuse substances or excitement or relationships – do anything, in fact, except take up the burden willingly. But when we focus outwards, as in sport, music, gardening and other activities requiring complete concentration, we are relieved of the burden for a while in a much less destructive manner.

We may not like the burden of daily life's demands. But, equally, getting caught up in a negative trance state also becomes a burden because, after a certain length of time, we start to get bored with it or dragged down by it. We start to realize that there are all kinds of pleasures we are no longer enjoying and suddenly life becomes meaningless. It's like becoming aware that we are dreaming the same dream over and over to a point where it becomes tedious. If we stay in a trance state, networks of the brain involved in thought and judgement may eventually become aware of how repetitive it is. We begin to think, "I'm not doing anything interesting in my life. My life is boring. I'm not enjoying my food as much as I used to. I have no energy. This is going to go on forever." When such a trance state becomes a burden, we sink into depression.

Once we understand what a trance state is and the various ways it can be induced, we have a useful way of observing and explaining much of our behaviour. We love many types of positive trance experiences that externally focus our attention, precisely because they release us from the need to switch our attention continually from demand to demand, with all the associated physiological arousal and effort that requires. It *is* lovely to switch off.

Uses and abuses of hypnosis

To recap briefly: there is often confusion in the literature about the apparently weird occurrences (hallucination, loss of sensory feeling, paralysis, regression, etc.) that can be associated with hypnotic states. These phenomena are easily understood, however, once it is realized that the hypnotist is activating the machinery of the dream state itself. Dreaming is concerned with our emotional and physical health, deactivating unresolved emotional arousals from the daytime. Whilst dreaming, we accept the often bizarre reality the brain presents us with, in the form of metaphorical representations of the concerns that are still arousing us. The contents of dreams are only strange because they are pure metaphor and, as we cannot reality check them, are accepted by us unquestioningly while dreaming, however odd they may be. This too can happen in stage hypnosis.[24] The most outrageous suggestions can be acted out by subjects, once the dream mechanism has been activated by the hypnotist, and can seem perfectly normal to the subjects – until they 'wake up'.

Just as dreams are always metaphorical[25] so using appropriate metaphors is central to good therapeutic practice, and lives can be changed for the better just by hearing stories that reframe experiences and provide a new unconscious mental map for charting the way through life's difficulties.[26]

Hypnosis is merely an artificial means of focusing attention, which involves both hemispheres of the brain. Ivan once asked a patient who was racked with Parkinsonism to give his full attention to the one part of his body that was not shaking – his left foot. Doing so engaged the left hemisphere of the patient's brain, which is concerned with details rather than the bigger picture. While the left hemisphere was distracted in this way, Ivan was able to make use of the focused attention of the trance state to engage the patient's right hemisphere in imagining positive expectations which could help him cope better with his disability. Similarly, inviting therapy clients to relax and guiding them to imagine themselves on a lovely beach or in the countryside on a fine day focuses the attention of the left hemisphere, while empowering ideas, preferably in metaphor, can be presented to the right hemisphere to absorb at an unconscious level.

Hypnosis not only helps us create alternative 'realities', as in dreams, it also makes it possible for us to bring about changes to our bodies. It can promote healing in skin and bones, reduce blood pressure, change the experience of pain, improve digestion and so on. There is nothing remarkable about all this when one sees the larger picture. If a hypnotist tells you, "You can't get out of your chair" and you can't get out of the chair, it is not magic. We are all 'stuck' for about two hours every night, when we are paralysed during REM sleep.

Some people have a terrible fear that a hypnotist can take control from them with some magical power. While, as just said, the power is not magical, hypnotists *do* have power. This is because they are providing a dream script for your brain to work from, and this is a serious form of influence. Therefore, great caution is needed – power can be corrupting. For many hundreds of years, Eastern psychologists have warned about the harm that can be done to human development by the ignorant or unscrupulous use of hypnosis.[27] We have seen the truth of this in tragic cases involving the generation of illusory memories of sexual abuse and multiple personalities by therapists, and the concern about the accidental triggering of schizophrenia by stage hypnotists.

We need to be clear about what is and what is not potentially harmful in the use of hypnosis. It is safe to evoke the natural anaesthesia that accompanies the REM state to carry out operations without chemical anaesthesia. It is safe to detraumatize a traumatic memory using hypnosis, if done properly. It is safe to use guided imagery to suggest life-enhancing behaviour changes to a hypnotized subject. However, if we use hypnosis so that, posthypnotically, a person conflates normal reality and an imaginary reality (as happens when stage hypnotists get people to hallucinate), then we are manipulating the very frames of reference through which that person's reality is experienced. This is potentially very harmful indeed. In a highly creative subject who has a predisposition to confuse 'normal' frames of reference and imagination, such an experience could precipitate a psychotic breakdown. Since the precursor to psychotic breakdown is excessive stress and depression, if the recollection of the hypnotically induced 'psychotic' experience were also stressful, then this would probably further damage the subject's ability to separate fantasy from reality. Such procedures are, of course, the very stuff of stage hypnosis and therefore carry a risk of triggering psychotic states in vulnerable individuals – the one per cent of the population genetically predisposed to schizophrenia.

There are also potential dangers attached to suggesting symptoms away, which is of course possible in a good hypnotic subject. This is because certain symptoms may be fulfilling a particular function for us, which we haven't yet learned, or relearned, to fulfil in a more constructive way. So we need to teach a client an alternative way to meet a need currently being fulfilled by a symptom; or help someone to see their concerns from a different perspective. This more sophisticated approach is much more likely to have beneficial results. It is perhaps not surprising that the dangers of hypnosis and the ways it can trigger psychosis are not widely recognized since, to recognize the dangers, one has to have specialized knowledge from several areas of study at one time: psychiatrists specializing in psychosis usually study pharmacological approaches to treatment and don't study why we dream or hypnotic phenomena, while stage hypnotists do not feel that they need to understand psychosis. Indeed, the experience of psychosis is often bewildering and may feel profoundly inexplicable, not only for sufferers but also for their families and for the caring professions. However, the insights from dream research that we have set out in this book throw light on the experience of psychosis, and point the way towards more effective treatments.

Dreams, hypnosis and psychosis

Several studies have shown that the outcome of schizophrenia is better in developing countries.[28,29] Although some such findings have also been challenged,[30] there is still something significant that we can deduce, when looking at this from the human givens perspective, as we shall see.

In developing countries, there is a much stronger tradition of emotional and family support, and greater tolerance for personal psychological crisis, which may therefore be less likely to spiral out of control. Also, there are more low-stress manual and handicraft jobs, and more meaningful tasks people need to perform for their subsistence, that facilitate recovery in a close-knit community. In these situations it is much easier for people to meet emotional needs for intimacy, support, status and validation than in the culture we have made for ourselves. Clearly, making sure the givens of our nature are fulfilled is a potent aid in helping people recover from psychological disorders, even ones as seriously incapacitating as schizophrenia.

An additional factor is that, in developing countries, the use of modern neuroleptic drugs to treat psychosis is minimal, whereas in the Western world they are the main treatment offered by the psychiatric profession, despite the strong evidence that these heavily promoted drugs do not aid recovery[31] and may even cause harm.[32,33,34,35,36]

Psychiatric theorists are at a loss to explain schizophrenia. Most scientists have stayed focused on the neurotransmitter dopamine ever since the discovery in the 1960s that reserpine, a drug used at the time for hypertension, lowered dopamine levels in the brain and reduced psychotic symptoms. However, there is little consensus about what exactly is going on, despite strident claims by some drug companies marketing antipsychotics.[37]

We have already described how the REM brain state, which underlies dreaming, is separate from the process of dreaming and dream content. It is also clear that the healthy brain is organized to keep the dream process separate from the waking state. We have shown how the behaviour of a person in a hypnotic state clearly mirrors phenomena of the REM state, such as muscle paralysis, dissociation, imperviousness to pain, and amnesia for the event after 'waking'. A psychotic breakdown is almost always preceded by an overload of stress and severe depression in a person's life, which, as we know, results in excessive REM sleep. We are now increasingly convinced that, when people are in psychosis, they are in fact trapped in the REM state, a separate state of consciousness with dreamlike qualities. In other words, schizophrenia is waking reality processed through the dreaming brain.

To illustrate this, we only have to look at a number of typical schizophrenic behaviours and experiences and see how they relate to the REM state.

Patients in a psychotic state often describe weird relationships with bodily feelings. One said that her legs felt empty, another that her arms didn't belong to her. This is a well-known REM state phenomenon and is also noted as a hypnotic phenomenon: patients may feel that their bodies are dissolving because, in the dream state, most sensory perceptions about the body are inaccessible.

It is also known that people with schizophrenia can be unusually resistant to pain, and even more so during severe psychotic episodes. One patient jumped out of a second storey window of a hospital, broke both his ankles and walked to the shops oblivious of the damage he had done – damage that would have caused excruciating pain for any person in a normal state of mind. Again, this imperviousness to pain occurs in the REM state while dreaming, as we are cut off from sensory information. (Anyone who has woken up in agony because a limb or ear has been lain on in an unnatural way for a long period during dreaming will recognize this. The pain this causes is only noticed after you wake up.) It is this phenomenon which is exploited when hypnosis is used for pain control or anaesthesia during surgery. Psychotic patients may also talk about hearing voices. In the dream state, which is largely the province of the right hemisphere of the brain, people are not usually capable of critical thought, the province of the left hemisphere, because the mind is 'locked' into the metaphorical script of the dream. But if an individual is trapped in a waking REM state, with waking reality happening around them, there is still likely to be activity in the left hemisphere of the brain. We suggest that, because the REM state operates through metaphor, the only way it could make sense of these independent left-brain thoughts would be to create the metaphor of hearing voices, or being watched, or spied upon by aliens – which easily becomes paranoia.

The visual illusions or delusions associated with schizophrenia are totally characteristic of the dream state, which generates hallucinatory realities that we believe in unquestioningly for the duration of the dream. Stage hypnotists make use of this when they put subjects into what is in effect a psychotic state, and induce them to believe that they are someone else or that non-existent people and objects exist.

Rapid eye movements are often seen to occur in psychotic states, which, of course, are the defining sign of the REM state. Psychotic patients also very quickly convert thought into sensory experience, with the result that they can become highly emotional almost instantly. When recalling a distressing memory, for example, they can be instantly transported right back into that memory and re-experience the emotions connected with it very strongly. That phenomenon, too, is a characteristic of the dream state, when emotional arousal triggers a thought pattern which is immediately converted into a sensory metaphor – the dream. It is not surprising, then, that psychotic patients not only talk in metaphors but live them out, which explains their often bizarre speech and behaviour.

The REM state, as we have explained, is in effect a reality generator. It creates all kinds of perceptions in our dreams, but these are illusory perceptions – vivid metaphors. One psychotic patient actually described herself as "being trapped in the land of illusion".[38] Indeed, we know from talking to psychotic patients in their saner moments that they readily recognize that they are trapped in a dreaming state.

We suggest that we can use this insight to help people make sense of their psychotic experience. Ordinarily, there is ongoing interplay between the left and right hemispheres of the brain. We can help psychotic patients dip out of the dream state into the more analytical side of their brains by the type of questions we ask them and by talking about what is concerning them; and by connecting with their metaphors and attempting to change the meanings these have for them. They can then start to better understand what is happening to them and spend more time in normal, waking reality.

When we have made these sorts of observations about psychosis at our seminars, they have on occasion been heard by people who themselves have had a psychotic breakdown and recovered. These people have all responded extremely positively, even thankfully, to this understanding of their experience. The following remarkable letter, sent to us by someone who had heard these ideas discussed and then read an article about them in our journal, *Human Givens*,[39] is a typical reaction.

> I was riveted by your article ... "Trapped in the land of illusion", which explored the connection between the dream state and psychosis – which might surely better be termed dream-walking.
>
> In the same issue, psychologist Daniel Nettle discussed the link between psychosis and creative thinking – asserting that psychosis is a physical process (hardware, not a software, problem, to borrow a computer term) and that environmental influences have chemical consequences. I would like to relate some of the elements of my own experience of psychosis 17 years ago, which may have

relevance to all this.

It was at a seminar this year, when Ivan Tyrrell first discussed the function of dreaming in the psychotic state, that I first 'came out' publicly about my own experience. I was so excited to find that someone else had noticed the similarity to dreaming that I wanted to contribute my own observations to support the idea. But I was also surprised to find I had an overwhelming surge of emotional reaction: heart pounding; a deafening ringing in my ears; my voice, barely audible, sounding far off as in a dream; words hard to form, just as in a dream. It was a ghastly flashback and insight into the high emotional state which was the (at the time) unperceived back-drop to the whole event. I am particularly interested in the notion that stress, anxiety, depression and psychosis may be on a continuum, and that a dreamlike state accounts for the altered thinking style of psychosis.

At the time of my original experience, I was suffering extreme anxiety, which made it impossible to sleep or eat. I was existing on coffee and cigarettes and, not surprisingly, although I would fall asleep exhausted, I would startle awake and find it impossible to get back to sleep till nearly time to get up again. After about a week of this I awoke one morning with a solid lump in my chest and totally bursting with energy. Something seemed to have happened, but what? I felt different; for the better: invincible, as if I had changed in some way. At first I thought it was just I who was different. But then I began to notice that people were looking at me strangely, meaningfully. I began to think they knew something about this too but weren't telling me what.

It was as if a veil had been peeled back to reveal a different world, like a dreamworld; one where everyone seemed to know what I was about and could see my inner thoughts. It was dark and frightening. There was nowhere to hide. People seemed to be in collusion, as if everyone was in telepathic communication with each other. Like secret agents. Dredging through memory banks for stories to explain this new order, suddenly I believed in magic, telepathy, and that this was a pilgrimage, a trial, some sort of test that I had to figure out for myself. Desperate for clues, I began to notice they were all around me, in overheard conversations, in supposedly casual gestures, even on the television.

My heightened emotional state was so intense and confused

that no single emotion could be distinguished any longer. This condition, created by insoluble conflict and paradox in my life, created a chemical cocktail that overloaded my brain and sent it into a frenzy of activity. It reached a sort of white-hot pitch which I experienced as feeling 'high' with a solid fist in the centre of my chest. In that heightened state I became hypervigilant: intensely sensitive and acutely perceptive of other people's responses to me. Observing people's minute micro-expressions as they observed me made me think that I could perceive their thoughts about me. The state had the self-centred character of depression. Add a little anxiety and you have paranoia. Seemingly being seen through by everyone you meet is terrifying, I assure you, as well as humiliating. Everything that happened seemed to add to the terror, making it more intense, and presumably exacerbating the condition.

It seems as if, at the time, thoughts were speeding so fast that they were not recognised as my own. (I have a mental picture of Winnie the Pooh circling an island and, coming upon his own footprints, thinking he had company.) It was as if thoughts were being 'picked up' from outside, because ideas seemed not to have been called up but just happened, unbidden. The suggestion, in the Griffin and Tyrrell article, that left-brain activity during the REM states could account for the phenomenon of hearing voices could perhaps explain such 'imposed' thoughts as well.

Eventually I said something totally bizarre to my spouse, whose look of horror was so obviously not faked that I decided to confide in him. After listening to my tales and questions, he managed to reassure me that people could not in fact read my thoughts. So then I was able to relax a little, and begin the long job of sorting out the 'real' from the dreamlike, and deconstructing the 'nightmare' world. Even after I had learned to identify which was which, for quite a while, I was conscious of the two 'worlds': the ordinary one, where people are separate and there is some privacy; and the other ghastly, dreamlike one, where I was transparent, exposed, and there was nowhere to hide.

With support and protection I was able to resume normal sleeping and eating and was lucky enough to be able to recover my balance in the safety of my own home, without medical intervention. My damage limitation strategy after this emotional rollercoaster was to aim for simplicity and calm and learn to ignore idle thoughts. The experience of having a stream of thoughts like so much tickertape just prattling away is something that I am still aware of when there is nothing more important to focus on, like being aware of the ticking of the clock once the telly is turned off. The fact that the brain consumes 20 per cent of our energy intake seems to support the imperative for appropriate fuel intake and is surely even more important where creativity is concerned.

If dreaming uses a huge amount of energy I hypothesise that consciously surfing one's imagination, as when writing poetry or music, designing, inventing or doing pure maths, also burns a lot of energy and can have an overheating effect because of the need to juggle ideas, hold lots of possibilities in the mind and employ different areas of the brain at once. Could it be that creative activity uses both sides of the brain, each interacting in harmony, but, in an emotionally 'overheated' state, the metaphorical mode is boosted, switched on persistently and the two modes become indistinguishable?

I also venture to suggest that, because of the speed and intensity of mental activity during the 'hot' phase, an abundance of new connections is made between brain areas not previously connected; and that, because of the circularity of thoughts, unhelpful circuits are created which remain forever tricky terrain. I have heard somewhere that it takes three goes to learn something but seven to unlearn it. So, if you learn a bad habit, it takes much more time and effort to undo it. I employed the tactic of starving it of attention and tried not to reuse those 'tangled' circuits.

I feel I now understand so much more about my own experience of psychosis. Pattern matching explains the thinking style. The brain's propensity for narrative helps explain the desperate attempt to link unrelated events. The information that dreaming takes a huge amount of energy explains the sensation of the head getting overheated to bursting point. Learning that there is an emotional accompaniment to all perceptions has freed me from fearing I was the only one guilty of ideas with an emotional tag. And the dreaming mode of psychosis explains being so gullible!

The beauty of the human givens perspective is that it identifies the fundamental role of heightened emotion in all psychological disorders.

Pinpointing the anxiety at the root of a psychotic experience is like finding the end of Ariadne's thread: a beginning point from which to unravel all the terrifying confusion, and find a way out of the maze.[40]

In our preliminary investigations, using these concepts, we have found that psychotic patients calm down when they realize there is an explanation for what is happening to them. When calm, the psychotic phenomena become less threatening and less intense. Then we can start doing what developing countries traditionally do so much better – re-orientating people towards getting their emotional needs met and creating strong support structures for them.

Being unhappy, stressed and depressed is a strong predictor of later mental illness. This new understanding of what psychosis is means we can set out practical guidelines for treating it and thereby reduce the prevalence of severe breakdowns and increase the recovery rate dramatically when they do occur.

We are saying, then, that extreme stress, anxiety and depression lead to psychosis, where the patient's brain can no longer distinguish between the metaphorical reality of the dreaming process and the way a brain normally manages to order reality. If we are right, it follows that, if people were treated more effectively for stress overload and depression by properly trained (human givens) psychotherapists, the depression would lift in most cases and not degenerate into psychosis. Because psychotic people are so hypersensitive to metaphor, health workers need to be trained, when working with these patients, to use metaphorical language that encourages left-hemisphere activity. They need to know how to reduce their patients' arousal levels with calming metaphors. Conversely, they need to consciously avoid metaphors that may remind patients of their predicament, flipping them back into their right hemisphere and psychosis. This is a specialist skill that can be taught. They also need to consider that their psychotic patients' metaphorical language and behaviour represent emotional needs not being met, or that they are attempts to express what it feels like to process waking reality directly through the REM state.

In addition, the skills of occupational therapists need to be given much greater prominence in the treatment of these patients, who need to connect to reality in disciplined, concrete, purposeful ways: by gardening, cooking, making things, doing craftwork, etc. Their daily routine also needs a clear structure and discipline.

But, above all, as a society we need to ensure these vulnerable people receive effective psychotherapy more quickly – before stress, anxiety and depression completely overload their dreaming mechanism and too much damage is done. Prevention is the better course wherever possible. Enormous savings could be made if all those who offer counselling and psychotherapy were trained so that they could act quickly to stop stress, anxiety and depression triggering major breakdowns in those genetically predisposed to developing psychosis. In other words, therapists need to work from the givens of human nature, not ideology, profit motives (drugs are not the only way to lower the arousal that puts pressure on the dreaming brain), or bureaucratic convenience.

A couple of decades after we first made these observations, our colleague Ezra Hewing, who holds an MSc in the psychology and neuroscience of mental health from the Institute of Psychology, Psychiatry & Neuroscience, King's College London, published a convincing account of how these ideas are supported by brain science and, taking them further, even explains the enigma of hallucinations and delusions (so-called positive symptoms of schizophrenia, because they add something on) and symptoms such as withdrawal and emotional flatness (termed negative because they take something away from the sufferer), experienced in the same person. His findings support our own recommendations for best ways to help someone with psychosis.[41]

The observing self

Some people may wonder why nature has made our brains so susceptible to influence. After all, scientists keep telling us that it is the most intelligent and complex organ that exists in the universe, but, if other people can influence it so easily and alter its functioning, surely this is a major defect? However, with the organizing idea that hypnosis is simply any artificial method used for accessing the programming state of the brain (REM), *which is absolutely vital for life itself* – for programming our instinctive knowledge and acting it out through posthypnotic suggestion – then you realize that hypnosis is tapping into the most basic programme of all: a programme without which we couldn't exist. So potent is this mechanism that our highest achievements, and civilization itself, grew out of it.

All of us *need* to have and retain a propensity to be programmed (conditioned) by other people and by the wider culture. All of us are conditioned by the values and belief systems we are immersed in.[42] Our politics, religion and moral values are an accident of birth and none of us chooses the bed we are born in. But, whilst programming instinctive templates (and the facility of being conditionable, so that we can add to them) are essential processes that enable us to adapt and survive wherever in the world we are born, there are also great dangers associated with them. This is because it seems natural to us to act out that programming. It's the most natural thing in the world to believe in the value system and the religious or cultural ideals we are brought up in and surrounded by.

One obvious danger is that we easily end up not being able to stand back and realize that we are programmed and therefore never question those values and see beyond the 'truth' of our own culture. In other words, if the conditioning is too rigid, we lose flexibility of thought and behaviour. All cultures are relative and see reality differently and are biased or prejudiced in favour of certain aspects of reality, while omitting others. This allows people to deny the rights and values of other cultures and makes it easier to commit atrocities against them. The process conditions us, limits our options, and, in addition, allows certain elements in society to take advantage of us – unscrupulous salesmen, politicians, dictators, cult leaders, cynical entertainers, trivializers – who, by preoccupying us, waste our time, exploit or even enslave us. And, by denying other people's reality, we can be taken to war. People in all cultures need to be more aware of this.[43]

The fact that we are so easily conditioned explains why so many people need psychotherapy. They accept the models they have been conditioned into by their family and, where their family is dysfunctional, it's difficult for them to spot the maladaptive patterns that they are operating from without the help of a therapist. It is important to remember that the chains by which conditioning enslaves us need not be all that strong. The integrity of our core instinctive personality is kept intact by the REM state. If we are willing to take a step back we can alter the distorting patterns installed by our environment and install more adaptive ones to express our instinctive impulses.

Fortunately therapists have an ally in nature, which has provided us with a mechanism for making it possible to step outside our conditioning. It is variously called 'the observing self', 'the transparent centre', and 'that which is aware'.[43] Our observing self is the natural opposite of the trance state. When our observing self is activated, we have stepped back from our trance state and thus widened the focus of our attention so that we can see from more than one viewpoint. Traditional Eastern psychology has long taught the art of flexible disengagement from emotional trance states so that the world can be seen more objectively. It is only when we are in our observing self that we can actually question our own conditioning. This is because the observing self is a more fundamental part of us than even our thinking and feeling selves. It is our awareness that everything else feeds into. A person could lose arms, legs, sight, hearing and yet still have that sense of 'I am', and being a centre of experience of reality – 'I am aware'. The observing self supersedes thought, feeling and action *because it experiences these functions*. As the psychiatrist, Dr Arthur Deikman, who coined the term, says, "No matter what takes place, no matter what we experience, nothing is as central as the self that observes ... It is incapable of being objectified; whatever you can notice or conceptualize is already an object of awareness, not awareness itself. Unlike every other aspect of experience – thoughts, emotions, desires and functions – the observing self can be known but not located, known but not 'seen'."[44]

As Deikman further points out, "The observing self is not part of the object world formed by our thoughts and sensory perceptions because, literally, it has no limits; everything else does. Thus, everyday consciousness contains a transcendent element that we seldom notice because that element is the very ground of our experience. The word *transcendent* is justified because, if subjective consciousness – the observing self – cannot itself be observed but remains forever apart from the contents of consciousness, it is likely to be of a different order from everything else. Its fundamentally different nature becomes evident when we realize that the observing self is featureless; it cannot be affected by the world any more than a mirror can be affected by the images it reflects."[45]

The evolution of the observing self in human beings is possibly the most important distinction between us and the rest of the animal kingdom. This was first recognized within Eastern psychology but only in the last few decades has it begun to be incorporated into Western psychology. All good therapists have the skill to help a client step back into their observing self (even if they don't call it by that name) to identify the patterns of conditioning that need to change.

Hypnotic ability

Going in and out of trance stays with us as a necessary function throughout our lives. When we give attention to people, and receive attention, we are going in and out of trance – internal focus, external focus, back and forth – and this serves a valuable need for us. It enables us to stay constantly in sync with the people around us, in our family, our society, our culture. If we didn't keep doing this, a process that paradoxically gives us flexibility, our own thought processes would become so bizarre that we would end up unable to operate within our culture. This is what happens to people with various types of mental disorders. The thinking of lonely, isolated people becomes more unstable and bizarre. Normal people's thinking is stabilized and kept congruent with the models of our culture by our going in and out of trance on a regular basis in the company of those around us. Yet, whilst this is a great aid to keeping us sane it is also our greatest weakness because the process limits our options.

This means that all the arguments about whether some people are hypnotizable or not are irrelevant because *every* undamaged person is hypnotizable. (Of course not everybody will believe this, however much evidence you give them. At a dinner party, Ivan was once sitting next to a psychologist who had authoritatively declared earlier that there was no such thing as hypnotic trance states. Late in the evening, it became clear that the man had gone into a profound trance whilst staring at a candle. After observing this for a few minutes, Ivan slowly passed his hand back and forth between the psychologist's eyes and the candle. It took several passes before the psychologist 'came back to the room'. Nevertheless, when challenged, he declared he had not been in trance!) We are all pre-programmed with instinctive templates and are activated by them – going in and out of trance – all day long. We hypnotize each other to varying degrees many times on a daily basis. Erickson showed that everybody could be hypnotized eventually, even though sometimes it took him days to do it. And somebody taking a different approach from Erickson might have been able to put that 'difficult' person into a trance straight away – perhaps the boss barking an order, for example. (Of course, people in a psychotic state are already largely in a trance, experiencing waking reality through the REM state, and what they need is help to engage more effectively with reality outside of that state.)

It is easy to hypnotize people once the principle is understood that it is simply a question of either mimicking the stages of relaxation before sleep, or any other part of the slide into the REM state. This can be done by inducing rapid eye movements through tracking a moving hand or pendulum, getting subjects to focus their attention in some way, or by other creative means. People can be hypnotized using their imagination, following a train of thought that they are intensively interested in, or by physical stimulus, sudden sound or shock. All have the common denominator of focusing attention, and different methods can be more or less effective with different people, as we are all individual.

Here is what happened when one particular highly stressed man came to see Joe for therapy. "He was clearly embarrassed, so when I started talking about relaxing, and he felt himself relaxing, he began to giggle. Of course, as Erickson would have done, I said immediately that, 'one of the best ways to relax is to giggle. In fact, the more you giggle the more deeply relaxed you go, and if you try to stop it now you will find yourself compelled to giggle even more …' and he started shaking with mirth! I said, 'I wouldn't be at all surprised now if you find that the shaking and giggling gets so intense that the shaking and giggling goes right down to your toes.' And it did! It was wonderful. Nevertheless, I was holding his attention. The more he laughed, the more he was allowing me to hold his attention. And that's all you need to do. If you can hold that attention mechanism for a minute or two minutes, the brain just assumes it is in some kind of a dream state and the cerebral cortex surrenders power to you, just as it surrenders two hours every night to allow itself to be directed by unresolved emotional arousals and dream them away.

"In the case of the giggling man I went from there into talking about his business and what he was doing in his business, because that was also something that was intensely interesting to him. As I talked about that, I was keeping his attention even more focused. Once I had his attention focused for several minutes, he was in quite a profound, deep hypnotic state. In other words, his brain had actually allowed me to take over its attention-directing mechanism and I could evoke all kinds of phenomena in him to help him overcome his difficulties. After about half an hour, when he came out of trance, he had amnesia about everything that happened after the giggling. It was as remote to him as most dreams are and dreams are notoriously difficult to remember.

"I am quite certain that, if he was being worked with in an experimental laboratory situation, many scientists would have concluded that he was unhypnotizable because he couldn't stop giggling, and the approach I used didn't conform to a standard procedure. If I were following a script, it wouldn't have worked. I had to work with what was there."

It needs to be understood that there are people who more easily surrender their ability to focus their attention than others. This is due partly to biological and partly to environmental factors. People who allow their attention to be focused easily *don't even need a trance induction*. On being told, "I want you to close your hand and when you try to open your hand you won't be able to open it", they will respond to the suggestion. That's how some stage hypnotists select the people they are going to work with. Commonly, they might say, "I want you all to put your hands tight together and when I count to three your hands will be stuck together". Then they pick out of the audience those who immediately respond to the suggestion – none of whom has had any form of induction. So if someone wants to prove that hypnosis doesn't exist, they will always be able to find people who will respond to a suggestion easily, and conclude that hypnosis is only suggestion. Conversely, there are people who are so psychically defensive or left-brain dominant that reassurance, flexibility and creativity are required on the part of the hypnotist in order to encourage them into a trance. We hope we have made it clear why we put hypnosis and hypnotic phenomena where they belong – right at the centre of human psychology and our understanding of what it means to be human.

PART TWO

Appreciating Our Biological Inheritance

CHAPTER FIVE

The human givens

WHAT, IN everyday terms, are the physical and emotional needs programmed into us from our genes? And how does nature set about helping us meet those needs? Some possible answers to these questions are what we will now put before you.

The law of all living organisms is that, to survive, they must take nourishment from the environment so that they can continually maintain and rebuild themselves. Like all animals, we need air to breathe, water to drink, nutritious food and sufficient amounts of the right quality of sleep (which, in turn, relies on having the right amount of exposure to light and dark and to temperatures conducive to sleep). These physical needs are easily apparent because, if they are not met, we quickly die – as many people sadly do in those parts of the world where clean water is scarce and food in short supply. We also need the freedom to stimulate our senses, hone our survival skills as youngsters through play, and exercise our muscles. In addition, we instinctively seek sufficient and secure shelter where we can grow and, as our sex drive rises, reproduce ourselves and bring up our young in safety.

Everyone can accept that these basic physical needs should be met and that they are 'givens'. But psychologists throughout the ages have also determined that there are other nutritional needs, emotional rather than physical, which are equally crucial for our wellbeing – and, sometimes, even for survival too.[1] These include the needs for:

- security – safe territory: an environment which enables us to lead our lives without experiencing excessive or undue fear and allows us to develop fully
- autonomy – control over what happens around and to us. Exercising volition gives us a form of feedback from the universe that we exist
- attention – receiving it from others, but also giving it: a form of

essential nutrition that fuels the development of each individual, family and culture

- emotional connection to other people – friendship, loving relationships, intimacy
- connection to the wider community – we are a group animal and we need to feel we belong to social groupings beyond our immediate family
- status – a sense that we are accepted by, and valued in, the various social groups we belong to
- privacy – time and space enough to reflect on and consolidate our experiences
- a sense of our own competence and achievements – which ensures we don't feel we are inadequate (and develop 'low self-esteem')
- meaning – which comes from being stretched in what we do and how we think. Meaning makes suffering tolerable. It is through 'stretching' ourselves mentally or physically – by service to others, learning new skills or being connected to ideas or philosophies bigger than ourselves – that our lives feel purposeful and full of meaning.

We come into the world with these innate but as yet unmet needs. How well they are fulfilled in the world determines many aspects of our personality, our character, how well we develop physically and emotionally, how we interact with other people and what we achieve in life.[2] If they are matched up in a fairly balanced way, life is good to us: we cannot be mentally unwell if our emotional needs are being met. If they are not, we soon get frustrated, stressed and angry and this can lead us to develop one or more of a range of disturbing psychological states: anxiety disorders, depression, addictions and even a complete psychotic breakdown.[3] And, as if that were not bad enough, our psychologically and emotionally disturbed behaviour impacts on those around us – family, friends, colleagues and the wider community. So-called 'anti-social behaviour', for example, clearly results from some of these innate needs not being met by the environment of the perpetrators.

Of course, our physical and emotional needs are not separate from each other but extremely closely interlinked. If the air we breathe is severely polluted, for instance, it impacts our ability to breathe easily, adversely affecting our ability to exercise (which itself affects mental health) and to engage in activities which require mental and physical energy. If we live or work in environments where there is little access to natural light, our mental health can be badly affected. Conversely, if life is not going well and we become miserable to the degree of sinking into a depression, we may stop engaging in activities, suffer poor sleep and not look after ourselves properly. If we terrify ourselves with fears of catastrophe, our bodies bear the brunt, leaving us susceptible to all sorts of ailments.

But our innate needs are only one half of the story. Nature has also provided us with a wealth of resources (refined over thousands of years) to help us get these needs met. We have, of course, basic physical resources, such as our ability to move/take action to achieve what we need and our ability to sleep and recharge our batteries, alongside our basic physical abilities to breathe, feed ourselves, eliminate waste, reproduce and so on. Our innate *psychological* resources, which can be usefully thought of as our internal guidance systems, include:

- the ability to develop complex long-term memory, which enables us to add to our innate knowledge and learn
- the ability to build rapport, empathize and connect with others
- imagination, which enables us to focus our attention away from our emotions and problem solve more creatively and objectively
- emotions and instincts – a guidance system whereby, through the release of a variety of neurotransmitters, hormones and other chemical messengers, we act to meet our survival needs
- the conscious, rational ability to check out emotions, question, analyze and plan
- the ability to 'know' – understand the world unconsciously through metaphorical pattern matching
- an observing self – that part of us which can step back, be more objective and recognize itself as a unique centre of awareness separate from intellect, emotion and conditioning (frontal lobes)
- a dreaming brain that preserves the integrity of our genetic inheritance every night by metaphorically defusing emotionally arousing expectations not acted out the previous day.

It is such needs and tools together that are the human givens, nature's genetic endowment to us. Over enormous stretches of time, they underwent continuous refinement as they drove our evolution on. They are best thought of as inbuilt patterns – biological templates – that continually interact with one another and (in undamaged people) seek their natural fulfilment, or completion, in the world in ways that allow us to survive, live together as many-faceted individuals in a great variety of different social groupings, and flourish. It is the way in which those needs are met, and the way we use the resources that nature has given us, that determine the physical, mental and moral health of an individual. GP and human givens practitioner Andrew Morrice, in his trainings delivered through Human Givens College, provides up-to-date research findings, showing how all this fits with current scientific knowledge.[4]

It follows naturally from the above that adequate fulfilment of the human givens should be the benchmark position for how we organize our own lives and those of others – for instance, in education, the workplace and the health services. Indeed, the Emotional Needs Audit, which we developed based on the needs described here (see opposite), has since been modified for use in specific settings within health, education and the workplace, and validated by university researchers.[5]

When we feel emotionally fulfilled and are operating effectively within society, we are more likely to be mentally healthy and stable. But when too many of our physical and emotional needs are not met or when our resources are used incorrectly – unwittingly or otherwise – we suffer considerable distress. And so do those around us.

From this perspective, there are three possible reasons for why someone may not be able to get the necessary physical and emotional nourishment they need.

ONE: The environment is sick and unable to provide proper nourishment at that time: crops don't grow in a drought; fish die when the water dries up; and so do people when there is nothing to eat and drink. And, just as crops won't flourish in poor soil, even if they have the water they need, a society that prevents people from getting any of their emotional needs met adequately is ensuring that we don't develop properly. An abusive home life that prevents children or adults from receiving the emotional nourishment they need for functioning

The Emotional Needs Audit

Nature has programmed all of us with physical and emotional needs. These are the 'human givens' that cannot be avoided. How stressed we are depends on how well our needs are being met, and how well we deal with the situation when they are not. Rate, in your judgement, how well the following emotional needs are being met in your life now, on a scale of one to seven (where 1 means not met at all, and 7 means being very well met), by ticking the appropriate boxes.

	NO	SOMETIMES	YES
	1	2 3 4 5 6	7

- Do you feel secure in all major areas of your life (such as your home, work, environment)?
- Do you feel you receive enough attention?
- Do you think you give other people enough attention?
- Do you feel in control of your life most of the time?
- Do you feel connected to some part of a wider community?
- Can you obtain privacy when you need to?
- Do you feel an emotional connection to others? For instance, do you have an intimate relationship in your life, one where you are totally physically and emotionally accepted for who you are by at least one person (this could be a close friend)?
- Do you feel you have status that is acknowledged?
- Are you achieving things and feeling competent in at least one major area of your life?
- Are you being mentally and/or physically stretched in ways which give you a sense that life is meaningful?

- If your scores are mostly low, you are more likely to be suffering stress symptoms.
- If any need is scored 3 or less this is likely to be a major stressor for you.
- Even if only one need is marked very low it can be enough of a problem to seriously affect your mental and emotional stability.

Stress, anxiety, anger, depression and addiction are the result of our innate needs not being met, either due to environmental factors, harmful conditioning or a misuse of imagination (worrying). People do not have mental health problems when their innate needs are being met in balanced, healthy ways. By highlighting areas in your life where your essential needs aren't being met as well as they could be, you can use this questionnaire to help you think constructively about how your life could be improved.

healthily is a sick environment. And so is anywhere that bullying takes place, whether on the street, at school or in the workplace. Furthermore, the very nature of modern life often disrupts our ability to use some of our resources, or internal guidance systems, effectively. For example, large institutions, and particularly governments, all too often impose innumerable inappropriate rules and regulations in an attempt to legislate for every possible eventuality. The constant stress that such context-blind or 'straight-line' thinking puts individuals, families and communities under is palpable and affects huge swathes of the population.

Another stressor is that we can no longer take it for granted, as past generations did, that our family, neighbourhood or political, religious and educational institutions will ensure social stability – those days are over and many people don't cope well with this. Only when new, more flexible organizations evolve, ones that constantly hold emotional needs in mind, whatever the changes (eg technological or financial) that occur, might we reduce the damage being done to people's emotional and physical health. Also, we need to be mindful of the damage that we ourselves have inflicted on the environment, causing many of the ills that have now come back to bite us, and support ways to live in better harmony with nature.

TWO: An individual's internal guidance system is damaged. Things can go wrong in the transmission of genetic knowledge and some children, unfortunately, are born damaged. Direct physical assaults on the brain due to attack, accident or poisoning by drug or alcohol use later in life can also seriously harm it. However, these represent a comparatively small number of cases. Overwhelmingly, the most frequent damage to human guidance systems arises from three sources: insufficient intake of the right physical nourishment; psychological damage due to trauma; and unhelpful conditioning. Fortunately, enough is known about the kind of food we should eat to be healthy and, fortunately too, human givens practitioners know how to decondition psychological trauma quickly (as will be discussed later). But the way we are conditioned by the culture we live in and the harm it can cause is more problematic and less widely realized; we don't often objectively recognize our own conditioned behaviour and responses, or examine them consciously.

THREE: Missing coping skills. Sometimes people don't know how to operate their internal guidance systems to help them to get their needs met. For instance, they may misuse their imagination by worrying, which leads them to become depressed. Or they may have been conditioned to expect rewards without putting in effort, so they never learn to take responsibility for their actions. The more complex any animal organism is, the more learning input from the environment, over and above what it inherits from its genes, is needed to survive. Higher mammals that hunt, for example, learn how to do this from older members of the pack. But humans, whose capacity for learning is vast, need much more complex input from the surrounding culture than, say, a wolf, and the input has to be sufficient and of the right quality for healthy development.

Alongside the tragic number of deaths incurred, the covid-19 pandemic in many ways illustrated what happens when essential emotional needs are not met. For instance, much of the traumatic stress and suicidal thoughts experienced by healthcare workers during the covid-19 pandemic can be attributed to unmet human needs and moral injury, according to researchers Sarah Hagerty and Leanne Williams, who analysed data collected from 1,122 health-care workers from across the United States between May 2020 and August 2020, to examine moral injury and unmet basic human needs in relation to traumatic stress and suicidal thinking. (Moral injury is defined as experiences in which someone perpetrates, fails to prevent, bears witness to, or learns about acts that go against deeply held moral beliefs and expectations.) Nearly one third of respondents reported elevated symptoms of psychological trauma, and the prevalence of suicidal thinking among healthcare workers in the sample was roughly three times higher than in the general population. Moral injury and loneliness predicted greater symptoms of traumatic stress and suicidality. Respondents commonly made comments about fearing social contact with families in case of passing on covid-19; too many patients to deal with safely; being obliged to decide who lived and who died; being unable to give adequate comfort; witnessing or participating in patients dying alone; and patients becoming depersonalized.

"We conclude that dehumanisation is a driving force behind the psychological injury resulting from moral incongruence in the context of the pandemic. Intrinsic moral imperatives, such as honouring the humanity in oneself and others, have been jeopardised," the researchers wrote.[6]

So we will now take a closer look at the most important of our emotional needs.

The need for security

At birth, like most mammals, we have a need for security, and we are dependent upon the protection of our parents and other older members of the species until we are old enough to look after ourselves. Our survival depends on their supplying warmth, safety and appropriate nutriment, including attention, so that we can develop well. This is a 'given' and the innate knowledge that dramatically increases the chances of our needs being met is also a given. Newborns, for example, know immediately how to develop rapport with the adults on whom they depend for food, warmth, safety and comfort. They know instinctively how to draw noisy attention to themselves to make sure they are fed and kept comfortable.

The need for this sort of security persists. Research has shown that, when we are fearful even as adults, the presence of someone we view as strongly supportive reduces the fear[7] and, indeed, that we continue to associate physical warmth with social support.[8]

Scientists have used many ingenious experimental techniques to find out what babies already know when they are born. For example, it was discovered that they know from birth to look for human facial features and even imitate what they see. If a mother looks at her newborn and sticks out her tongue, the baby will very commonly stick out its own tongue while looking back at her. (We say "very commonly" because some other researchers have failed to replicate this finding, yet those of us who have spent time with babies know how often it happens.) A baby quickly moves on from this to recognize different emotional expressions and other people's faces.[9] In other words, all babies have innate communication skills that they put to use immediately to 'pattern match' to parents' behaviour.

Three specialists in infant development had this to say 20 years ago about this particular human given and they made their point so vividly that we think it still relevant to quote here: "At first glance this ability to imitate might seem curious and cute but not deeply significant. But if you think about it a minute, it is actually amazing. There are no mirrors in the womb: newborns have never seen their own face. So how do they know whether their tongue is inside or outside their mouth? There is another way of knowing what your face is like. As you read this, you probably have a good idea of your facial expression (we hope intense concentration leavened by the occasional smile). Try sticking out your tongue (in a suitably private setting). The way you know you've succeeded is through kinaesthesia, your internal feeling of your own body.

"In order to imitate, newborn babies must somehow understand the similarity between that internal feeling and the external face they see, a round shape with a long pink thing at the bottom moving back and forth. Newborn babies not only distinguish and prefer faces, but they also seem to recognize that those faces are like their own face. They recognize that people are 'like me'. There is nothing more personal, more part of you, than this internal sense you have of your own body, your expressions and movements, your aches and tickles. And yet from the time we're born, we seem to link this deeply personal self to the bodily movements we can only see and not feel. Nature ingeniously gives us a jump-start on the 'Other Minds' problem. We know, quite directly, that we are like other people and they are like us."[10]

These researchers also came to the conclusion that, "trying to understand human nature is part of human nature".[11] Each individual human journey of discovery – our quest to understand other people and ourselves – begins as we struggle to connect, through this imitation process, with others like ourselves. So it follows that this given to imitate, triggered at birth by our need for security, is the beginning of the growth of rapport-building skills. If we do not learn how to build rapport early, our chances of being looked after and developing friendships in those first vital years are diminished. Building rapport only *begins* with the baby and its primary caregiver; it is the basic requirement in the formation of all future relationships. At its most fundamental level, it is created through a dance of matching movements, including body orientation, body moves, eye contact, facial expression and tone of voice.

All neurotypical babies are pre-primed to listen out for human language patterns and pay attention to them, and this pattern perception quickly extends to more sophisticated levels of pattern matching – to intonation, naming words, abstract words, etc. The genetic basis for the acquisition of language is a given but, because the process is a metaphorical one, it gives infants the flexibility to acquire the specific language of the country where they are raised. Most babies are born hearing linguistic information that the rest of us miss, although this ability to discriminate speech sounds and tones used in all the world's languages, including sign language, is lost at around 10 months, allowing them to learn their home language faster.[12] However, a child born of English parents who then moves with their family to, say, Japan, where they grow up surrounded by Japanese speakers, has no difficulty in becoming fluent in that language as well as the mother tongue – at least before the age of around 10, when that easy language-learning facility starts to be lost. This innate ability to acquire language is, therefore, an analogical process. The instinctive template for language acquisition is metaphorically matched up to whatever form of language the environment offers. Thus the pattern is completed.

As language develops, the speed, volume of word delivery, and range of words, phrases and descriptive images a person uses become incorporated into the rapport-building process, alongside body language. It is like a dance routine that gets more complicated as the music progresses.

Children who learn this dance of empathy in the first months of life – as their mothers, fathers and siblings match their tone of voice, degree of arousal, and expressed emotion – grow up more confident and better at establishing rapport with others.[13] The pattern for rapport building, genetically laid down in the child, has matched up with a pattern in the environment to complete itself. That this is a process of fulfilling a template becomes obvious when we study the behaviour of children where the pattern has *not* matched up as nature intended. When parents continually under- or over-respond to their children's emotional behaviour, perhaps by failing to listen to or hug them when they are upset, or by becoming angry when they are timid or too smothering when they are loving, it causes a distress reaction in the children – a strong feeling of insecurity – and they learn to repress their natural responses.[14]

Emotional uncertainty about the relationship with one's parents can have knock-on effects, even when a family is by no means uncaring or neglectful. The greater the matching of behaviours between two people, the more likely they are to feel themselves in emotional rapport, to like each other, be interested in what each other is saying and feel secure in each other's company. This pattern repeats itself in other realms of life. Studies show that the greater the degree of co-ordination between students' and teachers' movements, for example, the more friendly, happy and enthusiastic they feel during their encounters.

Couples have been video-taped discussing a contentious issue and, when the tape is played back and each partner is asked to identify what the other was feeling during the heated discussion, the most empathic accuracy is always shown by those whose non-verbal behaviour matches that of their spouses whilst watching the video. If, whilst watching the video, they react in the same non-matching way as they did when they were making it, they show poor ability to surmise what their partners were feeling and exhibit greater insecurity around the relationship. Only when body movements are in sync – often known as 'pacing' – is there empathy.

We now know that the dance of empathy has something to do with mirror neurons – nerve cells that fire both when we perform an action ourselves and also when we merely observe that action being made by someone else. Mirror neurons were discovered serendipitously in a laboratory at the University of Parma in 1995, when neurophysiologists using depth electrodes to study the premotor cortex in the brains of macaque monkeys realized that the neurons that fired when the macaques reached out and grasped a peanut also fired when a researcher absentmindedly reached out to eat a peanut himself.[15] Much more research followed and it has since been shown, through brain scan studies, that the same system operates in human brains. Although their effects appear less dramatic than originally thought (they were excitedly described as "the cells that read minds"), mirror neurons contribute to complex control systems, playing a role, for instance, in discriminating body movements; and they acquire – and alter – their mirror properties through sensorimotor learning.[16]

Each human given interacts with all the others in an increasingly complex, multilayered way that develops as we grow older. The need for security, for example, changes in quality the more we learn. After its being (it is to be hoped) satisfied initially by our parents, caregivers, childhood home and the familiar geographical environment we live in, it becomes increasingly fulfilled by ourselves as we learn that we can proactively understand and manipulate what is going on around us. Our sense of security, therefore, is in part generated from our knowledge that we are competent to deal with the kinds of situation that we are likely to find ourselves in. However, certain circumstances may undermine our getting it fulfilled, either gradually or in an instant. It can happen gradually if we slowly become aware that we have a serious illness; or we find ourselves living in an increasingly menacing neighbourhood, where the threat of physical attack grows; or we begin to realize that we have joined a workplace where overt or covert bullying is rife, or major threatening changes are going to occur – in the classic Whitehall studies, in which researchers followed up the health and wellbeing of thousands of civil servants for decades, the first study showed that those whose jobs had become insecure, in the course of major organizational changes, suffered far more serious ill health than those whose jobs were unaffected.[17] Our sense of security can plummet very suddenly if we experience a life-threatening event, such as a heart attack, car crash, mugging or earthquake, or if our country is threatened by war, any of which may result in post-traumatic stress. The need for security is a given, then, but our sense of security itself is never immutable. Thus it must be met in balance for us to be emotionally healthy at any given time.

The need for autonomy and control

Our need to feel secure is closely connected to our innate need for control. Having the ability to exercise willpower, and choose what happens to and around us, is one of the primary human psychological drives that operate in the service of our survival. We can easily see that this is so when we observe what happens to people who unexpectedly find an important aspect of their life suddenly turned upside down and no amount of willpower can do much about it. If their finances are compromised, for example, or a partner informs them that they are leaving, or an unforeseen health crisis strikes, they become panicky and anxious because they are losing control. When people talk about what is stressing them, whether at work, in a relationship or in their interactions with the wider community, it is common for them to say they feel that they have no control over a situation.

In some cases this has tragic consequences. Not being able to control noise levels and nuisance in our immediate environment, coupled with the frustration of not being able to sleep, can literally drive us crazy. It is no coincidence that a major form of punishment throughout the ages has included taking away control from people – whether by leaving them imprisoned and uncertain about if or when they will be released, or by torturing prisoners with sleep deprivation, thus denying them control over when they sleep.

Human beings need to feel a good measure of control over their own lives. All children, unless thwarted, move inexorably towards their own independence, first just gradually trying out what it is like to do things for themselves and eventually becoming fully self-sufficient. It is human nature to want our own slice of life to control as we like – whether the way we live, the way we arrange our living space or just having a drawer at the office in which to keep our personal effects and a surface to carry a photograph of our loved ones. (One of the reasons for the unpopularity of 'hot-desking', the practice of using whichever desk is free when one is in the office, is that it removes individual control over space and depersonalizes staff.)

Despite the widespread belief that too much responsibility and overwork is stressful and damaging to health, studies show just the opposite. It is having too little responsibility and control over one's work that is stressful, as one of the famous Whitehall studies of 10,000 London civil servants showed: those with low control over their work were more likely to become physically and/or mentally ill than those in higher status jobs with more autonomy.[18] Anxiety disorders often begin when individuals feel that control of some aspect of their lives is being removed from them. Then increasingly they come to fear that they cannot stop terrible things of any kind happening to them.[19]

When people are ill and in pain, anxiety about the outcome has been shown to increase the experience of pain. One of the world's leading authorities on pain, the late British professor Patrick Wall, has lucidly described the process: "Fear generates anxiety and anxiety focuses the attention. The more the attention is locked, the worse the pain. There is therefore a marked correlation between pain and anxiety. The anxiety here is not the free floating variety with a feeling of general disquiet that something is wrong but cannot be identified. The anxiety of pain is generated by the unknown, and grows worse as the pain persists and short-term expectations of relief fail to be fulfilled."[20]

Any anxiety associated with pain is generated by the fear of the unknown over which we have no control. If, however, we are told that we have done nothing seriously damaging to ourselves, that the pain will diminish shortly and we'll soon be right as rain, the pain can instantly lessen because its meaning has been clarified and changed and we are no longer in the hands of an indifferent Fate.

Fear of loss of control is also what exacerbates agoraphobia, an anxiety condition in which people find themselves panicking in particular places (often without knowing why but usually relating to past trauma) and gradually avoid going out at all.

In psychologist Martin Seligman's theory of learned helplessness, acute depression can arise as a consequence of perceiving oneself to have no control over situations. He and colleagues hit on this discovery when they were testing a learning theory on dogs. The test involved administering mild electric shocks to the dogs, which were strapped down and thus could not escape them. When the dogs were later placed in cages from which they could escape if they tried, and were given electric shocks, the dogs initially ran around trying to get out and then quickly gave up and whined quietly as they received the electric shocks.

The researchers were extremely surprised by this reaction, until they realized that the dogs were responding as if still in their previous condition, where they couldn't escape the shocks. They had, in effect, learned that their best efforts achieved nothing and that, therefore, they were helpless.[21]

Seligman then went on to test his theory with people. Students who had volunteered to carry out an experimental task, for which they were required to wear headphones, were subjected to a loud unpleasant noise through the headphones, which they couldn't turn off, even though pressing a particular button was supposed to be able to stop it. They soon stopped trying to control the noise and, on another occasion, didn't even bother to try. Later in the experiment, the students were asked to solve a difficult problem. Although they were all capable of solving it, the students who had been subjected to the interminable noise and were powerless to control it quickly gave up on the problem.

Research has shown that loss of sense of control during the restrictions imposed during the covid-19 epidemic significantly increased rates of depression. A cross-sectional survey study was carried out in Ireland to examine the relationship between the experience of public health restrictions, the sense of control and depression, both during and after restrictions were lifted. Data were collected at two time points, January 2022 and May 2022, with findings showing that both sense of control, in relation to perceived constraints, and the experience of restrictions predicted depression in January. Although participants overall were less likely to be depressed in May and had a stronger sense of control, strong loss of sense of control felt in January through perceived constraints predicted depression five months later. The researchers concluded, "Overall, these data show that public health restrictions and the sense of control are linked and that the sense of control has a powerful and long-lasting effect on depression status in restricted conditions, even once these have been lifted."[22]

It is an accepted fact that feeling helpless can help generate depression. As depression may then itself increase feelings of helplessness, an individual can be trapped in a vicious cycle. Helping to give people back an interest in and sense of control over their own lives is an important part of effective treatment for depression.

Coping with change

One major cause of both depression and anxiety, stemming in both cases from loss of control, is the rate at which change is occurring in our world. Our biology has not changed for tens of thousands of years, yet the changes in our environment and how we live our lives that have been made over a very short time have been nothing short of dramatic. For many people still alive today, television had not even been invented when they were young. Now we have 24-hour coverage on countless channels and streaming services; the whole world is computerized; and, increasingly, one is 'out of it' if lacking email, mobile phone or a presence on a social network site. Technological development and the ease with which capital investment in industry and commerce can be moved around the world in search of the most favourable deal has created job insecurity, even in professions where it was once the norm to expect a job for life. Unfortunately, our incredible ability to create always leaps ahead of our ability to adapt, and it may feel as if we are forever locked into a cycle of attempting to adjust to unprecedented situations. This difficulty may be coupled with an underlying general anxiety that even our creativeness is out of control. The contribution that human activity makes to climate change, increased pollution and dwindling natural reserves are clearly the unwanted and ill-considered consequences of human advances.

While it isn't possible to turn back the clock, it is certainly possible and desirable to do what we can to ensure, where possible, that we exert some degree of control over our lives. It has long been known, for instance, that a brief talk with the anaesthetist before an operation significantly reduces the need for post-operative pain relief.[23] The magic ingredient here is information. By telling a patient exactly what is going to happen, what pain to expect and what the stages of recovery will be, the disabling element of uncertainty is removed, and, for most people, the need for anxiety lessened.

The trend generally in health care nowadays is towards offering patients full information about their conditions, creating in effect a partnership in care, rather than expecting them to sit quietly and just take the pills. Not all patients welcome a plethora of information but most cite benefits to feeling more in control.

Many people diagnosed with serious conditions have found comfort and strength in seeking out their own sources of information and treatments. Increasingly, people turn to the internet to find out what they need to know, to arm themselves with choices.

The converse of learned helplessness, feeling positively about our ability to cope with life's adversities can have a significant impact on our actual ability to cope. Such beliefs are linked with what psychologists term 'locus of control', a term coined by American psychologist Julian B. Rotter in 1954.[24] Those who feel that they can make an impact on events in a positive way and are responsible for much of what happens to them (taking the view, for instance, that hard work brings rewards) are said to have an internal locus of control, while those who think that what happens to them is largely determined by forces outside their control ("people pick on me for no reason"), and so abdicate responsibility, are said to have an external locus of control. While patently we aren't responsible for, and can't control, everything that happens to us, believing that most things are beyond our control is disadvantageous for health. Belief in one's own ability to influence recovery is always advantageous, whether it is a case of speeding discharge from hospital, speeding recovery from an injury or adding a few more precious days to a terminal illness.

Sometimes very simple procedures can enable us to take or regain control over aspects of our lives. For instance, the introduction of patient-controlled anaesthesia, a painkiller-delivery system that allows post-operative patients to administer their own pain relief, up to a safe maximum level, *lessened* the amount of analgesia generally required after surgery. Being in control of when pain relief can be given removes anxiety and fear of pain, both of which, of course, increase pain. More generally, learning an effective relaxation technique and knowing how to put it quickly into practice, wherever one is, can take the power out of an unfounded fear response, including an overwhelming fear of panic attacks. Simple cognitive techniques whereby an individual is taught to question their automatic reactions (for instance, countering thoughts such as "I'm going to die if I stay in this room!" with thoughts such as "I've been in this situation before. If I breathe slowly, the fear will pass") are also powerfully effective.

Taking responsibility

Giving people responsibility is an effective means of restoring an individual's sense of control – not in terms of control over others but in the sense of being able to do whatever is required. Sufferers from mental illness have very often found the need to care for others, such as children or elderly relatives, a helpful aspect of their own recovery. It was discovered, long ago, in one nursing home for elderly people, that when a wild-bird feeder was placed outside one of the windows, those residents who were given the responsibility for keeping the feeder stocked with food reported being happier and more satisfied with their lives than those who could only watch the birds feeding.[25] Similarly, in another even older study, elderly residents in a home were given control over simple matters such as what meals they ate, how the furniture was arranged in their rooms and where in the house they would like to spend time with their visitors. They were also asked to choose a houseplant to take care of. These simple changes, which increased their control over and responsibility for elements of their own lives, not only had the effect of keeping them happier, more active and alert, but also kept them alive longer, compared with residents who did not have a say in their care.[26] Alas, such knowledge seems to get lost and has to get rediscovered and promoted again and again.[27]

Control does not have to be absolute to be positive for mental health. It was once found that people who best survived torture were those who had a cast of mind that enabled them to retain a modicum of control over what was happening to them, even to the limited extent of counting to 10 before screaming. One case described is of a man who was tortured by the Gestapo during interrogation, who knew that a point would come during the torture when he would lose consciousness and so, when he felt that point approaching, he would make the effort to last out for an additional 60 seconds.[28] In one account of the case, the comment was made that he didn't crack during several months of intense interrogation because he remained, in his own mind, "acting rather than acted upon".[29]

We can none of us escape from the fact that we have to live with uncertainty. "Expect the unexpected" is a wise old saying and we should not be surprised that all the major religions have teachings designed to ameliorate the pain suffered by people deluded into thinking they are masters of their destiny. In Islam, 'Insha Allāh' ('if God wills it') is said when speaking about plans being made and events expected to occur. Muslims are taught that things will happen only "if your endeavours are within God's plan". The same concept appears in Christianity, as a Bible passage illustrates: "Now listen, you who say, 'Today or tomorrow we will go to this or that city, spend a year there, carry on business and make money'. Why, you do not even know what will happen tomorrow. What is your life? You are a mist that appears for a little while and then vanishes. Instead, you ought to say, 'If it is the Lord's will we will live and do this or that'."[30] The great 20th century psychologist Erich Fromm described the evolutionary reason for such religious dictums: "The quest for certainty blocks the search for meaning," he said. "Uncertainty is the very condition to impel man to unfold his powers." Certainly the capacity to endure uncertainty indicates maturity of mind.

In the personal sphere, we cannot rely on accidents not happening or jobs being there forever. We cannot rely on our children turning out as we would have wished and on our marriage lasting. Whereas once a marriage might have been given a longer chance, or even seen as duty to uphold, increasingly individuals look for personal fulfilment and walk out on a relationship that has ceased to provide it. It has been argued that the current preoccupation with self in our society, with its firm focus on health, diet and fitness, reflects an attempt to take back, in some small way, a sense of control in this increasingly uncertain and insecure personal world. People may feel less able to control, or rely on, events and agencies outside of themselves, but they can control how much they eat, the exercise they take, what influences they expose themselves to and how effective they become at recognizing opportunities.[31,32]

To wake up to a new day is always a bonus and we cannot live our lives continually worrying whether a disaster may befall our family, a new war or pandemic may break out or a comet may hit Earth. No human being has ever known what is around the corner and we all live a transient life while pretending that life is constant. Living with uncertainty is complementary to our need for control. It puts it in perspective. Some things we can control, and are beneficial for us to control. Others we can't. Being prepared for change is a positive attribute, minimizing the risk of suffering stress reactions, anxiety, ill health and worse, when inevitable changes happen. Being able to tolerate ambiguity is an important aspect of mental health. Fortunately, the more we discover about the brain, the more we learn of its amazing ability to adapt to even the most trying of circumstances.

One cannot discuss control without referring to people who exhibit a particular extreme manifestation of it – they are colloquially known as 'control freaks'. We will look at this, along with other unhealthy ways of meeting essential needs, at the end of this chapter.

Attention: the need to give and receive it

Without nutriment we die. Western psychologists only discovered that attention is a vital nutriment in the first quarter of the 20th century. However, most adults today are still largely unaware of the significance of giving and receiving attention, and how that affects their own and other people's behaviour.

We all know that people draw attention to themselves in myriad ways – for instance, by being the most stylish, fashionable or expensively dressed, or the noisiest and most noticed at social gatherings. Some exhibit eccentric behaviours, wear garish clothes, sport deliberately odd hairstyles, boast about their achievements, pepper their conversation with vile swear words or swagger and strut, and so on. But the lure of attention seeking can be far more subtle than that. People are attracted, far more often than they realize, to *situations* that provide opportunities for getting attention. This might be so when someone publicly performs good deeds or carries out a job that requires the wearing of a uniform. The uniform ensures them attention, either in the wearing of it or for what they are doing in it, and this applies regardless of whether the wearer is a policeman, judge, nurse, traffic warden or vicar. Likewise, when individuals act as spokespeople for particular organizations or happily give a professional opinion whenever a relevant event is in the news, they enjoy the attention that brings. Some bask so much in such attention that they may even be happy to supply an opinion on a topic entirely unrelated to their professional expertise. The craving for attention easily overrides common sense about the limits of expertise, though few of us realize that it is our attention needs we are attempting to satisfy at the time.

Everyone wants to be the centre of attention at some time. It is normal to want to shine and be acknowledged when we do well or put a lot of effort into something. Children flourish when they are praised and made to feel special when they perform well at any task. Even shy children, who back away from being the centre of attention, desperately wish that they could have it and enjoy it.

In modern times, the first breakthrough into recognizing the importance of attention was made back in 1927 when, at the Western Electric Company's plant in Hawthorne, near Chicago, a remarkable experiment into productivity was carried out. Researchers wanted to know whether they could up productivity by simple measures such as introducing different systems of breaks or organizing working hours differently. Six women were chosen to be the subjects for this experiment and, for its duration, they were installed in a separate workroom away from the rest of their colleagues. The researchers then systematically altered the women's working arrangements in one way after another and monitored the effects this had on productivity. They introduced short rest periods twice a day, then increased the length of the rest periods, then tried no rest periods but a shorter working day, and so on. After each innovation, the women had to report what they thought about the new working condition.

A year later, productivity was much improved. At first, however, there was no clear reason that the researchers could identify to explain the success, as each innovation seemed to have the same level of beneficial effect. The explanation came when they realized that the only difference that was consistent throughout their experiment was the *attention* that they were giving the women. It was attention, not five-minute rest breaks or going home at 4pm, which was having a positive impact on productivity.[33] This finding, consequently known as the Hawthorne Effect, led the researchers to suggest that, if supervisors also gave workers due attention, and expressed interest in their work and their wellbeing, this in itself could promote an increase in motivation, and a corresponding increase in output – and so it proved.

The need for attention is an important given. That without it we cannot survive was shown in an horrific experiment carried out in the Middle Ages at the behest of the German emperor, Frederick II. He had newborn babies removed from their parents and cared for by nurses who fed and cleaned them and then left them isolated. The nurses were strictly forbidden to touch, talk or give them any attention whatsoever, in an attempt to satisfy the emperor's curiosity as to what language the children would speak if they didn't hear a native tongue. He never found out, because the children all died before they reached the age when children attempt language – they perished from attention starvation.[34]

Despite this 13th century experiment, and the discovery of the Hawthorne Effect in the 20th century, the concept of attention did not itself receive much attention from Western psychologists until relatively recently. (Indeed, the main thrust of the Hawthorne finding, as far as most psychologists were concerned, was that the act of being observed changes the way an individual normally behaves, and the consequences of this for experimental design.) It is, however, a phenomenon that has been well understood in Eastern psychology for a long time.

Idries Shah, who spent many years studying and exemplifying the Eastern heritage of Sufi knowledge and relating it to contemporary Western science, formulated a theory of attention from that tradition in which he made clear that many social and commercial transactions are in fact disguised attention situations. He also pointed out that, if individuals are unaware that what is driving them in certain circumstances is the demanding, extending or exchange of attention, believing they are engaged in something else – such as learning, informing, helping, buying or selling – they are likely to be less efficient in achieving their ends (both those they think they are serving and their genuine attention needs) and will be less able to act and react in ways that are appropriate to a situation, whatever it is.[35]

When asked to define the characteristics of attention, he suggested that humanity could benefit enormously by "studying the attracting, extending and reception, as well as the interchange, of attention".

He proposed that it is important for individuals to realize:

- that this attention-factor is operating in virtually all transactions
- that the apparent motivation of transactions may be other than it really is. And that it is often generated by the need or desire for attention-activity (giving, receiving, exchanging)
- that attention-activity, like any other demand for food, warmth, etc., when placed under volitional control, must result in increased scope for the human being who would then not be at the mercy of random sources of attention – or even more confused than usual if things do not pan out as they expect.

This is a profoundly more subtle understanding of the importance of attention than that commonly found in Western psychology. Shah also went on to enumerate principles that follow from this, which we quote in full.

1. Too much attention can be bad (inefficient).
2. Too little attention can be bad.
3. Attention may be 'hostile' or 'friendly' and still fulfil the appetite for attention. This is confused by the moral aspect.
4. When people need a great deal of attention they are vulnerable to the message that too often accompanies the exercise of attention towards them. E.g. someone wanting attention might be able to get it only from some person or organization, which might thereafter exercise (as 'its price') an undue influence upon the attention-starved individual's mind.
5. Present beliefs have often been inculcated at a time and under circumstances connected with attention-demand, and not arrived at by the method attributed to them.
6. Many paradoxical reversals of opinion, or of associates and commitments, may be seen as due to the change in a source of attention.
7. People are almost always stimulated by an offer of attention, since most people are frequently attention-deprived. This is one reason why new friends, or circumstances, for instance, may be preferred to old ones.
8. If people could learn to assuage attention-hunger, they would be in a better position than most present cultures allow them to attend to other things. They could extend the effectiveness of their learning capacity.
9. Among the things which unstarved people (in the sense of attention) could investigate is the comparative attraction of ideas, individuals, etc., apart from their purely attention-supplying function.
10. The desire for attention starts at an early stage of infancy. It is, of course, at that point linked with feeding and protection. This is not to say that this desire has no further nor future development value. But it can be adapted beyond its ordinary adult usage of mere satisfaction.
11. Even a cursory survey of human communities shows that, while the random eating tendency, possessiveness and other undifferentiated characteristics are very early trained or diverted – weaned

– the attention-factor does not get the same treatment. The consequence is that the adult human being, deprived of any method of handling his desire for attention, continues to be confused by it: as it usually remains primitive throughout life.

12. Very numerous individual observations of human transactions have been made. They show that an interchange between two people always has an attention-factor.

13. Observation shows that people's desires for attention ebb and flow. When in an ebb or flow of attention-desire, the human being, not realizing that this is his condition, attributes his actions and feelings to other factors, e.g. the hostility or pleasantness of others. He may even say that it is a 'lucky day', when his attention needs have been quickly and adequately met. Re-examination of such situations has shown that such experiences are best accounted for by the attention-theory.

14. Objections based upon the supposed pleasure of attention being strongest when it is randomly achieved do not stand up when carefully examined. 'I prefer to be surprised by attention' can be paraphrased by saying, 'I prefer not to know where my next meal is coming from'. It simply underlines a primitive stage of feeling and thinking on this subject.

15. Situations that seem different when viewed from an oversimplified perspective (which is the usual one) are seen to be the same by the application of attention-theory. E.g. people following an authority figure may be exercising the desire for attention or the desire to give it. The interchange between people and their authority-figure may be explained by mutual-attention behaviour. Some gain only attention from this interchange. Some can gain more.

16. Another confusion is caused by the fact that the object of attention may be a person, a cult, an object, an idea, interest, etc. Because the foci of attention can be so diverse, people in general have not yet identified the common factor – the desire for attention.

17. One of the advantages of this theory is that it allows the human mind to link in a coherent and easily understood way many things which it has always (wrongly) been taught are very different, not

susceptible to comparison, etc. This incorrect training has, of course, impaired the possible efficiency in functioning of the brain, though only culturally, not permanently.

18. The inability to feel when attention is extended, and also to encourage or to prevent its being called forth, makes man almost uniquely vulnerable to being influenced, especially in having ideas implanted in his brain, and being indoctrinated.

19. Raising the emotional pitch is the most primitive method of increasing attention towards the instrument that increased the emotion. It is the prelude to, or accompaniment of, almost every form of indoctrination.

20. Traditional philosophical and other teachings have been used to prescribe exercises in the control and focusing of attention. Their value, however, has been to a great measure lost because the individual exercises, prescribed for people in need of exercise, have been written down and repeated as unique truths and practised in a manner, with people and at a rate and under circumstances which, by their very randomness, have not been able to effect any change in the attention-training. This treatment has, however, produced obsession. It continues to do so.

21. Here and there proverbs and other pieces of literary material indicate that there has been at one time a widespread knowledge of attention on the lines now being described. Deprived, however, of context, these indications survive as fossil indicators rather than being a useful guide to attention-exercise for contemporary man.[36]

So one consequence of an excessive or inadequately met need for attention, as Shah points out, is a willingness to embrace behaviours or views which were anathema to an individual before. We may affect a deep desire to learn about whatever it is that the person from whom we seek attention enjoys or is knowledgeable about. We see this, for instance, when someone who is besotted with a new partner, willingly engages in activities the other person enjoys, whether it is going to football matches or opera or the ballet, treasure hunting with metal detectors, taking botany walks or joining a choir, which never interested them before and perhaps don't even genuinely interest them now.

Indeed, as Shah says, many sudden major changes of opinion, commitments or even the company one keeps are unconsciously instigated as a result of a change in a source of attention. So individuals who are desperate to be liked by another person, and to whom the offer of attention is being held out, are the more likely to embrace the ideals of that person, even if that means rejecting beliefs and tenets that they have never before questioned. People who join political parties and religious groups, even terrorist organizations, may do so because a need for attention has drawn them to the organization, or, initially, to an individual member of it, rather than because of any driving belief in the cause. That belief, or apparent belief, may follow but, tellingly, may last only as long as the organization can fully satisfy the individual's need for attention.

In the case of cults, there is a high price to be paid for having one's attention needs met by them. Lonely individuals are commonly sucked into a group's midst, enticed by promises of being loved and accepted, both by the creator and by those already in the group. To retain that good feeling, they must (and usually all too willingly do) embrace the beliefs and perform the practices the cult espouses. Attention needs are then being met on a mutual basis.

If attention is nutrition, what exactly is the nutriment we get from it? And why is it so important? One clue comes from a comment Shah made after listing the above 21 principles. He was referring to the difference between real teaching and the pseudoteaching found in many cults but what he said applies equally to any situation where people give up volition to others and sycophantic behaviour predominates.

"Attention upon oneself, or upon a teacher, without the exercise of securing what is being offered from beyond the immediate surroundings, is a sort of short-circuit. As [Persian poet and philosopher] Rumi said: 'Do not look at me, but take what is in my hand'." Where we focus our attention is, of course, critical in learning. If we are attention starved we may focus on the person rather than the meaning of what they are saying. This is especially so in a real learning encounter, rather than in a cult-like situation. Invariably, in cults, people are encouraged to focus on the personalities of those who are indoctrinating them with simplistic beliefs, rather than emphasizing content that students really need.

All this is true; we need attention, and how we get it can make us vulnerable to indoctrination, but there is more.

Clearly, in the attention exchange, we suspend our critical faculty. But, although this makes us vulnerable, it is also something that we have to do if we are to consider new patterns of information – the nutriment. To really understand new ideas, information and other people's perceptions, the brain first has to absorb them, and this is best done in a safe environment when in a receptive, open, uncritical state. Then, once patterns are absorbed and understood, we need to disengage from them. We need to step back into the observing self and consciously consider them, analyze them and 'check them out', as it were. Whether one does this or not is the difference between learning and conditioning. (One of the drawbacks of modern media is that, whenever new ideas or policies are proposed, plans presented or discoveries announced, they are immediately placed in the firing line of confrontational criticism – this is more emotionally arousing and therefore presumably considered to be 'good TV'. But the problem with this is that the absorption stage is bypassed. This explains why, for example, debating programmes on TV or radio or other media are so often unmemorable and unsatisfying and political debates in parliament seem so childish and lacking in depth.)

When attention is focused and we grasp what someone is telling us in an uncritical way, we have absorbed a pattern at an unconscious level. Its full meaning and ramifications may not become apparent at once but, once the pattern is in the brain, it will affect future actions and add to the sum total of our knowledge. Knowledge only becomes real in action, when it is experienced. This is how we learn.

As said, we need to learn the skill of disengaging from patterns and considering them critically, once they have been absorbed. Unfortunately, in our exchanges of attention within our immediate family or tribe, we often uncritically adopt their lifestyles and values and so can easily be conditioned into harmful behaviour and beliefs.

For this reason, therapists need to be very much aware of the role played by attention in the maintenance of their clients' symptoms. Clients often derive a massive amount of attention from having their symptoms, and the very act of focusing their attention on the symptoms helps to maintain them – whether they are manifested as anorexia, anxiety, anger disorder or anything else. Joe once had a female patient who maintained a belief that her husband was set upon murdering her. She had kept this belief for seven years, in spite of having extensive counselling before seeing Joe and continual reassurance from her husband and family. She freely admitted that part of her mind knew her husband was loving and supportive and that all her family was there for her – and yet she maintained this apparently psychotic belief. To make progress, the attention had to be withdrawn from the symptom. The family was taught by Joe to withdraw attention by ignoring her whenever she made these delusionary remarks about her husband being set on killing her. Instead, they were required to pay her attention only when she behaved and thought normally. The symptom then became unrewarding and faded away because her attention needs had become met in healthy ways. We have to realize that people do have a need for attention but the attention has to be given to normalcy. Typically, what we focus on is what we get. So, what a patient is encouraged to focus on – through receiving attention for kindness or humour or demonstrating cooking or computer skills – is more likely to be maintained.

Therapists also need to be aware that they themselves are highly vulnerable when exchanging attention with their patients. This is because, by continuously focusing on their patients' pathological models of reality, they are at risk of absorbing them uncritically, unless they take counter-measures to reduce the danger. This can be done in a few ways. Firstly, therapists need to be trained in how not to be passive recipients of patients' neuroticisms but to listen with a more objective enquiring mind as they search to see what function the patient's disturbed thinking has for them. What emotional needs are not being met? What innate resources are being misused? What kind of language is the patient favouring that might endanger the therapist? (Use of abstractions such as 'depression', 'misery', 'anger' and 'hopelessness' etc. have no intrinsic or sensory meaning, and thus necessarily send therapists on an inner search as their brains pattern match to what depression, misery, anger or hopelessness means to them in their own life experience. Inevitably, this generates emotional arousal and thus increases the risk of early burnout.) Taking a step outside of the situation as described enables therapists to keep challenging their patients' unrealistic models of reality – first in their own minds and then in that of their patients.

Secondly, for therapists to ensure that they are not conditioned by their patients' neuroticism, they need to have a life outside of therapy where they mix and exchange attention with people who are mentally healthy.

Thirdly, the recommended practice of brief therapy is itself a form of protection, focusing as it does on swift behaviour change and thus reducing both the time for, and likelihood of, adopting any unhealthy models of reality.

No culture can develop without attention exchange, but the quality of attention is critical because a culture, of any kind, amounts to the sum of the shared perceptions of its members as to what is collectively regarded as important and meaningful. We are now bombarded, via the internet and social media, with never-ending demands on our attention, which makes it all the harder to discriminate wisely. Perceptions are shared in society partly through conditioning and partly through the refining of shared perceptions, so that they become more nuanced, complex and objective. Whereas dysfunctional individuals and families cause chaos all around them, as do dysfunctional business organizations, governments, bureaucracies and cultures, the more developed and mature a family, culture or organization is, the more refined are the perceptions the majority of its members share.

This is ultimately why we need to study "the attracting, extending and reception, as well as the interchange, of attention".[37] Our species' very future may depend on it.

The need for intimacy

The need for intimate emotional, physical and sexual closeness to others is a strong one. Wherever we are and whatever happens to us, an important degree of security can be found in close relationships. We may not always recognize this pattern, and even consciously or unconsciously deny it, but when the world conspires against the proper enactment of this element of the genetic blueprint, emotional disturbance results. This is well illustrated in the case of a 25-year-old farmer, referred by his GP to Ivan for help because he was having suicidal thoughts. He had, until recently, lived with his parents and his much older brother on the family farm where they were all born, and which he and his brother now owned and worked. When asked what was troubling him, this strapping young man launched into a lengthy description of his day-to-day problems on the farm: how his brother dealt with the arable farming and he handled the cows; how his brother tended to interfere, as did his parents, who still lived in the main farm house. It was because he had become so fed up that he had moved to the nearby village to get away from them all, although he wanted to continue working on the farm and had no intention of leaving.

As the story went on and on, Ivan found himself struggling to get a clear picture of anything concrete to work on, and sensed that the young man was skirting around his real concerns. So he suddenly slammed his hand down loudly on the table – bang! – (which focused the young man's orientation response) and then quickly and clearly asked, "What's the problem?!" The man jumped up with shock and instantly blurted out, "I haven't got a girlfriend!"

Not only, it turned out, had he never had a girlfriend, but he was still a virgin and spent much of his waking time thinking about women and sex, and fantasizing about falling in love. Deep inside, he felt sad, unfulfilled, lonely – and desperate. These strong emotions locked his attention and prevented him from establishing normal social relations with the opposite sex. So strong were his feelings that he literally lost his voice whenever he tried to talk to any girl he was interested in. He was deeply depressed. He found life without intimacy unbearable, which he expressed by telling people he was thinking of killing himself. With the problem in the open, it could be broken down and solved. Therapy was short term, targeted at increasing his social and rapport building skills. It had a positive outcome.

The drive for intimacy with another person is powerful – so powerful that most people call it love. When we feel loved by someone else, it has a measurable effect upon our health, as various studies have shown. It has a particularly positive effect upon – appropriately perhaps – the heart. We have known since the 1980s that high risk factors for heart problems, such as unhealthy diet, smoking, taking exercise and family history of heart disease, have far less bearing on the outcome of heart disease than whether or not one feels emotionally supported by another person[38] and more evidence continues to accrue.[39]

Strong intimate attachments normally form when a baby is about six or seven months old, and this has been observed across cultures, regardless of child-rearing practices. Before this time, a baby tends not to mind who cuddles it. But, some time after seven months, a neurotypical baby easily becomes disturbed or upset if separated for even a short while from its primary carer.[40] Animal studies, and evidence of the outcome for children in orphanages left with little stimulation or human contact, indicate that the period between six months and three years is the sensitive time during which attachments optimally form. (After that time, it has been observed, there may be increasing withdrawal from social contact.) All living things require time to grow and develop and biologists have discovered that neuronal pathways in the human brain regions concerned with emotions, particularly fear and anxiety, are not sufficiently myelinised (sheathed in a material which allows more rapid conduction of nerve impulses) before six months of age.[41]

Much attention has been paid to 'attachment' since John Bowlby developed in the 1950s what he called 'attachment theory',[42] and ithas prompted countless psychological studies. Infants who are securely attached, so observations from some studies show, are happy to explore their surroundings as they grow and put their burgeoning independence to the test, confident that their caregiver will be there for them to return to. They are more likely to grow into popular, cooperative and competent children, whereas insecurely attached youngsters, who are far less certain that their caregiver will be there for them, either at all or in any positive way, are less likely to be comfortable with themselves and other people.[43]

But attachment theory is just that, a theory. Taken to its extremes, it has been used to induce guilt in dual-income families, whose infants spend their weekdays being cared for in nurseries or by nannies, and not by their primary caregivers. Though there are plenty of research findings to link an apparent failure to attach securely in infancy to emotional and social problems in adulthood, the findings by no means clearly show cause and effect, and often there are other different, perfectly reasonable explanations.

There are also many reasons for the different degrees of emotional bonding that occur between mothers/carers and babies, which can have significant effects on emotional development. For instance, whether present all the time or not, the way a mother behaves towards her baby and the way the baby behaves towards the mother may be the crucial element in whether or not a baby becomes emotionally responsive. When a mother smiles, a baby responds, making a mother more likely to smile more, and so on. Each is responsive to each other's positive actions. Having a depressed mother who doesn't engage in such behaviours can severely affect a child's emotional and cognitive development.[44] Conversely, a baby's own difficult temperament can have a bearing on whether a new mother becomes depressed, and therefore less likely to bond. It was shown decades ago that where a baby's motor control was rated as poor (the baby thus, perhaps, being less able to make and sustain eye contact with carers), the mother was at almost five times the normal risk of developing postnatal depression. When a baby was classed as 'irritable' (highly sensitive to slight stimulation, quick to become distressed and requiring a lot of help to become calm again), the mother's risk for depression was raised more than three and a half times.[45]

As Nancy Thomas, an internationally known specialist in therapeutic parenting, once eloquently put it, "It is by looking into each other's eyes that we learn to connect with other human beings. And it is as we connect and start to care about others that we start to develop conscience. So the children who scream when mum picks them up and become calm when put down need more holding, not less."[46]

If this crucial early need for intimate sharing is not met, an individual may fail to develop the emotional skills of empathy, or emotional literacy, as Daniel Goleman termed it in his seminal book, *Emotional Intelligence*.[47] This is what enables us to sense other people's moods and take them into account, and to act and react appropriately and sensitively. People who lack a developed sense of empathy, for whatever reason, have great difficulty in forming close relationships. Even in a healthy baby, the development of good empathy skills is drastically inhibited when the template is not matched up in the environment.

Love and resilience

The ability to love and receive love – to care and be cared for – by at least one other individual clearly has an important part to play in the development of a healthy emotional life, as the evidence continues to show.[48] This is *not* to say that everyone must seek a mate, and that only with a mate can one find fulfilment, but that the experience of loving and being cared for has a beneficial impact upon self-development and our sense of self-worth, whatever our chosen path.

For one thing, being loved makes us more resilient. The human brain is pliable and adaptable enough for people to be able to alter the future course of their life positively, even after a bad start.[49] This was well demonstrated in one particularly famous study. Researcher Emmy Werner and colleagues attempted to discover why only some children living in stressful or highly difficult circumstances appear to pay a lasting emotional price. They looked at around 600 children on an Hawaiian island, 200 of whom were deemed to be at high risk of developing psychological problems because of childhood difficulties, such as complicated birth, poverty, unstable family life and having parents who were mentally ill. They studied them at ages two, 10, 18 and 32, and found that, despite the odds, a third of these high-risk children became competent and confident adults.

When the researchers tried to account for this difference in outcome, they identified a number of discrepancies between the children who grew up emotionally healthy and those who did not. Those in the emotionally healthy group were easier as babies (and thus were easier for a parent figure to bond with). They were more loving, kind and affectionate, and ate and slept well. They achieved well at school, had diverse interests and were more popular and independent. All these children also had a close positive relationship with at least one parent or caregiver, and received emotional support from someone outside the family, such as a teacher or family friend. Having at least one strong, caring and supportive relationship was the key factor that enabled children to develop resilience to hardship in their early lives. The findings of this study speak volumes.[50]

Moreover, affectionate touching and stroking have many positive effects on the body and the psyche. This has always been known instinctively but was first explored scientifically as a result of chance observations made in the 1920s by an anatomist. As part of his work he removed rats' thyroid and parathyroid glands. He didn't expect the rats to survive the operation but, to his surprise, most of them did. On further investigation, it turned out that this was because the survivors had been regularly handled and petted by their keepers all through their lives. They were less nervous and less stressed than unpetted rats and more able to recover from the trauma of the operation.[51]

In another study carried out much later, rats removed from physical contact with their mothers slowed in growth but, when researchers stroked those rats with a wet brush (as a substitute for a mother's licking), the animals started to thrive and grow normally again.[52] Regular gentle stroking of rats' backs with a wet brush encouraged their brains to develop differently from those of unstroked rats and, as a result, as adults, they were mentally more able.[53] (The process works both ways. Many people get their need for intimacy met by owning a pet.[54])

We now know, of course, that touch is absolutely life giving. Massage of premature babies, for example, significantly increases their chances of survival, encouraging their metabolism and speeding weight gain. Since the importance for their development of touching and holding them has been recognized, they are no longer left the entire time in incubators attached only to tubes and apparatus.[55]

In adults, massage has long been shown to reduce stress and anxiety and help lift depression. It can banish tension headaches, and help ease abdominal complaints, joint conditions and back pain. By lowering emotional arousal, it causes a lessening of pain in various conditions such as cancer and heart disease, and can generally lift the spirit. Just as a mother's touch can distract a child from the pain of a grazed knee or a bumped toe, the comforting touch of another's hand can slow a speeding pulse rate, and reduce anxiety.[56]

The effects of touch can also be more subtle. In one famous experiment carried out by the head of anaesthetics at Harvard Medical School, a number of patients with similar symptoms, about to undergo the same operation, received a preparatory visit the night before by the anaesthetist who would be present the next day. For half of the patients, he provided just the usual brief information and checked that all was well. But, for the others, he varied his normal routine. He sat on their beds, held their hands, and was warm and sympathetic, spending five to ten minutes longer with each patient. After the operation, the patients who had received the warm approach asked for only half the amount of post-operative pain relief that the rest requested, and they were sufficiently well recovered to leave the hospital three days earlier than the 'untouched' patients.[57] Even brief affectionate touch has a demonstrably positive effect within relationships. In a study in which one partner was assigned to touch their partner briefly and affectionately at times throughout one day, shared activities experienced as positive increased that day and over the next week for couples who did not typically engage in such activities.[58]

Need for community: the search for social support

All needs are interrelated and nowhere is this more easily seen than in the powerful force that underlies and promotes the sharing of perceptions. This programme drives us to connect with *groups* of people – the wider social world beyond our immediate family. In the long distant past, it was crucial to belong to a group to ensure our survival. But there is much more to it than that. The individual brain only really thrives when in complex cooperation with a community of other brains. We wouldn't be where we are today if we had not evolved as social beings – tribal creatures – because meeting this need provides the optimum conditions for survival, thus perpetuating our genes through our children.

All networks, institutions and systems of education and government down the ages are extensions of the original means by which people ensured an effectively functioning society within which each individual could play a pertinent role. (Thus the disaffection, anger and despair of those who feel left out, and see no chance of attaining gainful employment or the wherewithal to acquire a decent home and build a fulfilling family life. The end result of emotional needs not being met in large numbers of the population is always civil strife. By contrast, good government is invisible. This is because it is getting on with making everything run smoothly for the benefit of those it serves, who consequently feel more fulfilled. You are only aware of government when it is noisily blustering about its failures.)

Because we are evolving far beyond other animals, our brains take approximately 20 years to develop fully and so, as we grow, we depend on the support of our families. Finely tuned social antennae are thus essential, if we are to learn the rules of survival.

The first interactions between a primary caregiver and a baby are, in effect, the beginnings of social orienting – the baby orients first to the primary caregiver, then to the family and then to the outside world. Even though, as the years pass, we become physically independent, our social dependence never disappears. The more complex societies become, the more this is so.

We need the contribution of other people to make and operate, to give just one example, various means of transport: cars, trains, buses and aeroplanes. None of these 'artificial mobility enhancers' (as zimmer frames and walking sticks are called in NHS hospitals!) would be possible without complex cooperation. An individual could not manufacture a jet plane, or the high tech communication system needed to fly it, from scratch and alone. The importance of our social functioning is also illustrated by the fact that humans are, on occasion, prepared to accept the risk of being killed, by fighting for the advantage of family, tribe or the country to which we belong.

Our brains evolved to respond to other people, to empathize and engage with them. We have already mentioned mirror neurons. Neuroscientists have also realized that even those parts of the brain originally assumed only to be concerned with 'lower' functions such as motor control, also have a vital part to play in our social development. Even the brain itself is intrinsically social: "The newest neurological findings suggest that the brain itself is a social organ; in the womb, neurons in the developing brain become functional only if they connect with other neurons. The brain's most primitive regions – the cerebellum and the amygdala – are the very ones involved in the brain's social processing. Indeed, the amygdala has neurons within it that only fire in response to other people's reactions. Furthermore, evolution shows that the brain has changed itself to survive, adapt and improve the success of its host person in a group of people."[59]

More and more information is emerging that shows just how fundamental our need for social connection is. Studies show that loneliness is as dangerous for our health as high blood pressure, lack of exercise, obesity and smoking. And it even alters the DNA transcription of immune cells.[60] The cells of chronically lonely people are less sensitive to signalling from the stress system, mediated by the stress hormone cortisol, which in turn dampens down immune responses.[61] When people are chronically lonely, they are, unsurprisingly, more likely to get depressed.[62]

Unquestionably, isolation kills – in all sorts of ways – and this has long been shown through research. For instance, among 100 bone marrow transplant patients, nearly three times as many of those who felt they had strong support from family or friends were still alive after two years, compared with those who experienced little support.[63] Elderly people who could rely on two or more people in their lives for emotional support survived longer after heart attacks than those with no such support.[64]

In 2020, Danilo Bzdok, associate professor at McGill University and Mila Quebec Artificial Intelligence Institute, and Robin Dunbar, emeritus professor at the University of Oxford, examined a broad range of studies to uncover the full picture of the severe impact of loneliness.

They found that having strong interpersonal relationships is critical for survival across the entire lifespan; social isolation is a significant predictor of the risk of death; insufficient social stimulation affects reasoning and memory performance, hormone homeostasis, brain grey/white-matter, connectivity and function, as well as resilience to physical and mental disease; and that feelings of loneliness can spread through a social network, causing negatively skewed social perception, escalating morbidity and mortality, and, in older people, precipitating the onset of dementia such as Alzheimer's disease.

Professor Robin Dunbar observed that loneliness has accelerated since 2010 and that "concerns can only be exacerbated if there are prolonged periods of social isolation imposed by national policy responses to extraordinary crises such as covid-19". He welcomed the "growing recognition and political will to confront this evolving societal challenge. As one consequence, the United Kingdom launched the Campaign to End Loneliness, a network of over 600 national, regional and local organisations to create the right conditions for reducing loneliness in later life."[65]

Because we are not 'closed systems' we can be impinged upon in a deep way by the warmth and friendship of others – and also be profoundly responsive to it. People with strong support networks of family, friends or community are happier and emotionally and physically healthier than people who feel isolated and unable to make connections with others. Feeling isolated and unable to make connections are operative words here. It is an individual's perception of being unloved and out of things that affects health and wellbeing, as many studies have shown[66] and continue to show.

For instance, one study investigated whether there was an association between overcrowding and loneliness. Using smartphone technology (hundreds of participants globally downloaded an app which prompted responses three times a day for 14 days), the researchers were able to collect 'real-time' information about perceptions of loneliness as people went about their lives. They found that perceived overcrowding made people feel lonely – i.e. they felt alienated and disconnected from others when population density was high.[67]

Like a retreating tide leaving fish stranded on the shore, the withdrawal of social support is disastrous for the individual concerned. And, alas, it is increasingly common as more people live apart from close family or friends and find themselves floundering. Some, for example, go where their job or career takes them, which may be far from any established social support structures. Others, such as young single mothers living on benefits, may be placed in council housing wherever it is available, which all too often is some distance from the help and support of families. Or the family unit itself may have disintegrated. Some lonely individuals' social world may shrink to the size of the computer in the bedroom, offering its seductive link to the inanimate and ultimately highly limited world of the internet, where 'friends' are people they have never met face to face.

Thus it is that so many people lose contact with others who care enough for them to support them through the inevitable uncertainties and heartbreaks of life. Increasingly, lonely people succumb to physical and mental illnesses and feel the need to turn to 'experts' for help in the art of living. Where once they would automatically have turned to relatives and friends for help, they now seek out counsellors or therapists. But, in modern living, we are less attuned to coping with other people's distress.

An article in the *Sunday Times*, written many years ago by our colleague Denise Winn, is still as relevant today, illustrating all too clearly this inability often either to hold out a helping hand or even just say the right words. One woman, widowed after 40 years of happy marriage, reported, for instance: "People I knew well would cross the road if they saw me coming, and if they did have to speak and ask me how I was, I learned to my cost that I mustn't really tell. They wanted me just to say, 'I'm fine'." Another woman, who had cancer and lived alone, said: "People tend to avoid coming to the house to help because it means acknowledging that I am ill. If I say, 'I have to go in [to hospital] again, could you feed the cat?', they are likely to start talking about some nice jumper they saw in Woolworths."[68]

Dr James Lynch's raw description of how not feeling seen or heard affects our mental health has never been bettered: "What emerges from the eyes of a bereaved individual is grief; what emerges from the eyes of those recently divorced is anxiety; what emerges from the eyes of those who live alone is loneliness; what emerges from the eyes of the unloved adolescent is frightened anger ... The dialogue of pain, anxiety, anger and loneliness is also part of life but it is a dialogue that can be both frightening and painful. How convenient to label these as scientific-medical problems, and therefore have others look into their eyes."[69]

The threats to community life

One of the most disempowering beliefs, from a mental health point of view, that still holds sway with many is the notion that evolution is propelled by selfish genes. The catchy phrase, 'selfish gene', was coined and vigorously promoted by the scientist Richard Dawkins. It is an attention grabber, just like a memorable advertising slogan. It could almost have been designed as a rallying cry for the 'me' generation. Our genes fight for power, and nature allows only the most dominating selfish genes to survive and rule.

In essence, selfish gene theory assigns to DNA the central role in the development of life. Our bodies are merely temporary hosts, enabling the survival and propagation of DNA, and most human behaviour is dominated by the selfish genes. In his book, *The Selfish Gene*, Dawkins asks us, "What on earth do you think you are, if not a robot, albeit a very complicated one?"[70] Fortunately this somewhat simplistic extension of the fundamentalist Darwinian viewpoint is not generally accepted in the scientific world, although it has certainly caught and held the popular imagination.

Nature always selects an *organism* that survives – not a gene that survives.[71] A gene can only survive by being part of an organism – part of a larger context. DNA cannot survive outside of a cell. It is not DNA on its own that passes from one generation to the next but the living cell of which DNA is but a part. This is vividly illustrated by examining the basic unit of biology in plants and animals: the cell. The cell itself evolved from the fusion of free-living bacteria. When these bacteria fused together, their combined abilities formed the basis for the living cell from which all plant and animal life arose. For example, mitochondria, the energy powerhouses of cells, evolved from free-living, oxygen-breathing bacteria that symbiotically integrated with other types of bacteria to form a more efficient complex cell.

This means that the very basic unit of life, the cell, came about through the cooperation, or the development of interdependence, between independent creatures.[72] It would seem to us far more likely, therefore, that evolution is not driven by selection of single genes, but works in a holistic way, increasing cooperation. This cooperation in a more complex environment furthers the survival chances of the individual creatures in it. In this case, the selfish gene theory, which seems to non-scientists to legitimize the idea that we are born to be cruel and tyrannical, hurting others if necessary to achieve our own ends, is based on a false premise. We can see the holistic setting of cooperation and interdependence everywhere we look in nature. It occurs all over the animal kingdom between different species. All animals depend on other creatures for various needs, such as maintaining their sources of food, keeping their skin clean, etc. Plants depend on insects for pollination. And so on, throughout nature. The principle of cooperation and increasing interdependence is equally as fundamental to nature as any principle based on greed and individual striving for dominance.[73]

The drive for cooperation may, in fact, be behind what has been termed reciprocal altruism as a means of explaining how altruistic gestures can be linked with survival needs. Doing something helpful for someone else, the theory goes, commonly results in someone doing something helpful for us in return, which eases our load. Quite simply, reciprocity oils the wheels of society. This truth is recognized and transmitted throughout the world in folk tales and stories where acts of kindness and cooperation play a part in the overcoming of apparently insurmountable obstacles.

The too many tribes problem

When 'tribes' first developed, it was in the interests of social evolution that individuals uncritically absorbed the moral laws, social habits and culture of their own tribes in order to maintain their membership of it. The ability to do this is bound up with the need for attention – giving and receiving it. As we have seen, the interchange of attention is nature's mechanism for enabling us to remain in tune with the mores of our family and the tribe and culture to which we belong. This ability also enables us to absorb uncritically the role models, morals, habits and culture of our tribe so that we can maintain our place as a member of it. This was a very necessary evolutionary development for our survival as social animals. But the downside of this necessary mechanism is that each culture is relative, omitting or distorting certain value systems.

This relativity is clearly seen when we look back over the history of past cultures – the preoccupations of an ancient Roman emperor were not the same as those of a Chinese emperor of the Han dynasty or a South Sea islander before the coming of Europeans – but it is equally applicable today, and not only between countries, religions and races. The values and culture of a London lawyer are not the same as those of a London taxi driver, Northumberland hill farmer, Welsh business executive, Scottish actor or motorway maintenance worker from the Midlands. Although we each inhabit a primary 'tribe' in our own country, often defined by our career, job or peer group, we are members of many other tribes, each with its own jargon, rituals and beliefs. Living like this, tribe piling on top of tribe, loosely coexisting but often uncomprehending of each other's reality, creates many opportunities for misunderstanding and conflict. It suggests that the need for greater adaptability is becoming ever more critical in a world where technology is forcing us to become one global village. Where once whole civilizations could exist without being aware of another, now each nation and tribe impinges ever more intrusively on the rest, putting ever greater demands on our collective tolerance and understanding. For many this creates a stress overload, which is why, despite our material wealth and the efforts of hugely expensive health services, mental illness is on the increase worldwide.

In traditional small, cohesive tribes – and only a few still survive – depression was virtually unknown. This is because the characteristic appearance and behaviour of depression is intended to convey a message to those around the depressed individual: "I am stuck, I am blocked, I don't know where to go from here". In a small society, such a message is readily heard and acted upon. Help and guidance become available. Studies of traditional New Guinea tribes and the Amish and Hutterite communities, for example, which still adhere to a slower, more human, 17th century lifestyle, show that, if a hut or barn burns down, everyone rallies round to rebuild it straight away. Out of disaster come closer human ties and social benefits, even pleasures. There is community support for individuals, balanced by an understanding that the individual has a responsibility to the community. In such societies, depression and suicide are almost unknown. But in our modern, technological society, where the world comes into our living room but we are increasingly separated from family and friends, a person can send out an emotional message that they are depressed for months or even years and nobody may actually notice.[74]

The law of 150

The loosening of traditional networks disturbs another ancient biological pattern – the 'law of 150'. The resultant disruption is negatively affecting communities around the world and raising the anxiety levels of millions of individuals.

The larger the cerebral cortex of any kind of primate, the bigger the social group they live in.[75] *Our* brains evolved to enable us to be more social – and the more complex the social arrangements we have to cope with, the more evolved our brains need to be. All primates, including monkeys, apes and humans have an *optimum* size of social group which each can cope with. As British anthropologist Robin Dunbar showed, in the case of humans, it appears to be 150. In surviving hunter-gatherer societies the average number of people in each group is around 149. In military organizations the basic unit of 'the company' is no more than 150, suggesting that, regardless of developments in modern technology, there is no genuine substitute for the small functional unit that can be effectively controlled in a personal manner. Larger organizations are usually dependent on hierarchies and rules in order to keep everyone marching to the same drumbeat, whereas, in smaller groups, peer pressure and personal loyalties to one's commander can create what faceless authority cannot: a sense of belonging and involvement, and of having a particular place within the whole.[76]

There is a similar cohesion to religious groups that keep their communities small. The Hutterites, a religious group which, for hundreds of years, lived in self-sufficient agricultural communities, first in

Europe and now also in North America, have had a policy of splitting each colony in two, when the number of inhabitants reaches 150. "Keeping things under 150 just seems to be the best and more efficient way to manage a group of people," one Hutterite leader said. The obvious deduction from this is that anyone wishing, for instance, to develop schools in disadvantaged areas, with the aim of creating a positive ethos and motivation to do well, would do better to establish several little schools, rather than one or two big ones. Similarly, commercial organizations that keep their basic units small are likely to be highly successful, because of their cohesiveness. Gore Associates, a multi-million-dollar high tech firm in Delaware, USA, with very low staff turnover, has no titles (everyone is an 'associate'), no bosses and no elaborate strategic plans, but is known as one of the best-managed companies in America. Founder Wilbert Gore discovered by trial and error that things were more likely to go pear-shaped if more than 150 people were working together. He decided to build small plants, which comfortably had room only for 150 people, and, if the business grew, to split, keeping each new venture within the 150-unit size.

In this age of technology and globalization, and without knowing anything about the law of 150, individuals still instinctively find it important to create a sense of community by founding small groups that better enable cooperation. Often it is projects set up to help others that are most successful at bringing people together. So charities set up soup kitchens; housing estates form tenants' committees; schools set up peer-group mentoring schemes, and social services departments initiate family-group conferencing – all designed to reassert the positive caring aspects of traditional support networks and fulfil this biological given of our nature.

This is not to say that large organisations with more than 150 people in them can't be fit for purpose. As business experts Gary Hamel and Michele Zanini say in their appositely titled book, *Humanocracy*, "If our organizations are inhuman, it is because we designed them to be – whether consciously or not", going on to show exactly how organisations can be both large and empowering – by, of course, taking the human needs of employer, employee and customers into account right at the design stage and maximizing human contribution throughout.[77]

By helping others we help ourselves

As organisms we evolved to cooperate, and nature so arranges it that cooperation leads to benefits for all parties concerned. Indeed, evidence has been accruing for many decades, showing that we can only fully enjoy true wellbeing when we are concerned with matters beyond our own needs and interests. A meta-analysis of more than 200 studies confirmed the link between prosocial behaviour and wellbeing, with behaviours such as altruism, cooperation and trust contributing to both mental and physical health and essential for a harmonious, well-functioning society.[78]

One striking early study showed that those whose voluntary work involved them in personal contact with the people they were helping were healthier than those who carried out only voluntary administrative tasks. (But even the administrators did better than those who did nothing at all.) As psychologist Robert Ornstein and physician David Sobel, the authors who cited this research, commented: "We need to meet the people we help, see their lives, connect with them". Indeed, it has now been scientifically shown that doing something nice for other people has more positive effect on people with moderate to severe symptoms of depression, anxiety, and stress than techniques such as planning social activities or cognitive reappraisal.[79] It may assuage our consciences to send money to good causes, but that, it would seem, is only half the story.

Why should it help us to help others? There have been many hypotheses. When we help others, we take our minds off ourselves (nothing deepens depression like dwelling on it). We briefly enter the world of another person or group of people we may not otherwise have met, and participate in a needier life, as they live it, thus gaining a new appreciation of our own competencies and talents, with a corresponding boost in mood. We may also feel nourished by the genuine gratitude and appreciation of others, and this metaphorical mental nourishment may be transduced by the brain into real physical nourishment of the immune system (in the same way that people have survived starvation in concentration camps by endlessly discussing wonderful meals they have eaten prior to their incarceration[80]). Clearly how we perceive the world, and our own and others' positions in it, affects our health in a powerful way.

So, from the human givens perspective, we can say that anything that improves social support should be encouraged, particularly when directed at distressed people. (Alas, many such interventions become bureaucratized and complicated, and, as a consequence, lose their power.) Simple instruction and rigorous practice are often all that is needed to transform a sad social outcast into an accepted member of the group. As psychotherapists working from the human givens, we have found that simple steps, such as engaging in more activities or practising social skills, often provide the quickest and most successful means of meeting important unmet needs and helping people to connect more fully and joyously with life.

In no common condition is our view of the world as distorted as it is in depression. The depressed person tends to think everything is wrong, will always be wrong, and it is all their fault. The world has it in for them and there's nothing that can be done about it. Just how dramatically this tunnel vision view can be turned around is vividly shown in Milton H. Erickson's account of the African violet lady.[81] One of Erickson's patients had asked him to visit his aunt, a middle-aged woman who had never married and who lived in Milwaukee. She had a private income and a housekeeper, maid and gardener to take care of her every need. But she had fallen out with her family and for the previous nine months had become deeply withdrawn and depressed. When Erickson called upon her, telling her he was a doctor and that the nephew had asked him to visit, she expressed no interest. Her behaviour was very passive so, to attempt to get at least some sense of her and her life, Erickson asked her for a guided tour of her house. "She led me from room to room," he said. "I looked around very carefully at everything. In the sun-room I saw three beautiful African violets of different colours in full bloom, and a potting shed in which she was propagating another African violet. African violets are very delicate plants. They are easily killed by the slightest amount of neglect."

Erickson also deduced from the presence of a large open bible and several church magazines that she had a keen interest in the church. He then challenged the true depth of her faith on the grounds that she wasn't using her God-given gifts in the way that she should. Although she had had no interest in anything he had said up till that point, this comment grabbed her attention.

Erickson said, "I am going to give you some medical orders and I want them carried out. Do you understand that? Will you agree that you will carry them out?" She passively agreed. So he continued, "Tomorrow you send your housekeeper to a nursery or florist and you get African violets of all different hues. Those will be *your* African violets and you are going to take good care of them. That's a medical order. [This was in the days when doctors' orders were much more likely to be respected and obeyed.]

"Then you tell your housekeeper to purchase 200 gift pots and 50 potting pots and enough potting soil. I want you to break off a leaf from each of your African violets and plant it in a potting pot, and grow additional African violets until they are mature. [These particular flowers propagate when the leaf is planted.] And when you have an adequate supply of African violets, I want you to send one to every baby that's born in any family in your church. I want you to be a good Christian and send an African violet to the family of every baby christened in your church. I want you to send a gift of an African violet to everyone who is sick in your church. When a girl announces her engagement, I want you to send her an African violet. When people get married, I want you to send them African violets. In cases of death, you send a condolence card with an African violet. And to the church bazaars – contribute a dozen or a score of African violets for sale."

With that Erickson left. It was soon reported that her depression had lifted. As Erickson said years later, "Anybody that takes care of that many African violets is too busy to be depressed. She died in her 70s and I have a newspaper cutting recording the fact that, 'The African Violet Queen of Milwaukee has died'. I saw her only once."

This case history illustrates clearly many of the human givens principles of therapy. First Erickson quickly assessed what needs were unfulfilled in the woman's life. Then he focused her attention and made her promise to do something that he knew would re-engage her with the community. He creatively drew on her own belief system and life resources. In this case it was her skill with African violets that he cleverly linked with the universal appreciation that the human community has for flowers. By precisely describing what he wanted her to do, he employed her imagination to rehearse success. He gave her enough work to do to ensure that her negative introspections would stop and her depression would lift. In other words he devised a therapy specifically for her: one that she could keep up independently.

This last point is particularly important. Therapists have to help depressed people use whatever skills they already possess to re-connect them to the community, so that their needs can be met autonomously. Erickson called this the utilization principle – whatever the patient brings to the situation is made use of to help them to move on. It doesn't matter whether traits are positive or negative. If someone is obsessive, positive use can still be made of that – perhaps, for instance, by asking the individual to keep careful records of how, when and where they carried out any tasks the therapist sets them. If they love travel, they might be required to take a journey for a particular purpose. Someone who believes their workaholic behaviour makes them more effective can be helped to see they are more effective if they conscientiously build periods of relaxation into their schedule. If they have a strong belief system, a therapist can work from that. If they grow African violets and are part of a Christian community, that can be made very good use of! Of course, some people may not have a particular skill they can use to help get needs met; they might be shy or poor at socializing, for example. Then the counsellor has to teach them social skills, or make sure that *someone* does.

It is important to make use of aspects of individuals' own personalities or the resources they have already developed, so that they can build on, or move on from, what they already know and feel comfortable with, and therefore adapt more easily to a positive change in circumstances. Imposing ways of being or doing from the outside does not help people to develop autonomy and make the most of who they already are.

The need for status

It doesn't matter how successful, wealthy or loved you are, if the sense that you have status in a particular area of your life is jeopardized and your reputation shattered it can plunge you into despair. A study of over 60,000 people from 123 countries found wellbeing "consistently depended on the degree to which people felt respected by others". Attainment or loss of status was "the strongest predictor of long-term positive and negative feelings".[82]

This desire for recognition and status is obviously related to our need to be connected to the wider community, and became encoded in our genes during the long evolutionary period when our only chance of survival was to belong with and stay in a group. This is because our early ancestors on the plains of Africa were easy meat for predators like lions and hyenas because we had no fangs or claws to fight with and no thick hairy hides to protect us: just juicy flesh that represented a tasty meal on two legs for other animals. It was only by banding together in large groups that our forerunners were able to survive, which they did by making a lot of noise and throwing sticks and stones to frighten away the wild predators that circled around. To be rejected by the group was as good as a death sentence. So being valued in it was critically important.

Having our status confirmed or denied actually colours how we perceive the world around us: the psychological experience of it provides a favourable lens through which to view one's social landscape.[83] By contrast, social difficulties, rejection or withdrawal of status during childhood, and especially in the developmentally sensitive period of adolescence, can have a life-long negative impact. Researchers studying human development at the University of British Columbia concluded that "...neurohormonal systems that play an important role in orchestrating the body's response to stress are highly plastic during puberty, making [young people] malleable to a variety of social–environmental influences. In addition, adolescence is a time when individuals begin assigning greater value to their status within peer social networks and reduce their involvement with family. With this combination of malleable physiology, focus on status within the peer group, and withdrawal from the family, adolescents may be especially vulnerable to the negative consequences of social stressors." They found that the most toxic challenge to social standing in adolescence is targeted rejection – in which someone experiences deliberate rejection by another person or a group, such as by being ostracized or taunted for sustained periods. Targeted rejection precipitates depression three times more quickly than other similarly negative life events. The effect was significantly more pronounced in those who perceived their social status to be higher before the toxic behaviour was directed at them.[84]

The importance of our perception of status was nicely captured in the report of the second in the classic series of studies on thousands of civil servants at Whitehall, which found that the higher one is up the hierarchy, the better the health: "The Whitehall studies have gone some way towards unravelling the mystery of why someone in the middle of the social hierarchy should have worse health than those above them and better health than those below them."[85] Indeed, it is lack of sense of status in societies where there is a huge equality gap between the best and worse off that has been found to account for not only much mental and physical ill health but for many other ills such as violence levels and illiteracy.[86] In other words, it is not lack of money per se – many poorer societies are happy societies – but the shame of feeling second class that is the defining factor in how healthy societies are.

Unfortunately, we may have unhelpfully fixed ideas about what signifies status in the outside world. In one US study, people were shown, in photo flashes that lasted 129 milliseconds, pictures of people wearing 'rich' or 'poor' clothes. They automatically assumed those in wealthier outfits were significantly more competent and higher status, even when informed that the clothes were irrelevant and that all the people worked in sales at a mid-size town in the Midwest and earned around $80,000 dollars a year.[87]

Real status is not necessarily visible and having status does not necessarily mean being 'top dog'. It is not about power, although it can be. But the best bosses are those confident enough in their own skills that they can encourage and confer a sense of status on those below them in the pecking order, as a result creating a happier and more motivated workforce. Real status is acquired only when you become valued for what you do or what you know. A good school cleaner has their need for status met just as much as a head teacher does, if the other members of staff respect what they do and consult them about school hygiene, for example. In other words people are valued when they contribute something to the common good – whether that is through work, skills, knowledge, child rearing, cooking, wealth, entertainment, protection against enemies, etc.

The need for privacy

People need people, as the saying goes, but there can be too much of a good thing. To be constantly in the company of others eventually raises stress levels in most people. We need to get away. It's wonderful to have guests staying for a few days but delightful when they leave, too. However, when we are not in control of how much privacy we have, the effects on our mental health can be dire.

There is considerable evidence, for instance, that the more people using or sharing a room in a house, the higher the psychological distress levels.[88,89,90,91] While much of this sort of research has focused on the impact of overcrowding on adults, inadequate housing also has adverse effects on children's wellbeing and one of the reasons may be over-stimulation.[92] Researchers have found that there are noticeably higher levels of chaos in crowded homes – and that some of the harmful effects of crowding are buffered when a child has a place somewhere in their home that they can take refuge. The effects of relentless overcrowding can be cumulative. For instance, children from crowded homes who attend crowded day centres have been found to be more aggressive, hyperactive or else withdrawn than children from a crowded home or attending a crowded day centre but not both.[93]

Overcrowding and resultant lack of privacy have unwelcome knock-on effects on our sense of control. In one study, researchers looked at 60 students living in halls of residence in large and medium-sized groups and found that those in the largest groups were likely to exhibit learned helplessness. They initially tried to do things that would help them create a bit of distance from all the others around them but fairly soon their inability to control social contact led them to feel helpless and hopeless and to cease to expect to be able to exert control.[94] In another study, students who were put into large groups in a small room for the purposes of an experiment were found to make less eye contact with others and reported feeling more discomfort and perceiving more crowding than students who were put in large rooms, or in small rooms but with fewer people.[95]

People in open-plan offices commonly suffer more stress, even when panels and bookshelves are strategically placed to create the perception of privacy. In such cases, it is the fact that others can be heard talking about irrelevant topics that adversely affects performance and even increases individuals' sense of work overload.[96] Loss of privacy and the increased disturbance appear to outweigh any positives of open-plan working, such as creating a more social atmosphere.[97]

As might be expected, overcrowding had been found to be a significant precursor of unrest and agitation in prisons.[98] In the US, lawyers have even won cases by persuading federal judges of overcrowding's negative impact on the physical and mental health and behaviour of prisoners. Overcrowding also increases aggression in psychiatric patients.[99]

It is findings such as these that first led therapist John Perry to contemplate just how far our need for privacy might stretch and how vital it is to our mental health, which we invited him to explore in our journal, *Human Givens*: "How many clients have therapists worked with whose major complaint is that they never seem able to get a break, that they are always 'on call' (a common complaint amongst new parents) or that they can't 'escape' from the pressures of the workplace or of the household? And things are getting worse, as mobile phones, email and 'instant messaging' intrude ever further into our personal lives, creating a climate in which it is almost impossible to be unavailable. As our ability to get our privacy needs met is eroded, so the toll on our mental health increases.

"I also know that this is a very common experience, from conversations I've had with ex-prisoners and from ex-boarding school students. The need for privacy – where it is overlooked – is a major cause of stress, in the face of which it is impossible to thrive. Interrogators have known this for centuries. (And yet still we expect prisoners to take advantage of the various opportunities for personal development they are offered during their incarceration – whilst housing them three to a cell, where they are unable even to use a lavatory in private.)

"This is not, of course, a new idea. The difficulty in getting one's privacy needs met has been cited as a reason for the high rates of mental distress in tower blocks with shared entrances; and, more generally, as an explanation for why human social behaviour frequently 'breaks down' in situations of chronic overcrowding. ... Perhaps this is why we tend to develop a fixed, middle-distance gaze in a lift or a tube train. And why so many people (particularly men) spend hours sitting alone fishing at a riverbank? Or take up long distance running?

Or retreat to their garden (or garden shed) whenever they feel stressed? The activity itself is largely unimportant – perhaps even merely an artefact.

"Whether it is fishing, running, gardening, model-making, painting, completing a jigsaw, playing computer games, seeking solace in a long hot bath, meditation, practising a musical instrument, train-spotting, hang-gliding, riding a motorbike, wind-surfing, metal-detecting, burying one's head in a book, studying for a research degree, enjoying a quiet pint in the corner of a bar, or storming out of the house following an argument (the list could go on and on), *all* of these activities may simply be means of achieving the same ends – getting one's needs for privacy met.

"Could this also be why the arrival of a new child into the household is so frequently experienced as a 'mixed blessing'? And why many young people report that their lives are transformed when their family move to a new house in which they, at last, have their own bedroom? And why someone who discovers that their diary has been read feels so violated? Perhaps this is also the reason why so many people find the process of counselling such a challenge. In revealing their 'private thoughts', they are also surrendering their need for privacy.

"One could develop the theme still further to take account of family dynamics – for example the need for the adults in a family to get their privacy needs met *as a couple*; and of the children's need to develop their own relationships with each other in the absence of a 'supervising' parent. ..."[100]

Since he wrote this article, in which he refers to the powerful impact of getting away from things, particularly outdoors, studies have suggested that being out in nature promotes general psychological wellbeing including greater sense of trust, acceptance and belonging.[101]

Of course, our privacy is under attack like never before, in the digital age we now live in. Social media insidiously reins people in – not to be on it, for many, is equivalent to not existing. A 2019 survey of nearly 2,000 US smartphone users found that they checked their phones on average 96 times a day, about once every 10 minutes.[102] Another survey of 1,200 smartphone users found that 23 per cent check their phones within a minute of waking and another 34 per cent hold out for five to 10 minutes. Only 6 per cent waited two hours or more.[103]

Web browsers store information about us via cookies, yielding valuable information for all sorts of organisations, not only retailers but governments. Our phones reveal our location; facial and voice recognition technologies become more and more prevalent; bots answer our questions online; and there is certainly no doubt there will be much more of this ilk now and in the future. Quoted on the Pew Research Center's website,[104] Leah Lievrouw, professor of information studies at the University of California-Los Angeles, has written, "To date, virtually no democratic state or system has sorted out how to deal with this challenge to the fundamental legitimacy of democratic processes, and my guess is that only a deep and destabilizing crisis (perhaps growing out of the rise of authoritarian, ethnic or cultural nationalism) will prompt a serious response."

Also quoted on the website, Robert Epstein, senior research psychologist at the American Institute for Behavioral Research and Technology, said, "As of 2015, the outcomes of upward of 25 of the national elections in the world were being determined by Google's search engine. Democracy as originally conceived cannot survive Big Tech as currently empowered. If authorities do not act to curtail the power of Big Tech companies – Google, Facebook and similar companies that might emerge in coming years – in 2030, democracy might look very much as it does now to the average citizen, but citizens will no longer have much say in who wins elections and how democracies are run. My research – dozens of randomized, controlled experiments involving tens of thousands of participants and five national elections – shows that Google search results alone can easily shift more than 20 per cent of undecided voters – up to 80 per cent in some demographic groups – without people knowing and without leaving a paper trail."[105]

We need privacy not just for all the reasons so far mentioned but also to enable us to reflect on the day's feelings and experiences, and to consolidate the lessons learned, and this is best done alone, preferably without interruption. It is hard, if not nearly impossible, to digest ideas and experiences when assailed by information of dubious quality from all sides and when surrounded by others who continually want our attention or from whom, in their presence, we wish to receive attention. While the psychological and physical need for privacy is now well established, we would suggest that the need for time to self-reflect is more recently evolved because it is connected to our need for meaning. Self-reflection requires imagination, which, in evolutionary terms, became widely incorporated into the human genome only relatively recently.

The need to become competent and achieve

The gaining of skills and competences by using our minds and bodies in new ways is deeply satisfying because our brains and bodies evolved to be used and are only at their healthiest when they are. The sense of our own competence and achievements gives us feedback that we have learned something. This is why the brain rewards learning or achievement of any kind by releasing dopamine, the brain's 'reward chemical'. We experience good feelings by learning something new and then, as we consolidate the achievement, the brain begins to turn down the reward chemical so we will strive to do better or learn something else. Competence is one of the triad of needs (along with autonomy and relatedness) which international research studies on self-determination theory have identified as important for emotional wellbeing.[106]

We can, however, most easily see the importance of experiencing a sense of competence and achievement if we look at what happens when it is denied us. A stark example emerged from research conducted many years ago into the effects on school children of being 'kept back' a year, if their results are not deemed to be up to standard. American studies have shown so-called 'retention' to be one of the strongest predictors for dropping out of school at a later point, getting lower paid jobs and earning less.[107] One particularly shocking piece of evidence for the negative effects on children's mental health of being kept back with younger children, behind their own peers, emerged from surveys of children's ratings of 20 stressful life events. In the 1980s, by the time children were in sixth grade (about 12 years old), they feared only the loss of a parent or going blind more than retention. When this study was repeated some 25 years later, children of the same age rated being kept back a year as the *most* stressful of all life events – even more stressful than losing a parent or going blind.[108] Not surprisingly, a number of studies have shown that being kept back has a strongly adverse effect on children's innate need for status.[109] Much more effective as a means of improving academic performance at school are interventions such as after-school programmes and holiday schools. Plenty of research also indicates that well-planned and well-implemented programmes to enhance social and emotional wellbeing can positively affect academic wellbeing.[110] Also, children's developmental competence is integral to their academic competence.[111]

Occupational psychologists and others have also paid a considerable amount of attention to the consequences of not experiencing a sense of competence, achievement and satisfaction at work. For instance, effort that is put into work but not rewarded by recognition and sense of achievement is associated with psychiatric disorders.[112] A large meta-analysis found "robust consistent evidence" that high efforts and low rewards are prospective risk factors for common mental disorders.[113] In one more specific example, a survey of the mental health of 882 consultant gastroenterologists, surgeons, radiologists and oncologists found a 27 per cent psychiatric morbidity level, with no significant differences between the individual specialties. However, job satisfaction significantly protected the consultants' mental health against job stress. Burnout (one of its three components being low sense of personal accomplishment) was more prevalent among consultants who felt inadequately trained in communication and management skills[114] – perhaps indicating again the close connection between psychosocial and intellectual abilities and the impact on our mental health. A startling 37 per cent of medical students suffer burnout globally, according to a meta-analysis of 42 studies involving nearly 27,000 people.[115]

Of course, we don't need research to tell us that feeling competent at what we do is important for mental health. No child is ever going to enjoy being the last one picked for a sports team in physical education sessions or never knowing the answers to questions posed to the class in maths and science lessons. However, it helps enormously if we can excel at one if not the other, or at something else. So less academic children may get their sense of achievement from sporting prowess or from acting, musical or horticultural skills.

The ghastly ideology known as 'non-competitive sport' that infected some schools many years ago undermined children who were good at sport by insisting that no one should be a winner and that every loser should have a prize. It demotivated sporty children. They stopped striving to exceed even their own previous level of achievement. What children need is to experience a sense of competence and satisfaction with achievement at least *somewhere* in their lives, if they are to stay mentally healthy. It doesn't matter if a child can't run fast if they are brilliant at art or mathematics. The same applies to adults – which is why many people who experience their main sense of satisfaction and achievement from activities outside of work can put up with jobs where they do not feel properly valued. They know that, come Saturday, everyone values their sporting prowess on the football pitch or their gardening skills or whatever, contributing also to their sense of status. Becoming competent by learning something that requires effort to master, whether a sport, craft, art or profession, is the best antidote to low self-esteem.

Sense of achievement is also, importantly, extremely subjective. Many people, for instance, consider raising a healthy, happy family or recovering and learning from the experience of a life-threatening illness to be their finest achievement, far more important to them than riches or qualifications, accrued or not accrued. Sense of achievement is also bound into context. There is a moving moment in Lisa Genova's best-selling novel *Still Alice*, a highly realistic account of a woman suffering from early-onset Alzheimer's disease, when Alice, previously a professor of cognitive psychology, smiles triumphantly at her husband at one of her assessments, after she manages to spell the word 'water' backwards; he, an equally renowned academic and all too well aware of her former achievements, can manage only a dispirited smile in return.

Context is significant. This is why setting small manageable goals is so important when working with people who are psychologically distressed, so that they can experience success. This might mean, for someone who is agoraphobic, walking to the post box at the end of the road to post a letter or, for someone with obsessive-compulsive disorder, not giving in, on three occasions in one day, to the desire to perform a certain action when a particular alarming thought comes into mind. Experiencing success breeds confidence and more success, as is also the case, of course, for people making slow recoveries from stroke and other catastrophic physical injuries. Without belief in our ability to do something well, however insignificant it may seem to others, we may find it hard to hold on to hope and our sense of meaning.

The need for meaning

Meaning makes suffering tolerable. Over and above the need to survive and the selfish pursuit of pleasure, it is the search for a higher meaning that drives humankind forward. And it is our curiosity that directs our search. We get the 'meaning feeling' whenever we are stretched in some way by what we experience, whether it is by being deeply moved by what we see or hear, or by what we do and how we think, or by the choices we make in life. It is through 'stretching' ourselves mentally, creatively or physically that our lives feel purposeful and full of meaning.

Many of us find meaning through the work we do, so it is perhaps not surprising that in the business world the very real benefits of making work more meaningful – increased motivation, better retention and a more diverse workforce – have been measured. One study, for example, asked what individuals would be prepared to offer in return to an organization that created meaning at work for them.

55.1 per cent would be more motivated

42.3 per cent would be more loyal

31.6 per cent would take more pride in their work

21.6 per cent would work harder

20.5 per cent would put in more hours to get the job done

18.4 per cent would be more creative.[116]

It has long been recognised that there is a relationship between sense of meaning and mental health. One study, involving 300 men and women ranging in age from young adult to elderly, found that life purpose, future meaning and a sense of life control all predicted psychological and physical wellbeing.[117] Similarly, a 25-year longitudinal study in Germany showed that the 'set-point' theory of happiness, which states that individuals have a genetically predetermined level of happiness, is wrong. It is the *choices* that individuals make which have an impact on their happiness, and those who choose meaningful activities can escape what the authors describe as the "hedonic treadmill".[118] This term describes the well-known problem that many pleasurable activities (those we would describe as "worldly", such as acquiring wealth, excitement, fame, etc.) become less and less valuable over time, so that people need more and more to have the same effect, and in the longer term they are no happier. An example of this is the widely replicated finding that, over time, lottery winners are no happier overall than they were before they won the money.[119,120] Choosing meaningful activity, on the other hand, increases an individual's happiness over time, in a way that is measurable and enduring.

More recent research has found that purpose in life predicts better recovery from negative events. "Purpose in life predicts both health and longevity, suggesting that the ability to find meaning from life's experiences, especially when confronting life's challenges, may be a mechanism underlying resilience," say its authors.[121] Pertinently, a different set of researchers found that a sense of meaningfulness served as a protective factor against psychological distress during the covid-19 pandemic.[122] And the link between purpose in life and ageing well was confirmed in later studies.[123]

Particular attention has been paid to the role of meaning and purpose in the lives of people who are seriously ill. It has long been shown that recovery from trauma often provokes positive psychological changes, including finding meaning in the experience.[124] Men who survived a heart attack and, as a result, perceived benefits to the attack, such as inducing a positive change in life values, were found less likely to have another attack.[125] Conversely, excessive rumination on traumatic experience to try to make sense of it but *without* eventually finding positive meaning has been shown to have a negative effect on health.[126] This finding was strongly borne out in another study, which followed up 40 HIV-positive partners or close friends of men who had died from AIDS and demonstrated that those who found meaning for themselves in their loved one's death – ie it led to a major shift in important values, priorities or perspective – maintained, over two to three years of follow up, the level of their own helper immune cells (independent of other factors such as smoking, drinking and other health habits), whereas those who did not find meaning in the death showed a reduction in helper cells. Only three of the 16 men who had found meaning in their bereavement died over the next four to nine years, whereas half of those who did not find meaning died.[127] Meaninglessness can even bring on illness, it would seem. One study found that participants who were free of cardiovascular disease when they joined the study were more likely to die in the follow-up period if they had reported, on entry to the study, that they were bored with their lives.[128]

People in the terminal phase of an illness who have a greater sense of meaning and purpose in life, have stronger faith and feel more comfortable about existential concerns are less likely to experience depression, which is otherwise a fairly common reaction, along with hopelessness and desire for hastened death.[129]

There is a definite link between sense of meaninglessness and suicide or suicidal thoughts and attempts.[130] It was even asserted by one academic investigator that the failure to create meaning for oneself underlies almost all suicide attempts.[131] One study found that distressed adolescents who found little meaning in their lives were also more likely to consider killing themselves.[132] Conversely, having a sense of meaning in life was protective against suicidal tendencies in university students.[133]

Clearly the finding of meaning and purpose is hugely important for both physical and psychological health. It even has an impact on the functioning of the brain, as a study with dementia patients has shown. As Dr Michael Thaut, senior author of the study, put it, "We have new brain-based evidence that autobiographically salient music – that is, music that holds special meaning for a person, like the song they danced to at their wedding – stimulates neural connectivity in ways that help maintain higher levels of functioning." The research team reported structural and functional changes in neural pathways of the 14 study participants (eight of whom were not musical), notably in the prefrontal cortex, the brain's control centre where deep cognitive processes occur. Exposing the brains of patients with early-stage cognitive decline to autobiographically significant music activated a distinct neural network that showed differences in activation after a period of daily music listening. Differences were also observed in the brain's connections and white matter, providing further evidence of neuroplasticity.[134]

The three basic ways through which we find meaning in our lives are: first, by being needed ourselves and serving those who need us (as in raising a family, working in a team, running a business, teaching, etc.); second, by learning new mental or physical skills (as in travelling, exploration, learning a language, academic study, joining a profession, exploring sport, craft, music, etc.); and third, by being connected in some way with philosophical, political, religious or spiritual ideas that are bigger than ourselves (as in pursuing a quest for scientific or spiritual truth). Extracting meaning in any one of these ways is all that most people need to keep relatively sane but getting the need for meaning met from all of them creates the richest life.

The second and third of these three ways are the most recently evolved. Interested readers may also like to see how we address the question of meaning in our book *Godhead: the brain's big bang*, which focuses on the origins of creativity, mysticism and mental illness, with special attention given to the nature of consciousness, the mystery of time, how consciousness may survive death, and how and why the material universe maintains itself – all meaningful issues that have preoccupied thoughtful members of humankind since the Stone Age.

Needs can be met unhealthily, too

From the human givens perspective we recognize that all organisms, including humans, have different needs and that, if those needs are met pretty well, they will mature in a fully rounded way. Our needs have to be met in balance, if we are to be mentally healthy. There may be times when certain needs are more important than others to an individual or when some cannot be met temporarily, for some reason. Someone attempting an around-the-world solo boat trip is not going to be meeting their needs for emotional and community connection but, for that period of time, fulfilling their need for autonomy and meaning and purpose takes precedence.

It is also relevant how we meet our needs. Needs that we meet at the expense of others are not healthily met (and also, of course, impede those others from best meeting their own), nor is excessive fulfilment of them healthy. All our needs can be met incorrectly, so we must be mindful of this.

For instance, someone who is so risk averse that they never dare leave the house or never try something new may seemingly be meeting their need for security but certainly fails to meet the human need to be stretched, face new challenges and grow. Someone who satisfies their need for control by over-controlling others (as is the case for the abuser in abusive relationships), apart from causing much misery, is not psychologically healthy. Nor are those colloquially referred to as control freaks. They tend to be people who, for whatever, reason, feel out of their depth and try to control the environment they live and work in, which of course includes how other people behave. In an attempt to hold their world together, they may intensely obsess about procedures, rules and regulations, quite oblivious that such inflexibility prevents others from exercising their own need for volition.

Others may overly seek to exert control by carrying out rituals and compulsive actions that they believe will prevent bad things happening to them and to those they love. Serious cases tend to earn the diagnosis of obsessive-compulsive disorder. Of course, what is behind all these extreme means of trying to exert control is a sense of insecurity, and it is this that needs to be tackled in order to redress the balance.

We have already discussed in some depth how our need for attention may often be met inappropriately, by adopting principles and practices only because these bring us the attention we seek from certain individuals. We can invest too much in intimate relationships, expecting these to meet not only our need for emotional connection but all other needs as well – how often is it the case that those newly in love drop their long-term friends and devote all their attention to the newly beloved? Or we may eschew emotional connection because we fear getting hurt and thus deprive ourselves of the joy of knowing and caring for another deeply.

Our need for community and belonging can be turned sour if we succumb to a 'them and us' mentality. In our long, long distant past, we needed to feel part of an ingroup in order to have the best chance of survival. But for ingroups to exist, there need to be outgroups, and their outgroup nature is reinforced by inculcated beliefs that the latter are inferior, dangerous or even subhuman, as much research into cults, religious and racist groups has shown. Indeed, when people feel threatened by a particular minority, they completely over-estimate the size of the 'threat' they represent,[135] adding to the fear and disconnect.

Also, despite what we might hope, especially in a world where global cooperation is increasingly important, people seem more likely to cooperate with those from their own country rather than with those outside it. This emerged from a study investigating how over 18,000 people from 42 different countries performed in a game in which participants had to choose whether to send money to a partner (a stranger to them) or keep it, in the hope of winning more. If both partners chose to send their money to each other, they would win most of all, but this was a gamble each had to take. Each participant played 12 times, with partners from their own or other countries (sometimes being given this information and sometimes not).

Players sent more money when their partners came from their own countries – a finding that was statistically significant for 39 of the 42 countries and still relevant in the other three. The extent to which this happened was also similar across countries and was not related to political or cultural factors. It also made no difference if people were told that their decisions would be published online or kept private. However, cooperation did vary overall and was stronger in countries with more egalitarian values.[136]

One disturbing side effect of our need to show that we adhere to a community's moral values is known as 'groupthink.' This phenomenon occurs when a group of individuals reaches agreement on an issue without critical reasoning, assessing alternatives or evaluating possible consequences, tending to refrain from expressing doubts and judgments or disagreeing with the consensus.[137]

William H. Whyte, influenced by George Orwell's *1984*, first proposed the term in the 1950s, and in the 1980s American psychologist Irving Janis set out the basis for studying it, pointing out that highly cohesive groups are likely to suffer from groupthink: a strong tendency that suppresses critical inquiry and results in faulty decision making processes and flawed outcomes.[138]

Groupthink is maintained through a common desire not to upset the balance of thinking or behaviour that the group has settled on. And so, like the courtiers in the tale of the emperor's new clothes, people will avoid risking their value to the group, and go so far as to denounce or distance themselves from anyone voicing opinions at odds with thinking and behaviour the group has deemed acceptable.

While it is most easily observed in the behaviour of cults, any group with a strong focus on adhering to a set of moral values, most obviously religious groups, political parties and military organisations, can unwittingly fall foul of groupthink. Historical examples of groupthink include the South Sea Bubble, Tulip Mania, Nazism, which many Germans believed was in the national interest, and Communism, which promised to resolve economic inequality. Present day examples are all around us.[139]

Groupthink can arise in all areas of society: academia, the media, the arts, education, health, politics, economics, agriculture, the corporate world – and psychotherapy. Indeed, one of the motives for developing our common sense approach to psychotherapy was the observation that many schools of therapy involved groupthink and cult-like behaviour that was harming both the practitioners and the people they were supposed to be treating.

Sense of status may be so important to some that they will go to any lengths to acquire it, even posing in some cases as a doctor when completely without qualifications – and in some cases getting away with it; or pretending to be wealthy aristocrats or business moguls, jetting around the world and sporting pricey jewellery at the expense of those they have conned out of their money. More ordinarily, need for status is unhealthily met by exerting power over others, by virtue (or vice) of one's position at work or in any kind of hierarchy. Many young, disadvantaged people may join gangs because this seems to offer them their only opportunity for gaining status, and sense of belonging, and, in turn, as they rise up the ranks, exert their power cruelly over others.

Need for privacy can be abused when it is taken at the expense of others – so, for instance, one parent may take for granted that they can go for a walk whenever they want to, enjoy a swim, have a long luxurious bath, without recognizing that this requires the other partner to be the one who looks after the children 24/7. Privacy can also be unwittingly abused, as when people turn their attention inwards and start ruminating excessively about aspects of their lives, generating anxiety and often descending into depression.

Our driving need for a sense of competence and achievement is powerful and sometimes it can appear to be met too effortlessly. Countless young people have sailed through school without problem till about the age of 16 and are then completely blindsided by the need to put in real effort to pass exams such as A Levels and to get a good degree at university. At this stage, their self-esteem may crumble.

Sometimes the need for achievement is stymied by what psychologist Carol Dweck termed a fixed mindset, as opposed to a growth mindset. She defines these terms thus: "In a fixed mindset, people believe their basic qualities, like their intelligence or talent, are simply fixed traits. They spend their time documenting their intelligence or talent instead of developing them. They also believe that talent alone creates success – without effort. In a growth mindset, people believe that their most basic abilities can be developed through dedication and hard work – brains and talent are just the starting point. This view creates a love of learning and a resilience that is essential for great accomplishment.

"A growth mindset isn't just about effort. Perhaps the most common misconception is simply equating the growth mindset with effort. Certainly, effort is key for students' achievement, but it's not the only thing. Students need to try new strategies and seek input from others when they're stuck. They need this repertoire of approaches – not just sheer effort – to learn and improve.

"We also need to remember that effort is a means to an end to the goal of learning and improving. Too often nowadays, praise is given to students who are putting forth effort, but *not learning*, in order to make them feel good in the moment: 'Great effort! You tried your best!' It's good that the students tried, but it's not good that they're not learning. The growth-mindset approach helps children feel good in the short *and* long terms, by helping them thrive on challenges and setbacks on their way to learning."[140]

A fixed mindset may be unhelpfully reinforced by many teachers who have lower expectations of certain students. Even a growth mindset may not flourish if it is not supported by teaching staff.[141]

Another way that fulfilment of the need for achievement can be striven for unhealthily is through perfectionism. This stems most usually from a feeling of not being good enough, a message often received during childhood from over-demanding parents or teachers. As a result, perfectionists are never satisfied with the work they produce, convinced it can be better – resulting often in procrastination, demotivation and the missing of deadlines. Seeking achievement too desperately thus commonly results in failure.

Finally, many people may seek meaning in unhealthy ways, often getting mixed up with the need for attention and connection. Thus people may join religious groups or political parties or other organisations for the wrong reasons. And sometimes people may allow their own thirst for a meaningful life to detract from the lives lived by loved ones – many are the children of celebrated philanthropists who privately complain, "I wish they had spent more time on *us*."

Keeping greed in check

What tends to dominate an individual or group when needs are not met in balance is *greed*. Greed feeds the ubiquitous confusion between needs and wants. When our need for attention is not met, for example, we become attention seekers, which can become destructive to relationships. We can become greedy for comfort, turn to food and overeat and become lazy. We can be greedy for status, if status has been denied us in childhood and adolescence, and this can develop into an aggressive drive to dominate others in order to extract status through power. Any healthy human need, if unnurtured, can swell into a destructive want. In a mature society, the process of getting people's needs met provides a natural rhythm of checks and balances to ensure no one becomes excessively greedy or cruel.

But greed draws its strength from the fact that, in a fundamental way, like all basic emotions, it is directly linked to survival. Every living thing *has* to take from the environment around it to stay alive. This is why our greeds can become overwhelmingly powerful. Like all emotional states, a greed for something, whatever it is, focuses and locks our attention so we are unable to see the bigger picture – what's really happening.

Greed, however, like an evil master of disguise, is not always easy to see in ourselves or in others. It sneakily pops up in a variety of ways – invariably causing havoc. For example: we can be greedy to have a problem solved or a difficulty 'lifted from our shoulders' and, at first sight, this doesn't seem too serious. However, the strength of emotion around wanting a solution to a problem can prevent us from stepping back and seeing that the first solution that presents is not necessarily the best one. It may, in fact, contain aspects that will make the problem worse, and therefore be a disastrous course to follow. Thus it is that people can take out a loan to pay off a fairly small debt but then be saddled with an exorbitant interest rate that incurs a much larger debt in the long run. Similarly, when we are greedy for attention, we are blinded to the motives of the person giving us that attention and can be manipulated, deceived or coerced against our interests. This is why con men and flatterers will always thrive.

In short, greed prevents us from standing back and taking the time to have a long, cool look at an issue – because greed, driven by emotional arousal, needs 'instant' satisfaction (the 'I want it now' syndrome). When we become greedy for emotional stimulation, for example, it makes us emotionally 'bloated'. The more we have of something, the more we want until we can no longer see, through the emotional smokescreen we have erected, any other options or connections we could develop. This is how many religions continue to exert a hold over mankind long after they have lost contact with the inner truth behind their teachings. The religious institutions that provide emotional stimulation, calling this 'spirituality', have simply discovered that, because such stimulation is addictive, people keep coming back for more. With too much emotional stimulation, of course, we effectively suffocate our potential for developing more refined perceptions. So greed plays a role in stopping us thinking for ourselves and becoming more objective. It steers us towards 'authorities' to tell us what to do and to putting 'heroes' on pedestals to guide us or allowing 'father-figures' to think for us, reassure us and tell us what to believe. This is why people so easily accept the tyranny of corrupt authority (authority is often corrupt because of the calibre of person attracted to – and greedy for – power). It is easier. Everything is simplified. Our greed always draws us towards what appears to be easy to get, even if this leads to immense complications later.

A study of over 2,000 Dutch people, half male, half female, found that having a tendency towards greed (as measured on a standard scale) correlated with having a higher household income, more sexual partners and fewer children – and shorter lasting romantic relationships and lower overall wellbeing.[142]

But nature, as always, performs a balancing act. To meet the needs of the individual and the wider group, natural regulation occurs, when given the chance. For instance, individuals will only have their own needs for intimacy met if they are not too greedy for attention for themselves: too much attention seeking detracts from the ability to give due attention to others, thereby preventing the desired intimacy from developing. In the same way, a corrective to selfishness exists in parts of the world where cultures require people to treat strangers well, to come to their aid without question, if necessary, share their last crust of bread with them and do such things for no material reward whatsoever. In this respect, perhaps our own successful culture, technologically advanced and sophisticated as it is in many ways, is psychologically and socially still immature by comparison.

Until it is more widely recognized that the need to be connected within the community is a human given, for instance, there will still be people who miss developing their potential because of the environment they find themselves in, fail to fit well into society, commit crimes and exploit or abuse themselves and others. The rise in serious social problems is the inevitable consequence of our collective ignorance.

In addition, without these understandings, the way we go about helping disturbed people will continue to be far less effective than is possible. Much counselling and therapy training, for example, is founded upon the unfounded assumption that people can 'self-actualize' and 'find themselves' through endless talking and introspecting long and deeply, and thereby overcome their neuroses. Trainee psychotherapists may be encouraged to undergo many sessions of 'psychotherapy' or 'counselling' as part of their training, despite important research which showed that this did not make people more psychotherapeutically effective.[143] This flies in the face of all the research findings, many of which have been cited in this chapter, which clearly show that mental health is connected to focusing outwards, developing a sense of meaning and purpose, fulfilling our potential and getting our needs met by being active members of a community, helping meet the needs of others.

CHAPTER SIX

Mind, brain, body

AS EMPHASISED in the last chapter, physical and emotional needs are highly interrelated and this is because there is no hard division between what goes on in the mind, brain and body. Philosophers have written reams on what differentiates brain from mind and we don't plan to get into that here. Suffice to say, for our purposes, that the brain enables consciousness while the mind represents the contents of consciousness, generating energy through thinking and feeling, which the brain responds to in physical terms, impacting the body. What impinges on one very commonly has an impact on one of the others.

This becomes relevant in the ways we attempt to meet our needs. GP Andrew Morrice has illustrated vividly in his teaching for Human Givens College how people in sedentary jobs are advised to take 'exercise' to keep healthy, whereas those who do physical work, and certainly our hunter-gatherer forbears, quite naturally meet that need in the course of their daily activities. If exercise has to be incorporated specially into our lives, that can be a sticking point. So, as he points out, what motivates us to keep on with 'exercise', be it dance or kick-boxing classes, rambling or playing sports, is that the activity has a meaning or purpose for us, and/or it is fun, and/or it is done with others, and/or it is carried out in a green space – all, as we have shown, elements of healthy meeting of our emotional needs. Conversely, seeking to meet our needs for meaning, connection, fun and privacy may happen to occur through activities that involve movement.

It is very hard to draw clear lines of distinction between brain and body. Listening to music, for instance, is food for the mind and has also been shown to lower blood pressure, reduce anxiety, lessen the experience of pain, and improve sleep quality, mental alertness and memory.[1] It can even prevent seizures.[2] Dancing not only improves fitness and is fun but can play a part in helping with cardiovascular conditions, diabetes, arthritis and back pain, reducing inflammation and regulating the immune system. As Julia Christensen and Dong-Seon Chang, authors of *Dancing is the Best Medicine*, point out, the ancient Greek god Apollo was god of dance, music and healing, and gods and goddesses in many other mythologies are also in charge of both dancing and health.[3]

Security, an important emotional need, is very much linked with physical safety. We cannot feel secure if we can't reliably find food or clean water or shelter or healthy air to breathe. In developed countries, that may be linked with having enough money to secure these basic needs – and other comforts. If a person is at risk of losing their home or job, then worrying about whether or how these needs will be met will also impact upon security.

Worrying about needs not met is one of the prime causes of depression, as we shall see. The first manifestation of this is usually insomnia, which brings us on to the importance of sleep for both physical and mental health. Andrew Morrice has made the case for sleep as both a need and a resource and we are indebted to him for his simplified explanation of new understandings about the relevance of the three stages of sleep, which go in cycles throughout the night.[4] The first is mainly a transition stage, when we 'drop off' to sleep and enter stage 2, which is when consolidation of memories occurs – earlier sleep cycles are more associated with consolidating factual information and later ones with physical skills – enabling us to retrieve these when awake. Stage 3 occurs mainly in the first two hours of the night, is colloquially known as deep sleep, and is when the brain is flushed of waste products and damaged proteins, and tissue repair takes place. The last stage is rapid-eye-movement (REM) sleep, during which most dreaming takes place. We have already discussed this in some depth as the stage in which emotional flushing takes place. What is now understood is that having 'enough' sleep means having enough quality sleep so that all these processes can reliably take place.

As Morrice describes it, "A good proportion of people who say they 'sleep well', meaning that they are 'out for the count' for a good number of hours at night, nevertheless wake up feeling dreadful, foggy, tired, anxious or depressed and struggle with their memory. On the other hand, some who complain of lying awake or waking frequently at night are in fact fully readied for the next day by the time they get up in the morning. This demonstrates that we can be unconscious for eight hours at a stretch without properly accessing the various functions of sleep in healthy cycles, or can wake several times at night between really healthy sleep processes."[5] As Morrice goes on to explain, disruption of deep sleep is strongly associated with profound fatigue and malaise, and can be caused by the intrusion of alpha waves into the delta waves of deep sleep (so-called alpha-delta sleep), which is commonly associated with fatigue, fibromyalgia, chronic pain, depression and traumatic childhoods, but also may occur as a result of sleep apnoea, restless legs and being too hot or cold. There is also likely to be a link between loss of deep sleep and the inflammatory state that is seen in depression but the takeaway, here, is the importance of getting as much good sleep as we can.

Another HG colleague, Ezra Hewing, has brought together the research that shows how too little REM sleep can have a serious impact on both mental and physical health, such as increasing likelihood of suicidal thoughts and self harm, severity of obsessive thoughts, poor ability to regulate emotions (when insomnia or recurring nightmares have been experienced during adolescence); triggering of the manic phase of bipolar disorder; and increasing risk of dementia. Too much REM sleep leads depression to persist and exacerbates exhaustion and low mood, while psychosis risk is greater if there is disturbed sleep and depression in early years and schizophrenia risk is greater when a loss of deep sleep during adolescence interrupts neural development.[6]

Much research has been carried out in recent decades which establishes the gut as the second brain, as some like to put it. More technically, it has been shown that the bidirectional communication between the central nervous system and gut microbiota, known as "the gut-brain axis", plays a significant role in mental health, with poor functioning of the gut linked with anxiety and depression.[7] Much of the scientific work has been carried out with animals but effects of the benefits of probiotics on brain connectivity and mental health and the effect of pregnancy-related stress on gut microbiota in newborns have been shown in humans.[8]

The stress factor

The common denominator in all this is stress[9] – all organisms have to respond to stress from the environment and the earliest mammals evolved the 'fight-or-flight' response to help them escape from predators – the triggering of hormonal and other changes which enabled them to breathe faster and move faster and to cut down on internal activity unconnected with immediate survival, such as digestion. It is theorized that immune responses to such stresses were part and parcel of this, as fight and flight both increase the risk of injury and infection. Nowadays, although most of the threats we face are social rather than physical, threats such as losing social approval or failing to achieve academic success can have physical consequences, including immune system changes.

Yet until at least three-quarters of the way through the last century, the idea that our attitudes and reactions to events in our lives could have an impact on our bodily defence systems was anathema to most mainstream physicians. The Russian scientist Pavlov had discovered in the 1920s that the immune system could be conditioned by experience. Fifty years later an American scientist made a similar discovery[10] – rats given immune-system-suppressing drugs with saccharine-flavoured water continued to experience a lowering of immunity when given the saccharine-flavoured water alone. And suddenly there was an explosion of interest in the understanding that the healing response is a rich system of mind/body connections.

Whereas once it was thought that the brain and the immune system carried out their separate businesses, unable to influence each other, what research revealed was that there are strong interconnections, enabling our thoughts and our feelings to play an important part in our physical health. The hormones that course through our bodies when we are under chronic stress can impair immune function. And emotional reactions, by equally complex routes, can impair the functioning of specific organs. A meta-analysis of about a hundred smaller studies confirmed in the late 1980s that certain emotional 'attitudes' (i.e. emotions experienced long term, almost as a character trait, such as chronic anxiety, prolonged grief, tension, hostility, suspicion and pessimism) could double the risk of a whole range of diseases, including heart disease, headache, asthma, arthritis, peptic ulcers and skin disorders.[11]

Many books have been written about this fascinating subject, and indeed we have been covering it ourselves in this book – we have looked, for instance, in some depth at the impact on health of having close relationships and strong social support systems, and the ability of the mind to enhance its own health and healing powers. Indeed, it is impossible to write a book about mental health without extensive references to mind and body connections. The research findings have built up over the years and continue to be replicated and extended.

Since the laboratory findings showing how rats' immune systems react to stress, it has been impossible to ignore the impact on the body of chronic stress and anxiety. Our bodies are designed to handle brief bursts of stress to help us manage difficult situations (that is what the fight-or-flight response is all about), but if all the energy which is generated is not expressed in appropriate physical action, it doesn't quickly disperse. If we remain on the equivalent of constant alert, through anxious worrying, the chemical cocktail of stress hormones that maintain the ongoing arousal weakens our immune system.

Excessive anxiety compromises the immune system to the point where it can speed development of cancer, increase vulnerability to viral infections, and exacerbate plaque formation, leading to atherosclerosis, and blood clotting which may in turn lead to myocardial infarction. Stress overload can accelerate the onset of insulin-dependent diabetes and influence the course of non-insulin-dependent diabetes. It can lead to ulceration of the gastrointestinal tract and trigger symptoms of ulcerative colitis (inflammatory bowel disease). Even the brain is susceptible to the effects of long-sustained stress. Damage can be caused to the hippocampus and, therefore, to memory. All this has been known for several decades.[12]

There have been many studies that show the adverse effects of stress on the body's ability to fight infections. In one particularly famous one, carried out at the (now long defunct) Common Cold Unit in Wiltshire, people were asked in detail about the amount and nature of stress in their lives and were then exposed to the common cold virus. Those who saw themselves as being under the greater stress were the more likely to catch the colds. People with fewer social supports were also more likely to catch colds.[13] Similarly, people have been shown to be more susceptible to outbreaks of the herpes virus when they are under stress,[14] and to the onset of symptoms, if HIV-positive.[15]

Other research studies have shown that people under stress have a poorer response to vaccines and that wounds are slower to heal when people are stressed. When small wounds were inflicted on the arms of (willing) carers of spouses with Alzheimer's disease, for example, these took longer to heal than those inflicted on non-carers. The same effect was found in students taking exams. Oral wounds healed 40 per cent more quickly when the students were on vacation than when they were taking exams. The slower-healing effect persisted after the exam as well. This is a highly relevant finding for surgeons, as anxiety commonly persists after surgery, as well as being rampant before it.[16] A study carried out during the covid-19 pandemic showed that stress lowered immunity against infection with the virus – also the case with flu.[17]

One study revealed more than 50 years ago just how important it is to have a sense of being able to cope with one's life and have an element of control over it. Rats that were exposed to electric shocks experienced a lowering in immunity if they couldn't escape those shocks, whereas this didn't happen if they could escape the shocks. When they were injected with tumour preparations, those that could escape shocks were more often able to reject the tumours, whereas those that couldn't more often developed cancer.[18]

Of course, not everyone who is under stress, even extreme stress, develops serious illness and it may well be the coping mechanisms that we use which play an important part in maintaining our health. However, just *being* under stress can make problems seem bigger. In one study conducted by cognitive neuroscientist Tali Sharot and her students, firefighters who had had a stressful day with lots of call-outs were made more anxious by information the researchers gave them, such as the likelihood of being a victim of credit card fraud or robbery, than firefighters who had had a slow day and spent most of it quietly at the station.[19]

All the rage

When we get angry, we are activating the body's fight-or-flight mechanism as effectively as anxiety does. The whole process of stress hormones being released, heart rate rising, blood pressure shooting up, etc. gets into gear. As with anxiety, all this is all right if it happens only every so often. But when it keeps happening, the body stays in an unhealthy state of alert. Over 40 years ago, a link was established between hostility and coronary heart disease.[20] Those at most risk, it seemed, were those who were quickly roused to anger a great deal of the time or who almost permanently harboured feelings of hostility – "Why should he have a better job and bigger house than me? Why didn't I get that promotion? Who does she think she is, telling me what to do? How dare they keep taking more of my hard-earned money in taxes!" Many people become addicted to being angry. It is a seductive, apparently uncomplicated response: "I am right. You are wrong!"

With the passing of the years and more research, it seems the finding is not so robust. Although hostility definitely does have a part to play in heart disease, it accounts for a relatively small increase in risk of coronary heart disease and some of that may be due to other unhealthy associated behaviours, such as physical inactivity.[21] But, of course, hostility could only ever be part of the story in the development of heart disease. Drs Robert Ornstein and David Sobel, in their book *Healthy Pleasures*, lucidly show how hostility ties in with social isolation and lack of connection with the community – crucial emotional needs, as we now know. "There is a strong sense of self-involvement underlying hostility. A person who thinks of himself or herself as better than others in many ways is vulnerable to anyone who confronts such claims. Hostility may be a strategy for coping with such challenges by saying, 'Who do you think you are to challenge me like this!' To the self-involved, almost any event can be viewed as a personal threat: the turn of the stock market, the prospects for one's company, and the daily difficulties in a marriage. Individuals who think that everything is theirs – my wife, my kids, my company, my car, my neighbourhood, my church – have a lot of territory to defend.

"Those who are hostile use more self-references in conversation; they use the words 'me', 'my', 'mine' and 'I' more frequently. The 'mine' expression is the aspect of the self that claims ownership – 'that's my money!' When we begin to look at the world through these eyes, a viewpoint usually considered egocentric, there are consequences within the brain and the heart. Heart-attack survivors are usually less self-involved than those who die from a heart attack. Blood pressure reactions to challenges are higher, too, in self-involved individuals. The self-centred, hostile person tears his heart out because he or she is likely to have intense reactions to stress. Such a person responds to everything as challenge and mobilizes to face it.

"Self-centred, hostile people set themselves apart from the world rather than see themselves as a part of it. They have seceded from the social union, and cut themselves off from the life-sustaining, give-and-take of social intercourse. The result may literally break their hearts."[22]

Anger, of course, is an emotion and, like all emotions, it is a tool given to us by nature. It is neither good nor bad in itself. It is how we use it that needs looking at. Anger tells us that we feel our rights are being trespassed upon in some way. It alerts us to this perception, which arises as a result of unconscious pattern matching from what is happening now to something that happened in the past. Now, that pattern match may be close enough and the threat real. Or it could be inappropriate – we are, say, matching a constructive criticism from a boss to a criticism we received from a teacher when we were young, which we perceived as unfair but were unable to defend ourselves against it. Or it may be that the person we are angry with does not realize that they are upsetting us. This is where we need the skills to step back, lower the emotional arousal and give ourselves a chance to take a wider view to see whether the feeling of anger is really justified and our rights are being trespassed upon or not – and, if they are, to decide on a constructive (and safe) way to assert them, if possible. We all need to have anger management skills and we teach these during therapy, if appropriate (see page 255).

Why depression is linked to disease

There has long been evidence that depression also suppresses the immune system.[23] We saw earlier how rats that had no chance to escape from electric shocks were more vulnerable to cancer tumours. Depressed people commonly perceive themselves as having no options, no way out of their depressed thinking. People who are already ill with serious conditions and who are depressed about their illness or their chances of recovery are more likely not to recover. This has been shown in patients receiving bone marrow transplants[24] and in dialysis patients:[25] depression was a good predictor of which patients would not come through the treatments.

In a study carried out in Wales, researchers assessed the states of mind of 37 people who had had a first heart attack, and elicited their beliefs and intentions about adopting healthier behaviours such as better diets, taking more exercise or stopping smoking. Those who didn't believe in their own ability to change were, unsurprisingly, the least likely to have made any changes three months later. Depressed people were the least likely to take charge of their health.[26] People who are depressed after a first heart attack have also been found to react more poorly to minor day-to-day stresses; blood pressure rises more than that of non-depressed patients who have had a heart attack.[27]

One study's findings suggested that early treatment for depression before the development of symptoms of cardiovascular disease could decrease risk of heart attacks and stroke by almost half.[28] A direct connection between depression and heart disease was shown by Dr Dominique Musselman from Emory University in Atlanta, Georgia. She found that depressed people have 41 per cent more sticky platelets in their blood (increasing the likelihood of clots) than non-depressed people. Getting rid of the depression was sufficient to return their blood almost to normal. Interestingly, when she gave them an antidepressant, the recovery effect on the blood only occurred if the individuals felt happier on taking the medication. Similarly, those who responded to a placebo drug by becoming happier also experienced the anti-clotting effect.[29] Those who did not respond to either drug or placebo continued to have sticky blood.

Even relatively minor conditions may be affected by depression. Outbreaks of herpes are found to be more common when people who already have the virus are feeling down. Depressed people also get sick more often than others, have more colds and have more sleep problems.[30]

When people are depressed, they are in a negative trance state, trapped in the tunnel vision of black-and-white thinking. Just having this sort of mindset itself increases risk of illness. In one study, head teachers were interviewed and classified as 'absolutist' or 'non-absolutist', according to the way they handled two work problems set as a test. Absolutist head teachers, those who saw life in terms of rights and wrongs and viewed the opinions and actions of others as acceptable or unacceptable, were less satisfied with their jobs and had poorer mental and physical health. Non-absolutist head teachers, who were more flexible in their approaches, found problem solving easier and enjoyed better health.[31]

It has now been known for some time that chronic inflammation is linked with depression, although the exact mechanisms are still unclear. Suffice it to say that chronic inflammation is stress related – and ongoing stress, caused by emotional needs not being met, is at the heart of the HG explanation for depression.

The great addiction mystery

Even addictions are not diseases with neat physical causes. Any successful ex-smoker, for instance, will know that the most uncomfortable aspect of giving up smoking is psychological, not physical. This is so, even with drugs such as heroin.

We all know people who take drugs or drink too much during a bad phase in their lives; we may even have done so ourselves – after a divorce, a redundancy or other major upset. We are most vulnerable at those times when we lose our moorings. The phase in life where people most commonly lose their moorings, drift and feel rudderless – willing to try anything – is when they are young. For some groups of adolescents and young adults, drug or alcohol abuse is almost an obligatory rite of passage. But in most cases, no matter how bad the addiction seems at the time, people recover from such a phase without too much difficulty when they move on to the next stage in their lives and get their needs met in more natural ways. They mature out of it.

A remarkable discovery about the dynamics of addiction came about as a result of the Vietnam War. American soldiers in Vietnam frequently took narcotics, and nearly all those who did became addicted. The authorities were worried about the social consequences for American life when tens of thousands of young heroin addicts returned home. They charged a group of medical epidemiologists to study these soldiers and follow them up for a long period. To their amazement, the researchers found that most of the soldiers stopped taking drugs addictively when they returned to normal life. Only a small percentage of these former addicts became re-addicted.[32] Life for the soldiers in Vietnam epitomized the kind of barren, stressful, and out-of-control situation that encourages addiction. When they came home and could lead a fulfilling life among friends, family and colleagues, the soldiers didn't need drugs.[33]

The puzzling question is: why does nature, which clearly applied so much intelligence to the evolution of human beings, enabling us to become the most creative and adaptive of any species on this planet, also make us so vulnerable to addiction? Why do so many people wilfully indulge in self-destructive behaviour, and risk damaging their relationships, their children and their work prospects? Why do they let addictions make them behave immorally, against all principles that they may have held prior to the addiction – resorting to stealing, prostituting themselves, and so on? At first sight it seems incredible that this could happen to such 'advanced' creatures as ourselves.

The answer lies in a highly adaptive mechanism, the 'carrot and stick effect', which is built in to all life forms and which is nature's way of motivating us to seek meaningful activities and thereby learn. Alas, however, it is a mechanism that can be 'hijacked' by addictive behaviour, as we will explain.

The mechanism works like this: when we engage in any experience or activity that is challenging and that we learn from, the brain provides the experience of pleasure. This reward, the 'carrot', spurs us on to repeat and become more proficient at whatever it is, giving enjoyment to what we are learning and encouraging mastery through practice. In this way, we are helped to meet one of our fundamental needs – the need for purpose or meaning. It is the brain chemical dopamine which drives us to pursue new skills and activities – it motivates us to seek the reward of pleasure in achievement. The pleasure is provided by other brain chemicals called endorphins, released when satisfaction is achieved. However, the brain doesn't continue to provide the same amount of pleasure every time we repeat that experience or activity, otherwise, we would not move on to seek yet more challenging experiences or learning situations. We would just keep doing what we can do well. For the sake of evolution, there has to be a way to encourage creatures to keep stretching themselves – to explore, experience differences, learn, develop new skills, etc. – so that they can adapt to environmental changes. So, once we have mastered some new experience, the brain turns down the reward and the pleasure begins to lessen. But we miss that pleasure and crave to experience it again – suffering, in effect, withdrawal symptoms. We can stop feeling the pain, and start feeling the pleasure again, if we proceed to challenge ourselves further – in the same or a different field. The withdrawal symptoms serve, in effect, as a stick to drive us on.

Whenever we need to keep on doing whatever it is we have learned to do, even if it is no longer so pleasurable, then the withdrawal symptoms serve as the stick, if we stop. For instance, if an overweight man decides to start taking regular exercise for the sake of his health, he may start walking a mile each evening and initially derive enormous pleasure from becoming more fit. After a while, though, it starts to become a boring routine experience – he doesn't get quite the same pleasure out of doing it. On wet nights, he is tempted to stay in front of the television. And yet, if he does, something feels wrong. He feels guilty and uncomfortable slobbing about in the evening, knowing how much better it will be for his body if he takes his usual walk.

Feeling bad or empty or that something is missing is the stick that the brain uses to goad us into maintaining worthwhile behaviours. Different brain chemicals help us to maintain what we have achieved (with the stick of painful withdrawal symptoms), while at the same time motivating us to stretch ourselves in ways that further our development (with the carrot of pleasure). It is a wonderful mechanism that enables all life forms, from single-celled organisms upwards, to progress.

However, in addiction, this process goes disastrously wrong. This is because, when we ingest a pleasure-inducing addictive chemical, it hijacks the receptors designed for the chemicals that the brain uses for rewarding us and making us feel good when we make an effort. When we pump them in from outside, the same pleasurable feelings are released in the brain. However, if we keep taking the drug, in the search to re-experience the 'high', the mechanism that we have just described kicks in and cancels out that pleasure. Then, if we want more pleasure, we have to increase the dosage of the drug. But, if we then stop taking the drug at any point, the 'stick' comes into use – we suffer withdrawal symptoms, which can only be assuaged (we think) by taking more and more of the drug. However, in keeping with the valuable principle of 'utilization', we can actually make effective use of this very same human given – the brain mechanism of the carrot and stick effect – to cure people of addictions (see page 257).

Functional disorders

After a major abdominal operation many years ago, Ivan had to stay in hospital to recover. In the bed next to him, another man was also recovering from a similar operation. In his case, the operation was exploratory; after many months of irritable bowel syndrome, severe abdominal pains, constipation, etc, with no relief provided by laxatives or other treatments, the decision had been taken to open him up and examine his bowels and other organs to see if there was some blockage or tumour that wasn't showing up on scans. The operation turned up nothing abnormal. There was absolutely nothing physically wrong with him. So he was put back on laxatives.

Ivan couldn't help overhearing this man's conversations with his family, when they visited, and with nurses and doctors. It became apparent that he was a highly anxious individual. His anxiety had been exacerbated on learning that his wife needed a new heart, and she was waiting for a heart transplant. Moreover, the stomach problem started after he had been told by a doctor that his wife could literally drop dead at any moment. This was his biggest concern, and a constant one. Whilst in hospital, he became highly anxious about whether or not his wife was well enough to keep visiting him and whether or not she was well enough to have him at home whilst he recovered from his operation. Clearly, his alarm response was permanently activated, with all the consequent bowel problems that can be caused when the body is on high alert. He needed psychotherapy, not surgery.

But when Ivan asked staff in the hospital whether they took account of the psychological profile of patients with these kinds of conditions, the answer was a resounding 'no'. They said that the surgeons who operated on this man had not even considered that there might be a psychological component to his symptoms. And, to be fair, even if it crossed their minds, they did not have ready access to anyone who would be competent in using psychological techniques to help him.

Fortunately we have moved on a long way since then and what are now termed 'functional disorders' are more widely recognized. Functional disorders are characterized by symptoms which do not have an organic cause. The pain or disability is real enough but the source of the problem is not physical disease or infection. Irritable bowel syndrome is a classic example of a functional disorder, and this should be no surprise, taking account of what is now known about the strong communication between brain and gut.

Backache can be a functional disorder, the cause lying in mental distress. Unfortunately, while it is true that such causes are much more commonly known about these days, specialists may still tend to view symptoms through the lens of their own specialty. Dr Grahame Brown, a former NHS consultant in musculoskeletal medicine, has described how arthritis or disc abnormalities which show up on MRI scans may be assumed by surgeons to be the cause of the pain a patient is presenting with, even though a great many people in the population who do not have pain would also show the same or even worse wear and tear on their spines.[34]

A significant proportion of people referred to neurologists have functional disorders, including limb paralysis or weakness, tremor, abnormal movements, dissociative seizures, cognitive impairment, urinary retention and 'scan negative' cauda equine syndrome.[35] One multicentre investigation found that 16 per cent of new outpatients had a functional neurological disorder (FND), making it the second most common diagnosis after headache.[36] This is likely to be an underestimate, with individual neurologists often estimating that up to a third of their patients have FND. Often, however, multiple organs are involved, with patients being referred to several different clinics – which may or may not communicate with each other. A new illness category termed bodily distress disorder, in which patients complain of several persistent medically unexplained symptoms, has been added to the latest edition of *International Statistical Classification of Diseases and Related Health Problems*, published in 2022.[37]

In her excellent (if misleadingly entitled) book, *It's All in Your Head*, consultant neurologist Suzanne O'Sullivan (she is one who estimates that a third of neurology patients have functional disorders) describes a wide variety of cases in which it becomes clear that the neurological symptoms experienced reflect or mask emotional distress of many kinds – such as that caused by relationship breakdown, fear of failure or domestic violence. Pauline became ill at 15 and what started out as an apparent urinary infection became joint pain, food intolerance, leg paralysis and then convulsions. No medical causes were found but each manifestation of illness occurred whenever Pauline was faced with a new challenge.[38]

Sadly, as is the case for many that O'Sullivan describes, patients may see so many specialists who find 'nothing wrong' and who suggest, overtly or otherwise, that it is 'all in their heads' that patients become resistant against a potentially effective psychological approach to helping reduce their symptoms, fearing they are being dismissed as mad. Also, for those who have care packages in place or receive special attention from loved ones because of their disabilities, there can be unconscious secondary gain in retaining their symptoms.

Far from ignoring FND, as neurologists were accused of in the past, they now have a flourishing interdisciplinary international society and FND can increasingly be found in the training curriculum for neurologists.[39] However this comes with a warning that FND should be diagnosed only when every other likely possibility has been ruled out.[40] Alarmingly, this message does not seem to be getting through in the case of symptoms associated with anti-depressant withdrawal, which is an acknowledged potential cause of, or contributory factor to, FND symptoms.[41] Twenty-five per cent of a sample of 158 patients participating in the Voice of Patients research group, comprising those experiencing severe and enduring withdrawal effects, found themselves diagnosed with FND when seeking help for their symptoms.[42] To add insult to injury, antidepressants may even be prescribed as the treatment.[43]

Stress can even be contagious

Perhaps, as we are social animals, it is not so surprising that we can even catch stress from other people, as a neuroscientist showed some years ago, when he measured the physiological response of study participants observing others experiencing stress and found they showed a spike in their own cortisol levels.[44] Emotional reaction to stress experienced at work can spread to partners, family and close friends, "transmitting through social networks similarly to pathogens", according to the findings of another academic paper.[45]

More dramatically, whole collections of the same symptoms can manifest in groups, a phenomenon once dubbed mass hysteria and now termed mass psychogenic disorders. There have been many examples throughout history and a classic example in modern times is that of hundreds of children in Sweden identified as suffering from 'resignation syndrome'. Children even as young as three would became anxious and depressed, gradually stopping their usual activities and then taking to their beds, no longer wanting food or even opening their eyes. Although they didn't move and appeared unconscious, their brain waves were normal. Symptoms in many cases persisted into adolescence. Crucially resignation syndrome was experienced only among children from specific communities, mainly Yazidis from Syria, Iraq or Turkey, and Uyghurs, all of whom had been severely persecuted in their own countries, were granted temporary asylum in Sweden and then were turned down forpermanent asylum, often not until after many years, when their families thought they were settled.

Neurologist Suzanne O'Sullivan was invited to examine some of the girls and wrote about them in her book *The Sleeping Beauties*,[46] along with accounts of other equally strange contagious non-organic symptoms that affected significant parts of different communities. She makes the case that the symptoms are an expression of societal or cultural distress and that they emerge from something going on in a shared environment against which the sufferers feel powerless. Problems at government or global level are just so big sometimes that we have to "psychologise and biologise" to cope with them, she has said.[47]

Using the mind to help the body

It should now be clear that how people respond to what happens to them in their lives and what people believe about themselves play a large part in helping them conquer pain or worsen it, recover from disease or succumb to it. Belief and attitude also appear to have an impact on our susceptibility to illness. These are strong cards to work with, whether in therapeutic settings, business organisations, schools or anywhere else that is concerned with human resources and the nurturing and care of others. What could be more empowering than being helped to see just how much control we can have over our own health, whether in preventing illness or speeding recovery?

Small things also make a big difference. For instance, small pleasures are not a luxury but a gateway to better health: little enjoyments

– such as stopping to really savour a cup of aromatic coffee or the taste of country-fresh vegetables, having flowers on the kitchen table to admire, taking an early evening stroll or having a leisurely bath perfumed with an exotic bath oil – all serve to help empower our immune systems. People may need 'permission' to relax and encouragement or motivation to take up exercise, both of which work wonders for mind and body too. Exercise, as we know, lifts mood by stimulating the production of brain chemicals called endorphins and providing an outlet for high circulating levels of adrenaline caused by chronic anxiety. Exercise also turns the attention outward – away from the constant negative and harmful introspections that characterize depression. It is a perfect example of the physical impinging upon the mental (and vice versa, as mentioned at the start of this chapter) and certainly something that every human givens practitioner will keep in mind, when working with anxious or depressed clients. Fortunately, exercise is also now increasingly likely to be recommended by GPs, via their 'social prescribers', for people whose mental difficulties are recognized to be more rooted in their environmental circumstances than in anything 'treatable' by a doctor.

In therapy it is our job, we believe, to do whatever is needed to help people develop a more positive outlook and re-engage with life at all levels. Creativity may be needed to enable this to happen. This is exactly what Milton Erickson did when he helped the 'African violet queen' reconnect with friends and community, from whom she had withdrawn, by the task he set her of growing and distributing African violets.

Effective therapies work only to the degree that they are in tune with the human givens and the fulfilment of those givens in the environment. Being able to see the patterns connecting all behaviour allows the provision of a much more powerful and creative form of therapy than any single approach taken on its own. Everything that science is finding out about the impact of mind and body systems upon each other urges us to take a more holistic approach to mental and physical health.

So psychotherapists, while concerned with mental health, need to make use of both physical and mental resources to achieve it. In the final part of this book, we will be looking at how the APET model, and its various practical applications, makes it much easier to do this.

CHAPTER SEVEN

Understanding difference: gender, identity and neurodivergence

A LOT of the thinking about differences in human behaviour that was taken for granted years ago has come under increasing scrutiny in the 21st century. Even what constitutes a male and what constitutes a female has become contentious in various circles, including academia and politics. Similarly, many people who previously were diagnosed as suffering a deficit or disability in neurological functioning increasingly embrace, and are encouraged to embrace, their difference as strengths. In the human givens approach to therapy, we always focus on strengths, so we applaud this. However, while some brain differences may be mild and bring compensatory gifts, others may be more incapacitating, and help with coping skills can only enhance individuals' ability to meet their needs successfully. Similarly, some of the yearning to reinterpret or embrace a different gender may be rooted in needs not well met. In this chapter, we take a brief look at relevant aspects of difference which may impact on individuals' mental health, and then focus specifically on autistic spectrum behaviours, presenting theories that we feel make sense of the otherwise puzzlingly enormous divide between one end of the spectrum and the other.

Not so gendered brain

In the last edition of this book, we had a chapter which looked at all the findings which seemed to support the idea that differences in brain structures – whether in size, density or connections – accounted for observed differences between male and female brains. At the time, it wasn't contentious to make the assumption that people were typically born male or female, with just some very few individuals born with anomalies that made their sex less definitive.

What constitutes male and female is known to be more fluid in many other parts of the animal kingdom. The normal female mole, for instance, has ovotestes, comprising ovarian tissue at one end and testicular tissue at the other, the latter not capable of producing sperm but increasing the mole's ability to dig for longer and defend her pups. A female hyena has an eight-inch clitoris that looks exactly like a penis and even gets erections, while the labia look like male gonads.[1] However, we don't find such exotic differences in the human species.

When the research tool known as functional magnetic resonance imaging (fMRI) became accessible in the 1990s, many neuroscientists keenly set about examining male and female brains to see if there were, indeed, physical differences that might explain observed variations in behaviour, and they appeared to find quite a lot. However, in her book *The Gendered Brain: the new neuroscience that shatters the myth of the female brain*, cognitive neuroscientist Gina Rippon shows how very many of the physical differences between male and female brains purportedly identified through these scans emerged from small, poor quality studies, with questionable methodology, very low statistical differences and ambiguous interpretation of results. As a whole, the differences were, in reality, very small and not explanatory (or even contradictory) of observed differences in behaviour – for instance, women tending towards more emotionality than men or appearing to multitask better. Any greater emotionality or multitasking ability on the part of women, she argues, rather than being innate, is more likely to have been learned in accordance with cultural and social norms.

Rippon describes and cites a large number of studies which show that behaviours which earn societal approval are those which we tend to adopt – and society still largely approves different behaviours for males and females.[2]

Such cultural processes do change the brain, but not because of some inherited biological template. However, as Rippon is at pains to point out, it is still all about biology. "The social, cultural aspects I mention in the book are all processes that will change the brain. I think it is all biology. It is a matter of where those differences in the biology came from, and it is not necessarily from some biological template we inherited but maybe because of continual exposure to cultural expectations of our social world."³ As she points out, from a very young age we are looking to fit into a social network, which will welcome and care for us, and thus ensure our survival. The brain is geared to pick up on the social rules that bring approval and, as she illustrates with an anecdote from her own life, that process starts very early. (When she was in the labour ward with other new mothers after giving birth to her second daughter, a nurse wheeled in two noisy babies and handed the boy to another mother, commenting "Cracking pair of lungs!" and the girl to Rippon, saying, "The loudest of the lot. Not very ladylike.")

Since then, a comprehensive synthesis of three decades of human fMRI and post-mortem data, led by neuroscientist Lise Eliot and focusing most particularly on meta-analyses and large studies, found, "few reliable sex gender differences and a history of unreplicated claims". The fact that male brains are larger than female brainsright from birth apparently accounted for brain sex differences such as higher white/gray matter ratio. And when identifiable structural and lateralisation differences were found even after accounting for brain size difference, sex or gender explained just one per cent of the variance.⁴

Whether specific differences between typical male and typical female behaviour (there have always been and always will be people who don't conform to the stereotype) are biological or cultural, it cannot be disputed that behavioural differences commonly exist and it is important, where they do, to address them in couples therapy.

In general, for instance, men tend to talk to *give* information or to report on events and establish their status. They talk about things – cars, work, politics, ideas, research, sport, food, drink – rather than relationships between people. They are more interested in conveying facts, not emotional responses. They are goal oriented. They focus on solving problems and find it more productive to concentrate on one task at a time. They are less likely to ask for help or directions. Men compete.

Women, on the other hand, talk to *get* information and to get into rapport and connect with other people. They talk about *people* rather than *things*. They convey feelings and details and are relationship oriented. Who they know and what they know about other people is more interesting to them.

But, although the thinking strategies do commonly differ between the sexes, they don't differ nearly so much as the emotional strategies we each use.

Because women, on average, are more in touch with their feelings, they are generally regarded as being more sensitive, *warmer* and, as the current phrase has it, emotionally intelligent. Indeed, the acts of reading the subtleties in children's mood changes, and comforting and nurturing them, are in all cultures better done (on the whole) by mothers. The father's role is nurturing but usually in a different manner. As their children grow, men play with them in a more physical and adventurous way, with emphasis on risk taking predominating, rather than female concerns for security and safety. The male interaction with offspring has the quality of apprenticeship about it. Consequently, for this and other reasons, men are typically characterized as being *colder* and less emotional than women.

Young boys are encouraged by parents and wider society to show emotional restraint, thus keeping their attention off their emotions and their focus outwards. Girls, on the other hand, are allowed, and indeed encouraged, to express their emotions. This difference between the sexes, with men on the whole more skilled in controlling and holding back emotions and women more skilled at expressing and putting emotions into words, is at the root of much contemporary marital conflict.[5]

The fact that, in arguments, male blood pressure and heart rate tend to rise significantly higher than in females, and stay higher for much longer, is at the root of why a man typically prefers to stonewall or withdraw when his female partner is upset about something. Men may stay silent or leave the room because they are trying desperately to keep a lid on emotional arousal. They have learned that, if they verbalize their feelings and get angry, they will lose control of the ability to think straight; their blood pressure will go up even more; and they will put themselves in danger of having a heart attack or even of becoming violent, in a crude attempt to resolve their distress. But, because women have an equal need to do exactly the opposite and so want to vent their feelings, this typical male behaviour winds females up and a spiral of misunderstanding can easily develop.

Identifying as...

We have been talking here about heterosexual behaviour differences. Behaviours typically associated with males and with females are on a continuum, and, therefore, much that has been said above will apply to individuals in homosexual relationships, too. Increasingly, it seems, there is an acceptance that there are an extraordinary number of genders, with, at the time of writing, the acronym LGBTQIA+ used as a collective term for people identifying as gay, lesbian, bisexual, transgender, queer, intersex, asexual and pansexual. Gender identity, from this perspective, is viewed as something that is not fixed, can change over time and reflects how one sees oneself, rather than the sexual characteristics one was born with. This may be empowering for some and possibly clutched at desperately as a lifeline by others who, for many reasons, often unrecognized even by themselves, are struggling to fit in with the norms of their society. What is important is that they are supported to feel *truly* comfortable with themselves, whatever that might mean. As we have seen, adopting an identity for reasons such as the need for attention, for belonging and for status is not a healthy way to get these needs met.

'Identifying' as something is a concept that has gained much currency, albeit its validity is disputed by many as well. So men who identify as women, for instance, may be allowed into women-only spaces. In Scotland, MSPs voted at the end of 2022 to require people to be legally treated as the opposite sex on the basis of self-identification only (ie no need, as previously, to have a medical diagnosis of gender dysphoria and show proof of having lived as a member of the desired gender for at least two years previously). This led to political shamefacedness early in 2023, when Scotland's then First Minister Nicola Sturgeon was forced to back down as a result of uproar and reject the right of a rapist, convicted as a male and then identifying as female, to serve the sentence in a women's jail.

Identifying as someone of the opposite sex leads some to want to change gender, either to live entirely as a person of the chosen sex while still physically a member of the opposite one, or having surgery to make the transition more complete. While there have always been people who feel that they were born into the wrong sex, the number has rocketed, particularly since the rise of organisations keen to support/encourage transitioning, the easy access to such information through social media and, as noted at least anecdotally by therapists, the unprecedented restraints of the covid-19 lockdown period, which led to much mental upheaval among young people, as described earlier in this book. Many girls who express a wish to transition have been noted to be on the autistic spectrum and, therefore, quite likely to be experiencing a sense of 'not fitting in', the source of which they may or may not have correctly identified. The National Autistic Society has stated that there is some evidence of a link between autism and gender dysphoria.

But it isn't just about gender. An analysis of 168 million Americans' census forms between 2000 and 2010 indicated that 10 million people identified their racial or ethnic background differently from one census to the next.[6] And, according to an item on the UK Radio 4 statistics programme, *More or Less*, in January 2023, very many people identify as being of the religion they were born into, even when they don't follow its teaching. This was found to be most commonly the case across the world for Catholics who no longer went to mass.

Whatever one's personal views on all this (and personal views are exceedingly polarized), clearly there is now considerable fluidity in how people view themselves, with identities far from fixed in their own minds. This is not always benign. Alarmingly, in 2023, a condition previously known as body integrity identity disorder (whereby someone rejects one of their limbs or organs, such as their eyes – commonly a result of damage to the area of the brain concerned with body configuration) started to garner a lot of mainstream publicity and attract unhealthy attention as a movement known as transableism (identifying as disabled), which had previously been little known. Some people might choose to identify as disabled by using a wheelchair when physically unnecessary; others might beg surgeons to remove the offending limb, in the name of transabled rights, or take drastic action themselves, as in the case of a woman who deliberately blinded herself with bleach. Clearly certain forms of 'identification' are likely to reflect serious underlying psychological distress and should not be accepted at face value. In *Time to Think*, a forensic analysis of the debacle that unfolded at the Tavistock Clinic's Gender Identity Development Service (GIDS), which was closed down in 2022), the author mentions the case of a young person identifying both as another gender and another ethnicity completely different from their own, who was prescribed potentially damaging puberty blockers after the briefest of assessments.[7]

Another concept associated with identity that has now found its way into common usage is 'neurodivergence', which describes people whose brains work differently from those who are deemed neurotypical. The word derives from the term 'neurodiversity', which was coined decades ago, in 1998, by Australian sociologist Judy Singer, who used it to make the case that people's brains develop very differently and therefore there can be no 'normal'.[8] It didn't catch on at the time. She has since updated her definition to claim for it a place within biodiversity, saying that neurodiversity is a feature of Earth as a whole, since humans have colonized all Earth's ecosystems. She also clarifies that she coined the term neurodiversity as a political term, to empower neurological minorities, and that it isn't a scientific term, nor is it a diagnosis.[9]

While a group of people can be described as neurodiverse, an individual in this category is referred to as neurodivergent. However, neurodiversity does not appear to be used to include what is often called neurotypical behaviour; nor, indeed, other relatively recently identified differences such as aphantasia, a term applied to those who do not imagine in the conventional way by visualization.[10] Instead it encompasses conditions such as autism, Asperger's (now termed, in the American Psychiatric Association's *Diagnostic and Statistical Manual of Mental Disorders* autistic spectrum disorder level 1), dyslexia, dyscalculia, dyspraxia, attention deficit hyperactivity disorder (ADHD), Tourette syndrome and even obsessive compulsive disorder (OCD), which might more usually be thought of as a treatable anxiety disorder.

It is, of course, empowering to celebrate difference and to focus on the strengths that individuals possess, rather than the deficits, and there is now much help and advice on this available, particularly on the internet. For instance, people diagnosed with ADHD may be highly creative and empathetic and have strong problem-solving abilities, even while struggling with traits such as impulsivity and paying attention. People with dyslexia may struggle to read but excel at picturing 3D objects, leading them to do well in jobs like graphic design and engineering. Some psychiatrists and psychologists, however, have also argued that ADHD or, indeed, autistic spectrum disorder, is not a valid diagnosis and reflects differences in behaviour across different populations.[11] And there can be extremes to each presentation, which makes it much harder, sometimes perhaps impossible, to reap any benefit from 'difference'. This is most marked in the condition currently termed autism, and it is to autism and Asperger's (as we shall continue to call the latter, as it is still the term most used in common parlance) that we shall turn now. For the rest of this chapter we shall be putting forward an explanation for the behaviours found at either end of the autistic spectrum, which may be useful in terms of conceptualizing these conditions and helping those who struggle with them.

Water babies and our distant aquatic past

Marie is Joe's autistic sister. "I remember, as a little boy," he says, "that, whenever my mother went out with my little sister, people stopped to admire her golden ringlets and beautiful face. She was about two years old. My mother felt very proud. But it soon became apparent that Marie had problems. She spoke of herself always in the third person, then gradually lost her speech altogether and began making strange, ritualistic movements, continually whirling and turning. She was also endlessly fascinated by water. At every opportunity, she made for the stream that ran close to our home and my mother was terrified she would drown. Back then, in the 1950s, we were given no name for Marie's condition. It was only a quarter of a century later, when I became a psychologist, that I recognized Marie was autistic. Even her outstanding beauty was a classic feature."

Autism is still viewed as a mysterious condition. The National Autistic Society describes it as "a lifelong developmental disability which affects how people communicate and interact with the world." The many different symptoms can occur by themselves or in combination with other conditions and, because children with autism – like all children – vary widely in their abilities and behaviour, each symptom may manifest differently in each child. It used to be thought that boys were four times more likely than girls to be autistic. However, it is now recognised that symptoms can be masked in girls, as they may be better able to do what is socially required of them to fit in, although finding the effort exhausting.[12] Still, boys are three times more likely to be diagnosed with autism than girls.[13]

In more than 40 years of extensive research into autism, no insights have been developed to explain the full range of strange, ritualistic, self-obsessed and sometimes very destructive behaviours associated with the condition. Joe's theory, for the first time, does explain them, and also suggests which approaches to treatment are most likely to be successful. Furthermore, it explains the origin of many normal human gestures, feelings and emotional expressions. It has become known as the 'water babies' theory.

The central argument is that childhood autism results from a human infant's failure to develop the responses and patterns of behaviour common to mammals, but specifically the human responses that orientate children in their environment and form the basis for all subsequent learning. As we have seen, one of the greatest achievements of mammalian evolution was the development of social life – in other words, the development of communication and cooperation between members of the group, which afforded greater protection to the group as a whole and allowed a longer period of development for the group's young. This, in turn, enabled more learning to take place during the lengthier maturing period, resulting in greater flexibility and potential for further evolution.

But in autistic children, premature brain changes alter the course of their development.[14] As well as an overall increase in size, there is a change in the white matter connections between areas in the brain.[15,16] One area which is particularly affected is the orbitofrontal cortex, which in humans and primates, and to a lesser extent in rodents, governs how we respond to the emotions, appetites and urges which direct our behaviour in social situations.[17] The premature growth of the orbitofrontal cortex and its white matter connections appears to reduce the window of opportunity for autistic children to learn flexible social responses.[18,19] And in the absence of these responses, autistic children have to rely on a more basic system of orientations that are present in normal development but usually play a very minor part.

In the transition state between fish and reptiles, which subsequently allowed evolution into mammals, there was an amphibious phase. The amphibians, of course, needed two sets of responses: those appropriate for land and those appropriate for water. As mammals evolved more and more responses appropriate for the land, those responses became ever more dominant. But they did not lose entirely the earlier responses that were suited for the sea. Instead, these more primitive responses continued to play an important role in evolution, in many cases providing the initial behavioural response on which adaptations could be built. Evolution does not start from scratch to construct each new species. Rather it builds on, and holds on to, whatever was found useful in the ancestral life force. This is an important point.

Fishy features

One obvious example of fishlike behaviour, which almost all mammals seem to perform without learning, is swimming. Most mammals' spines, and therefore their bodily bulk, are parallel to the ground when walking – the natural position for swimming. Primates are among the least successful at swimming because they have evolved to stand upright. Very young children, however, show a swimming reflex up till the age of six months, at which point it is repressed to allow walking to develop.

There are some features of the human embryo and foetus that are also present in other mammals and in fish. The gill arches, for example, which appear at a certain stage of foetal development, support breathing in a fish but go on to become the bones of the inner ear in humans. The arteries of the human embryo are at first very similar to those of fish and the human embryo also has a tail.[20] By stroking the sole of a 14-week-old foetus's foot with a hair, it is possible to elicit quite complex and coordinated movements. These include bending of the big toe, slight bending of the sole of the foot, fanning of the other toes (creating a lobe-like shape typical of the fish that mammals descended from) and stretching of the leg.[21] This is exactly the movement a fish would make if it wanted to move its pelvic fin away from something dangerous or unpleasant.

Interestingly, young children make a similar movement and shape with their hands when they want to be rejecting. The renowned ethologist Niko Tinbergen published a photograph that showed how a very young child showing displeasure with his mother adopted the same unusual posture commonly used by autistic children – hands raised in front of the head with fingers fanned out, one palm facing inwards, the other outwards, the end fingers slightly bent and the child's head leaning towards the outward pointing hand.[22] Tinbergen's point was that behaviours typical of autistic children can also be seen in neurotypical children when they are under stress. The position described, however, is exactly that which we would expect if the hands were fins and the child were in water and wanted to swim away. Again, the hands are held in a lobe shape, characteristic of our fish ancestors' fins.

Adults, particularly from cultures given to gesticulation, often adopt a similar gesture as a non-verbal signal of disagreement during conversation. One palm is brought up to the face, palm outwards, with the head turned sideways from the other person, while the other hand makes a swift downward movement, often ending by striking a desk or some other object. The effect of these movements in water would be movement away from the speaker.

Adults may use this sort of gesticulation when they are agreeing with each other too; they lean forwards and make circular flicking movements of their hands towards the speaker. If sitting down, the gesture may finish with the slapping of a thigh. Waving in greeting or farewell, the ritualized way we show our warm feelings towards the person approaching or departing, is also based on the instinctive fishlike movement of the fins which in water would bring us closer to them.

Although these gestures are clearly communication signals, they are nevertheless built upon the more basic instinctive response of automatically moving towards or away from different stimuli. Fish use either bodily movements or movements of their fins to propel themselves through water. The former is their main method of movement, although the fins are in constant use because they act as brakes and aerofoils as well. While we humans can consciously inhibit gesticulatory movements if we wish, and express our reactions with words, the ancient part of our brain still urges us towards some form of movement. We may not physically move away from someone when we disagree, but we may still do the equivalent of moving our fins, because we are not consciously aware of what such actions mean any more.

If autism results from a baby's failure to develop the mammalian behavioural response patterns (templates) appropriate for it, then, it could be that the aquatic response patterns, which are always present but peripheral in a neurotypical baby, will come to the fore and provide the basis of the child's perception of reality and its place within it. It would follow that such an outcome must be due to a failure in the programming of the instinctive basis of these patterns into the child. Michel Jouvet's findings[23] that the role of rapid eye movement (REM) sleep in the foetus, newborn and young is to programme the central nervous system to organize instinctive behaviour is, therefore, crucial to understanding why these mammalian patterns are missing in autism.

As we have explained at length, the REM state is not only concerned with the programming of genetic knowledge in the brain before birth and in early life. It also plays an important role throughout our lives, when we dream each night, in maintaining our instinctual mammalian integrity. We would therefore expect children with autism to have primitive patterns of REM sleep compared with those of normally developing children of the same age. This is exactly what has been found.[24]

We have shown that instincts are programmed in the form of analogues, such as the instinctive template for language, for example, which has to be matched to the languages spoken in a particular culture. But when this programming is compromised or damaged in some way, as it is with autistic children who are missing typical social and perceptual orientations, they are obliged to fall back on whatever instinctive templates or orientations are available to them as a means to connect to reality. These will necessarily be non-mammalian. And if those templates are suited to a water environment, then autistic children are going to show behaviour that appears to be puzzling and bizarre to the rest of the human race. They are likely to feel as though they are living in a totally alien world. Indeed, if we read the self-descriptions of those exceptionally talented autistic people that have been able to communicate something of their experience to us, it is obvious that this is so.

Jim Sinclair, an autistic adult, has said: "Being autistic does not mean being inhuman. But it does mean being alien. It means that what is normal for other people is not normal for me and what is normal for me is not normal for other people. In some ways, I am terribly ill equipped to survive in this world, like an extraterrestrial stranded without an orientation model."[25]

Temple Grandin, acknowledged superstar among autistic people, early on described herself as "an anthropologist on Mars", providing Oliver Sacks with the title of his bestselling book on autism.[26]

The five areas of disturbance identified in the 1970s as typical characteristic symptoms of autism are: motility, perception, relating, speech and language, and developmental rate.[27] It is possible to look at the typical behaviours of an autistic child and relate them very closely to behaviours that would have been typical of our aquatic ancestors.

Autistic fishlike behaviours

Motility disturbances are characterized by both excitable and inhibited behaviours that have been described as follows: "The motor excitation involves hand flapping, excited whirling and circling, darting and lunging movements and toe walking. In contrast, motor inhibition is manifested by posturing and prolonged inhibition."[28] A better description of fishlike behaviour is hard to imagine. Toe walking makes sense, as the feet have evolved from fishes' fins, which were unbent. There would consequently be a desire to have feet bent as little as possible – or at least not more than that required for a lobe shape, the shape of the fins in our fish ancestors.

Descriptions of autistic children's behaviours almost always include a fascination with spinning, flicking and rocking movements. They are not interested in the real purpose of different objects and toys but in the role something might play in their own ritualistic, stereotyped movements. A toy car may, for instance, be used solely for spinning its wheels. Autistic children often become extremely dextrous at manipulating objects so that they spin. Plates, boxes and assorted other objects will be sent twirling across the floor to the evident delight of the child. Not only will autistic children spin objects, but they will also spin themselves around for long periods and without any apparent dizziness.

The tail fin of a fish works a bit like a propeller but with the tail being swept from side to side instead of being on a rotary screw. It would seem highly plausible that the spinning dance of autistic children is an attempt to replicate this movement. Their pleasure in spinning objects may spring from an innate pleasure in the perception of spinning movements similar to that of fins. This can clearly be seen in the following description of an autistic child's behaviour: "As Raum leaned over the objects he set in motion, he would rock as if one with them. His hands and fingers responded with erratic and jerky patterns of movement."[29]

The flicking movement which autistic children often make when holding string or other suitable objects can be seen as an effort to replicate the snakelike undulating movements of a fish as it courses through water. The following description of an autistic child's behaviour illustrates this vividly: "She sits with a long chain in her hand. Snaking it up and down, up and down for 20 minutes, half an hour – until someone comes, moves her or feeds her."[30]

Some autistic children learn to stimulate themselves with only partly circular movements, for instance by rapidly turning the pages of a book – reflecting, perhaps, the fins' only partly circular motions. Some, before they have even learned to stand, perform a circular dance on their knees; "circling round and round a spot on the floor in mysterious self-absorbed delight," as the same author described it.[31]

Unusual movements of the hands are often most noticeable when autistic children become excited; they may flap their hands and arms, jump up and down and make facial grimaces. (This sort of behaviour is also seen in neurotypical children when they are intensely excited while watching an event they cannot participate in.) When fish get excited, they gulp in more water to obtain more oxygen, appearing, as they do so, to make facial grimaces. They flap their fins more too, to create more speed. Interestingly, excited hand flapping, posturing and twirling have been noted as the usual reactions of an autistic child to spinning objects; as a result, spinning objects were often presented by experts as an aid to diagnosis of the condition.[32]

Autistic children usually withdraw from human contact, failing to raise their arms when they are about to be picked up and frequently showing an aversion to physical contact.[33] Yet they love certain types of rough games that involve contact; these include being thrown into the air, bounced on someone's knee and being tickled. The movement of the fish's tail fin, which repeatedly kicks the fish forward, must be a bit like being bounced on a knee. Fish have most of their sense organs running along the side of the body and it may be that, for the autistic child, being tickled along the sides of the body and under the arms represents an innate anticipated source of stimulation.

Autistic children's love of rocking back and forth may be seen as a gross attempt to replicate the fish's primary body movement when swimming. The fact that they frequently make a backwards and forwards movement, as well as the side to side swaying movement of fish, can be explained by evolutionary changes: our main muscles are now in front and behind the spinal column rather than laterally sited as in fish, and therefore forward and backward rocking may provide more powerful stimulation than sideways movement.

The sudden lunging and darting movements of autistic children are clearly characteristic of fish behaviour and the position in which many hold their arms when unoccupied is very similar to that of the lobe-shaped pectoral fins of our fish ancestors. The following description illustrates this vividly: "Many of these children hold their arms in a special way when unoccupied. They have their elbows bent and their hands near together in front of them, dropping at the wrists with fingers slightly curled."[34]

Autistic children are fascinated by surfaces; they love to feel cool, smooth plastic, smooth wood and soft fur (sometimes rubbing their faces against someone's fur coat while ignoring the wearer). The cool, smooth textureless sensations which they evoke may resemble the sensation we experience when we place our faces or hands in water. Autistic children are highly fascinated by water too. They like to pour it endlessly through their fingers or, sometimes, from one container to another. Their love of water is so pronounced that they may without thought take off their clothes in public so that they may sit in an inviting pool of water.

When, as an adult, Joe went to visit his sister Marie, she didn't recognize him as her brother but she was keen to persuade him to follow her, which she achieved by staring at the knobs of doors they arrived at, to encourage him to open them for her. In this way they progressed down many dark corridors until eventually they came to a little room, empty except for a sink and a single tap. She indicated that she wanted Joe to turn on the tap (neither in the opening of doors or turning on of taps was it natural for her to use her own hands as tools). When the water was running, she was deliriously happy.

Autistic children commonly refuse to eat any but two or three specific foods.[35] Young fish also eat only certain foods and continue to seek these foods out from an abundant supply of food items.[36] Difficulties in getting autistic children to eat solid food have frequently been reported over the decades[37] and one father has described how his son nearly choked to death when he was given solid food at an age when normally developing children can chew without difficulty.[38] Interestingly, a classic book on Palaeozoic fish[39] states that rhipidistian fish, believed to be our ancestors, were predators that swallowed their food whole, without chewing.

An insensitivity to cold is common in autistic children. They may happily run out of doors in winter with no clothes on. Fish, of course, are cold-blooded creatures not as sensitive to cold as warm-blooded animals.

Autistic children may indulge in self-mutilation, biting or picking at parts of their own bodies or bashing their heads against walls or floors. Such self-destructive behaviours are usually performed as a form of aggression, designed to keep others away and prevent interference from them. In this respect, their behaviour is similar to that of fish, which, in normal circumstances, rarely fight another fish. Instead they put on aggressive displays by beating the water with their tail fins, after which one or other withdraws. (One researcher has pointed out that autistic children may begin the action of striking someone who has aroused their anger but can never actually go through with it.[40])

Not surprisingly, then, the best way of treating self-destructive behaviour is to leave the child alone. When mild electric shocks were applied by one researcher as a deterrent, the undesirable activity increased – which is explained in this theory as an increase in aggressive display in the face of increased 'aggression' from the researcher.[41]

The parallels between aggressive behaviour in autistic children and aggressive displays in fish may not be so obvious when it comes to other forms of self-abuse, such as pulling out their own hair and biting their own hands. However, if the 'water babies' theory is right, these could be attempts to provide the kind of stimulation usually provided by being in water – for instance, the experience of resistance and of water being taken in by mouth (and exhaled through the gills).

A summary of motility disturbances compiled in the 1970s for the National Society for Autistic Children (now National Autistic Society) cited the following habits common to autistic children: rocking; head banging; jumping; twisting, flapping and writhing of arms and legs, especially when excited; spinning; facial grimaces of all kinds; odd ways of walking, especially on tiptoe; unusual hand movements, e.g. turning hand with outstretched fingers in front of the face; and extreme pleasure in bodily movement such as swinging, rocking, riding in cars, etc. We suggest that all these behaviours are well explained by Joe's 'water babies' theory.

The second category of disturbance identified is autistic children's disturbances of perception. These children are frequently thought to be deaf because they show no response to loud noises such as the sound of plates crashing to the floor, yet turn sharply at the slight rustle of a favourite sweet being unwrapped behind them.[42] (Curiously, scientists at one time thought fish were deaf.)

The explanation for the autistic child's apparent deafness may lie in a characteristic that is common to all of their behaviour – that is, their responses do not seem to generalize. For example, they may readily grasp an object that they can spin but will let fall most other objects that are handed to them, as if they lacked the ability to hold on to them. Many writers have commented on the autistic child's reluctance to grasp an object firmly to use it as a tool (clearly, Marie demonstrated that behaviour). So hearing and grasping may only occur when there is something the child particularly wants to do with an object. (In Marie's case, even though the doors and taps served as means to an end, it was only the water she was interested in.) There is no generalized reflex to use hand dexterity to explore or interact with the environment. Fish don't use their fins to explore their environment, nor do they use them as tools. It may therefore be that autistic children's reluctance to explore the environment may be due to the absence of an instinct to use limbs for that purpose.

They may also lack the mammalian-developed ability to localize sound, responding only to associations that have been conditioned. Fish have a very poor ability to locate sound but do have sensitivity to frequency vibrations. An increase in vibrations would very likely mean the fast approach of another fish, therefore one likely to be a predator. Similarly, sounds an autistic child enjoys at a lower level often cause distress when increased. Autistic children love various types of music, responding particularly to the rhythm and vibration. So, it seems, do fish. On an edition of the BBC's *That's Life* programme many years ago, a variety of music was played through a microphone placed in an aquarium. The fish huddled excitedly round the microphone for the most rhythmic, vibrating music and showed little interest in other types.

Autistic children also appear to have problems seeing, and are sometimes thought to be shortsighted or even blind. They very commonly give the impression of looking through people and may show no reaction to new people or new things. They often also walk or even ride a bicycle without looking where they are going, bumping into objects as if they didn't see them. Contrary to the impression given, however, they do not actively avoid looking at people and in fact look at them longer than they look at objects.[43] The mistaken impression is due to their habit of darting glances and then looking away. This is quite alien to the way neurotypical people use sight when relating to others.

What autistic children are particularly sensitive to is movement and outline, which is how they tend to recognize objects.[44] Fish, in an ever-moving environment, are of course especially sensitive to movement, and a sensitivity to outline helps in a fish's fantastic ability to find its way and recognize other fish and food in an environment where it is frequently difficult to see. When autistic children are spun round in a chair, they, unlike neurotypical children, do not show nystagmus (involuntary jerky movements of the eye), unless the spinning is being done in the dark. This accords with the 'water babies' theory, whereby autistic children would naturally use their eyes to observe movement and outline, which would not be possible in the dark.

Autistic children also pay more attention to what they can touch, taste and smell, rather than to what they can hear or see.[45] One pair of researchers found that: "if a buzzer was sounded and simultaneously a small tug was given on a piece of string tied around the child's ankle, autistic children, unlike other children tested, were more likely to attend to the thing they felt rather than the thing they heard".[46]

Autistic children's fascination with anything that shines or twinkles, such as silver or shiny paper, may be explained by a predisposition to encounter the patterning of light refracted in water. Fish view the world through a medium that has very different optical properties from those of the atmosphere. Light rays entering the water are refracted. Our fish ancestors had a pineal opening on the top of their heads which was sensitive to light and which possibly helped protect them from overhead attack, in that an approaching predator would block out some of that light. Interestingly, autistic children often react to sudden changes in illumination with great fear.[47]

Autistic children are endlessly fascinated by their own hands and feet, looking at them as if they are strange and puzzling. They frequently, as already described, place their hands under their faces in the position and shape of the pectoral fins of our fish ancestors. It might well be, then, that they are confounded by their hands' ability to appear in places other than those in which they expect them to be permanently located. Similarly, their legs can do so much more than instinctively they expect them to be able to do. Their fascination may be rather akin to what our own would be if we found our limbs could suddenly detach themselves and perform actions some distance away from us.

As might be expected, autistic children usually lack the mammalian reflex of lifting the arms in anticipation of being picked up. Their aversion to human contact, other than in tickling and rough play, has its counterpart in fish behaviour. Fish avoid physical contact except in the spawning season.[48]

It would be surprising, in terms of the 'water babies' theory, if language, that most recent of evolutionary acquisitions and one uniquely geared to social interaction, should have its development unimpeded in autistic children. Fish have a limited sound production capability, which has been shown to have some communication value for some species. The sounds are made by such means as the expulsion of air and the grinding of teeth.[49] Some autistic children never learn to speak, while about a half learn to say a few words or phrases, often tending to repeat these at random (echolalia). Repetitious sound, such as that induced by the fish's body moving through water, may be innately satisfying. In children who do progress from this stage of speech, most continue to show severe disturbance in their pattern of language acquisition, compared with normally developing children.

Disturbed rate of development, the fifth and final category identified as symptomatic of autism, shows itself in deviations from the normal sequences in motor, social and language milestones. For instance, an autistic child can sit without support very early on but shows delay in being able to pull up to a stand. This makes sense in terms of the theory: the autistic child usually shows no orientation to use hands as tools or legs to stand upright on.

Spatial intelligence can be precocious, with autistic children able to do jigsaws upside down – in other words, paying attention only to the shapes, not the clues in the pattern and picture. Many fish species have an excellent ability to recognize a variety of shapes.[50] Autistic children have a remarkable ability to find their way back to places after just one visit or to locate objects they haven't seen for years. This calls to mind the equally remarkable ability of some species of fish to return to their spawning ground after crossing many thousands of miles.

Oceanic feelings of transcendence

In descriptions of autism, there are frequent references to the Buddha-like serenity which autistic children show during their periods of self-absorption. One parent said of his son: "In almost every way his contentment and solitude seem to suggest a profound and inner peace. He was a 17-month-old Buddha contemplating another dimension."[51] The meditation practices of the East could easily have been inspired by autistic behaviour. The whirling dervishes, for instance, induced trance by spinning themselves. Certain types of meditation involve staring at a certain object for a long period of time or the repetition of a mantra. The state that these practices induce has been described as a state of thoughtless awareness in which the emotions have been stilled – an apt description of much of the autistic child's reality. In *Ecstasy*,[52] a cult book in the 1960s, the phrase "oceanic feeling" was used to describe the feelings of transcendence which adherents of these techniques claim to induce, and identified walking by water as one of the triggers.

Aldous Huxley's thesis that there is a functional similarity between certain transcendental experiences and the effects of certain hallucinogenic drugs is also relevant, and would fit with the water babies hypothesis that the more basic part of the brain stimulated, though normally inhibited, is sensitive to the interrelationship between rhythm and form. Autistic children often flap their hands up and down and make lunging or jumping movements while standing on their toes. In our remote evolutionary past, such movements may have been associated with swimming. Some particularly sensitive people may, under the influence of hallucinogenic drugs, have an overwhelming desire to carry out such movements. Unaware that these movements were evolved for free passage through water, they may conclude they can fly. This might explain why some people, under the influence of these drugs, have tragically leapt to their deaths.

If, as Joe's theory argues, autistic behaviours are the legacy of our evolutionary past, we should expect to see significant correlations between human bodies and those of our aquatic ancestors. And this is indeed the case. In his beautifully written book, *Your Inner Fish*, paleontologist and evolutionary biologist Neil Shubin describes the discovery of Tiktaalik, an extinct, fossilised, bony four-limbed fish.[53] The organisation of Tiktaalik's body reveals that when it crawled ashore, approximately 375 million years ago, the pattern of a fish's body was preserved and passed on by amphibians, to those of land-dwelling vertebrates [54,55,56,57] So, fish fins were the precursor for the wrists and connected bones which later became human hands, while our heads are organised like long extinct jawless fish. And, while at an early stage the human foetus has gill arches just like fish, these develop into the top lip, palate and jaw. The torturous path that our cranial nerves take is closely related to the development of fish brains in our ancestors.

Help for the 'water babies'

If autistic children are almost inhabiting another world, this one unfortunately leaves them handicapped – like fish out of water. How much an autistic child can be helped may depend upon whether certain templates aren't present at all or whether they are present but the ability to read them has been blocked by some insult to the brain experienced before or after birth. If it is only the ability to read the templates which is blocked, then it should sometimes be possible to stimulate those templates and create significantly improved functioning. A successful therapeutic approach must therefore involve making behaviours that are rewarding to the neurotypical child, because of instinctive mammalian orientations, also rewarding to the autistic child. To do this we must build a bridge between the autistic child's world and the neurotypical human world. In other words, the therapist or parent must enter the autistic child's world, using whatever orientations the child has access to, in order to connect them to our world.

Spinning alongside an autistic child, for instance, encourages them to notice you. That can be the first step towards building rapport and leading them, in their turn, to mirror more usual behaviours.

In another graphic example of this technique, a mother involved herself in the activity of a two-year-old autistic child who spent hours staring into space while rubbing the pile on a particular spot of carpet. "We had the girl's mother place her hand next to her, right on the favourite stretch of floor. The child pushed it away but her mother gently pushed it back. Again she pushed, again the hand returned. A cat and mouse game ensued and, by the third day of this rudimentary interaction, the little girl was smiling while pushing her mother's hand away. From this tiny beginning grew emotional connection and relationship."[58]

Methods which concentrate on the systematic application of conditioning techniques to produce in sequence those orientations necessary for the natural development of intelligence and emotional behaviour have, in some cases, resulted in significant improvements, including intellectual, emotional and linguistic ability comparable to or higher than that of neurotypical children. These have included the Lovaas technique, the most coercive of this kind of approach. A gentler approach, known originally as the Option Method, adapted many of behaviour therapy's techniques and made particular use of imitating the child's behaviour[59] but can be overly demanding on those delivering it. Authors of one critique of the method wrote, "The approach stresses the need to accept behaviour and impute meaning. Within the Option approach adults act on what children do rather than on interpretations of behaviour, they are interventionists and use rewards to reinforce desired behaviour. Option states that no behaviour is judged, yet in practice some behaviours are deliberately misinterpreted, or almost ignored, while others are welcomed and acted upon enthusiastically. A noted feature of the approach is the intensity of the intervention as well as the demand on parents to organize and run such an intensive programme over an extended period of months or years."[60]

Some approaches concentrate on only one of the deficits experienced by autistic children. Holding therapy was developed in 1983 as a means of combating the autistic child's tendency to avoid physical contact. The parent or carer is encouraged to hold the child on their lap, wrapping their arms firmly around them and gazing at them in a positive loving way. If the child struggles, even this is praised. Famous animal behaviourist Temple Grandin, who was diagnosed with autism as a child, developed a 'squeeze machine' to provide a firm pressure sensation which, she found, reduced her own stress levels. Machines which help regulate the sensory system in a similar way have since become commercially available for children with sensory processing difficulties, suggesting that being held or restrained in a self-chosen way can indeed be enormously helpful.

As we have seen, tantrums and self-mutilation can most effectively be dealt with by removing the child and placing him or her somewhere on their own. Similarly, stereotyped behaviour in young children is most likely to decrease if ignored, as the child finds increasing satisfaction in more usual human behaviours.

Older autistic children often develop bizarre fears and behaviours acquired as a result of associations with some experience they find unpleasant. In such cases, the technique of 'flooding' can work. One little girl, for instance, was terrified of the colour red and threw a screaming fit if ever she was put on a red bus. It is possible the fear developed on an occasion when she heard a red bus revving up, a sound many autistic children find frightening. Her parents cured her of her fear by saturating their house with red, despite her protestations, so that it became a major and unavoidable factor in her life.

All such approaches help induce the orientations that the autistic child is missing and, in turn, may stimulate the interactions necessary for the normal mental and emotional development of the child.

Of course, many other interventions have been developed, and will continue to be developed, which may help young people with severe autism, and guidance on this can be found on the National Autistic Society website. Importantly, the society stresses that all interventions should be person-centred, promote the individual's dignity, keep them safe, healthy and happy and enable them to do the things they love, never trying to make someone less 'autistic' and never involving punishment.[61]

Autism is a continuum disorder and we can learn a lot from people at the high end, like Temple Grandin, who function in some ways highly effectively and creatively. Such people are usually said to have Asperger's syndrome. Civilisation owes much to the original thinking of gifted people on the less severe end of the spectrum. Professor Michael Fitzgerald of Trinity College, Dublin, published a series of books outlining this contribution, which includes such people as Charles Darwin, Isaac Newton, Albert Einstein, William Butler Yeats, Lewis Carroll and numerous other creative geniuses.[62]

A highly eloquent and knowledgeable former colleague and friend of ours, Tim Jacobs, has Asperger's syndrome and wrote an article for the journal *Human Givens* about what living with the syndrome is like.[63] (This led to his appearance on a BBC radio programme on the subject.)

He told us that one of the chief limitations he experienced was 'straight-line thinking', a term he coined. He had gradually become aware that his mind leapt from one thing to another without any moderating influence. This, of course, had a significant impact on his behaviour. Everyone who worked with him knew this to be true, merely by observation. He found it almost impossible to hold two or more lines of thought in his mind at the same time and appraise and prioritize them to see how one thought or perception might be affecting the other. It is this aspect of the other end of the autistic spectrum that we will now consider.

When context is missing

Most people realize instinctively that there is no single, always correct answer to any of the following questions: Where is a good place to live? What is the polite way to greet someone? What is a good gift for a neighbour? What will a person feel like when being looked at? Is it all right to touch someone's hair? Which job shall I do first?

This is because answers to such questions depend upon context: it is context that lights up our perception about a situation and influences our responses to it. Most of us just know this and read context instinctively. There are some people, however, who don't; reading context is *always* difficult for them. We spent several years puzzling over clients who did not respond well to normal psychological interventions and also about some of the behaviour of our more eccentric acquaintances. Over a number of years we came to realize that the common denominator was that, as well as exhibiting other signs of being on the autistic spectrum, they continually showed context blindness.

Of course, everyone can be context blind on occasion, especially when highly emotional, tired or behaving selfishly, but most of us revert to recognizing context fairly easily when circumstances change our state again. We are talking here about the *enduring* condition of being unable to see how one variable influences another.

Context blindness explains what people across the autistic spectrum have in common, whether they are physicists or engineers with high-functioning autism (or Asperger's syndrome) or severely autistic people who are unable either to communicate or take care of themselves. It seemed remarkably odd to us that a person who needs constant specialist help and assisted housing can be included in the same category as a professor of physics, say, or a gifted poet or musician, or a computer programmer who is married with a family – all individuals who, despite having Asperger's syndrome, have managed to make an accommodation with the world and have learned enough of the 'rules' to function fairly efficiently and relate to people to some degree. The one factor that unites everyone on the spectrum is that they are missing the ability to read context reliably.

Professor Simon Baron-Cohen of Cambridge University, one of the world's leading authorities on autism, has suggested that there is a systemizing brain (usually associated with the male thinking style) and an empathizing brain (traditionally associated with female behaviour) and that we all have varying amounts of each. He has provided much evidence for this claim, showing how these sex differences arise more from biological than cultural causes, and goes so far as to support Dr. Asperger's suggestion that the syndrome is an extreme form of the male brain.[64] However, the case he makes has also been disputed on several grounds.[65] And, after many years of working therapeutically with male and female adults with Asperger's syndrome, as well as interacting with them socially and in business, we also believe that the extreme male brain theory of autism, which does at first seem persuasive, is an insufficient explanation for the various deficiencies seen in this syndrome.

Whilst it is true that men are, generally speaking, more interested in systems than women, and that women are, generally speaking, more interested in human relationships than men, this does not get to the heart of the matter of what is missing in people with autistic spectrum disorder. It does not explain, for example, why many otherwise extremely feminine women show Asperger's traits but many men who are good systematizers don't. It was this sense that the puzzle of autism remained just that, a puzzle, that led us to look back to our evolutionary past to search for new clues.

How does a brain become aware of context?

As we saw in Chapter 2, the evolution of mammals and birds began when creatures developed the ability to generate and maintain a constant internal body temperature, irrespective of the external environmental temperature – popularly known as 'warm-bloodedness'. Reptiles regulate their body temperatures by moving to different places in their environment to get warm or cool down; they can move around quickly only when their blood has heated up and are sluggish when their blood is cold. In contrast, mammals can respond quickly and move around whatever the external temperature.[66] But this greater mobility, flexibility and freedom of behaviour came at a high price: a staggering 80 to 90 per cent of a mammal's energy is spent on maintaining its constant internal temperature. Compared with a similar-sized reptile, which controls its temperature by external means, this means a five-fold increase in energy requirement. Early mammals needed to get around to find plentiful food but also conserve energy wherever possible. They couldn't afford to give way to impulses that would waste energy unnecessarily. So they had to evolve a mechanism that would make them more intelligent in their reactions. If a wild animal automatically chased anything that moved, in case it might be food, it would use up the precious energy required to catch prey and obtain the protein essential for its survival. Mammals had to develop the facility to subject every arousing event to a risk analysis: "Does that noise signify potential food – or danger? Should I hide? Am I likely to succeed in catching that rabbit?" They had to make decisions based on the specific circumstances or *context* they found themselves in – and do so swiftly, as their survival might depend on it. Even if a rabbit might be near enough to chase, it would be wasted effort if a rival could get there first – or fatal, if a bigger predator appeared on the scene, saw you and decided that you would make a better meal than the rabbit.

To see context, we need to be able to attach and detach attention from different objects and events and see them from different viewpoints. The early behaviourists believed that mammals and birds simply responded mechanically to stimuli, but more sophisticated experiments revealed that there is a cognitive component involved in their response, which relates to prior experience. One significant experiment demonstrated that there is a mammalian intelligence that searches for and assesses relationships between different events – some part of the brain has reviewed the history of past experiences of a similar kind.[67] Many subsequent experiments have substantiated this finding. So, millions of years ago, mammals evolved, in effect, a biological form of what computer buffs today call 'parallel processing': a mechanism capable of gauging risk by processing multiple streams of current information, at the same time as unconsciously comparing similar, previous experiences to each new one.

Our colleague Ezra Hewing, in the course of his research into explanations for schizophrenia,[68] brought to our attention the following scientific information, which explains how an early form of parallel processing first arose in vertebrates. Over half a billion years ago, simple vertebrates used to go about their business, chasing rewards, without any means of weighing up the risks and benefits. Then came the evolution of the lamprey worm, a jawless parasite fish with startlingly large teeth, which feeds on the body fluids of fish. These worms were the first known creatures to have evolved basal ganglia, brain structures which allowed them to weigh up risk versus reward – ie when they were likely to become lunch rather than find lunch. All vertebrates alive today have basal ganglia, through which a series of complex chemical messages enable them to encode memories of rewards and memories of dangerous outcomes, so that they can make more informed decisions about whether to chase that rabbit or eat that berry.[69,70,71,72,73,74] They thus have a greater appreciation of context than early predecessors.

Ability to determine context depends upon need. As Hewing has explained, "Fish brains allow for some appreciation of social context, but this appears to be more focused on competition and hierarchy, not cooperation. By contrast, mammals, and especially primates and early humans, had to *collaborate* in social groups in order to have a better chance of survival, which required much greater appreciation of social context. To collaborate we need to appreciate the value of each other's roles and contributions and suppress self-interest. This may well constitute theory of mind, which of course Baron-Cohen identified as lacking in autism."[75]

Context blindness

Appreciating context is something that we take completely for granted today but, millions of years ago, it was the key to surviving and thriving. When we say that the profoundly disabling impairment found throughout the whole autistic spectrum is the inability to perceive context, we mean this mammalian ability to maintain separate streams of attention and switch effortlessly between them to assess the relevance of each to what is currently happening. This can be done only if the brain can dissociate so as to review what it knows about something it has come across before, while still paying attention to that something in the here and now. This function has been ascribed to the structure in the brain known as the anterior cingulate gyrus. However, as shown earlier in the chapter, in autistic children, premature brain changes affect connections between certain brain areas and particularly affected is the orbitofrontal cortex, which, along with the anterior cingulate gyrus, is involved in reward processing and emotion.[76] We contend that this inability to appreciate context is likely to be a common factor across the autistic spectrum.

As one neuroscientist puts it, "This region is active when we need controlled, distributed attention, such as listening to our friend at the party while also watching our colleague dance. It also tells us to forget both of those people and pay close attention to the other side of the room when we sense that potential combatants may start a fight."[77]

'Context blindness' – the inability to switch easily between several foci of attention and track them – is clearly seen, alongside other symptoms, in severe forms of autism (the child transfixed by spinning the wheels on a toy car has no sense of a car's real purpose, for instance) but is the most dominant manifestation in high-achieving people with Asperger's syndrome.

If you can read context, it seems like the most natural thing in the world. You might be talking to Jack about something, for example, but another part of your attention is aware that Jill is listening as well and could read implications into what you are saying that you didn't intend. So, straight away, because you have this awareness, you are able to alter the way you are speaking to take into account Jill's possible reactions too. When you can do this easily, it's difficult to imagine not being able to do it. But people with context blindness can't. As a consequence, they continually misread social cues, upset other people by saying or doing inappropriate things and cause confusion because they mainly rely on literalism and logical thinking or random associations. They also have difficulties understanding complex metaphors.

Other theories

Leading researchers in the field of autism have also linked the word 'context' to Asperger's syndrome. Cognitive psychologist Uta Frith, along with others, has put forward a theory of 'central coherence', which suggests that, when carrying out tasks, people with autism show a relative failure to process information for context-dependent meaning.[78] For instance, it was found that, if a high-performing person with Asperger's syndrome was asked to retell a story which they had been told, they were likely to focus intensely on the small details in it – whole sections of whatever they could recall, almost verbatim – but would completely miss the overarching idea, meaning or metaphor. They failed to extract the main idea because they were not sensing context. Frith pointed out that, if someone not on the autistic spectrum was told a story and asked to retell it, they could invariably give the gist: its central meaning.

Another theory to explain Asperger's syndrome and autism was developed by Simon Baron-Cohen, Uta Frith and their colleague Alan Leslie, while all were working at the Medical Research Council's Cognitive Development Unit in London in the 1980s. It proposed that people with autism lacked 'theory of mind': what is missing in autism is the ability to read other people's minds and, from that, to predict other people's behaviour.[79] As Frith described it, "Thinking about what others think, rather than what is going on in the physical world outside, is essential for engaging in complex social activity because it underpins our ability to cooperate and to learn from each other. Our research has shown that theory of mind is either absent or severely delayed in autistic individuals and that this can explain their difficulties in social communication."[80]

Frith wanted to find a way to relate the theory of 'central coherence' to the theory of 'theory of mind'. We propose that the theory we put forward does just that and also provides a much richer view of context than the theory of central coherence. To us, 'central coherence' and 'theory of mind' are limited examples of the deeper principle we are describing, which is the crippling inability to see the world from multiple perspectives and to recognize how sudden change can alter a current situation.

After reading about our theory when we first published it, Belgian researcher, Dr Peter Vermeulen, then co-director of the Centre for Concrete Communication, got in touch. He also recognizes that the inability to read context is a key factor and has since published extensively about it.[81] As he has written, "What makes social interaction so difficult for people with autism spectrum disorders (ASD)? Traditionally, we have attributed it to both brain physiology (different 'wiring' of the brain) and social skill/social understanding challenges, often referred to as impaired perspective taking or 'theory of mind' (ToM). We use the term 'mind blind' with this population and assume it is this mind blindness that makes it difficult for individuals to relate to others ... The human brain, through its evolution, has learned to interpret situations by taking context into account. These basic processes occur within the first 50 to 400 milliseconds in the unconscious phases of information processing. For instance, neurotypical brains use the contextual information coming from the shadow of an object to quickly recognize that object. Studies using ERPs (event-related potentials) indicate many of these early, unconscious brain processes are affected in individuals with ASD. On a conscious level context helps us think through how we should react and what choices ... we should make. Context gives meaning to the stimuli our brains receive."[82]

Examples of context blindness

A friend of Joe's, who had Asperger's syndrome, used to stand in front of a mirror and brush the front of his hair, but never the back. The image he saw in the mirror didn't show the back of his head and, clearly, he was not relating the image he saw to a bigger 'picture' of his head as a whole. He was genuinely unaware, at the time, that a human being can be seen from all angles and that, therefore, he should comb his hair back and front, if he wanted to make a neat impression. Clearly, there was a major category of information missing in his mind: being able to view a situation from different perspectives (context).

Sarah, a woman with Asperger's syndrome, was asked by a friend what she thought of an expensive fancy handbag the friend had just bought. Sarah didn't like the bag and was completely nonplussed as to how to respond. She could see only two possibilities: to tell the truth, which was that she disliked it, or to say nothing. She was unable effortlessly to juggle in her mind conflicting perspectives (not liking the bag, liking the friend) and choose an appropriate one to communicate, on the basis of a wider knowledge of the possible consequences (upsetting or pleasing her friend). She was unable to see, for example, that an honest opinion is not always required in such circumstances; she could have pretended to like the bag, complimented her friend for buying it, or told her that it was a bargain. In fact, she said nothing at all, which totally perplexed and unsettled her friend. (This inability of people with Asperger's syndrome to be tactful or diplomatic is often interpreted as frank honesty.)

A very intelligent man who had Asperger's syndrome used to come out in a rash whenever he was anxious, which bothered him. One day, he read in a health magazine that mustard was good for skin rashes and promptly bought an industrial-sized pot of it, so he could plaster mustard over his face every day. It never occurred to him that customers in the shop he managed would think it odd to see him walking around with a bright yellow face and mustard smears on his collar.

Another man with Asperger's syndrome, also highly intelligent, described to us how his wife gave him a little box of chocolates just before they went out to celebrate his birthday and said, "You can eat the whole box while I go upstairs to get ready". When she came down a little later, dressed for their night out, she found him eating the cardboard box. She immediately got angry and shouted at him – but he had absolutely no idea why. After telling this anecdote, he said, "It seems as though other people have a concept to follow that I am missing. I just follow the instruction." If he had had instant access to the knowledge that humans are not expected to eat cardboard boxes, just the contents of the box, he would not have engaged in this bizarre behaviour. (Interestingly, such literalism can also be observed in people in deep trance.)

Another example: a professional woman who came to see one of us had decided to give up her job in a bank and go and live in a Buddhist meditation centre. Although she was keen to do this, she was also very sad and upset because she would never see her mother again. When asked why, she said, "My mother's a Catholic". She assumed that, if she went to visit her mother, she would have to tell her about her own change in religious belief, and that her mother wouldn't be able to cope with it. It didn't occur to her that people of different faiths *can* still know and love one another, especially if they are family; or that she could choose to protect her mother from what she thought would be devastating information for her, and just continue to go to Mass with her mother whenever she was home.

Clearly, in such cases, people lack the information necessary to inform their judgements about the choices and actions available to them in different situations.

Struggling to cope

It is, therefore, easy to see why people with context blindness experience high levels of frustration, anxiety and anger when other streams of information keep intruding into whatever they are trying to do – especially when their needs for structure, rules and rituals are transgressed. Because they don't know instinctively that multiple factors affect any given situation, they may be nonplussed even when just two simple interacting factors require attention. We saw this clearly in the jerky way a colleague with Asperger's syndrome would drive. Whenever he became aware that a gap between his car and the one in front was closing or widening, he responded by jamming on his brakes or speeding up inappropriately, instead of gently moderating his speed to accommodate what is, after all, a continually fluctuating situation when driving. He found it difficult to negotiate varying circumstances smoothly – other drivers changing speed, closeness to other vehicles, the curve of the road, weather conditions, etc. – all of which need constant simultaneous attention.

On one occasion, he was in the wrong lane when approaching a set of traffic lights. When it was pointed out to him that he needed to move over to the right lane, he refocused his attention on this new task and was unable at the same time to continue processing and prioritizing other relevant information – such as the fact that the light had changed to red and that driving through it could get him and his passengers killed. Indeed, he proceeded to drive on through the red light, causing us much alarm and consternation! Although he was aware of this deficit, and described it as 'straight-line thinking', he was unable to do anything about it.

Dancing with horses

A dream, by chance related to Joe by his then-teenage daughter Liley-Beth, served to crystallize our thinking about the role of context. In the dream, she went to a club with a horse; all the other girls there were dancing with horses and she, too, started dancing with a horse; it seemed the most natural thing in the world. Then the horse asked her out and she was just wondering whether to accept when she woke up. When Liley-Beth described the dream over breakfast, she said that what astonished her most about it was her unquestioning acceptance while she was dreaming that humans can go out with horses. Everyone who remembers dreams will recognize this feeling of accepting as perfectly natural a phenomenon that is actually distinctly odd: it is the same as that described by the man who had felt it was natural to eat the cardboard box instead of the chocolates inside it – except that he was awake.

So why did Liley-Beth unquestioningly accept, as we all do in dreams, such bizarre happenings? The reason has to be that in dreams we have access to emotions and metaphor but not context because, when we are dreaming, the prefrontal cortex, which the right hemisphere draws on for background information, is largely switched off. The context missing in this dream was the information that humans do not go on dates and dance with horses; horses can't walk around on two legs and speak like humans. Because, in the dream, Liley-Beth was cut off from the background information usually available to her, she was totally accepting of the validity of the dream imagery. Exactly the same thing appears to be happening in the experience of people with Asperger's syndrome. They may accept absurdities as true and make judgements about them, without the background information and knowledge to apply to the context they find themselves in.

For those of us not permanently suffering from context blindness (as we have said, it can be a temporary phenomenon, too, induced by stress and anxiety and depression), our minds can unconsciously draw on a vast hinterland of information that informs different aspects of any situation we find ourselves in. People who are context blind cannot do that because, although they may have collected millions of individual 'facts' in their memories, they are missing the ability to scan instantly for patterns in that rich background of information. Consequently, when something changes, they can't evaluate the importance of the change and how it affects what is going on in the wider environment. They can no more do a reality check while awake than anyone else can while dreaming.

Chaotic emotions

For sufferers from context blindness, one of the main consequences of not being able to manage separate streams of attention simultaneously is that they have no easy way to control their emotions. They cannot detach from a conditioned response pattern and see the possible consequences of that response or consider other more beneficial ways of reacting. Thus they feel confused and out of control, suffer extreme anxiety and anger, and can swing between wild mania and the blackest depression. They may also have trouble with sexual emotions and their sexual identity. Enduring this emotional turmoil must sometimes feel like living with an unpredictable wild creature. Indeed, some people who are context blind have told us that this is exactly how it feels. Maybe the sensory overload that many people on the autistic spectrum experience is because of their inability to process within themselves the changes going on around and within them. As they struggle to moderate their feelings, the only hope they have of reducing the pain that this sensory overload causes them is to try and control the environment and other people as much as possible. Because exercising control keeps their arousal down, and thus makes them feel better, they tend to do it obsessively. Unfortunately, as reducing their stress levels in this way involves exerting control over others, this raises the stress levels of everyone around them.

Left- and right-brained context blindness

As the intelligence system evolved in humans, our cerebral cortex became more complex and its left and right hemispheres developed specializations for different processes. Whilst maintaining the ability to interact with and complement each other, the hemispheres developed exponentially to support rational and contextual thinking. The corpus callosum, the thick bundle of neurons which joins the two, also serves to keep them apart, in that it prevents over-involvement by either hemisphere. So human language and thought, for example, are primarily ordered through the left hemisphere, which sequences and structures information moment by moment in a way that fosters reason. But our logical thinking is informed, and also coloured, by associative thinking and imagination, both faculties that emanate from the right hemisphere. Whereas previously we had relied on instinctive responses to keep us safe, once the cortex developed in modern humans we became able consciously to review feelings and not just act on them. In other words, we could investigate what was going on around us with a more refined reasoning ability.

But when people are missing the 'parallel processing' template for handling multiple streams of information, they are forced to try and resolve problems by other means. If a person is left-brain dominant, we see Asperger's behaviour as traditionally recognized: literal, logical, analytical reactions with difficulties in communication and empathy because of a severely diminished ability to think contextually. This happens because the left hemisphere is itself 'autistic' – it doesn't have access to the feelings that create context. But if a person is right-brain dominant and is missing the template for reading context, we suggest that this may express itself through an undisciplined, very strong imagination. The right hemisphere looks always for associations, so, without a strong left hemisphere to moderate the myriad associations that the right hemisphere makes, a person with context blindness cannot discipline them and check them out. The associations made are unlikely to be the right ones because, without access to a personal emotional history, they are not anchored in reality. The constant, undisciplined association-making can lead not only to inappropriate thoughts and behaviour but often quite bizarre ones.

Right-brained context blindness is caused by a lack of instinctive feelings to moderate the person's thoughts and behaviour, leaving the mind to run free, making directionless, random associations. Because a right-brained person with context blindness is more emotional, it may seem odd to suggest that their condition is due to a lack of instinctive feelings, but it is the *lack* of emotional instincts to discipline associations that gives rise to problems. Scientists researching decision-making have determined that it is emotion, fired by imagination, that prioritizes decision-making, not logic. "Emotions arise when events or outcomes are relevant for one's concerns or preferences and they *prioritize behaviour* that acts in service of these concerns"[83] (our italics).

Both right- and left-brained context blindness result in black-and-white thinking. Indeed, as already said, when heavily stressed, we can all become temporarily context blind: prone to black-and-white, crazy, irrational behaviour and faulty reasoning.

More women than men

We suggest, from our own experience as psychotherapists, that females are much more likely than males to suffer from *right-brain* context blindness, and that clinicians are not yet recognizing this expression of Asperger's syndrome. This could be because, although in *right-brain* context blindness we see the same inability to track multiple foci of attention and think contextually, such people have ready access to emotions in a way that people who are left-brain dominant and context blind – who, in our experience, are predominantly male – do not. The right-brain context blind can become emotional quickly and very, very easily – crying at the slightest upset, for instance. This accessibility of emotion, much more common in women generally, disguises the context blindness. However, they are sometimes just as poor at interpersonal intelligence as those diagnosed with Asperger's syndrome. They may also lack empathy and are quite unable to see how inappropriate their behaviour or beliefs appear to others.

Sense of self

When, in our evolutionary past, humans gained conscious access to the right hemisphere of the brain (the source of imagination), complex language with a past, present and future tense could develop.[10] Only with the arrival of complex language could we escape from the present and describe things that were not there in front of us. It was this that opened up the possibility of universal reasoning: discovering the underlying patterns and rules by which matter and life operate. Only then could we begin to develop and test hypotheses and start to unravel the cause-and-effect sequences in the world around us – water enables plants to grow; sunshine facilitates growth; days are shorter in the winter and longer in the summer; there is a rhythm to the seasons and the movement of the planets and stars, and so on.

Although missing the template for parallel processing, the more intelligent a person with context blindness is, the more likely they are to have access to universal reason. They may then be able to use thought to reflect back consciously on whatever has happened and construct another perspective. But this is a slow process and, without instant access to their own reinforcement history, their sense of self will be impaired – that sense of 'I-ness', of being separate from whatever context we happen to be in. People on the autistic spectrum, lacking this ability, may struggle to develop a sense of self and typically feel insecure in a world where everything is constantly changing. It may be this impoverished sense of self that keeps driving the more creative people with this condition to find out who they are, trying out roles to play in life and reinventing themselves, etc. Since scientists began studying Asperger's syndrome in the 1940s, it has been repeatedly remarked upon that sufferers lack a sense of who they are. "I feel like an outsider, and I always will feel like one," the autistic writer Anne Rice once said in an internet interview. "I've always felt that I wasn't a member of any particular group."[85]

Perhaps because they feel like outsiders, people who are context blind may be attracted to professions that give them an off-the-peg identity, very often one that comes with a uniform that announces that identity, such as army fatigues, police uniform, church regalia or even the more eccentric costumes of 'artists' and 'intellectuals'. Uniforms confer status. Professions that require uniforms also tend to have more tightly defined structures – rules, rituals and coded modes of speech – all of which render life more predictable and make people who lack a sense of context feel more secure. In a well-ordered life, the sensory overload feared by autistic people can better be kept at bay.

The observing self

For some years, whilst teaching psychotherapy, we have been using the term observing self – awareness of awareness itself. The observing self is different from our thinking self, emotional self or functioning (physical) self. It is outside these, yet experiences all of them. Arthur Deikman expressed this beautifully as follows: "The most important fact about the observing self is that it is incapable of being objectified. The reader is invited to try and locate that self to establish its boundaries. The task is impossible; whatever we can notice or conceptualize is already an object of awareness, not awareness itself, which seems to jump a step back when we experience an object. Unlike every other aspect of experience – thoughts, emotions, desires, and functions – the observing self can be known but not located, not 'seen'."[86]

The observing self is a waking state in which we dissociate from the external world and become aware of being aware, entering the daydreaming (REM) state just enough to allow us to review different aspects of reality – to see multiple contexts. But if we were to become absorbed to the same extent as when we are dreaming, our sense of reality would disappear. While daydreaming, our brains are still contextually aware, so that, when we stop introspecting, we know very quickly where we are and can reorient ourselves. Conversely, in the dream state, we are totally 'associated': completely lost in the dream.

Accessing the observing self is something that context-blind people have great difficulty doing because it involves focusing on something specific and then defocusing, to see a bigger context; then, whilst holding the bigger focus in mind, focusing back down again. When we gave our lectures for Human Givens College, for example, we were totally focused on the point we were making at any one time but, every so often, we had to defocus: we had to open up our minds to see where we were in terms of the work that has to be covered that day, assess whether we were being fully understood, whether it would soon be time to stop for lunch, etc. This continual process of focusing, defocusing and re-focusing kept us aware of the bigger context.

Those who struggle to see context cannot detach or dissociate. This is why certain psychotherapy techniques are ineffective with some context-blind clients. The powerful technique we know as the rewind technique, which can effectively neutralize even the most severe symptoms of post-traumatic stress disorder (PTSD) and phobias, involves guided imagery and dissociation. First, we intentionally arouse the client emotionally, by momentarily focusing them on the traumatic memory that is affecting them, and then help them to achieve a state of physiological calm in which they are guided to defocus, so that they can view the traumatic memories in a dissociated way. The technique requires the client to set up two different streams of attention: first, seeing themselves on a screen and 'fast forwarding' through the traumatizing event(s), then going backwards very fast through the same event(s), until there is no longer emotional arousal associated with the memories. This technique, when correctly carried out, is highly successful for most people, leading to a cessation of their post-traumatic stress symptoms, such as panic attacks and nightmares. However, the reason that it doesn't seem to work for many people with context blindness must be because the process is dependent on the patient's ability to maintain different perspectives simultaneously.

Context blindness as an organizing idea

The term Asperger's syndrome was derived from the name of the doctor who first described its traits, and means nothing in itself, whereas the term context blindness represents the underlying condition. Because the name is innately descriptive, it points to more effective ways that we can work with and relate to people who are context blind. When therapists find that their usual interventions don't work with particular clients, it could be because they are assuming that those clients can read context. Because they can't read context and can't, therefore, take certain necessary cognitive leaps for themselves, context-blind people can benefit from 'borrowing' someone else's brain to help them learn how to do what others can do instinctively. Someone has to explain the rules of behaviour to them, using clear, concrete terms and train them in how to keep to those rules. As people with context blindness are very literal minded, metaphors, when used, must be extremely simple. (For instance, Ivan used the metaphor of a train switching between tracks to convey to the woman who wanted to become a Buddhist that she could choose to 'switch' to behaviour that would please her Catholic mother – ie. go to Mass just during her brief visits.)

Many people with context blindness have little or no facility with guided imagery and it works less effectively, if at all, with them. However, we have often found that teaching them breathing techniques to lower anxiety can help them a lot. Those vulnerable to outbursts of extreme anger have also sometimes found it helpful to identify the anger as a wild animal that they need to let calm down (by taking time out and doing some aerobic exercise, such as brisk walking, jogging or other energetic activity).

Undoubtedly, many highly imaginative right-brained people, who may be vulnerable to psychotic thinking, display context-blind tendencies that compromise their ability to connect to the 'ordinary' world.

It is not unusual in psychotherapy to come across people who are emotionally intense and self-absorbed, with strong imaginations that are not moderated by their left hemisphere. They may spend much of the time disconnected from reality and are often eccentrically involved with arts and crafts, alternative health or magical beliefs and practices. Despite showing undoubted signs of creativity, they might not be able to discriminate good work from bad and can take their work intensely seriously, even if it isn't particularly good. It is important to recognize, however, that context blindness does not necessarily accompany psychosis; vulnerability to the condition commonly arises from traumatic experiences and an imaginative mind. It is also important to recognize the developmental potential in creative people with context blindness. Some, as they grow older, improve their ability to read emotional contexts, resolve their emotional problems and become more secure in themselves, whilst still retaining their creative faculty.

Context blindness is a significant disability yet, much of the time, manages to go unnoticed. This is because, when a person at the higher end of the autistic spectrum becomes familiar with an environment, and what is expected of them in it, they may become sufficiently competent and confident in that role, so the context blindness remains concealed. A mild version of the same thing occurs with somebody who has a poor sense of direction. When that person is in an environment that is familiar to them, their poor sense of direction does not reveal itself. It is only when they find themselves in unfamiliar territory that it becomes obvious that they cannot naturally find their way around it, whereas the brain of someone with a good sense of direction automatically maps it. For instance, in a large, unfamiliar hotel, when someone with a good sense of direction makes their way to the bedroom that they have been allocated, their brain automatically not only records the route but, when they come out of their room, automatically alters its mental map, so that they walk the right way to get back to the reception area. But, if someone has a poor sense of direction, the brain will only remember the direction taken to the room. It hasn't recorded an internal 'map' and can't reorient position accordingly. So, when the person leaves the room, they can easily find themselves going in the wrong direction.

Of course, lacking a sense of direction is incomparable in its consequences to the inability to recognize context. Thus it is that many people with unrecognized context blindness end up seeking therapy because of difficulties with primal emotions such as anger, anxiety or depression – aroused by problems in new relationships, confusion about sexual identity, unmet sexual needs, obsessions, being a control freak, inability to hold down a job, managing money, etc.

But it goes wider than that. Elsewhere we have explored the extent to which context blindness was an inevitable consequence of the evolution of daydreaming and how context-blind behaviour is behind many of the frustrations we face in the modern world, especially in the way governments and organizations try to relate to, control and influence people, not only those who work in them but also individuals and families in the wider world they are supposed to be serving.[87] We called this organizational context blindness.[88] Others trying to make sense of puzzling behaviour have also found our reasoning helpful, leading, for example, to the cannabis-induced theory of context blindness. This was first proposed by Ezra Hewing, who had worked with substance abusers, to explain the paradoxical effects of cannabis use, namely why using cannabis increases the risk of developing mental health problems such as depression and schizophrenia; why some people find that cannabis helps them to relax, reduce stress and alleviate the symptoms of mental disorders such as depression, anxiety and PTSD; and why some people find that using cannabis gives rise to unusual thoughts and access to imagination and creativity.[89]

So context blindness, we argue, not only plays a role in autism and is the key deficit in high-functioning Asperger's syndrome but also affects, in various ways, many individuals not thought of as suffering from an autistic spectrum disorder. This has crucial ramifications for our society.

PART THREE

Emotional Health And Clear Thinking

CHAPTER EIGHT

The APET model: the key to effective psychotherapy

WHEN emotional needs are not met, for whatever reason, anyone can suffer distress. If the situation persists, more serious emotional disorders are easily triggered: anxiety, obsessional or addictive behaviour, depression, bipolar disorder (manic depression), psychosis, etc. At this point, people often decide to seek help to alleviate the emotional pain they are suffering. That brings a new problem: where to go for effective treatment.

Psychiatry tends to medicalize conditions and predominantly relies on drug treatments, with all their attendant risks – not least that taking drugs is psychologically disempowering. This 'medical model' ideology is under increasing attack as evidence mounts about the harmful side effects of drugs.[1] Although, for instance, it has long been known by sufferers that the antidepressants known as SSRIs (selective serotonin reuptake inhibitors) can cause prolonged withdrawal effects,[2] this was acknowledged by the Royal College of Psychiatrists only in 2020, when they finally updated their website guidance to include the significant possibility of this occurring.

Complicating this further is the fact that what constitutes mental unwellness is not agreed on, either. The American Psychiatric Association's *Diagnostic and Statistical Manual of Mental Disorders (DSM)* and the World Health Organization's *International Classification of Diseases (ICD)* are regularly updated to incorporate 'new', sometimes questionable, mental disorders which may in fact just reflect aspects of the human condition, such as sadness and grief and embarrassment. Meanwhile, neuroscientists delve into the brain itself to try to find abnormalities that might explain identified conditions (even though, after three decades of intense neuroimaging research, no neurobiological account for any psychiatric condition has ever been unearthed[3]) or that might explain the fact that some people seem to suffer several conditions (such as schizophrenia, depression and obsessive-compulsive disorder) at once.[4] According to the *DSM*, every mental disorder must have different symptoms from every other one (for no reason other than that this was what was agreed by the committee that decided on the system clusters), so people may end up appearing to suffer from several illnesses at the same time. This would cease to be a problem if less attention was paid to classifying symptoms and more paid to the range of each client's actual experience, as should happen in good psychotherapy.

However, even here is there is no agreement. The often confusing world of psychotherapy and counselling has also consistently come under attack down the years.[5] One systematic review two decades ago showed that neither of these disciplines, as we traditionally know them, did much good: "Pulling findings from the trials, it seems that patients referred to counsellors felt themselves better understood and listened to and were more likely to declare themselves satisfied with their treatment but there was no actual difference in patients' ways of coping with their difficulties or their knowledge of what needed to be changed in their lives. There was no difference in social adjustment between those who were counselled and those cared for just by GPs."[6] There has even been evidence that they may sometimes do more harm than good.[7] There are also ongoing arguments within the profession as to the difference, if any, between counselling and psychotherapy and who should be considered qualified, and on what grounds, to practise. At the time of writing, several psychotherapy/counselling organisations are engaged in a very large and ongoing piece of work to define basic competencies that should be expected of psychotherapists/counsellors (the terms are not defined because even these groups can't agree on a definition) and what level of training they should have received in order to demonstrate these competencies. This is known as the SCoPEd (The Scope of Practice and Education) Framework. As the therapy organisations involved are from very different schools of therapy, it has been impossible for them to reach true agreement, although they have made valiant efforts to recognise each other's strengths.

There are an enormous number of therapies on offer throughout the world – Wikipedia publishes a mind-boggling list[8] – which in itself indicates the general lack of shared perceptions about how best to help people. Yet, as each new therapy for dealing with human distress is launched upon the world, it tends to begin a process of entrenchment, digging itself into a rut by developing a systematic philosophy to be applied mechanically to every person with a problem.

All major therapies seemed wonderful to some people in their heyday. Perhaps the most valuable aspect of Sigmund Freud's psychoanalytical therapy at the beginning of the 20th century, for example, was to draw the attention of the Western world to the ancient insight that many of our everyday behaviours are largely controlled by unconscious processes. However, the value of incorporating this simple but important truth into our culture was then largely undermined by Freud himself. Driven as he was by messianic ambition and paranoia, and working from invented, unrealistic models of human functioning and psychology, based largely upon the mechanistic 19th century understanding of biology, he mounted a propaganda campaign for his bizarre ideas. Thus he effectively muddied the waters of psychiatry, psychotherapy and counselling for the remainder of that century. The development of complex psychoanalytical theories (which were never scientifically tested by Freud or his followers, only asserted as true) had their roots in just six case histories – which were all that Freud ever published, and all of which were disasters from the point of view of his patients.[9] The legacy of psychoanalysis and its offshoots is a disturbing story of misguided, often harmful, treatment.[10]

Behaviour therapy, which developed partly in reaction against the absurdities of psychoanalysis, also contained a profound insight. While others were still grappling with the 'deep unconscious', behaviourists discovered that changing behaviour was often able to help people resolve problems. They made use of the knowledge that there are innate pleasure circuits in the brain that can be stimulated by certain behaviours. When people were shown how to replace destructive behaviours with more rewarding positive behaviours, they found it easier to make healthy changes. The method often worked because any counsellor who clearly targets the elimination of behaviours that are stopping a person's needs being met, while fostering behaviours that increase the likelihood they will be met, is bound to have success. Encouraging depressed people to become more physically and socially active, for example, helps to lift clinical depression. That is powerful therapy.

Unfortunately, behaviourism soon swelled into a total philosophy that would brook no dissenters. Students were told: *there is no such thing as consciousness. There is no such thing as mind. What you think has no effect upon you. You are your behaviour and nothing else.* Pure behaviourism became a gross distortion of what humanity is about. It undermined values and meaning in life and took away people's personal autonomy. In his classic text *The Origin of Consciousness in the Breakdown of the Bicameral Mind*, Julian Jaynes had this to say about behaviourism:

"But the single inherent reason for its success was not its truth, but its programme ... with its promise of reducing all conduct to a handful of reflexes and conditional responses developed from them, and generalizing the spinal reflex terminology of stimulus and response and reinforcement to the puzzles of headed behaviour and so seeming to solve them ... In all this there was a heady excitement that is difficult to relate at this remove.

"Complexity would be made simple, darkness would be made light, and philosophy would be a thing of the past ... off the printed page, behaviourism was only a refusal to talk about consciousness. Nobody really believed he was not conscious, and there was a very real hypocrisy abroad, as those interested in its problems were forcibly excluded from academic psychology."[10]

Then came the growth of client-centred therapy ('active listening'), developed by humanistic psychologist Carl Rogers. His idea was that, if you truly listen to somebody with a problem, and let them know that you *are* really listening, by feeding back your understanding of what their problem is, people can move forward from a stuck position. Patients do need to have their stories heard in a respectful, non-judgemental atmosphere. Sometimes, when a person is temporarily emotionally overloaded, just being heard in a supportive way is all it takes for them to calm down, view their situation from a wider perspective and chart a way forward. Most people coming to therapy, however, need more than support. They have to borrow someone else's brain for a while to help them lower their emotional arousal *and* think clearly and learn, so that they can move on. Counselling them effectively may involve social skills training, teaching anxiety or anger management skills, giving help with an addiction or detraumatizing them from terrible past experiences that are influencing their present behaviour. So, although active listening is an important component of therapy, it is usually only a small part. But, with person-centred counselling, again the inevitable happened. Active listening expanded into a philosophy which said: *all anybody needs is for someone to really listen to them and a 'self-actualizing principle' inside them will then manifest itself and sort all their problems out.*[12] (The irritating trite fashion for saying, "I hear you" during conversations arose from this.) This is beautiful idealism but, as we have seen, painfully wrong. Someone with depression can be listened to sympathetically for ever and a day, and still they may not come out of it – in fact, they are more likely to become even more deeply depressed. The depressive trance state has to be broken, not deepened as in psychodynamic 'insight' therapy.

One of the main reasons for counselling being found, in some studies, to be ineffective in helping people move on with their lives could well be that counselling training is still largely based on this active listening/self-actualization philosophy. As made clear, knowing how to listen is a vitally important skill, but much more is needed to provide effective help for people with emotional problems.

Cognitive-behavioural therapy (CBT), a more recent and somewhat more successful approach, has also headed in an unhelpful direction. It is based on the straightforward idea that, if people can be helped to use their rational ability to question the evidence for their damaging negative belief systems, they can change their behaviour. Helping people to make more realistic assessments of their life *is* powerfully effective, especially if they suffer from depression or anxiety. But in the spread of CBT we have seen the same degeneration at work. The original brilliant insight, which could be grasped at a single workshop and that generated an enthusiastic following, attracted pedants who then made it the subject of complex books. Academics have written manuals specifying exactly how it should be carried out in different settings and most people who practise it now are clinical psychologists, who are obliged to study for some years for their qualifications.

This mental thickening process seems to happen with every school of therapy – psychodynamic, Rogerian, behavioural, biomedical, gestalt, cognitive, etc. Many of them began with a useful insight but then became closed systems of thought, unable to incorporate the totality of what it is to function as a human being. CBT, for instance, focuses primarily on the rational aspect of the human mind as a means of lifting depression or anxiety or any other form of mental ill health. We could equally accurately say that problems are caused by a misuse of imagination and that a solution is to help people use their imagination more effectively. Interestingly, for some years, increasing numbers of practitioners of CBT have seen this for themselves and have started incorporating use of imagery and also mindfulness techniques into their practice.[13]

As therapies become complex, so they develop jargon that makes them incomprehensible to outsiders. Hakim Jami, commenting back in the 15th century on this perennial tendency, encapsulated the problem succinctly: "If the scissors are not used daily on the beard, it will not be long before the beard, by its luxuriant growth, begins to think it is the head".

As a rule, when an approach starts getting really complex, you can be certain it is going wrong – perhaps trying to make up for what it lacks by inventing ever more complex jargon to explain away its failure to get significant results. CBT, however, has established a firm, if unfounded, base and has built itself into an unstoppable force. As its proponents very commonly work in universities and can command research funds, many randomized controlled trials of CBT have been carried out, variously showing mild to moderate benefits in certain settings. Results of randomized controlled trials carry most weight with NICE (National Institute for Health and Care Excellence), the UK body which issues treatment guidelines which primary and secondary health providers follow. Thus it is CBT which is usually recommended for all sorts of mental disorders, and CBT is the leading therapy offered within the Improving Access to Psychological Therapies (IAPT) programme (now known as NHS Talking Therapies), which has been rolled out across the country. Unfortunately, the impressive results it claimed are not genuine but often the result of clever presentation.

As set out in an opinion piece in the leading medical journal *BMJ*, around a quarter of people who are referred to IAPT don't ever get that far and nearly a third of those that do start treatment drop out. Out of those who complete a course of treatment, half achieve recovery. However, when this figure is unpacked, this 50 per cent actually represents just 19 per cent of the total referred. So only one in five of those referred moves to recovery.[14] Psychotherapist Farhad Dalal identifies what he terms nine "corruptions" in the science behind CBT (amplification; overgeneralizing; objectifying the subjective; spinning, lying and hacking; desire-driven results; 'treatment as usual' treated as equivalent to placebo; restriction of research; treatment as a package; and researchers' needs prioritized over those of clinicians), with evidence provided to back up his assertions.[15] A comprehensive 2023 meta-analysis of CBT versus other treatments for depression (looking at 409 trials involving 52,702 patients) found that, although the efficacy of CBT has been *documented* across different formats, ages, target groups and settings, in the meta-analysis its superiority over other psychotherapies for depression did *not* emerge clearly. It did, however, appear to be more effective in the long-term than treatment for depression with drugs.[16]

People coming from a psychodynamic perspective have sometimes said that the human givens approach deals only with symptoms, not the underlying problem. But research and experience do not support them. When time is spent digging up everything people can remember about what went wrong in their lives, and exploring problematic past relationships in an effort to 'understand', it does not improve confidence or give them the skills to deal with life today. And yet such psychological archaeology was the dominant approach in therapy for a long time. It still lingers on in many quarters and is often the basis for the way psychotherapy is portrayed in literature, the media and by the entertainment industry, despite being long out of date. When many hundreds of efficacy studies were looked at together, in a meta-analysis published back in the 1990s, brief, solution-focused therapy was proved more effective for the treatment of anxiety disorders, depression, phobias, trauma and addictive behaviour than any long-term psychoanalytic style of therapy or drug treatments.[17,18,19]

The birth of the APET model

Clearly a fresh approach to mental health is needed, as we said at the start – one that puts mental ill health in the context of the way that human beings function, the lives that they live and the environments that they live in. This includes looking at the barriers that may get in the way of mental health, such as living in unsafe environments (for example, a home where there is domestic violence or a street where there is high traffic pollution); being widely discriminated against because of one's beliefs or background or behaviour; living in poverty, with all its knock-on adverse effects on mental and physical wellbeing; and so on. Unlike in physical conditions, such as, say, osteoarthritis and glaucoma, which occur regardless of what else is going on in one's life, life circumstances cannot be separated out from the experience of mental disorders such as depression, anxiety, so-called borderline personality disorder (which usually means having had multiple adverse childhood experiences) and psychotic conditions such as schizophrenia.

When, back in the early 1990s, we first considered how we could teach psychiatrists, clinical psychologists, psychotherapists and counsellors to work within the givens of human nature, we puzzled over how to find ways that could encompass all the current understandings about brain functioning in a model that had clarity, was true to the new knowledge and could draw on the most effective elements of existing therapies. We needed to find a way that showed the key role of emotion in determining what happens to us, internally and in the external world – and stress the pattern-matching nature of the brain and how it produces emotional arousal. One morning, as we set off to the Redhill Hospital Post Graduate Centre to teach our approach to the first pioneering group of aspiring human givens therapists, Joe announced that he had hardly slept all night from thinking about this problem. As a consequence, when he woke up, he had found the answer and planned to lecture on it that very morning.

His inspired talk was electric. Everyone in the room knew this was a significant moment. For the first time, he described the APET model, a psychologically and physiologically accurate view of mind/body functioning that could provide a clear, practical framework which therapists could work from.

The **A** in APET stands for the activating stimulus, something internal or external which gets our attention. (The term was inspired by the A for activating agent which was used in the ABC model developed by psychotherapist Albert Ellis in the late 1960s. Originator of rational-emotive behaviour therapy, the first form of cognitive therapy, he taught that activating agents (A) led to beliefs/thoughts (B), which in turn led to emotional consequences (C).[20] This incorrect formulation drove cognitive therapy and CBT for decades.) In the APET model, information about a stimulus, taken in through our senses, is first pattern matched by the mind to innate knowledge and past learnings, hence the **P**, which in turn gives rise to an emotion or an expectation, **E**. This, in turn, may lead to certain thoughts, represented by the **T**. It is important to point out, though, that thought is not an inevitable consequence of emotional arousal. People often talk of a red mist descending and being taken over by something overwhelming, without awareness of any thought at all. So, as the emotion certainly leads to physical changes in the body and often an action, we can also consider the **T** as standing for 'Things-happen'.

This model, which underpins HG therapy, is completely in tune with reality and is one which can be easily understood. It not only helps therapists be more effective, but throws light on numerous other phenomena: how a virtuoso violinist performs the immense complexities of a concerto – the ethereal harmonies, melodies, tones, changing rhythms and moods – and thereby transports an audience to more subtle realms; how we recognize an old friend we haven't seen for 20 years; why there are not millions more car crashes every day, as motorized populations around the world negotiate complex urban road systems at speed; how a farmer knows exactly the right moment to begin harvesting; how we learn; why placebos work; what happens in our minds when we start to laugh *before* something funny happens; how a craftsman knows when a work of fine art is finally complete; how we pick up what someone else is feeling; and why we sometimes feel anxious without a conscious reason for it. The key to it all is pattern-matching – the process of matching up innate or learned templates, which is constantly occurring as we interact with our environment.

The importance of perception

Good therapy and counselling *always* centre around meaning – changing meaning from negative to positive, from harmful to helpful, is what effective counsellors do. To change the meaning is to change the template through which we experience reality. When we do this, it literally changes consciousness. So the APET model is a way of reminding us of this because it symbolizes the order in which the brain perceives meaning and reacts to what it perceives. Perception, and the way we react to our perceptions, always depends on pattern matching to innate and learned knowledge. The inborn patterns – templates – are so fundamental that no reality can exist without nature presetting them into organisms in the first place. Pattern matching, we could say, means pattern *perception* because we perceive reality through those templates. In other words, what we perceive are the *meanings* that we attribute to certain stimuli.

This has been demonstrated startlingly clearly in cases where cataracts are removed from people blind from birth. Arthur Zajonc vividly described the outcome of one such operation: "In 1910, the surgeons Moreau and LePrince wrote about their successful operation on an eight-year-old boy who had been blind since birth because of cataracts. Following the operation, they were anxious to discover how well the child could see. When the boy's eyes were healed, they removed the bandages. Waving a hand in front of the child's physically perfect eyes, they asked him what he saw. He replied weakly, 'I don't know.' 'Don't you see it moving?' they asked. 'I don't know,' was his only reply. The boy's eyes were clearly not following the slowly moving hand. What he saw was only a varying brightness in front of him. He was then allowed to touch the hand as it began to move; he cried out in a voice of triumph: 'It's moving!' He could feel it move, and even, as he said, 'hear it move', but he still needed laboriously to learn to see it move. Light and eyes were not enough to grant him sight. Passing through the now clear black pupil of the child's eye, that first light called forth no echoing image from within. The child's sight began as a hollow, silent, dark and frightening kind of seeing. The light of day beckoned, but no light of mind replied within the boy's anxious, open eyes.

"The lights of nature and of mind entwine within the eye and call forth vision. Yet separately, each light is mysterious and dark. Even the brightest light can escape our sight."[21]

It is always easiest to see such effects when illness or disability prevents a normal reaction. So, again, we can see the fundamental significance of meaning illustrated in the actions of people with ideo-motor apraxia (IMA), a condition that occurs as a result of certain diseases of the central nervous system and affects a person's ability to grasp or use objects. Research has shown that, if people with IMA are asked to pick up a cylinder the size of a cup and pretend to drink, they cannot do it. If, however, they are asked to make this same imitative movement while actually eating a meal, they are much better able to grasp and raise the cylinder. Suddenly the task is more meaningful. It has a context.

For everything we become aware of, there is a pre-existing, partially completed, inner template, innate or learned, through which we literally organize the incoming stimuli and complete it in a way that gives it meaning. These metaphorical templates are the basis of all animal and human perception. Without them no world would exist for us. They organize our reality. (This idea is explored more fully in our book, *Godhead: the brain's big bang*.)

With this understanding we can see how crucial *meaning* is when helping people who are using inappropriate patterns through which to understand their own reality. Obviously, if people's attention is locked by strong emotions – depression, anxiety, lust, anger, awe, greed, etc. – those emotions frame the meaning of life for them. That is why lowering emotional arousal is so important and needs to be done *before* attempting to adjust the patterns to bring them closer to reality. If a person has the belief or template that the world owes them a living, for example, they need an input to correct that; otherwise they will always see their interactions with other people through this parasitic viewpoint and fall foul of the people around them. Likewise, someone who idealizes the opposite sex is doomed to disappointment until a more realistic template is set in place.

Emotions before thought

Patterns of perception in our brain always seek completion in the environment and each perception is shaped by emotion. Strong emotions are feelings that create distinctive psychobiological states, a propensity for action and simplified thinking styles, and they arise from a network of interconnected brain structures, which coordinate our feelings, moods, memories and physiological sensations. These anticipate physical danger and monitor what our senses register from our environment. And they do so before we become fully aware that it is happening.

Early on, anything which signals a potential threat is sent by our senses to our amygdalae, two small organs, one in each hemisphere of the brain. (They are not the only parts of the brain involved in this but, for simplicity, we will focus on them and because they are usually referred to in the singular, we will do that too.) The amygdala can usefully be thought of as our internal 'security officer'. When our organism is under threat, it can receive sensory information directly, instead of via the cortex, allowing the triggering of the fight-or-flight response to be quicker.[22] Neuroscientist Joseph Le Doux, who carried out the experimental work which showed this,[23] used to express these pathways in layman's terms as the 'low road' and the 'high road' of communicating with the amygdala. However, it led to misunderstandings that the 'low road' meant unconscious processing and the 'high road' involved conscious processing. In fact, both sensory input routes to the amygdala are non-conscious.[24] Threats are brought to conscious attention a moment afterwards, and that is when we realize that the stick is not a snake and that the cracking sound was a twig, not a gunshot.

In other words, we first unconsciously interpret each new stimulus in terms of, "Does it represent a danger, or is it safe?" Perhaps even more fundamentally, "Is this something I can eat, or is it something that can eat me?" or, "Is it something I can approach or something I should get away from?" The conscious mind is presented with the end result of this analysis – whatever the reactive networks of the brain have considered the significant highlights.

We need here to say a word about 'emotion', as it is a surprisingly contentious term. Most neuroscientists used to believe (and many still do) that different emotions are hardwired into the brain.[25] More current is the thinking that the specific emotions we feel are psychological or social constructions which we create when we interact with our physical or social environments. The bigger our emotional 'vocabulary' (which comes from the language we hear and information given to us by adults when we are children), the more sophisticated the emotions we might interpret ourselves as experiencing[26] (irritation or frustration in slightly annoying situations for, instance, rather than full-blown anger, which, in someone with a lesser emotional vocabulary, might lead to serious over-reaction in the same situation). In the context of threat responses, which we are talking about here, LeDoux now prefers to talk about amygdala-based defensive survival circuits rather than defensive circuits triggered by emotion. As he has put it, "The human brain may be able to categorize emotional states in broad strokes without language but it is unlikely that specific emotions (fear, anger, sadness, joy) could come about without words."[27] In other words, what we feel and identify as different emotions is determined by the patterns already in our brains.

Very many neuroscientists today argue that the brain works by prediction. It can't wait for things to happen and then react. On the basis of similar situations that have happened before, countless neurons communicate through electrical and chemical signalling in an attempt to predict what is going to happen to us next – i.e. how to make sense of the information we receive through our senses – and how best to react.[28] If, for instance, we are walking up a wide staircase and, at the next landing, it becomes narrower and steeper, without our even knowing it, our brains will register (predict) that we need to step differently and send this message to our feet via the relevant motor neurons. In the case of the snake or the cracking sound, we have already jumped or taken evasive action before we are fully aware of it.

So our brains are wired to initiate actions before we consciously realize what is happening. Our conscious reality is accompanied by emotions – expectations that exist at a stage prior to language – ranging from very subtle to extremely strong. They are the only language available to the subconscious mind for communicating the significance of patterns. Something happens – perhaps we wake up in the morning with an unpleasant feeling in our stomachs. It could be that we are thirsty or hungry or still tired. But someone who is habitually very anxious is more likely to interpret the sensation as dread or fear, and quickly start thinking about what, that coming day, could go wrong. This is the point at which thoughts come into play – and it may be as a result of a prediction error.

As well as this happening when someone suddenly feels anxiety in a dark alley and runs away from a possible attacker in the shadows, it is also what happens in non-emergency situations which certain individuals respond to *as if* they were emergencies, because they haven't learned to adjust an outdated pattern from the past: for instance, when someone might hit out aggressively if a tall, red-bearded man comes near them because of a traumatic history of being restrained and abused by a tall, red-bearded man. They hit out before they have even had time to think what they are doing and why. It is the job of the conscious mind to discriminate, fill in the detail and arrive at a more intelligent analysis of the patterns offered up to it by non-conscious pattern matching.

We have said several times that, when we are highly emotionally aroused, we can no longer think straight. If we look around the world today, wherever we see prejudice, discrimination, conflict, violence, torture and inhumane behaviour it is invariably accompanied by high levels of emotional arousal. The people doing these things are not different from the rest of us. Even the most intelligent person can behave like an ignoramus when emotionally aroused. And an atmosphere of continuous emotional arousal maintains ignorance because, when reasoning power is inhibited, no one can see the bigger picture. Black-or-white, emotional logic eliminates fine discrimination. As the old saying goes, "The coarse drives out the fine". Or, to put it more colloquially, high emotional arousal makes us stupid.

Our cerebral cortex evolved to such an advanced degree partly as a means to discriminate the thousands of colourful shades that exist between black and white. It has the capacity to modulate emotional responses – all brain networks are interconnected – and explore subtle implications and complexities, look at bigger contexts and makes analyses, but *this is only possible if we are not too highly emotionally aroused.*

We cannot communicate with people who are too highly aroused because, in their aroused state, they cannot process data contradictory to their black-or-white thinking. They cannot give attention to another viewpoint. As we've seen, high emotional arousal locks the attention mechanism, effectively putting the person into a trance state where they are confined to viewing the world through an inappropriate pattern or template, limiting their perception of reality. The best tactic when trying to communicate with a highly aroused person is to buy time and do whatever is necessary to bring their arousal level down first. Presenting rational arguments will be fruitless before that.

There is one important proviso. Some people need to be in a state of enhanced emotional arousal to perform specific tasks well. For them, emotional arousal itself is an essential tool because it is focusing their attention on the task at hand. For example, at a great sporting event, world-class athletes rise to the occasion and give a better performance than ever before. They need the extra emotional arousal (caused by the big occasion) to focus their attention to help them to go into a state of flow. Getting the degree of arousal right has to be learned because it is normal to be more anxious at such times and emotional arousal (put in place by the big occasion) can rise to such an extent that performance disintegrates. That is what happens to anxious individuals when taking an exam; however intelligent they are, their minds go blank. (The solution is to use relaxation and guided imagery techniques several times before the event, to rehearse being more relaxed on such occasions. The more often we can experience positive rather than disabling levels of arousal and associate them with exam taking, the more likely it is that this state can be achieved in the exam room.)

Nearly all great actors say that they feel nervous before a public performance. Yet, they also say that without that nervousness they don't produce their best; the anxiety they have prior to going on stage enables them to focus their minds more intensely and produce their best work. But it's a fine line. At the height of his powers, Sir Lawrence Olivier once spent almost an entire performance with his back to the audience because he was so nervous. He couldn't get into flow. So it is always a question of the right amount of arousal for the job in hand.

Even in learning, a certain amount of emotion is involved. A good teacher knows to focus their pupils' attention and, as we know, what focuses attention better than anything is emotion. But the teacher doesn't over-arouse the pupils; instead he or she will present the subject matter in a way that is so intrinsically interesting it causes sufficient emotional engagement in the pupils to focus their attention.

So, emotional arousal should by no means be viewed as negative or destructive. That would be black-or-white thinking in itself. It is always a question of the *right* degree of emotional arousal for the task at hand.

Counsellors and psychotherapists who recognize that people with emotional problems are locked into tunnel vision know that their key role is to open up that view. An effective counsellor has the skills to disengage the templates that 'lock' individuals into disabling viewpoints and help them access ones that widen their vision. This is known as reframing.

When we take account of brain physiology, we can see that the fastest way to begin helping distressed people is to calm them down first, thus overcoming the mental paralysis caused by excessive emotional arousal. Clients are then more able to respond to help in escaping from their predicament.

Three vital principles

From what has been explained so far about brain function, we suggest that we can draw out the three principles from the APET model that are vital for therapists and counsellors to understand if they are to deal effectively with the most common emotional disorders, such as phobias, post-traumatic stress, anxiety, anger, clinical depression and addictions:

- the brain works principally through an infinitely rich pattern-matching process
- emotion comes before thought – all perceptions and all thought are shaped by emotion
- the higher the emotional arousal, the more limited the emotional/mental pattern that is engaged.

By studying therapy models with these fundamental principles in mind, we can more easily see their strengths and weaknesses. Any therapy that encourages emotional introspection, for example, is unlikely to offer the most helpful or quickest way out of most common problems.

That there is emotional accompaniment to *all* perceptions may not seem obvious. It is now known that emotions are not neatly restricted to one area of the brain but are mixed up with both cognitive and bodily processes. However, we may only notice the emotional element when it stands out in bizarre ways. For example, Capgras syndrome, which results from right-hemisphere brain damage to connections between the temporal lobes and the amygdala, has the effect of making sufferers think that people they love and care about are impostors.[29,30] Although the left-hemisphere elements of the brain that pattern match and recognize familiar people are still working, the damage prevents the integration of the emotional responses, feelings and meanings associated with, for instance, one's parents or spouse, which are right-hemisphere properties. Because these are not activated, someone who suffers from the syndrome jumps to the conclusion that "This person *can't* be my father/mother/husband/wife!"

Normally, people don't give a second thought to the feelings that accompany seeing their parents or partners. The feelings are normal, routine, and so the brain doesn't bring them into consciousness. All unremarkable emotions are neutralized in this way – a fact that makes the phenomenon difficult to observe until an exception demonstrates it. So, even though the most common of perceptions have feelings associated with them, we only become aware of feelings, and our thoughts about feelings, when they are somehow unexpected – surprising. Surprise is the common element.

The power of thought

Finally, the T in the APET model, which refers to Thought or Things-happen. (It should be noted that Thought or Things-happen can also be the activating stimulus (**A**), creating a kind of APET 'loop'.) Undoubtedly, emotions affect thinking. However, this is not usually a negative thing. When our brains are not over-emotionally aroused, we can employ exceptionally subtle evaluation procedures. As theoretical physicist and science writer Leonard Mlodinow has put it, "Our emotional state influences our mental calculations as much as the objective data or circumstances we are pondering ... and that is usually for the best. ... indeed, if we were free from all emotion, we would hardly be able to function because our brains would have to be hopelessly cluttered with rules governing the simple decisions we must constantly make to react to the everyday circumstances of life."[31] Our 'executive control network', as neuroscientists now tend to term sites in the executive prefrontal cortex, which include areas involved in attention and working memory, are closely connected up with the 'emotional salience network' (representing awareness brought to things that have significance or meaning for us) – tiny nodes anchored in structures such as the insula, anterior cingulate gyrus and the amygdala.

Again, Mlodinow describes the connection vividly: the job of the emotional salience network is "to monitor our internal emotions and our external environment and take note of what is important. [It] identifies the most relevant among those inputs and spurs you to act (or not act) on that basis. The executive control network has the job of keeping you focused on what is relevant to your goals while ignoring distractions. It jumps into action once the salience network has been activated. It then marshals the brain's resources to enable you to act if necessary."[32]

The networks of the brain are in a state of continual flux from second to second, minute to minute and hour to hour.[33] This has to be so. We would not be the adaptable creatures we are otherwise. These networks are nature's solution to the need for adaptable responses to an ever-changing environment. By gifting us with innate instinctive patterns that are not totally programmed, and giving us the ability to add to these patterns almost infinitely, nature made us into the remarkably flexible, talented creatures we are, able to explore ever deeper into the nature of our world.

Every researcher and writer on the subject describes this incredibly complex organ, the brain, in awed tones. It has literally billions of potential neuronal connections and the almost inconceivable ability to remodel itself according to the richness of input coming in through the senses from the environment. It continually makes new connections, strengthening valuable ones and withering old ones that it no longer finds useful. It can hold on to and store whatever information is pertinent to its current reality and use that store of connections to modify old patterns – a complex fine-tuning operation. It is this continual refining of the metaphorical pattern-matching process that allows us to discriminate ever more accurately between the polarized extremes of over-emotional responses and sophisticated understandings.

Before all these new understandings were brought to light, we used to talk in terms of 'emotional brains' and 'rational brains', as if they were almost two distinct entities, the latter busily attempting to temper the former. But, as we can see, this is entirely wrong. As Iain McGilchrist has argued, in his profound works, *The Master and His Emissary*[34] and, more recently, *The Matter with Things*,[35] it is not a distinction between emotional and rational which has bearing on how the brain works but the interplay between the focus of the left and right hemispheres of the brain. He describes the left hemisphere as needing to manipulate the world, see fragments, focus in on detail, to put together a picture which is largely inert, unchanging, like a map. This has its place, as too much information would be counterproductive when trying to get to grips with a particular circumstance. The right hemisphere, however, recognises that the bits we focus on are merely what we have chosen to focus on, not separate at all but part of a seamless whole, within which things are constantly changing and evolving.[36] Both ways of seeing the world are needed but the left has a tendency to want to take over and dominate, leading to the kind of straight-line thinking that sends us down rabbit holes and prevents us from seeing the bigger picture.

As McGilchrist puts it, "Reason suggests a linear way of thinking, seeking chains of causation, which makes sense only in a limited environment. Its mode of operation is local, one bit at a time. Reason suggests a global, holistic understanding, which makes sense only in the round. It is a seamless apprehension of the world. Yes, you read that correctly. Reason means different things" and reasoning of the second kind "can be offered only by a living, fully feeling, embodied being, since it draws on value, and on the vast complex store of human experience, reflecting an understanding of how particular cases always differ by virtue of context."[37]

We shall look next at how we can make best use of all these in-built mechanisms of brain functioning.

Using the APET model

Using the APET approach – activating stimulus processed through pattern-matching, giving rise to emotion/expection, giving rise to thought or some activity (things-happen) – provides therapists with many points of intervention.

Human givens therapists are acutely aware, for example, of how influencing the activating stimulus (the A in APET) can in itself dramatically improve people's lives. If someone is depressed because of being relentlessly bullied at work or because the ethos of a company does not accord with their own, a therapist can encourage the discussion of options, including changing jobs.

One young married woman suffered vomiting fits during her critical and somewhat interfering mother-in-law's all too frequent visits to her home. The young woman was encouraged (by Joe) to be sick on the kitchen floor in front of her mother-in-law (instead of running to the bathroom), and then rush to her room, leaving her mother-in-law to clear up. This had the effect of reducing the frequency of the mother-in-law's visits (the activating stimulus) and gave the younger woman back control in her own home. The vomiting stopped.

The powerful effect of changing the activating stimulus can also be seen at work in social contexts. Social workers may particularly need to work with the activating stimulus that causes distress, with one of their roles being to ensure that people who are poor or ill have a roof over their heads, warmth, clothing and sufficient food. However, this is something HG therapists would expect to engage with, to a degree, too. One therapist realized she could get no further in helping her client handle her overwhelming anxiety until she had helped her sort out the faulty boiler in her shared house. Her client was responsible for organizing the repair of this fault but was so intimidated by two of her flatmates that she was too paralysed with fear to act, worsening the home situation further.

A rather dramatic example of the impact of changing the activating stimulus on reducing (or, in this case, eliminating) mental distress was described to us by a psychiatrist. He had been asked to see a woman suffering from severe panic attacks and an inability to engage with almost any task, even at home. She had been reluctant to attend and only did so after being repeatedly cajoled by her husband to do so.

Her panic attacks were so severe that she could no longer leave the house, unless she went out in the car with her husband. (It is relevant that the car was kept in their drive, which was concealed from view by trees and fencing.) Once the woman had established the confidentiality of the session, she opened up and revealed that she had had an affair with the man next door, which she bitterly regretted and had ended. But she was now terrified that, if she saw him, he would remonstrate with her or in some way give her away. Quite separately from this, she and her husband had been discussing the benefits of moving to a nicer area. As it wasn't, to her, an option to confess to her husband, the psychiatrist encouraged her to put her energies into finding a new place for them to live. This gave her hope, got her out of her frozen state, absorbed her attention and, once they had moved, she was fine again.

Importantly, an activating stimulus is not necessarily external. A fast-beating heart or sudden dizziness, for instance, may be the trigger for a cascade of pattern matches and interpretations which may or may not be appropriate. In one study, it was found that judges are more likely to deny parole to defendants just before lunch than just after breakfast. They were misinterpreting the discomfort of hunger pangs as unease about defendants' trustworthiness.[38] Some people are extra-sensitive to internal sensations, such as faster heart rate, and may tend to respond with panic. Helping people recognise their own 'normal' and learn to respond differently to such internal cues may be what is required. Conversely, former HG practitioner Chris Dyas has written movingly about the feeling of dread he started to wake to every night, which soon spread into the day and led him to cast around desperately for explanations, such as serious mistakes he must have made. It resulted in severe anxiety and depression. In fact, it was a symptom of complete heart block and it was only when other symptoms recognisable to medical professionals occurred that he was rushed into surgery and saved.[39]

Other examples of internal activating stimuli can include hormonal changes that occur during pregnancy or perimenopause, which for a number of women may lead to marked and, to them, seemingly inexplicable, personality change, anxiety and depression; or hormonal imbalances caused by ageing or illness that can affect men as well as women.

Human givens therapists pay considerable attention to changing inappropriate patterns (the **P** in APET) that cause individuals distress. As we have shown, pattern matching leads to expectations, usually in the form of emotions, and then things happening. Working with patterns can help change the **E** and the **T** of APET into helpful, rather than harmful, outcomes, and can be done in a variety of ways. For instance, when someone is stuck, a time-honoured way to change the patterns in their mind is through telling stories, using metaphors and appropriate humour. In this way, their imagination can be stimulated and experiences reframed (changing their expectations, the **E** in APET). This is why very many highly effective counsellors and psychotherapists tend to be natural storytellers.

Indeed, the benefits of this essential skill extend even further. When a more useful metaphorical pattern is offered to clients, for instance, they have the capacity, through the brain's own pattern-matching process, to decipher the metaphor for themselves, with the result that their solution is 'owned' by them rather than imposed on them by the therapist. Because it is the clients themselves who have made the connection, the connections are all the more 'hard-wired' and more firmly established. The method also enables rapport to be maintained because, if a client doesn't feel that a particular story or metaphor is relevant to them, they can just let it go past them, without feeling they have rejected 'advice' from the therapist. (Often, however, the meaning of a pertinent story will penetrate at a later date.)

Human givens therapists are particularly aware of the pattern-matching process in the phenomenon once known by philosophers as 'reification' and by linguists as 'nominalization'. This is the act of turning a verb or adjective into an abstract noun. A politician, for example, might change the verb to *modernize* into the noun *modernization*, claiming that "what we need is *modernization*", as though the process of modernization were something concrete that you could buy, see or touch. Similarly, we might be told that "we need to deliver *innovations*" as if they were parcels. The problem with these words is that they contain no sensory information – nothing specific such as who should be doing precisely what to whom. They are content-free, which is why they hypnotize both the listener *and* the speaker. To make sense of them, we have to go on an inner search to find a pattern match for what such words mean *to us* before we can give meaning to them. Consequently, they always mean something different to every listener while simultaneously giving each the feeling that they understand what the speaker means. That is why they are the stock-in-trade words of politicians, preachers and gurus.

For example, if a political leader says, "I am going to put more *resources* into *education*", everyone may applaud and be supportive. (The rhetorical trick, 'Education, Education, Education', was a New Labour party slogan.) But 'putting *resources into education*' means something quite different to every teacher, child or parent. And, to assign a personal meaning to these abstractions, listeners are forced to search inwards for a corresponding pattern. Because this happens unconsciously, they don't notice the con trick being played on them. One person might think the politician is going to instigate research into what exactly is the best way to educate a child. Another might think teachers are going to be paid more, or better schools will be built, or class sizes reduced, or schools made safer, or that there will be more exams, or that there will be fewer exams, or that the curriculum will be widened, or teachers trained better, and so on. The politician is trying to get support and credit by using these abstract terms to appeal to the different individual concerns of all those listening. This is an illusion. THE POLITICIAN HAS NOT PROMISED ANYTHING SPECIFIC AT ALL. You do not 'supply', 'give' or 'input' an abstract noun like *education*. You educate. And what people are educated about, why, how, where and by whom, are the questions that must be asked. So it is our duty to make politicians define exactly what they mean and to not let them off the hook until they do.

Likewise, a guru might say to his congregation, "We are gathered here in *spirit* today because we all share the same *profound values* and seek *peace*, *harmony* and eternal happiness from the divine blessing, which is to be found only by following the path of *truth* and *love* to *enlightenment*". When gurus or preachers keep up such hypnotic abstract language for any length of time, it makes their listeners feel special, as if the gurus are addressing their remarks directly to their 'hearts'. What is actually happening, of course, is that they are arousing emotions in them, softening them up for further conditioning or to make a sale.

It is because there are no precise, commonly shared perceptions about the meaning of such abstract words that they readily confuse us, making us vulnerable to self-deception and manipulation by others.

The only way to prevent this is, first, to learn to spot abstract nouns. (You can tell if a word is an abstract noun by asking yourself, "Does this have substance? Can I touch it/see it/feel it/taste it? Can I pick this up or move it?" If you can't answer yes to any of that, it is an abstract noun.) Second, we need to learn how to challenge these abstract terms, which is easily done by turning them back into verbs and asking people to be more precise.

For instance, if someone says, "My *expectations* must come first", we might respond by asking, "What exactly do you expect?"

If someone says they have *anger* in them, we should ask, "What exactly is making you angry?" (People do not have *anger* in them. It is not a substance like blood. In the same way, people do not have *depression* or *fear*. They are depressed *by* something or afraid *of* something.)

If politicians claim they are going to put more *resources* into the health services or transport or whatever, they should be challenged as to precisely how much they are planning to spend, on what, why and when. Similarly, if they say they are going to take *responsibility*, we need to know what exactly they are going to be responsible for, how this will be measured and what the penalties are if they fail.

The point we are making here is that operating through metaphor and generalizations, as we all must, is a vulnerability as well as an advantage. People use this kind of abstract language to hide ignorance, protect territory and deceive and manipulate people. Jargon, psychobabble, political and 'culty' language are almost entirely made up of it. It is important to be aware of this because we are social creatures and, unless we have perceptions more or less in common with those around us, it is difficult to cooperate with one another, and our interactions at all levels become cruder. That makes it harder to ensure our proper needs are met and makes selfish, unethical behaviour more likely.

One of the first to emphasize the importance within psychotherapy of recognizing abstract nouns, which he termed nominalizations, was the psycholinguist John Grinder, one of the founders of Neurolinguistic Programming (NLP).[40] Patients very commonly use these because they can't think straight and are ignorant about why this is so. They throw them out as a cry for help. It is the counsellor's job to dispel the ignorance so that they can be more realistic about their situation. Examples of negative abstractions (some are disguised as adjectives) that patients might use include: *anger, black cloud, evil, misery, doom, despair, depression, worthless, useless, hopeless, fear, gloom, low self-esteem*. If therapists are not aware of the pattern-matching process, such words can lead them to identify closely with the misery of their clients. Again, the way to deal with them is to challenge them. When a patient says, for example, "I'm full of misery," the most useful response is "What exactly is making you miserable? When did this feeling start? What was going on at the time?"

However, abstractions can also be used to positive effect. Positive ones, such as *happiness, strengths, love, creativity, resources, joy, principles, insight, learning, power, awareness, truth, beauty* and *possibilities*, although they may be used by advertisers, gurus and politicians to manipulate people, may also be employed by therapists and counsellors to send clients on a constructive, inner search to help them access positive patterns of behaviour. For instance, saying something like the following can have a powerful therapeutic effect: "After listening to you, I know that your *unconscious mind* has many *strengths* and *resources* that you can bring to bear on your situation which, coupled with your *integrity* and *creativity*, can open up new possibilities and bring *satisfaction* and *happiness* to your life once more."

Thus the pattern-matching process can subtly be used to change thoughts and perceptions. Thought patterns *can* be changed directly and consciously, of course, provided a person is not overly emotionally aroused. The new thought helps moderate or change any inappropriate pattern matches that are creating undesired emotional consequences. (For instance, someone who finds it hard to form a relationship with a new partner because of pattern matching to an abusive relationship in the past might be asked to think of 50 ways in which this relationship differs from the previous one.) This means, when people are highly emotionally aroused, the most effective thing to do is to calm down their emotions so that they can think more intelligently. They can then more easily see all the shades of grey between the emotionally driven black and white frames of reference they are stuck in.

The rewind detraumatisation technique, which will be described in the final chapter, offers a powerful, non-invasive means of changing outdated patterns by neutralizing the strong emotion still attached to a previous traumatic experience. Most commonly, for instance, human givens therapists would use this technique, which involves deep relaxation and tailored guided imagery, to help a client in the situation just described above – being unable to commit to a new healthy relationship because of being stuck in the emotion attached to the previous abusive relationship they suffered.

Therapy delivered from the APET model usually produces fast results. Once people are calmed down and no longer prey to heightened emotions, they can be given the information they need, either directly or through metaphor, to help them see their situation from multiple viewpoints. This helps them learn for themselves how calming down enables finer discrimination and a more accurate picture of the world.

The APET model offers a unifying theoretical basis for why any technique that is successful works. For example, with an understanding of the metaphorical pattern-matching function of the brain, and of how our instinctive templates are first programmed in the womb and after birth during REM, we can see how any therapy that directly accesses the REM state – guided imagery for example – can help clients reprogramme unhelpful patterns of responses. Until recently hypnosis (which, as we explained, simply means any artificial way of accessing the REM state) was treated with awe, incredulity or hostility within the psychotherapeutic community. However, as leading exponent psychiatrist Milton H. Erickson and others have long ago shown, hypnosis is the single most powerful psychotherapeutic tool available to us. It is so powerful precisely because it accesses the state of consciousness in which nature programmes the brain and can *reprogramme* it.[41] (As discussed earlier, of course, this also means that, like any powerful tool, hypnosis can be misused – and frequently is. So it is important that a therapist who uses it knows and respects its power and ensures using it for good.)

Reframing is another powerful technique, widely recognized as a core skill in effective counselling, that can be put in context through the APET model. A reframe replaces a pattern that is outdated or inappropriate with a richer one that opens us up to new possibilities we hadn't previously realized were there.

All effective therapy involves reframing. The determining factor in a person's flourishing is not just what happens to them in life but how they interpret experience, or how they 'frame', or put meaning to, life events – their expectations. Some 'frames' empower us and some disempower us. When someone unconsciously assumes that their way of perceiving reality is the only way, then a major shift can occur when another view is unexpectedly demonstrated to them. After a powerful reframe it is virtually impossible to maintain the problem behaviour in the same way.

Panic attacks

As well as providing an organic basis for understanding and integrating whatever works from the more potent therapeutic methodologies used today, the APET model also provides a clear theoretical understanding of why certain psychological conditions arise. With this understanding we can look afresh at such debilitating conditions and see how they could be better treated.

A panic attack, for example, is the inappropriate activation of the fight-or-flight response, the emergency reaction that prepares the body to deal with physical danger. Nowadays most of us are rarely in the presence of life-threatening events and yet that doesn't stop many people experiencing panic attacks. These usually come about as a result of a progressive rising in background stress levels until the point where one more stress – the straw that breaks the camel's back – sets off the alarm reaction, triggering the fight-or-flight response.

When this first occurs, not surprisingly, people don't understand why their heart is pounding, why they are sweating, why their breathing is accelerated, why their hands or face seem to have gone numb, etc, so they jump to the alarming conclusion that something must be seriously wrong and that perhaps they are having a heart attack or a stroke. This causes a further rise in the alarm reaction, release of more stress hormones, and even more intensified panic symptoms.

When we experience extreme alarm during a panic attack, the

brain, naturally enough, desperately scans the environment to find out where the 'threat' to its survival might be. Not surprisingly, many people then make an association with an element in the environment where the panic attack occurs. If it first occurs in a supermarket, for example, an individual may avoid supermarkets in future, even though the panic attack was caused not by the supermarket but by raised stress levels. Once the faulty association has been made, the fight-or-flight response will continue to fire off every so often, pattern matching to any environment that has similar elements to that of the supermarket: a post office, a bank, anywhere with bright lights or crowds or queues. People thus affected may then progressively avoid all these places and gradually the noose of agoraphobia grips them, hindering their interaction with life itself. In the worst cases, they become confined to home, terrified of the outside world.

A combination of relaxation, behavioural therapy and cognitive therapy is useful in treating this condition. Sufferers are taught to calm themselves down, address the emotional needs not being met that triggered the disorder, and progressively re-engage with life. With CBT this can take several sessions of therapy and practice but, with the human givens approach, progress is accelerated by first detraumatizing the memories of the most frightening panic attacks (using the rewind technique). As a result, the brain ceases to pattern match in a destructive way when people enter a new, previously frightening but in fact innocuous situation. Once the disabling emotional memories are processed, guided imagery is used to help people safely rehearse going through situations comfortably that they had previously been avoiding.

More empowering pattern matching can help with overwhelming or troubling anxiety of any kind (see, for instance, the following section on obsessions). In generalized anxiety conditions, people tend to catastrophise and tell themselves unhelpful stories with dire outcomes; giving them appropriate metaphors, telling them apposite stories and helping them make use of their imaginations to rehearse more realistic expectations, along with the practising of new skills, is the way to bring change about quickly.

Obsessions

Obsessive-compulsive disorder (OCD) can take many forms but is most often seen in repeated washing and checking behaviours. Again, often the background trigger is raised stress levels, which may be due to anything from physical illness, a fright, not getting enough sleep due to business worries, a relationship breakdown, a fear of loss, or stress around examinations – anything that prevents innate emotional needs from being met. Some people have a particular propensity to develop this disorder in response to raised stress levels. It is estimated that between 1 per cent and 3 per cent of the population have OCD.[42]

OCD is a complex neuropsychiatric process usually characterized by a homogeneous core of three main symptoms:

1. intrusive, forceful and repetitive thoughts, images, or sounds that dwell in the mind without the possibility of rejecting them
2. imperative needs to perform motor or mental acts
3. doubt or chronic questioning about major or minor matters.[43]

In more recent times, however, a variant known as Pure O has been identified, which refers to obsessive thoughts that do not lead to actions.

Sufferers of OCD may, in effect, be responding to posthypnotic suggestions accidentally implanted by environmental factors (for instance, seeing a white cat on the day that a loved one died and feeling obliged to perform a specific ritual to ward off new loss any time afterwards that they see a white cat). They may lose track of time and forget how long they have been performing the obsessive behaviour, or whether they have performed it fully, and so start all over again. Losing track of time and amnesia are common hypnotic phenomena.

Clearly, a pattern match is fired up in the brain and then embedded deeper and deeper by repetition – much as in addiction behaviour. Changing such deeply entrenched patterns is not easy but is possible in many cases, and working from the APET model offers multiple ways in which to go about it.

One key step, for example, is to help sufferers take a step back so that they can observe themselves and their behaviour. Once the patient's core identity has been separated from the problem and they recognize that the OCD behaviour is not who they are, and that the OCD thought is a bully, it is possible to stop the behaviour. (Indeed, dramatic recoveries from many conditions can occur by helping a person separate themselves from it.) Alarming memories of days when the intrusive thoughts (and compulsive behaviour) were very disabling can be put in the past, emotionally, by the rewind technique. Guided imagery can then be used to rehearse choosing not to act on, or give attention to, the bullying thought and calming down without performing the behaviour, if any. Innate emotional needs not being met when the condition began can then be addressed.

Negative ruminations

Depression is associated with memory bias – either a better memory for negative events or a poorer memory for positive events and experiences. This has led to the widely accepted theory that the onset of depression somehow facilitates access to negative memories which, once recalled, serve to exacerbate and extend the depression,[44] a finding consistent with network theories of emotion.[45] The more that we go back over the stories in our lives the more we are increasing and programming in the saliency of those patterns. Ask a depressed person about their childhood and they will describe it as though they had a terrible time but ask them again when they are out of the depression and they will describe a completely different upbringing. A depressed person who continually resurrects negative life experiences is programming those negative templates ever deeper into their unconscious mind. Therefore, new stimuli coming into their conscious minds, before ever reaching consciousness, are being matched up and scanned by negative templates to draw out what is negative in those experiences. Perceptions are continuously biased by the negative templates that are programmed in as a result of negative rumination. It is no surprise that depressed people also have false memories for negative material – they remember seeing or reading miserable things that they actually didn't even see.[46]

An emotion is like a lens through which we view the past. When we are feeling good, it is easy to pattern match to happy times. And the reverse is true. In cognitive therapy, people may be asked to challenge their conviction that everything they do is always wrong or hopeless by recalling successes and achievements. But the memory bias and reinforcing of negative patterns make it hard for a depressed person to recall good memories, so it isn't easy for them to generate a more positive attitude to life, however much they are willed to. Therapy based on the APET model, working from the human givens, can take a more diverse and creative approach to shifting unhelpful patterns, particularly through the use of metaphor and story, which impact on the unconscious mind more directly and powerfully than reason. Depression is such an important and fascinating topic we devote the next chapter to it.

Anger disorders

Anger disorders are also accelerating as the rate of environmental change overtaxes many people's ability to adapt. There are a number of physical states that lower the threshold for triggering anger. These include: dementia, physical illness, over-tiredness, hunger, hormonal changes during puberty, menopause, birth of a baby, physically craving for an addictive substance such as nicotine, alcohol, caffeine or other drugs, chronic or acute pain, intoxication and sexual frustration.

We all know that, because high emotional arousal affects our ability to think clearly, a chronically angry person is a stupid person. Fortunately everyone who is capable of concentration and motivated to learn can be taught to control their anger and reduce their stupidity.

There may be a variety of reasons why a person has a problem with inappropriate anger. In the majority of cases, when people lose their temper, it is simply a result of 'the straw that breaks the camel's back' – they are just currently over-stressed. Because of this they see reality in black-and-white terms, and a small infringement can seem like a huge one. As mentioned, some people develop an addiction to anger. They actually enjoy the feeling of certainty and the emotional high it gives them – they are 'emotional junkies'. In such circumstances, this has to be treated like any other addiction; they have to learn to see how, overall, anger outbursts have more of a destructive effect upon their lives than a constructive one. And they have to be willing to learn how to manage that behaviour responsibly. Sometimes excessive anger is a response to some traumatic life experience, and such individuals would benefit from treatment for post-traumatic stress. In other cases, it may be driven by a cause that is hidden from consciousness, as a result of a 'molar memory'. (See "Molar memories" on page 261 for a full explanation of this.)

In a properly matured human being, anger is a tool in the service of the observing self. As Aristotle said, "Anyone can become angry – that is easy; but to be angry with the right person, to the right degree, at the right time, for the right purpose and in the right way – that is not easy."

In the 1970s, a fashion arose whereby unhappy people were encouraged to 'get their anger out', in a reaction against the controlling tendencies of psychoanalysis. Research on anger management has long shown, however, that hitting punch bags or pillows, shouting louder and louder and so on, and thereby getting more and more angry whilst doing so, only serve to make a person more unhappy and dysfunctional, even though it appears in the short term as if the exhaustion that all this induces is satisfying. As a therapeutic technique, it was a disaster.[47]

Anger management skills connect far more closely with how the mind/body system works. People can learn to recognize when they are starting to lose their temper, and how to withdraw from an explosive situation with another person before emotion stops them from thinking straight. This might take the form of acknowledging to the other person the seriousness of the issue and explaining that they are getting too worked up to think clearly about it and that they need to be able to address it in a calmer state of mind. Withdrawing from the situation for at least 20 or 30 minutes and doing something calming, such as taking a walk, can give the stress hormones a chance to flow out of the system. At this calming-down stage, it is important people do not use it rehearse the reasons for their excessive emotional response or attempt to justify their anger, as this will just pump it up again. Only once calm is it possible to go back and work at resolving the problem. It is important not to leave the issue unresolved, as that will just let it fester and thus further undermine the relationship.

Another important point which is helpful to take on board is that most arguments are not really about right and wrong. They are really about 'my needs' versus 'your needs'. When we can take that approach in a calm manner it is usually possible to begin negotiating so that both sets of needs are met, or a reasonable compromise is found.

An important skill, which we think young people should be taught as a matter of course, is the use of calming techniques on ourselves. This is sometimes, fortunately, now taught in schools – indeed, we know of many human givens therapists who work with young people being invited to do so. There is also a trend for some schools to teach mindfulness techniques, which in principle is good but can sometimes be counter-productive, if anxious children worry about not being able to let go of their thoughts.

There are times when *everybody* needs to know how to relax. Breathing techniques, such as the 7:11 technique, are invaluable: this involves breathing into the diaphragm to the count of seven and out to a count of 11. When the out-breath is kept longer, it stimulates the parasympathetic nervous system, the relaxation response. Aerobic exercise can also calm us down. When we are calmed down, we are more able to look at a difficult situation differently and reframe it.

An essential skill, when on the receiving end of anger, is not to escalate it. Even if receiving an undeserved amount of vitriol, it is not the time to try to reason, because angry individuals are not in a state of mind where they can process a viewpoint that contradicts their own. Arguing with angry people is futile. They need help to calm down because, when angry, they cannot help but see life in a distorted way through their emotional black-and-white thinking. Their outbursts need not be taken too personally once that is recognized.

Addictions

Most people realize that, if they indulge too heavily in any potentially addictive form of pleasure – whether alcohol, drugs, gambling, shopping or even work, it will interfere with getting other needs met, as addiction usually results in disintegrating relationships, low self-esteem and insecurity created by debt. Young people may often experiment with drugs but, as they mature, form relationships, take on responsibilities, build a family, etc., drug use tends to drop off. In other words, there is a natural counterweight to overindulgence in any appetite built in to us. If we over-indulge in one pleasure, we lessen the likelihood of other important needs being met. Knowing that provides the motivation to keep any single pleasure from getting out of hand and dominating our lives.

So nature has built this lovely balance into us. But there is a complication: the counterweight must be in place, if tendencies towards addiction are to be thwarted, and that is not always the case. People who are lonely, isolated, involuntarily unemployed, suddenly bereaved, or who, for whatever reason, lack the ability to generate the self-esteem that comes from being involved in work, building a family and involvement in meaningful community activities, are clearly not getting their needs met, and are therefore highly vulnerable to addiction. Many of them lack relationship skills or don't know how to manage their anxiety and stress other than through taking drugs or drink. Some have been traumatized in war or been subject to violent domestic attacks or sexual abuse. Any such cause can damage human beings and make them vulnerable to addiction.

It might seem that this doesn't always apply. What about high achievers who reach a stage in life where they have great wealth, a family and, to all intents and purposes, seem successful, but then become addicts? They are not 'down and outs' or social failures. They are exemplars, however, of the carrot-and-stick principle we discussed earlier. If they no longer derive pleasure, a healthy, natural reward, from having to stretch themselves to build their career, in the way that they were used to, they may start to try and put pleasure back into their lives by drinking too much or indulging excessively in other pleasures.

The first step in combating an addiction is to help people to recognize that they have one. They must come to realize that this behaviour is, in the overall economy of their life, causing them more pain than pleasure. This cannot be done by being critical of them. Criticizing or arguing with an addict only puts them on the defensive and drives them back into emotional black-and-white thinking. They need to be helped to see, in a sympathetic, supportive way, how destructive the addiction is in their life, and how it creates an emotional wasteland leading to nowhere except an early grave. Only when this is seen to be the case, and an undesirable state of affairs, can the next step be taken.

Human givens therapists will explain to clients the expectation theory of addiction, devised by Joe Griffin.[48] Understanding and managing expectations (E of APET) is the most powerful ally in helping addicts quit. In our book *Freedom from Addiction*,[49] we clearly explain the physiological component of expectation – how believing that the addictive substance will bring us pleasure affects the associations that we bring to mind and the strength of the physical discomfort of cravings experienced. Physically, withdrawal symptoms are mild. It is when the brain gets involved and reacts over-emotionally that the experience may become unbearable.

In deep relaxation, clients can be helped to reprogramme their associations with the addictive activity, so that, when they think of engaging in it, negative memories or fears (such as illness, death, financial or relationship ruin) are pulled up instead of false positive ones. Then they can be guided to visualize a future in which they are healthy, happy, have more money or family time – or whatever it is that makes them want to quit the addictive activity in the first place.

Addicts must be helped to build their self-esteem, so that they can believe it possible to change their lifestyle and rebuild their lives. Our colleague Ezra Hewing has drawn together the scientific evidence to explain why and how guided imagery is so valuable for helping them engage deeply with this.[50] All vertebrates have structures in their brains called basal ganglia, which enable creatures to weigh up whether a particular goal is safe to pursue (a tasty food) or a threat to their survival (a predator will get them first). Obviously the relevant structures in human brains are much more complex than those in simple vertebrates and, to keep this explanation simple, involve what are known as D1 and D2 brain receptors for the neurotransmitter dopamine (the D stands for dopamine), which is concerned with motivation. The DI receptors encode rewarding experiences (in this case, the positives associated with the addictive activity); the more pleasant memories there are, the more D1 receptors are in place. The D2 receptors encode memories of all possible adverse outcomes, and the more *unpleasant* memories there are, the more D2 receptors are in place.[51,52,53] Guided visualization which encourages extremely vivid imagining of the negative consequences increases the numbers of D2 receptors, inhibiting the encoded D1 reward memories and making it less likely that the person will want to succumb to the addictive behaviour.

As addiction clients' sense of self-empowerment grows, whatever blocks are in the way of getting their needs met more constructively must be removed. This is a problem-solving focus. If it is post-traumatic stress that is disabling, they will need to be detraumatized. If it is clinical depression, they will need to be lifted out of it. If they lack social interaction skills, they need to be taught them.

It is also important to keep the attention mechanism in mind when treating addictions. Because all views and beliefs are determined in part by those we interact with, someone who spends much of their time with people who indulge in an addictive lifestyle will inevitably reactivate that mindset in themselves. Because the brain is a pattern-matching organ, any time a person encounters something in the environment that in the past was positively associated with their addiction, it will automaticaly reactivate the desire for the substance or behaviour.

The actual chemical need for an addictive substance is usually gone in a matter of days; the body rebalances itself. But the tendency to relapse comes with perceiving a pattern in the environment that recalls the addiction state. There may be a compulsion to complete the pattern – by taking drugs again or whatever the addictive substance is.

This means that the ex-addict has literally got to wear the pattern out. When enough time goes by, the brain finds other uses for the neurons involved in that behaviour. Some people achieve this by withdrawing as much as possible from any environment or actions that might activate those patterns. An alcoholic may need to avoid the pub for example. A heroin user would be best advised not to go to places where heroin is used or mix with people whose main point of connection is their drug use. Otherwise, strong desires will be triggered off again.

Clearly, a part of recovery must involve helping someone meet or spend more time with people who have a healthier attitude towards life. In such company, they will be able to get their needs met in more wholesome ways.

Rituals associated with addiction also need to be avoided, or at least the ex-user must be very conscious and wary of them, so the resolve not to give in is kept strong. For example, if the *last* time you went on holiday you were still a cigarette smoker, you have to be wary that, the *next* time you go, the pattern match might trigger off the desire for a cigarette. If you anticipate this, and know it is something temporary (part of wearing out old patterns), you don't have to give in. You are forearmed, and that's the essential element.

Addiction distorts thought processes, fooling us into thinking that life would be the better for indulging in it. So it is helpful for people to know that most people do not beat an addiction on the first attempt. The skills involved in learning how to overcome addiction take time to build, just as learning to ride a bicycle involves a few tumbles. So, if in the past a man had always got drunk whenever he got angry and, on one occasion, got blotto again, he should be helped to view his lapse as a slip up, not a failure. The therapist's task is to make sure he doesn't give up trying; to help him make good use of the slip up – by seeing that getting drunk didn't actually do anything to solve whatever had made him angry; and to work with him to develop the skills to deal with testing situations more successfully.

So a human givens approach contains essential knowledge for treating addiction. Treatment involves sociological and environmental as well as psychological elements. In summary, to come back from addiction a person first needs help to see what is blocking a better lifestyle, and then help to think more realistically about the addictive substance and to work out a package of skills and behaviours to enable their needs to be met more effectively – creating the counterweight against relapsing into addiction.

Molar memories

In some cases, addictive behaviours can have a hidden cause. An individual acts compulsively and has no real understanding of why this is happening. In fact, the explanation can be found in something that Joe Griffin has termed a molar memory – a memory that has two emotional roots, one positive and one negative, which can drive addictive behaviours, including anger.[54]

As the theory explains, a molar memory evokes excessive *positive/pleasurable* emotions (anger, sexual arousal, eating, drinking, greed for money, attention, new clothes, etc.) when it is *unconsciously* activated by pattern matching to certain stimuli in the present. So, for instance, it could be that someone struggling with compulsive eating sees a plate of cakes belonging to someone else and grabs one. But, in therapy, it produces *negative/painful* emotions when the memory of the original event is first *consciously* pattern matched to (using a technique explained below). In our example, the person recalls as a very young child reaching for a delicious cake on a plate intended for visitors and being yelled at and sent to her room, which she found both terrifying and confusing. Only by focusing on the memory further, and allowing the initial negative feelings to abate, will the positive/pleasurable emotion also associated with the original event be consciously evoked (taking the cake in the expectation of enjoying eating it). It is pattern matching to this unconscious, positive root of the memory that drives the compulsive and seemingly irrational behaviour in the present.

Why? Well, when an experience is both intensely pleasurable and intensely painful, the pain memories encoded in the D2 receptors (described earlier) are stronger than the pleasure memories encoded in the D1 receptors, so the irrational or compulsive behaviour will not be acted on. However, if it appears that there is currently no risk of hurt if the pleasurable action is indulged in (the person is an adult now and no one will stop her taking the cake), the pleasure memory will be acted on. A molar memory is never a 'suppressed memory', as in psychodynamic theory; only one part of a molar memory is initially outside of consciousness – the positive root.

A molar memory can be accessed using the 'affect bridge' technique, a powerful way of accessing a pattern match from the past that needs de-conditioning. A person simply has to relax and focus on experiencing whatever feeling seems to be excessive (in our example, greed for a cake), to see what memories it brings up. If the person then identifies a memory that involves a negative emotion (e.g. shame, humiliation, anxiety, fear or pain) *but not the troublesome excessive emotion*, a molar memory is present. Most commonly, the original event that created the molar memory will have occurred in childhood. A human givens therapist will ask the person to relive the memory that has been triggered and acknowledge the negative emotion, so that this emotion abates. Then the person will be asked to go back to earlier in the memory, to see if they also experienced the troublesome excessive positive emotion *before* the negative one led to its suppression. If this is so, the person is asked to experience the positive emotion as intensely as possible and express it (verbally or silently). Doing this puts the feeling back in its correct context. Then the therapist will normalize the emotion by saying something like "It was perfectly normal for a young child to feel greed in those circumstances and you didn't know it was wrong to take a cake without asking". This process, once complete, should prevent the inappropriate feelings or behaviours occurring in the future. It can effectively be used on oneself, as well as others.

Joe once worked with a man who came to see him about his drink problem. The man routinely downed eight or more bottles of real ale at home at night. When Joe asked him what he found so pleasurable about drinking, the man described the wonderful feeling he experienced when he drained the warm beer, which he always drank straight from the bottle.

Joe relaxed him deeply and then, using the affect bridge technique, asked him to relive that exquisite feeling of draining the bottle and stay with the feeling, to see if any event from the past came into mind. After a while, the client recalled the memory of when he was four years old and was bawled at by his furious mother, who had caught him drinking from his baby sister's bottle. He had been jealous of his sister for being allowed to drink milk from a bottle with a teat, when he was no longer allowed to do so. So, one day, when his mother was not in the room, he had sneaked a prepared bottle of warm milk and drained it. The pleasure was supreme, until his mum came into the room and terrified him with her anger.

Clearly, the memory of the pleasurable experience (draining the bottle) had been superseded by the memory of intense humiliation and fear. So, whenever he was in a situation when he *didn't* risk humiliation and fear if he drained the bottle (and, of course, as an adult, there was no such risk), he would find himself drinking excessively. Once the client had re-experienced the guilty pleasure, Joe had normalized it by saying, "It was only natural that you wanted to drink from your sister's bottle. You were feeling jealous and wanted to be the baby again yourself and do what babies do. But now you are grown up and you are not prevented from drinking from a bottle. So you can choose to have just one or two bottles of real ale and then stop drinking." After that, the man didn't drink excessively again.

This technique is successfully used by many human givens therapists to treat addictive activities ranging from eating problems, gambling and compulsive shopping to watching pornography. Findings from neurobiology explain why the treatment works so well.[55]

Placebo – nocebo

The placebo response has baffled scientists and puzzled thoughtful human beings since perhaps the dawn of civilization. It was certainly referred to by Chaucer in his writings. The word comes from *placebo domino*, "I will please the Lord", a term that was associated with travelling friars who demanded money from poor people to say prayers for their dead – in effect, a form of emotional blackmail. For centuries, the word placebo was a term of abuse. But gradually doctors started using it to describe the response whereby some patients recovered from illnesses even when medicine was ineffectual, as if some kind of faith healing had taken place.

One of the functions of modern double-blind trials is to find whether a medicine is the cause of a person's cure or whether they might have got better because of a doctor's implicit 'suggestion' that a medicine will work. Double-blind means that neither the doctors nor the patients in a trial know who is receiving the active treatment and who is receiving the placebo. And somebody neutral must hand out the pills because, when doctors know which pill contains the genuine drug, their own beliefs about it somehow transmit to the patients and the patients often improve because of that.

The remarkable thing, however, is that, even with the most stringent double-blind trials, there is still an effect on the control group (those not receiving the active treatment). A significant number of the control group invariably get better, even when taking an inert substance. To be considered effective a new drug must be significantly superior in effect to the placebo response experienced by the control group. What wasn't realized till a couple of decades ago, however, is that there is a placebo effect to active medicines too.[56] Indeed, as indefatigable psychologist and academic researcher Irving Kirsch has shown, analyses of published and unpublished data that were hidden by drug companies reveal that most, if not all, the benefits they attributed to antidepressants were due to the placebo effect.[57]

The power of placebo continues to amaze. The British Psychological

Society's *Research Digest* carried a round-up of 10 "amazing placebo-related findings",[58] which, alongside the long-known fact that branding, colour of pills or sham use of medical apparatus associated with the conventional treatment can have a part to play in placebo effectiveness, included less familiar findings, such as that placebos can boost both physical and mental performance. In one of the studies covered, cyclists who had been asked to train to the point of exhaustion were found able to persist significantly longer when timers had been altered to run slower, so that the participants thought they had been cycling for less time than they really had. In another study, participants who thought that their brains had been stimulated by a mild electrical current intended to boost mental functioning were quicker to react and more accurate in their answers in a learning task.

Intriguingly, as the compiler Christian Jarrett observed, there is even such a thing as a placebo sleep effect. Study participants who had been tricked into thinking they had had more sleep than was really the case performed better on language and maths tests. Another fascinating finding which he said might be attributed to the placebo effect was that people who believed they exercised more than their peers tend to live longer, regardless of how much they really exercised.

But the most striking discovery is that placebos can work to ease physical symptoms even if they are *known* to be placebos. A study published in 2010 showed that a significant number of people with irritable bowel syndrome experienced improvement in their symptoms even when given what they knew to be placebo pills, in a bottle clearly marked 'placebo'.[59] The same result was found in a similar study of people with chronic back pain.[60] In both, participants were told that the placebo effect could be powerful; that the body could respond automatically to taking placebo pills, like Pavlov's dogs, which salivated when they heard a bell; that a positive attitude could be helpful but was not necessary; and that taking the pills faithfully for the 21 days was critical.

Openly prescribed placebos have now also been shown to have a positive effect for cancer-related fatigue (those randomized to receive 'open label' placebo reported 29 per cent improvement compared with 10 per cent in those receiving usual treatment, while disruption of quality of life caused by fatigue improved by 39 per cent, compared with 5 per cent). They also helped with episodic migraine attacks (15 per cent reduction in pain when taking placebo compared with 15 per cent worsening of pain with no treatment). The researchers suggest that openly prescribed placebo may be valuable for conditions with "self-reported outcomes", and thus may also help other cancer-related symptoms such as nausea, pain and hot flushes, but is unlikely to be beneficial for patients with, say, malaria or high cholesterol levels.[61]

Knowingly drinking decaf coffee can help reduce symptoms of caffeine withdrawal. Study participants, who normally drank more than three cups of coffee a day, abstained for 24 hours and then drank coffee freshly brewed in front of them but only half knew it was made with decaf beans, while a control group drank water. When all described the effect afterwards on their withdrawal symptoms, there was, unsurprisingly, no change for the water drinkers. Those who thought they had had normal coffee reported a significant reduction in symptoms and those who knowingly drank decaf experienced a lesser but still substantial drop in symptoms.

The authors attribute the effect to pattern matching, although they don't use that word. They suggest that the sounds and associations – eg the coffee grinding, the coffee smell, the liquid pouring and the warmth of the filled cup – were sufficient to trigger the expected physiological effects of drinking coffee, including, as would be expected, a cessation of any withdrawal effects.[62]

These finding strongly suggest that the placebo effect must reflect an innate capacity within human beings for self-healing: if we could find a way of tapping into this, we might be able to tap into nature's own way of healing itself. This might open the door to powerful new treatments with no side effects.

Indeed, it *is* possible to tap into the placebo effect. We would suggest that pattern matching – the **P** in APET – is at its basis, along with expectation – the **E** in APET – and can help us understand the mind/body connections involved. Three conditions must be fulfilled before a placebo can work. There must be a pattern that can be matched to, however crudely (we have seen how even just one or two elements of similarity is enough); the treatment must seem plausible enough for the brain to interpret it as capable of bringing about a healing reaction; and the emotions must be engaged – the individual must accept that the treatment could work.

So, the placebo, first and foremost, generates a pattern that corresponds to a pattern the brain already knows. Matching to this pattern gives the brain the ability to alter the body's reactions. When a person is offered a pill (dummy or otherwise) to cure a headache, the pattern being matched to is "I've had headaches before and I feel better when I take a pill/this colour pill/this shape of pill" or whatever.

When the treatment is a novel one, for instance a treatment for cancer, the patient's belief in the plausibility of its working must be stronger, as there is no past success to match to. The pattern to which the brain must match is one of wellbeing or the experience that doctors are trustworthy. It may be sufficient that the patient places great store in the fact that the doctor has an international reputation or that they successfully treated a family member or friend.

For the placebo effect to work, there must be only one pattern for the brain to try to match to. The pattern must be "This can make me feel better", and even a little scepticism is not sufficient to undermine the power of this.[63] For the brain to focus on the one pattern, the emotions must be aroused, creating in effect a trance state of belief and conviction. Expectation, desire for the treatment to work, faith in the doctor and a sense of urgency, for instance, all help arouse the emotions and create the desired focusing of attention. When a credible pattern is focused on with a level of emotional arousal that locks the attention onto the required outcome, the brain then does all it can to pattern match to that result.

Joe tells the tale of his own experience of a placebo response which bears out the above. He once heard, from what he considered a fairly reliable source, that aspirin could stop a hangover. "As I was curious to know whether this could be true, I promised myself that I would try it out when appropriate. But I don't drink to excess very often nowadays – although anybody who knows me knows you don't have to force a drink into my hand! This meant my frustration levels about satisfying my curiosity were building up the more I was denied an opportunity to put the method to the test. Eventually, however, after a family celebration, I had drunk enough to cause a hangover. So I eagerly took an aspirin and went to bed.

"I woke up the next morning on cloud nine – not a trace of a hangover. I felt as if I were walking on air in a way similar to how I had heard some of my heroin addict patients describe feeling after taking heroin. In fact I suspect that is exactly what I *was* experiencing: the release of my body's own endogenous heroin, namely endorphins."

If we look at the mechanics of what had occurred here we can see a clear illustration of how the placebo response works. First there was a credible theory – that taking an aspirin could prevent a hangover – but there was also a build up of emotional arousal because of the frustration while waiting for a chance to put the theory to the test. So the placebo effect was triggered and Joe woke the next morning after a release of endorphins that made him feel very positive indeed.

However, the story doesn't end there. Joe took an aspirin on another occasion, later, when he thought he might have a hangover. But this time it didn't work! The only difference was that the second time he took the aspirin there was no emotional arousal and Joe's attention was not focused on the outcome.

The emotional arousal and focusing of attention is enormously important. It explains why, for instance, some people who attend accident and emergency departments for crippling headaches respond to placebo tablets.[64] Being in an accident and emergency department is an unusual experience. Just being there sends a powerful message to the brain that there is something seriously wrong, which raises emotional levels and locks attention onto whatever tablet is given. The tablet is a physical metaphor that seeks a pattern match. The pattern match provokes an endorphin release that relieves pain.

Other research has shown that, if a placebo is given by injection, it is more effective than if it is given by tablet.[65] This is probably because an injection is seen as stronger medicine. Also, smaller tablets have been found more powerful than standard tablets, probably because patients are subliminally influenced to believe that they must be receiving a very concentrated essence of the 'medicine'. This unconsciously focuses their attention even more. Such methods give the rituals more credibility.

The placebo effect is an enormously powerful one, as we have seen, but it is definitely not magic. Even when all the conditions are right, as described above, healing cannot occur in, for instance, the case of advanced cancer or when the immune system is compromised. This, along with any lack of conviction, explains why placebos often do *not* work.

The reverse of the placebo effect also exists. Known as the 'nocebo' effect or medical hexing, patients' conditions worsen as a result of doctors unintentionally conveying negative suggestions to which the patients respond. Simple instances might be "I haven't had a patient respond to this treatment yet, but ...", "I don't know much about this treatment personally ...", "Well, it might be worth a try", "This doesn't work for 40 per cent of people". Whenever a doctor focuses a patient's attention on a possible negative outcome, even with a throwaway remark, the emotion the remark arouses in the patient's brain will lock attention onto it and increase the chances of a negative outcome. This effect has been shown scientifically, too. In one study, participants were told that their pain would increase after a pain-relieving treatment was stopped. In actual fact, the analgesia effect would normally persist but, in those given the misinformation, the pain relief came to an immediate end once treatment was stopped, overriding the usual physiological effects.[66]

This is why it is important that doctors are careful with the language they use when giving prognoses or life expectancy projections. In very many cases, their patients may fulfil the predictions that have been suggested to them.

So, to recap, the placebo response is most likely to work when a credible ritual is offered with positive endorsement from the relevant health professional that raises the patient's expectations of improvement or cure. A placebo is an undifferentiated metaphor. Once the brain's attention mechanism is locked onto a pattern, it does everything it can to try to complete that pattern – to find a match to it.

It has been shown, unsurprisingly, that those who are most susceptible to hypnosis are also most likely to respond to well-delivered placebos. The credible ritual is a metaphor. It can be a physical metaphor like a tablet, injection or procedure, or it can be a mental metaphor, like a phrase, theory or story. Tablets are fairly crude metaphors. The giving of one doesn't convey much guidance about how the patient should use it to mobilize his or her own immune system. A story, however, especially when delivered while a client is in the focused attention state of trance, can provide a disguised means of giving highly detailed instructions for kick-starting the immune system.

The following is an example of how Ivan used this means to help a depressed woman whose feet were deformed by dozens of painful verrucas. One of the verrucas was as big as a 50 pence piece and some days she could barely stand with the pain. Over the previous years she had attended chiropodists at different hospitals and received a variety of treatments, even surgery, all to no avail. But, within a few weeks of putting her into a trance and telling her this story, her verrucas had gone and her depression had lifted. Three months later, her feet were completely smooth.

ONCE UPON a time there was a wonderful land ruled over by a wise and popular king. He kept his people safe from enemies and helped them prosper and thus he earned their respect. But, as happens, the king died and his only daughter inherited the kingdom and became queen. At first all went well for she possessed her father's wisdom and worked hard for the good of the people who consequently loved her.

Then calamity struck. Alien barbarians invaded the southern regions of the kingdom and built ugly castles from where they sallied forth, pillaging the surrounding countryside, making life unbearable for the people. The young queen didn't know what to do as the invaders drained the lifeblood of her country, causing more and more pain and the people lost their spirit.

As the months and years passed the invaders entrenched themselves deeper and deeper and the queen grew more desperate.

One day, an old warrior rode up to her palace and begged an audience. The queen bade him welcome and asked him what he wanted.

"You are a good queen beset by troubles," he said. "And I am here to help you. The troubles come about because, unlike your father, who I knew as a young man, you are not skilled in the arts of war."

"Then what must I do to rid my country of these evil parasites?" the queen asked.

"It is not difficult," said the old warrior. "With your permission, I can do it on your behalf using the tried and tested techniques of siege warfare. But you must give me command of your people to do it."

The queen felt she had nothing to lose and the old warrior set about mobilizing her people and turning them into armies, one for each castle. He showed each army how to surround the barbarian castles – lay siege to them – and stressed how important it was that the occupants were prevented from getting any sustenance or nutriment from the surrounding countryside.

"You will soon see," said the old warrior, "that the enemy will either die off in the castles or retreat whence they came."

And so it was. Soon the land was cleared of the invaders and their ugly castles quickly decayed or were destroyed. Peace and prosperity returned to the kingdom.

The queen thanked the old warrior and rewarded him well and he settled nearby in case she ever needed him again.

The story is clearly a metaphor for the client's problem and for the solution (her immune system needed to "mobilize" itself for a big effort and "lay siege" to the verrucas). She had no conscious recollection of the story after coming out of trance.[67]

Not only does the pattern-matching concept open up an understanding of how the placebo effect works but also, as in the above example, it explains why its conscious use as a psychotherapeutic procedure is often so effective.

Nocebo counselling

Once one understands the APET model it is easy to see why some counselling can be ineffective or harmful. Many counsellors are trained to encourage emotionally arousing introspection in their clients about what might be 'causing' their problems. The emotional arousal this produces locks the client's attention onto negative patterns of thought and behaviour. This leads, almost inevitably, to a period of negative rumination and the cycle of depression can set in. The process, however unintentional, can, in effect, be characterized as nocebo therapy.

When counsellors encourage people to remember, and get emotional about, negative life experiences – bringing to the fore destructive patterns – they are actually going against nature's inclination to promote survival, health and wellbeing. And that's why some people say they go to see their counsellor feeling miserable and come out feeling suicidal. The essence of good therapy, on the other hand, is placebo therapy – focusing clients' attention on problem solving and solutions, using their own innate powers.

Metaphor, storytelling and learning

As the brain is fundamentally concerned with matching metaphorical patterns, it follows that metaphors are the most wonderful natural tool for learning. Learning is a process of refining patterns of perception built upon a foundation of both instinctive patterns and learned patterns. All learning is an extension of existing patterns in the student. We are referring here not to learning facts by rote, in effect just storing up a series of bits of information, but to real learning – interacting more effectively with the environment, and developing through experience the ability to discriminate and discern a greater subtlety of the patterns therein and how they connect up with our own inner perceptions.

The way creative breakthroughs are made in science well illustrates this. The breakthrough 'ah hah' experience comes when scientists recognize that a pattern which works in one area of reality can also be applied in another. They take a pattern that explains one phenomenon and use it as a metaphor to explain what is going on in a different phenomenon. One of the most famous metaphorical insights led to Kekulé's discovery of the structure of the benzene ring: one of the most important discoveries in the history of chemistry. He had been trying for years to solve the problem of the molecular structure of benzene. Then one afternoon, as he was puzzling over the problem, he began to doze. He saw atoms gambolling before his eyes. Then he saw larger structures in long rows, twisting and entwining in a snakelike motion, until they looked just like snakes. One of the 'snakes' proceeded to seize its own tail. He awoke with a jolt to realize that the structure of benzene must be a closed ring – a solution suggested to him by the image of the snake swallowing its own tail.

Conveying new, desired patterns in a metaphor or story is perhaps the most effective way of all to refine patterns (although there are other effective methods, such as modelling desired behaviours). Milton H. Erickson, whom many regard as the most significant clinician and psychotherapist of the 20th century, was a master storyteller who put this skill to good effect in his work.[68] Often the teachers who most influence pupils' education are those who use anecdotes and stories to make their lessons come alive. In the human givens training context we ourselves use stories and case histories to illustrate our theoretical principles in order to bring those principles to life in the minds of students. All good communicators use stories for that reason.

If clients are missing some piece of the jigsaw puzzle of life we could offer them a story about another (anonymous) client with a similar problem that shows how *their* behaviour changed, and thus convey the desired new pattern in an indirect way, or we could tell an appropriate traditional story. The world's stories, oral and written, contain a fantastic cornucopia of wonderful patterns, which chart the possibilities of understanding ourselves more profoundly and help us engage with the world more fruitfully.

Our former colleague Pat Williams, a founder–director of the former College of Storytellers, has described how she helped somebody who was struggling with an addiction by telling them the ancient Greek myth about Odysseus who, on his way home to Greece after the battle of Troy, had to pass the island of the sirens. He had been told by the enchantress Circe that all sailors who passed that island were lured to their death on the rocks if they heard the sirens' song. But she had also told him a way to hear the sirens' magical music and survive. She told him to order his sailors to put softened beeswax in their ears, to stop them hearing the singing, and then have them tie him fast to the mast, giving them instructions that, no matter how much he urged or pleaded with them to turn the boat towards the island, they should merely bind him faster and continue on their course, past the island. This was done. When Odysseus heard the sirens' song, he wanted with every cell in his body to go to the island but, because he had forewarned his crew, they ignored his signals to change direction, bound him even more tightly to the mast, and eventually they passed the island. Odysseus was released by the crew, enormously grateful that he had been enabled to survive – and that he had escaped being dragged to his doom.

This powerful metaphorical template, with all its allusions and implications, can be used to show how a drug or addictive experience may be extremely seductive and yet ultimately is destructive. The story also metaphorically sets in place a template for how people can reorganize their internal resources to fight it.

This form of learning can be used if appropriate in conjunction with cognitive-behavioural approaches to increase the chances of a successful outcome.

To recap, to help educate clients who are stuck we have to help them understand what is blocking them from getting their needs met. This is done through refining their patterns of perception, helping incorporate these patterns into their own perceptual apparatus and creating a healthier, outward focus on life. If those patterns are not already active, the job of the counsellor is to help draw them forth, thus providing a stronger and more accurate lens through which the client can perceive reality. Using metaphor is one of the most powerful ways this can be done.

This whole process can be greatly speeded up by using nature's own tool for accelerated learning. This is the state of consciousness characterized by REM sleep, in which, as described in Part I, in the foetus and early months of life, nature lays down the instinctive templates that will later seek out their completion in the environment.[69]

We now know that we can directly access that same cortical organization through guided imagery. (This state, when entered deeply, is analogous to that of REM sleep.) People can be put into trance by replicating any part of the pattern by which nature triggers the REM state. These include muscle relaxation; inducing rapid eye movements, (as in the 'focus your eyes on my swinging watch' technique and as used in Eye Movement Desensitization and Reprocessing, [EMDR]); or by firing off the brain's orientation response, as when a stage hypnotist suddenly pushes down on his subject's shoulder and gives the instruction "Sleep!" The orientation response focuses attention and is firing continually during dreaming.[70] The brain absorbs new ideas and information best when in a receptive, open, uncritical trance state. Once patterns have been absorbed and understood, they can be looked at consciously and 'checked out'. In counselling, when we relax people and focus their attention, we have some degree of access to their REM state in which the brain is at its most receptive and able to absorb information uncritically. This is, therefore, the ideal time to offer constructive stories and metaphors to clients' unconscious minds to help them transform their perceptions.

The bigger pattern

Understanding the importance of pattern matching, metaphor and story is fundamental to making teaching more effective and our children more able to develop their full potential in life. Down the ages all good teachers have been great storytellers, but only now do we have a physiological understanding of why it is necessary for them to be so. Research by Dr Robert Ornstein and others shows that, when people are listening to stories, their right hemisphere is very actively engaged in the process. Our left hemisphere processes facts and factual information, whereas the right hemisphere is involved in creating and revising the 'context' – the bigger pattern – through which facts make sense.[71]

In our technological civilization we are flooded with factual information from a myriad of sources. But facts on their own don't make us wise. And an excess of facts just raises our stress levels. What makes us wise is fitting facts into a meaningful context, and that is the job of the brain's right hemisphere. We, therefore, firmly believe that children need an education that involves history and stories – the patterns that give context and make learning a real experience. It has long been known that children and adults exposed to 'classical' stories (brimming with rich psychological templates) become more flexible in their thought processes, more creative and more intelligent as adults. As Idries Shah wrote in his introduction to his major collection of stories, *World Tales*, "Many traditional tales have a surface meaning (perhaps just a socially uplifting one) and a secondary, inner significance, which is rarely glimpsed consciously, but which nevertheless acts powerfully upon our minds. Perhaps, above all, the tale fulfils the function not of escape but of hope. The suspending of ordinary constraints helps people to reclaim optimism and to fuel the imagination with energy for the attainment of goals: whether moral or material."[72]

The quality of stories is important. Our whole culture is saturated with stories – television soap operas, streaming services, newspapers, magazines, films, plays and popular songs all contain stories about what's going on in people's lives, fictional or otherwise. Our brains crave stories and metaphors. Once a story starts we want to hear it through; the pattern has to be completed. But the stories our brains receive are not just entertainment. They can have a creative or destructive impact on how we understand life and live our lives.

Some metaphors in our culture come from ideas put forward by scientists and spread through the media and educational institutions to the wider population. (As historian Yuval Noah Harari shows in his powerful book *Sapiens*, our belief in gods, nations, human rights, trust in money, laws and much more all derive from the stories created about them to make them 'real', as none has an independent existence – they are all abstract concepts.[73]) These metaphors can have a powerful effect – creative or destructive. The view that evolution is the story of 'the survival of the fittest', for example, was used by racial supremacists to justify exploitative colonial policies. This evolutionary theory is only a story, not an actual explanation based on facts.

The 'selfish gene' theory is another attempt to supply a metaphor to explain certain biological processes which quickly took on a devastating life of its own, maintaining the forces of pessimism and hopelessness.[74] What the metaphor says to our culture is that 'life is meaningless'. It can be seen as a cultural form of nocebo. Whilst few serious scientists question evolution, the over-emphasis on the selfish gene idea neglects the cooperative principle found throughout nature for furthering survival. This is evidenced between members of the same species and also in symbiotic relationships between different species, and in the huge variety of subtle feedback processes that maintain life in the biosphere.[75]

There is no doubt that stories are powerful. One reason they can have a *positive* effect in influencing behaviour is that, when we give them attention, we actively engage the imaginative side of the mind and go into trance. We open up the part of the brain that can programme in new templates. When children hear a story, the pattern is absorbed into their unconscious minds where it will remain available, awaiting opportunities to interpret and unfold more of reality, until the pattern is completed.

It is often said that stories carry in them all the wisdom of the world because knowledge is metaphorically expressed through them and transmitted orally down the generations. As an example, and to demonstrate the levels of meaning and the values that can be extracted from such a story, we can look at a familiar one that adults could easily dismiss as trivial – the story of the Ugly Duckling.

> ON A FARM a little bird is raised by a duck but feels itself to be very different from all the other ducklings who keep mocking it for being big and ugly. In due course, the ugly duckling becomes so unhappy it decides to run away, leaves the farm and goes in search of his destiny. But every animal it meets laughs at him for being so ugly and he learns that he can ignore them and not get upset by their stupidity. Eventually he finds a little pond where, despite feeling isolated and lonely, he learns to look after himself and survive through the long, cold winter.
>
> As the months pass by, changes happen within him, although he is unaware of this. One day, in early spring, the pond is still and calm, and in the water he sees the reflection of a line of beautiful swans flying high overhead. He wishes with all his heart that he could somehow be with them. The swans call down saying: "Why don't you join us?" And he said: "How can I, an ugly duckling, fly with beautiful birds like you?" And the swans laugh and say, "But look at your reflection," and the duckling looks at his own reflection in the still pool and realises that he has transformed into a swan. The former ugly duckling is able to join the swans as an equal on their journey.

That story resonates with all children because, at some time, every child feels isolated from their fellows – an outsider who doesn't fit in. There *are* times in life when we feel rejected, when we have to go it alone, when we have got to find the courage to last the course, when our emotional needs are not being properly met. But the template in the story contains more than that. It shows us that, if we approach those times with courage, changes will occur. We can learn from the very deprivations that seem so problematical and, if we persevere and seek out an appropriate environment, our talents and potential can blossom. The story holds out the optimistic prospect that the individual, and perhaps the human species, has somewhere to go; that there is a destiny awaiting us, if we have the courage to seek it, to stretch ourselves and sustain our spirit during troubled times.

Further subtleties include the profound truth *that we can only see clearly when we are calm.* If the water on the pond had been disturbed the ugly duckling would not have been able to see what he was like. In other words, children hearing this story are given the template that they need to be in a calm emotional state before they can accurately perceive what they actually are.

At an even deeper level, we might draw out the idea that high emotional arousal is like an ugly duckling, but, if we are willing to retrain our responses and cultivate and refine our perceptions, we can become more intelligent and raise ourselves up. It's only, as it were, by escaping the world of the ugly duckling that the true potential of the individual can emerge. And the price that has to be paid is that we may have to go against some of the prevailing orthodoxies within society and tread a lonely path for a while.

The patterns in such a rich story stay with us all, like a protective talisman, for the rest of our lives.

A therapeutic metaphor provides a map for clients, showing them where they are at and what resources they need, and where they can go. It gives them information in a non-threatening way. We all need a map for any endeavour we are about to undertake. We need a sense of form and structure to what we are attempting to achieve. It is surprising, however, how many therapists we meet go into a therapy session *without* a sense of structure, without a 'road map' of what a good therapy session should entail. They may have great ideas and tremendous therapeutic techniques but, unless they know how to apply them at the right time, the results can be as disastrous as taking a wrong turning on a mountain track in the dark.

The RIGAAR model

There is a form, a shape, to a good therapy session – just like a musical composition. It begins with rapport building (**R** of RIGAAR) – the counsellor entering the client's model of reality. This is done by listening to the patient's story in an empathetic and sympathetic way and every so often summarizing back to the client our understanding of what we have been told. It is the skill that Carl Rogers called active listening[76] and involves a therapist listening to a person and then responding to them using techniques such as paraphrasing. In this way the listener restates what has been said in order to demonstrate empathy and show that he or she was really listening and understanding what was being said, which has a calming effect. It is an essential part of psychotherapy and counselling but we think a more descriptive term to use for it is 'reflective listening' because the process allows patients to see the emotional content of their preoccupations *reflected* in the therapist's responses to them.

The reason reflective listening calms people down is that emotional arousal is the first part of a two-part autonomic nervous system process – arousal followed by de-arousal. This process is a pattern that can only be completed when action is taken or when something else happens to lower arousal. So, for instance, the emotion of hunger is aroused until we eat some food and de-arouse it. And if a child in a supermarket is temporarily separated from their mother and fears they are lost, seeing her approaching them from the next aisle is sufficient to discharge the arousal the fear had created. Similarly, when a person sees a reflection of their emotional state in the therapist's response, it completes the incomplete patterns of arousal, allowing them to calm down and access more of their thinking capacities.

Once the patient has unloaded their story and felt heard, the effective therapist will begin to reframe their situation slightly. Thus therapy can begin straight away without disrupting the necessary initial unloading of emotion and information. For example, if a woman says in the course of explaining why she has come to therapy, "I am so lonely since I moved here; I have no friends", a good counsellor would reflect back by gently saying, "So you feel sad and lonely at the moment and haven't discovered how to make friends in the area yet". (The crucial words are 'at the moment' and 'yet'.) This is known as a reflective reframe. It accurately reflects back to the person that the counsellor understands how she is feeling but also builds in hope with a reframe that implies things will change for her soon.

This is the first step in a therapy session and, having established rapport, and whilst establishing it, we gather information that is relevant to the therapy (the I of RIGAAR). We need to know, for example, where and when the problem occurs, who else is involved, when the problem doesn't occur and so on. We need accurate information in order to build up our understanding about any needs in life that are not being met, or to see if someone is misusing their imagination (worrying) or has been conditioned in an inappropriate way that is stopping them moving on. As this information is gathered rapport has to be maintained.

The next step is to establish clear goals and make sure both therapist and patient are clear about them. Without goal setting (the **G** in RIGAAR), therapy can go on forever. The goals, of course, have to be specific and relate to the client's needs because, when their needs are met, the problem will be solved in most cases. The goals may be such things as learning certain social skills and practising them on predetermined occasions, or to take exercise, or learn how to reduce stress levels before going for a job interview. If something is worrying someone, making them depressed and affecting their relationships, then the goal is to put in place specific ways that will lift the depression so that they can connect better to their family, friends and colleagues.

Goals must not be couched in abstract terms. If a patient says, "I just want to be happy", the therapist needs to ask, "What exactly would make you happy? How would you know you were happy?" Clear goals are necessary because the brain needs specific patterns to work upon. Once it has a pattern, it can then endeavour to match that pattern up in the outside world. Our job as therapists is to create a new template in the client's imagination that will make this possible.

Goals give a positive focus to the therapy and allow the measurement of progress week by week.

During information gathering we would also be accessing life resources (the first **A** in RIGAAR): finding out what people are good at, what they have achieved in their life, their successes, their qualities, such as a sense of humour or determination, or examples of when they have been creative. We need to know about the times in our clients' lives when they have felt good about themselves, so that later in the session we can access those positive emotions again to fuel the changes they need to make in the present.

The next step is to agree ways to get the client to reach that goal. This is called agreeing a strategy (the second **A** in RIGAAR). The strategy has to be realistic and one that the counsellor and client can agree is likely to help them achieve their goal. It will involve a combination of the elements delineated in the APET model.

Finally, having developed strategies and accessed resources, we need to talk the patient through the ways that they can change their situation to reach their goals. This we refer to as rehearsal or rehearsing success (the final **R** in RIGAAR) and is best done through guided imagery, metaphorical reframes and by helping clients vividly conjure up images of themselves coping with their life in more helpful ways and feeling good. By making these patterns vivid, people become more impelled to match them up in reality and, providing the goals have been realistic and they are genuinely motivated, it is likely that they will make the changes in the real world. They have the template activated in their mind. They are focused on the 'map' they need to use to make the changes.

The acronym RIGAAR (**R**apport building, **I**nformation gathering, **G**oal setting, **A**greeing a strategy, **A**ccessing resources, **R**ehearsal) makes it easy to remember this structure. However, no one can learn how to do therapy from reading a book – learning only happens in action, when skills are demonstrated and then practised by the student.

To summarize: the APET model is at the heart of human givens therapy. The letters stand for specific processes through which the mind/body system works. These processes are currently being explored by neuroscience and psychology in many direct ways and are not dependent on ideologies.

The **A** is for an activating stimulus from the environment. The **P** is for the pattern-matching part of the mind, which in turn gives rise to an emotion or expectation, **E**, that can produce thought, **T**, or some other consequence (things-happen).

But these letters also contain a powerful metaphor that enriches the idea. The first three letters spell 'ape'

APE T

and can be thought of as representing a mixture of primitive instincts and conditioned responses. If we let emotionally arousing greeds and selfish desires control us, we are cutting ourselves off from the richer and more subtle templates located in our highly developed frontal lobes, through which we can experience more of reality than an ape can.

On the other hand, if we emphasize the letters slightly differently, we have 'a pet'.

A PET

As we know, a pet is an animal that was originally wild, but its nature has been constrained – domesticated to serve the needs of a master. This is a cooperative relationship. The pet serves the needs of the master and, in return, the master takes care of the needs of the pet. That is the same civilizing process we humans have to go through too – domesticating the wild, instinctive more primitive parts of ourselves.

So, whilst the individual letters symbolize the way the brain processes information, they also describe the essence of the therapeutic process – helping people to 'master' the mind/body system, particularly the more instinctive, emotional elements of it, and fulfil our human needs and potential.

Why human givens therapy should be more widely available

There is a wonderful section in Idries Shah's book *Knowing how to know* where he describes a characteristic of almost all human societies as "the general belief, hallowed by institutions and uncritically accepted, that something must be: convenient; plausible; believed; allowed by precedent; accepted as true; capable of 'proof' within confines laid down by self-appointed authorities or their successors; admitted by some established body of experts: otherwise it is not allowed to be 'true'." He then goes on to say, "The fact is, of course, as we can immediately see once we pause to analyze it: an idea, scheme, or almost anything else, really needs no other qualification than that it is true."[77]

After *Human Givens* was first published in 2003 and we had started training therapists and others in how to use the human givens approach, people have said it should be considered by the NHS as a bona fide model of therapy in its own right and become central to education: its main tenets were so obviously 'true'. This was obvious to those who took the trouble to understand it and who witnessed how quickly it helps many people. But our culture does not like to act on what it can directly observe. It requires academically acquired 'evidence'. So there was a delay of some years before the right kind of material acceptable to institutions began to accumulate. In 2011, The British Psychological Society's leading peer-reviewed journal, *Psychology and Psychotherapy:*

Theory, Research and Practice published a 12-month evaluation of the human givens approach in primary care at a general medical practice, showing that more than three out of four patients were either symptom-free or reliably changed as a result of human givens therapy. This was accomplished in an average of only 3.6 sessions, significantly better than the recovery rate published for the UK government's flagship IAPT (Improving Access to Psychological Therapies) programme, which uses therapists trained in cognitive behavioural therapy (CBT).[78]

The same year, another paper appeared in a peer-reviewed academic journal, the first to show the efficacy of the human givens approach with adolescents.[79]

The conclusion of another peer reviewed study published in *Mental Health Review* in 2012 declared that the National Institute for Health and Care Excellence (NICE) should be made aware of some of the techniques used in the approach and that training in human givens methodology and concepts should be formally accepted as a mainstream option for continuing professional development within the mental health community.[80]

These are the strong recommendations that resulted from research commissioned by Sandwell Primary Care Trust to assess a new pilot human givens mental health service within primary care, in an area of considerable socioeconomic deprivation in Staffordshire. Local primary care groups (predecessors to the later primary care trusts) had already invested in human givens therapy but, when NICE guidelines on depression recommended, in 2004, a mainly CBT approach, it was felt necessary to carry out research to show whether the human givens service was as or more effective.

The research used the 'non-equivalent groups design', commonly used in health research when randomization is problematic – and it was problematic in this case because the GP practices already offering human givens therapy would not let their patients be randomized to different treatment groups, as they were so satisfied with the outcomes for their patients. Nineteen GP practices referred moderately depressed patients into the study – 14 offering human givens therapy (with or without medication) and five offering standard care (such as CBT, counselling and medication). All potentially suitable participants were invited to complete three questionnaires (life satisfaction, clinical outcomes and emotional needs). At the outset, the trial involved 106 people receiving human givens therapy and 70 receiving 'control' interventions. (As indicated, it was found difficult to recruit adequate numbers of controls.) Life satisfaction and emotional wellbeing scores were similar in each group as were age range, sex, employment status (mainly unemployment) and previous history of depression. The three questionnaires were to be completed again four, eight and 12 months after treatment.

The majority of those who had human givens therapy finished their treatment within four months of referral and, on average, needed just one to two sessions, compared with four to six in the control group. All patients who completed the study showed similar levels of improvement but lasting effects were more marked in the human givens group, as far fewer in the control group were able to complete a year's follow up. Whether patients received antidepressants alongside human givens therapy or not made no difference to outcomes.

The researchers, from Staffordshire University, suggest that the speedy effectiveness of the human givens method may be explicable in terms of its biopsychosocial approach and its emphasis on psychoeducation, "providing the patient with a superior understanding of their condition and ways to deal with it independently of the therapy session". They conclude that integrating human givens therapy into the NHS as a standard treatment choice would be highly cost-effective, as it would reduce both waiting and treatment times.[81]

In the course of the research, the human givens Emotional Needs Audit (ENA) was assessed for reliability and validity. ENA aims to identify areas of potential problems and distress in a person's life, on the understanding that quality of life and mental health are related to emotional needs being adequately met and in balance. As the researchers comment, there is thus a difference between ENA, which looks for causes of problems, and other instruments that focus on the results of ill health.

After rigorous testing, the researchers concluded that, "the Emotional Needs Audit is acceptable in the domains of internal consistency, concurrent validity, discriminant validity, predictive validity, sensitivity and specificity. This suggests that it is a valid instrument in clinical populations for measuring emotional wellbeing, quality of life and emotional distress."[82]

They also suggest that the ENA scale has additional advantages over the Satisfaction with Life Scale and the Clinical Outcomes in Routine Evaluation – Outcome Measure (better known as CORE-OM), which were also used in the research. "Our observations suggest that, when faced with a patient in distress, it is necessary to evaluate not only the level of distress but the causes of distress. The ENA allows the practitioner to evaluate such causes.

"We conclude that in addition to measuring symptoms and satisfaction with life, the ENA is capable of providing greater understanding of the causes of any problems, and therefore has the potential to be the more useful instrument in clinical practice. Indeed we would argue that the results from ENA might allow a practitioner to develop a level of communication that might therapeutically assist the start of treatment."[83]

In 2016 researchers at Kings College published a report showing that treatment offered to army veterans suffering PTSD and other conditions by the charity PTSD Resolution, which refers clients only to human givens practitioners, led to slightly higher improvement than that achieved within the NHS Improving Access to Psychotherapies (IAPT) services. This might not sound like a ringing endorsement of our methods but, in effect, it is. For, as the researchers acknowledged, the clientele for the two services differed quite dramatically, with those attending the former experiencing much higher distress at the outset and likely to have gone through a number of different, unhelpful therapies previously, while those attending the latter were just members of the general population.[84]

As researchers become more and more interested in examining our approach, because of the consistent high levels of success achieved by practitioners, we expect to see an even stronger growth of evidence of this kind, which statutory bodies all too often require before they will fund services. This can only help make human givens therapy more widely available, so that many more people will benefit from it.

In the meantime the following sums up what we believe clients should look for in a therapist.

An effective counsellor or psychotherapist:
- understands depression and how to set about lifting it straight away
- can help immediately with anxiety problems including panic attacks, nightmares, post-traumatic stress disorder, phobias or other fear-related symptoms
- is prepared to give advice if needed or asked for
- will not use jargon or 'psychobabble'
- will not tell you that therapy is likely to be 'painful' (it definitely does not have to be painful)
- will not dwell unduly on the past
- will be supportive when difficult feelings emerge, but will not encourage you to get emotional beyond the normal need to 'let go' of any bottled-up problems
- will assist you, if necessary, to develop your social skills so that your needs for affection, friendship, pleasure, intimacy, connection to the wider community, etc. can be better fulfilled
- will help you to draw on your own resources (which may prove greater than you thought)
- will be considerate of the effects of counselling on the people close to you
- will teach you to relax deeply
- will help you think about your problems in new, more empowering ways
- will use a wide range of techniques
- may ask you to do things between sessions
- will take as few sessions as possible
- will increase your self-confidence and independence and make sure you feel better after every consultation.

CHAPTER NINE

A very human vulnerability – depression (and how to lift it)

WITHOUT motivation, human beings cannot find meaning in what they do and are left wandering feebly in the joyless grey limbo between a healthy, fulfilling life and insanity.

Why, at any one time, are so many people in the grip of this debilitating mental state – one characterized by lack of meaning and motivation, coupled with total exhaustion? Our understandings about the role of the REM state, set out in the first part of this book, provides the answer.

Anxiety and depression are the two most common mental disorders worldwide. In 2019, the global prevalence of anxiety was 31 per cent and depression 29 per cent[1] and, among adults, depression is the most prevalent of all mental disorders.[2] Although anxiety and depression are separated out in statistics, our many years as psychotherapists have shown us that there is rarely depression without anxiety.

In 2019, 280 million people worldwide were living with depressive disorders, a figure which rose significantly in 2020, as a result of the covid-19 pandemic.[3] Globally, 4.5 per cent of women and 3 per cent of males, had depression, with numbers highest in the over-50s.[4] And mental disorders are generally more common in high-income countries[5] which certainly helps overturn any belief that it is circumstances that cause depression.

Up to 10 per cent of people in England can be expected to suffer from depression in their lifetime, according to statistics current at the time of writing.[6] Epidemiological studies show that the rate of increase in depression has grown in *all* age groups, but is growing fastest in young people, with 17 per cent of adolescents in the US experiencing at least one depressive episode in 2020.[7] Depression also significantly affects the elderly. Around 22 per cent of men and 28 per cent of women over 65 have depression in the UK, and it is estimated that around 85 per cent receive no help whatsoever from the NHS.[8]

Suicidal thinking is a common symptom of depression and, in 2021, there were 5,583 suicides registered in England and Wales, an increase of almost 7 per cent over the previous year.[9] The number of people self-harming more than doubled between 2000 and 2014 and, shockingly, the same survey reported that the numbers of those reporting self-harm or suicidal thoughts have been rising faster than the numbers of those experiencing mental health problems overall.[10] Alas, the statistics could go on and on and on.

According to the American Psychiatric Association, women are 1.5–3 per cent more likely than men to develop depression, with gender-specific causes including fluctuating hormone levels, menstruation, pregnancy, menopause and side effects of birth control and hormone replacement medications likely to account for some of the difference. One report found that women on average take 50 per cent longer than men to recover spontaneously from depression.[11] Symptoms tend to differ too, whether for biological or, more likely, cultural reasons: women, for instance, are more likely to feel stress, sadness and sleep problems, while men are more likely to experience irritability and impulsive anger.[12]

Depression is so serious because it is a strong emotion. Sustained states of high emotional arousal stop affected individuals from being capable of reflecting on what is really happening to them, seeing their problems in context and setting about solving them creatively. In effect, depression acts as a brake on the development both of individuals and, when very many people are depressed, of the wider society. The use of the word 'arousal' may seem odd when linked with depression, but, even though depressed people often look 'flat' and inactive, their blood levels of the stress hormone cortisol are much higher than normal.[13]

As we've seen, all emotions – anger, hate, fear, love, sexual desire and greed (in all its forms) hypnotically lock us into a confined viewpoint which we refer to as focusing attention. So, a person in the grip of *any* powerful emotion can be said to be locked in an emotionally driven trance state. Depression is no exception.

When we are highly emotionally aroused and flooded with stress hormones, the networks in the brain most concerned with cognitive functioning can't operate properly. We can't 'think straight'. A curious aspect of this is that the strong emotions that focus our attention and lock us into a confined, trancelike, viewpoint by focusing our attention, can just as easily be stimulated by the misuse of our imagination as by real events. This is what happens in anxiety, when people worry too much and upset themselves by imagining what might go wrong in some situation, or when a person gets angry by reliving in their mind some injustice they once suffered. Sexual daydreaming also raises arousal levels. The importance of all this for depression will become clear shortly.

As mentioned in the last chapter, very many modern-day neuroscientists now believe that the brain works according to prediction.[14] Imagine that we are struggling with a number of chronic stresses, such as threatened redundancy or marriage breakdown – or even a whole series of imagined ones. The brain will be trying to predict what will happen and 'correct' it by signalling for more metabolic energy in order to deal with these stresses, but to no avail because there is no physical action we can take that can make things better. The likely end result is that the overwhelmed brain ends up 'protecting' us by opting to save energy instead, initiating the sickness behaviours such as fatigue and withdrawal which feature strongly in depression.[15]

These sickness behaviours are initially valuable. Like all emotions, depression is a form of communication conveying a two-way message: outwards, to the people around the emotional person, and inwards, to the individual concerned. Depression's message is, "Something is seriously wrong. I am stuck. I am blocked in my life. I don't know where to go from here."

For most of our existence human beings lived in small, cohesive tribal groups, so when somebody gave out that message, it was readily identified. Living with a depressed person is difficult and everyone knew intuitively that they had to work hard to protect themselves from being sucked into the depressed person's deeply pessimistic and barren world view, devoid of all the stimuli that make life interesting and pleasurable. The group would understand how and why the person was blocked *and be able to do something about it.*

In healthy, traditional, so-called primitive, non-westernized societies

– and a few still survive – major clinical depression is almost unknown. Such people live in cohesive communities where they are kept busy with meaningful activity and where practical problems are dealt with quickly. As we have seen, studies of traditional New Guinea tribes and the Amish community (which still tries to live a 17th century lifestyle) show that if somebody suffers a crisis, everyone rallies round to help them straight away. There is real community support for individuals, balanced by an understanding that the individual has a responsibility to the community.[16] But depression always increases in developing countries when rising uncertainty caused by political violence, population increase, intense urbanization, unemployment, food shortages, disease etc., makes them unstable.[17]

Our modern technological society, despite the benefits it brings, is an increasingly complex and stressful culture in which more and more people find it difficult to get their emotional needs met. Today a person can send out an emotional message for months, or even years, and nobody around them may actually notice or, if they do, may lack the wisdom to do anything about it.

So, what is different about modern living that might account for so much depression? Here are some suggestions.

Technology and consumerism: In technologically advanced societies, the loosening of social structures has increased the incidence of family and community breakdown. Modern communications technology, in the service of industries that require people endlessly to buy things they don't really need, plays a big role in this. So the media, in a consumerist society, increasingly emphasize the acquisition of material goods and place more emphasis on satisfying the selfish wants and desires of 'me', with a decreasing lack of commitment to other people and wider social responsibilities. This has encouraged much more obsessional preoccupation with the self, with which depression is linked.

It is normal for toddlers to scream "I want it now!" As far as they are concerned they are at the centre of the universe and delayed gratification is not an option. But, in healthy families, as children grow, they are taught to have a more realistic expectation of how things happen. They learn that people have to wait their turn, that success in life is earned, that wants are not the same as needs, that the needs of others should be considered and that they themselves are *not* the centre of the universe. But, in this consumerist age, it suits many vested interests to keep as much of the population as possible behaving like selfish four-year-olds by undermining more healthy developmental processes. Political parties now retain power by manipulating their messages according to the short-term whims of 'focus groups', supposedly sample representatives of the public, instead of by inspiring people with long-term policies and plans that might improve and strengthen society. Politics is now largely reduced to a specialization of the public relations industry.[18]

"Take the waiting out of wanting" was the famous advertising slogan used long ago to launch credit cards in the UK. Television programmes and the advertisements that intersperse them or which border web pages, coupled with corresponding peer group pressure, raise expectations in the population. These expectations stimulate in many a desire for the 'good' life NOW, as if it were a right, undermining the necessity for learning, work and patience in due proportion. The media also imbue people with simplistic ideas about how we should educate children, what we should wear, how much attention we should receive, what love is and what we should enjoy and be moved by. Because most people are unable to avoid the influences of the entertainment and advertising industries, which constantly assail us, cleverly stimulating our greed for their own profit, there is constant manipulation of the way we live our lives. In other words, we have largely become a new peasantry, a vast international community of peasants. (A peasantry does not refer only, as many might think, to impoverished people ruled by rich ones. It is a population that is 'owned', whose beliefs are engineered by propaganda, and whose activities and diversions are largely provided for other people's gain.[19] Throughout history, there have always been plenty of comparatively rich peasants.)

Time pressures: While technology can clearly remove pressures, it can also create new ones. Cars were wonderful inventions, for example, allowing us to keep dry and comfortable as we moved all over the land. But spending time stuck in traffic jams is not so wonderful, nor is the pollution they cause. Since the invention of the mechanical clock we have increasingly segmented days into hours and minutes, and driven ourselves by this artificial measurement. The consequence is that we pack more into the day and organize the way we cooperate with one another more efficiently. This brilliant innovation made industrialization and modern, organized society possible, but it has also brought many subtle problems with it, not least an increase in time-related stress. It tends to leave, for example, no time for reflection or spontaneous relaxation. We, the new peasantry, are now 'sold' leisure packages.

This has more serious consequences than might at first be apparent. When we are driven by the clock we become more intolerant of people who work in a more relaxed timeframe. We also tend to pay less attention to, or ignore altogether, our own, highly evolved and infinitely subtle internal biological clocks – our natural ultradian rhythms.[20] For example, it is quite normal to 'switch off' for 20 minutes every hour and a half, as the brain swaps hemispherical dominance from left to right in order to process information, lay down long-term memories and make internal mental and physical repairs. Indeed, we are designed to do this and, whenever we override our natural need for a 20-minute break every 90 minutes or so, it always involves the production of stress hormones to keep us alert. It has been shown that, if we continually and inappropriately override this need for regular relaxation, as many do in the modern, target-focused workplace, we become highly stressed, mentally unstable and, eventually, physically ill.[21]

Many people now find it difficult to wind down without the aid of phones, TV, music, drugs or alcohol to change their mood. The ubiquitous presence of TV, computers and mobile digital devices in homes around the world has had some deleterious effects as well as good ones. It was long ago shown that, when TV is introduced into a community, both adults and children become less creative in problem-solving, less able to persevere at tasks, and less tolerant of unstructured time.[22] Heavy users of TV and computer games have reported feeling significantly more anxious and less happy than light users.[23] This is because these media vastly over-employ multiple fast cuts, quick zooming in and out, wobbling cameras and change of focus, as well as sudden sounds and unexpected images, which have the effect of continually alerting the orientation response, and thus keeping attention focused on the screen.[24] The activity becomes addictive because, once aroused, the pattern of arousal has to be completed by the dénouement – hence the success of soap operas. Increasingly too, watching television and playing computer games restrict the amount of time children spend talking among themselves and with their parents – which steadily retards the development of their social skills. In recent years, social media site usage has led to a huge rise in cyberbullying and also to obsessive behaviour. People may suffer stress when no one is texting them and often behave as if they have lost a limb if they lose their mobile phone or tablet.

Another time-related stressor is our heightened expectation for instant solutions to every problem. Enormous amounts of information are now available cheaply and easily through the internet. We are bombarded with news and gossip from around the world. 'Crisis' is the watchword. It can seem as though every natural catastrophe, every man-made disaster and cruelty, every political, scientific and social ethical dilemma is paraded before us by news media.[25] But there is no corresponding mental and emotional education in how to discriminate the usefulness and meaning of this information.

There are no solutions to disasters once they have happened. Wars are not tidy problems with neat resolutions. Corruption and injustice require more than a wish that the world were not so. Expectations are seldom realized and when we allow expectations to rage like a fever it is deeply frustrating for people. That life is full of surprises is one of the three certainties. (The other two, as we all know, are death and taxes.) Expectation and disappointment go hand in hand. We are swept along first by expectation – then by disappointment or surprise. And, once in the disappointed or surprised stage, we quickly forget our earlier expectation. We are not masters of ourselves when swept along like this and although, as we are human, expectation and disappointment will always be with us, they are major handicaps that stop us from seeing situations clearly. Hence the growth in cynicism, which fuels the creeping feeling that life has no purpose.

Uncertainty: Consider for a moment some of the changes in workplace practices that unsettle us. There is a widely perceived sense of uncertainty and injustice in the world about job stability, which has been generated by technological development and the ease with which capital investment in industry and commerce can move around the world, ruthlessly seeking a better deal. This is often cited as a cause of stress and depression. Certainly, short-term employment contracts have become the norm in professions where one used to consider one could 'have a job for life'. Zero-hours contracts, usually poorly paid and with no guarantee of any hours at all, are another modern source of stress. Increasingly, too, redundancy and the lesser likelihood of getting another job, particularly after the age of 40, or the fear of never getting a job at all, in the case of very many young people, lower self-esteem. So too does the realization that many large corporations and the banking system are more corrupt and unstable than we used to believe, and that the pension fund system that depends on them is proving inadequate for retirement needs, increasing financial difficulties and debt. All this creates mental and physical burdens that overwhelm many, as does the growing taste for unreasonable litigation, where people are encouraged to sue for every minor misfortune or accident, forcing the law to apportion blame and put a price on it. Control over how we work and live is slipping from our grasp – yet a sense of being in control is essential for mental stability and physical health.[26] There is a paradox here however. Although we have a need to feel in control, no human being has *ever* known what lies around the corner. This was brought starkly home to the entire world when the covid-19 pandemic began in 2019. We all, in fact, live a transient life whilst pretending that life is permanent. Consequently, being prepared for change is a positive attribute that minimizes the risk of suffering stress reactions, anxiety, ill-health and worse when the inevitable changes happen.

Defeatism: A common but largely invisible thread running through current cultures is that we impart to our children, along with all the positive praise and problem-solving skills we like to think we are teaching them, a strong trait of defeatism and negativity. Children quickly emulate their parents' rationalizations for why certain tasks are not attempted; they are 'too tired', or doing such-and-such is not 'worthwhile', or 'there's no point', or 'some other day'. This unspoken conditioning is passed on in many families like some sort of contact disease, alongside other, more positive manifestations of belief and action. The dangers inherent in this have not been widely realized and so nothing is done about it.

Mobility: Travel has never been easier, which in many ways is a huge plus, but we are paying dearly for opening up the world with modern transport. One outcome, which relates directly to depression, is the ease with which it is now possible to move away from our geographical roots and work and live elsewhere. (To be adaptable enough to do this is, of course, a sign of maturity. But many people are not sufficiently mature and mentally stable enough to make the necessary adjustments.) This has contributed to the breakdown of close extended family support in times of trouble.

Relationship breakdown: Research long ago showed that children can be damaged more by the strife leading up to divorce and its subsequent effects than by the death of a parent.[27] For instance, in the UK, children of middle-class parents who were born in 1958 and whose parents divorced before they were 16 were twice as likely to leave school without any qualifications as those whose parents remained married. They showed more behaviour problems in school, were more likely to be unhappy and worried, and were behind their schoolmates at reading and arithmetic. They were also much less likely to go to university or to be in a job when they were 23 years of age. They were four times more likely to live in subsidized social housing and were much more likely to smoke than were other middle-class young adults whose parents had not split up. They were also, on average, less emotionally stable, left home earlier and themselves divorced or separated more frequently later in life.[28] This research was published 25 years ago and its findings are still being endorsed today, with children of divorced parents experiencing increased psychological problems, regardless of age, gender and culture.[29] Such findings are significant because there is no reduction in numbers of broken families we are seeing nowadays, throughout society.

Of course, there are many reasons for why single-parent families exist; very many children brought up in single-parent families do well; and not all two-parent families confer benefits. One study compared outcomes for children living with both parents, sometimes in households where there was strife, with outcomes for children in stepfather and single-mother households. Parental conflict was associated with children's poorer academic outcomes, increased substance use, early sex, early parenthood, and break up of the relationship.[30]

These are just some of the stressors peculiar to the modern world. But we must not forget that hardship, accident, famine, war and disease have been the common lot of human beings since we appeared on the planet and the majority of people adapt and cope fairly well, whatever the range of pressures. This is not too surprising since we have evolved to be adaptable. Nevertheless, whilst the majority copes, even thrives, many do not. The increasing rate of technological and social change is creating a more psychologically disturbed population and the rapid rise in anxiety disorders, depression, addictions and selfish antisocial behaviour illustrates, reflects and compounds this trend.

Depression is not a genetic illness

Because of the massive medicalization of depression we need to spend a little time showing why depression is not, in fact, a biological disease. The marked increase in the rate of depression revealed in epidemiological studies itself shows that depression cannot be a biological disease carried in our genes. Genes do not change that quickly. Despite the explosion in genetic research and gene mapping, and high hopes of finding a gene for everything, no 'depression gene' has been found, because genes don't work that way. Indeed, a relatively recent analysis of multiple large samples has confirmed this.[31] But it is not for want of trying, on other researchers' parts.[32]

Over the decades conclusive evidence has mounted to show that the vast majority of depressions are learned, created by the way we interact with our environment.[33] Only quite recently, researchers showed that having a fixed mindset – believing that people cannot change – is linked to greater likelihood of depression in adolescents.[34] We know that depression is not an event-driven phenomenon because the majority of people exposed to adverse life circumstances do not develop it. Those who react to events in their lives by getting depressed do so because that is how they have learned to respond to adverse life experiences.

There has long been support for the environmentally learned view of depression through evidence that depression responds well, and often very quickly, to psychotherapeutic interventions that concentrate on stopping negative introspection and helping people get their emotional needs met.[35] Such interventions also greatly reduce the rate of relapse compared to drug treatments based on the biological model. They work precisely because of the human brain's ability to be conditioned by experiences, and *reconditioned*. When depressed people are helped to adapt more effectively to the pressures and uncertainties of modern living by *learning* to respond to adverse life circumstances in better ways, they get better.

That there is a biological *component* to depression is undisputed, since all our emotions are expressed in the language of biochemistry. Also, depression affects our biology by, for example, impairing the proper functioning of our immune system. But the idea that depression is the result of a chemical imbalance in the brain, so disempowering and yet so fervently promoted by self-serving drug manufacturers, is wrong. Indeed, the final nail in the coffin of the chemical imbalance myth should have been hammered down by the findings of research, led by Dr Joanna Moncrieff, professor of psychiatry at University College London.[36] Commenting on the research findings, she said, "Our view is that patients should not be led to believe that antidepressants work by targeting these unproven abnormalities. We do not understand what antidepressants are doing to the brain exactly, and giving people this sort of misinformation prevents them from making an informed decision about whether to take antidepressants or not." Co-author training psychiatrist and clinical research fellow Mark Horowitz said, "I had been taught in my psychiatry training that depression was caused by low serotonin and had even taught this to students in my own lectures. Being involved in this research was eye-opening and feels like everything I thought I knew has been flipped upside down."[37]

Although doctors saturated by drug company propaganda will probably still continue to believe the serotonin imbalance myth and tell it to patients, it now seems clear that changes in serotonin levels in the brains of depressed people are a *consequence* of depression, not the *cause* of it. Serotonin levels fluctuate constantly and are directly correlated with the effectiveness with which we all live our lives. Life-enhancing experiences raise serotonin levels at least as effectively as drugs, with no adverse side effects, and more instantaneously.

As Ezra Hewing pointed out in his article on how REM sleep, not chemical imbalance, explains depression,[38] if depression reduced serotonin in the brain, giving drugs to block serotonin production should *cause* depression. Research has shown that this was not the case.[39] Nor do all antidepressants act on serotonin anyway, some acting instead on other neurotransmitters, such as noradrenaline.[40]

It has long been established that the types of psychological treatment that are effective in lifting depression are brief, short-term therapies that concentrate on problem solving, changing people's attributional style of thinking, focusing their attention away from their emotions and helping them get their needs met by, for example, helping them to improve their relationship skills.[41] The same research clearly showed that the least successful forms of psychotherapy were those operating from psychoanalytical and psychodynamic perspectives (so-called insight counselling), and non-directive, person-centred counselling – all of which tend to encourage emotional introspection and thereby may maintain and deepen depression. (The term 'insight' counselling is generally associated with the methods of various psychodynamic schools of therapy but, if they *were* providing insight, surely they would be more successful than they actually are. *True* insight is an important part of any therapy.[42])

It is also well established that antidepressants can lift the symptoms of clinical depression – completely in a third of those who take them and partially in another third – although they are not nearly as effective in preventing further episodes of depression as the right type of psychotherapy. Antidepressants don't work at all in a third of those who are prescribed them, and for many people the side effects are more unpleasant than the depression, so they stop taking them. It was long thought to take between four and six weeks for the drugs to exert their maximum effect (and probably most doctors still believe this to be the case). But a meta-analysis of large and small trials of antidepressants found, in 2006, that the response, if there was one, was greater in weeks one and two than in weeks three and four or weeks five and six. In fact, if patients had shown no improvement within two weeks, they were unlikely to experience any benefits.[43] There is, as yet, no widely accepted agreement as to why antidepressants sometimes work, although the placebo effect is known to play a part.[44] Indeed, it is now known that the difference in effect between antidepressants and placebo may be "minimal or non-existent" in patients with mild or moderate symptoms of depression.[45]

Antidepressants like the 'modern' selective serotonin reuptake inhibitors (SSRIs), a class of drugs which includes fluoxetine (Prozac), can cause dizziness, nausea, anxiety, facial and body tics, muscle spasms, parkinsonism (symptoms similar to those seen in Parkinson's disease), brain damage, sexual dysfunction, memory loss, neurotoxicity and debilitating withdrawal symptoms that are often mistaken for the original symptoms returning. There is also a direct link between suicide and violent behaviour and their use.[46,47] Antidepressants cause immediate changes in the brain,[48] which would strongly seem to indicate that it is not a good idea for them to be given to children – the brain does not fully mature until the mid-20s. And, because of the common toxic side effects, they should not be prescribed to older people who have any sign of brain deterioration. A great deal of alarming information about the effects of these drugs has been documented over recent years – not least the fact that many have found their way onto the market on the strength of questionable data.[49]

St John's wort, a popular natural remedy often recommended for depression, has evidence for and against it. One meta-analysis showed that St John's wort (Hypericum) can be as effective as antidepressants in lifting mild-to-moderate depression and is safer.[50] However, other studies showed that placebo was just as effective as both St John's wort, and, in one case, the antidepressant SSRI sertraline, in treating moderate depression.[51,52] A 2008 review of 29 international studies suggested that St John's wort *might* be better than a placebo and as effective as standard antidepressants for mild-to-moderate depression, with fewer side effects. However, the studies that were conducted in German-speaking countries, where St John's wort has long been used by medical professionals, reported more positive results than those carried out in other countries.[53]

Most experts now recommend a combination of medicine and psychotherapy. However, more and more studies, including those carried out on our own methods, show that medication is unnecessary if the depressed person receives *appropriate* help.[54]

Building on all the above information, and considering it from the human givens perspective, it is clear to us why depression occurs and takes the form it does; why some forms of therapy are more effective than others; and how psychotherapists and counsellors can learn to apply the most effective treatment approach in each individual case.

The human givens approach to therapy looks at each person holistically, using an understanding of the psychobiological needs and resources that human beings have evolved over millions of years throughout their animal ancestry to cope with the environment.[55] We look for what is missing in patients' lives and work towards correcting this imbalance so that needs are met. We use a particular blend of the cognitive, behavioural and interpersonal approaches that are proven to be effective, plus other elements such as stimulating the imagination of patients, using guided imagery. We also clearly distinguish *needs* from *wants* and build on individuals' life resources and innate abilities to add to, and thereby improve, their cognitive, emotional and behavioural skills base where necessary. Therapists and counsellors who learn to work in this way quickly get results that last with most of their clients.

As we have shown, one of the tools nature has given us is the dreaming process, through which metaphorically we act out unresolved patterns of autonomic arousal each night so that they are not carried over from one day to the next. This new knowledge about why we dream is the key to understanding the psychobiology of why people can become depressed.

Dreaming and depression

The link between dreaming and depression became clear when we considered the following cluster of research findings in the light of Joe's discoveries about the function of dreams. The majority of depressed people, when they go to sleep, enter REM sleep (dream sleep) more quickly and have more prolonged and physiologically more intense REM sleep.[56,57,58] Although most depressed people sleep less than non-depressed people, they may spend a higher proportion of their overall sleep time dreaming. A significant proportion of depressed people dream excessively. It has been known for many decades that severe low mood lifts if REM sleep is prevented.[59,60,61,62] (Unfortunately the depressed state may return once the person resumes normal sleeping, or may even worsen because of extra compensatory REM sleep, so this is not a reliable treatment method.) Antidepressant drugs reduce REM sleep.[63,64] So why should a reduction in REM sleep lead to a reduction in depression? The answer lies in the way the brain stimulates itself during REM sleep, a process that involves the PGO spike. As we explained in the chapter on dreams, the PGO spike is the orientation response that draws our attention to changes in the environment, startling changes such as a loud bang or sudden movement, or changes that arouse curiosity – anything that focuses our attention. It first evolved in mammals to activate the flight-or-fight response to potential danger and is the system which manages the body's responses to stress.

During REM sleep, and just before it starts, there is a massive firing of the orientation response. There has never been a satisfactory explanation for why the eyes dart about during REM sleep, and do so in the womb from about 10 weeks after conception, but we suggest that there could be a simple reason: the eyes automatically scan the environment at speed, in response to the firing of the orientation response. The PGO spike is signalling, "something vitally important is happening now", and so the eyes keep on trying to look, darting about in all directions. However, when we are asleep there is no information coming in from the external world. The source of the arousal is internal – the unexpressed emotional expectations from the previous day, major or minor, which are still occupying space in the brain, trapped, as it were, in the autonomic nervous system. As we have shown, the act of dreaming, by metaphorically acting out those unresolved expectations, discharges those arousals and frees the brain to be ready for the concerns of the following day.

But what happens when the emotional arousal level is extreme, as in depressed and anxious people? Hundreds of studies have long-shown that the fight-or-flight stress response is hyperactive in such patients.[65] In other words, the morbid and prolonged introspection and self examination, which tends to characterize depressed people, leads to above-normal levels of emotional expectations, which then need to be discharged during their dreams. In fact, the pressure for emotional discharge caused by excessive emotionally arousing negative introspection is so great that the first REM period of the night occurs earlier in most depressed people, is more prolonged and shows an especially high rate of discharge. This amount of discharge not only reduces the level of arousal in the brain but also actually exhausts it, leaving the person more likely to lack motivation the next day. It is no wonder that so many depressed people say they wake up exhausted from a night's sleep.

In hundreds of interviews and therapy sessions, many of which we have filmed, depressed patients readily talk to us about waking up exhausted and finding it difficult to motivate themselves. The more severe the depression the more exhaustion they experience. As therapists we find talking to depressed patients about their sleep patterns is the quickest way to build rapport with them. They seem to recognize instinctively that we know something about what they are going through. Many of them report waking up early and being unable to get back to sleep, even though exhausted. Since the early hours of the morning are when we have our longest period of dreaming, we can surmise that this early morning awakening is the body's way of preventing any further discharge of arousal caused by excessive self-analysis. In other words, the brain is losing energy so fast it is trying to protect itself by waking early.

So depressed people who introspect too much are tired and lacking in energy when they wake up because their orientation response mechanism is over-worked. It has fired off so much during excessive dream sleep that it is exhausted. And, without this response effectively alerting them to what is happening around them, and enabling them to switch attention from one thing to another, they find it very difficult, and in severe cases impossible, to motivate themselves to do anything.

This explains the common complaint of depressed people: that they feel that 'everything is meaningless ... pointless ... not worth bothering about'. It is a given that, to feel well, fulfilled and mentally healthy, we need a sense of meaning and purpose in our lives. But depressed people no longer have the means to generate such a positive outlook because their attention-switching mechanism is exhausted, leaving them unable to refocus on the bigger picture. It is a closed circle. Although the orientation response gradually recovers as the day goes on, typically the depressed person begins to introspect on that feeling of emptiness, the tiredness, the lack of pleasure and joy or enthusiasm in their lives, and is driven into another intense period of dreaming the following night – piling misery on misery – and becoming even more depressed.

Depression, we are saying, is not a disease; it is a natural response to certain types of emotional introspection that result in excessive dreaming. What is more, there are clear therapeutic implications suggested by this understanding of the causal sequence in depression. The trigger factor for depression is always around emotional needs not being met. It may be some experience of loss: redundancy, failed relationship, divorce, death of a loved one, loss of health, loss of status or a financial setback – all situations where someone feels they have lost, or are losing, control over their lives. If the person tends to be of a pessimistic disposition, this will lead them to excessive negative emotional introspection about the loss, which in turn leads to an excess of emotional arousal discharge through the dream state. In a minority of cases, in a predisposed person, genetic influences may contribute to triggering an excess of negative introspections, though there is absolutely no conclusive evidence for this. (When depression runs in families, conditioning could easily cause it. A defeatist, pessimistic world view is readily passed from one generation to the next, as is the more romantic 'soul in torment' view of depression common among artistic types, some of whom may deepen their torment through psychoanalytic explorations of their condition.) But, in either case, research conclusively shows that the most long-lasting benefit derives from psychological interventions that alleviate the negative introspections, particularly ones that teach depressed people how to do this for themselves. As already covered, such interventions are more effective than antidepressants in reducing further episodes of depression.[66]

Some important provisos

As GP and human givens practitioner Andrew Morrice has shown, through indefatigable trawling of the research, sleep is much more complex an event than we might think, not least where it concerns depression.[67] It appears that the classic pattern of excess REM sleep, leading to reduced slow-wave recuperative sleep, is present in only 50–70 per cent of sufferers from depression,[68] and can also be found in some people who aren't depressed at all. This sleep pattern is thought to be related to chronic stress and adverse past experiences, which means that REM sleep excess (and deep sleep deficit) is, indeed, a strong predictor of depression. While it is certainly possible that depression can arise as a result of lack of deep sleep,[69] which itself may have other causes, what has been clearly shown is that there is a link between rumination and introspection and excess REM sleep,[70] which is what we have been talking about here. However, the approaches we use for working with depressed people, based in helping them meet their physical and emotional needs effectively and make best use of their innate resources, work just as well whatever the other underlying causes of depression in a minority of people.

Why some people get depressed and others don't

So what exactly is a pessimistic disposition? Why do some people get locked into depression while others, with equal or more hardship in their lives, don't? It is, of course, natural from time to time to experience temporary sadness or depression when we feel overwhelmed by stressful events and that we are losing control. But it is what happens next – how individuals continue to react – that is crucial in the long term. Worrying, deep grief or sadness, like any other form of emotional arousal, forces the brain back into primitive black-or-white modes of thinking and locks our attention. When we are highly emotionally aroused, with our capacities to think straight swamped, everything is either good or bad, right or wrong, safe or dangerous, happy or sad, perfect or irretrievably imperfect. And, when emotional arousal is maintained, it prevents other networks within the brain from exercising our ability to tolerate ambiguity and take a wider perspective.

People who are not habitual black-or-white thinkers can usually 'snap' out of this arousal fairly quickly. However, people who tend towards analyzing what has gone wrong in their lives, reviewing the past selectively (picking out the negative aspects), catastrophizing every little setback, dreaming up future disasters or engaging in self-blame, tend to stay locked into the state of depression instead of rising above it. This explains something observed for some time – that depressed people habitually adopt a particular way of thinking to explain things that happen to and around them. This tendency was termed 'attributional style' by psychologist Martin Seligman and colleagues.[71] We all have an inbuilt need to make sense of our world and explain to ourselves why things happen the way that they do. The type of explanation we give ourselves – our attributional style – is critical, determining whether or not we will get depressed when bad things happen to us. The three important types of attributional style identified are:

- How *personally* we take events. (Do we tend to blame ourselves for every setback rather than considering other possible reasons for something going wrong? If a relationship breaks down, for example, is it always our fault?)
- How *pervasive* we view events to be. (If we lose a job, do we think our whole life is ruined or do we view the damage as limited to a short period of time and consider the possibility that other career opportunities may open up?)
- How *permanent* we think an event is. (Do we think a setback will be short lived or go on forever? If we don't get the house we have set our heart upon, for example, do we say, "Oh well, perhaps something else even better will turn up" or, "I will never be happy again as long as I live"?)

If we take things personally, interpret events as all pervasive or all encompassing and think setbacks last forever, we are candidates for depression. This is because these emotionally driven black-or-white thinking styles inevitably generate more emotion by repeatedly turning on the fight-or-flight response that makes us angry (fight) or anxious (flight). In other words, when people catastrophize the 'bad' things that happen to them, magnifying them so that the whole of their life is affected, they are either making themselves feel very hostile or frightening themselves.

What this means, of course, is that they have formed an inner template that says their future is full of pain and misery. They continually match that pattern to painful aspects of their present and past to validate their catastrophic view of their future. This leads to an excessive turning on of the fight-or-flight response which results in the 'all-or-nothing' reaction to life events found in depressed people and explains why they find it difficult to break the whole down into relevant component parts. When the brain is highly emotionally aroused it stops us from thinking clearly because it cannot see the infinite shades of grey between different viewpoints. That is why so many depressed people are perfectionists: if an event they anticipated didn't go totally as planned, for example, they view it as a disaster; if a relationship isn't perfect, it is terrible. This same tendency makes some depressed people prone to excessive jealousy.

Most things that happen in life have multiple causes. When we are more objective we can see the truth of this and we don't have to blame ourselves unreasonably when things go wrong. But depressed people, because of their high emotional arousal, cannot think clearly. That is why they plump for the big, simple-minded, single cause to explain a setback – "either I am to blame or somebody else is". They either get unreasonably angry with someone else for their difficulties or only ever see themselves as the cause of their difficulties, generating self-blame and low self-esteem.

By contrast, healthy people are not driven by these emotional hijacks of our abilities to think straight, weigh things up, get things into perspective. They moderate the assessments they make, as circumstances change, whereas the black-or-white thinker will often make fixed judgements with lifelong implications. For example, a woman emotionally hurt when her partner left her might decide never to embark on a relationship again. She thinks *all* potential romantic partners are untrustworthy, leading her need for intimacy to remain unmet and she withdraws into herself. A person's subjective view of reality is known to be highly correlative with their parents' view of reality. As we've said, this doesn't mean that depression is a genetically transmitted disease; it simply means that we tend to model ourselves on our parents' emotional behaviour and mimic, at least in part, their way of envisaging what is going to happen. Personality research shows that genetics make a 50 per cent contribution to our personality. This means that 50 per cent of our personality is environmentally determined. Good therapy involves working with the relationship between both, helping people use genetic traits (for example, a tendency towards obsessive attention to detail) in a positive rather than a negative way, and helping people change the way they react to, and deal with, their environment and life circumstances.

Because people prone to depression tend to see the difficulties that arise in life as permanent, they become pessimists. It takes considerable and consistent effort on the part of others to resist such a view. A depressed person's cynical pessimism about everything can be absorbed by whoever they live or work with, particularly if they are of a similar disposition. As a consequence it can spread like a virus. Whole families can become pessimistic and depressed.[72]

A frequently indulged-in pessimistic view of the future is a major risk factor for depression. A significant proportion of people who are clinically depressed are unlikely even to go to their GPs, because their pessimism convinces them that their situation is hopeless. If they do go, it may be only because somebody has nagged them into it. This means that, if they do then agree to attend counselling, it is terribly important that the pessimism – the hopelessness – is challenged in the first session. The whole session should never be given over to history-taking because the patient might not come back, or might even commit suicide, before the next appointment. It must be demonstrated to the patient in the first session that change is possible. This is summed up in the phrase coined by solution-focused therapists: "Do something that makes a difference *today*".

Curiously, pessimism is not only a high risk factor for clinical depression; it is also a major risk factor for *all* kinds of illnesses later on in life, including cardiovascular disease, and can be a predictor of a shortened lifespan.[73,74,75]

In the treatment of depression we can again see why an important part of any therapist's skill is the ability to calm people's emotions down.[76] Only when they are no longer aroused by the emotion of depression can a patient begin to reason, analyze or imagine different scenarios sufficiently well to perceive that life is complex, that there are multiple reasons for why things happen and that their excessive self-blame, or anger at others, is unrealistic.

People who don't get depressed can see different perspectives to situations – the various shades of colour between the extremes of emotionally driven black-and-white thinking. They have the ability to limit the damage done by a particular negative experience so that they can concentrate on the good parts of their life. They might think, for example, "It's terrible that I've lost this relationship, but other parts of my life are working. I've got a good job. I have a loving family to support me. And, of course, I'm free to get into another relationship again in the future." Or they might say, "I was extremely unlucky to have had a difficult start in life – but I didn't choose the bed I was born in. I can see that other parents make a much better job of it than mine did and I'm going to use my experience to do better by *my* children."

Mentally healthy people are flexible thinkers who limit the damage of a setback by *not* globalizing. They recognize what is within their control and what is not. They don't get sucked into the illusion that they have total control in any situation, nor that they have none at all. This is the opposite of what depressed people do.

When pessimists have a setback, they amplify it by dramatically exaggerating the hopelessness of the situation and the number of difficulties they have – catastrophic thinking. They often blame themselves when bad things happen, and worry. They emotionally introspect and, consequently, because of the excessive dreaming this causes, feel tired when they wake up and so begin progressively to eliminate all sources of pleasurable stimulation from their lives. Their exhausted state soon means that it becomes too much of an effort for them to go out and socialize, to exercise, make love, keep up their hobbies and interests or celebrate anything. Every time they back out of doing something pleasurable they feel a brief sense of relief and comfort, but never connect this to the fact that a couple of hours later they are even more depressed. And it is the progressive elimination of positive stimulation from their lives that drops them deeper into the black pit of despair.

To recap: depression is an emotion that narrows down thinking patterns which, in turn, encourages emotionally arousing, worrying introspections that can give rise to distorted and excessive amounts of REM sleep. Dreaming is a prolonged firing of the orientation response and uses up enormous reserves of energy. The intense excessive dreaming of a depressed person drains the energy they need for normal arousal of attention, leaving them unable to motivate themselves or draw any sense of meaning out of their everyday activities. This is the only explanation for depression that accounts for *all* of the symptoms of severe depression – depressed mood, disturbed sleep, exhaustion, loss of pleasure or interest in usual activities, disturbance of appetite, sluggishness or agitation, loss of energy, feelings of worthlessness and guilt, difficulties in thinking, and recurrent thoughts of death or suicide. In other words, it explains the complete psychobiological cycle of depression.

This knowledge derived from human givens understandings explains many other things – including why some treatments work and others don't. Up until now there has never been a satisfactory explanation for why, when people are given antidepressants, they nevertheless do work for a proportion of people. We can now see that this is because, as mentioned earlier, they either reduce REM sleep or help correct disordered REM sleep, bringing the sleeping pattern back to normal. The reason there is such a high rate of relapse when people stop taking antidepressant drugs, compared with effective psychotherapy or counselling, is that drugs don't teach people to build a realistic, empowering inner template with which to engage with reality. Also, antidepressants have many unpleasant side effects and often persistent withdrawal effects, as is now acknowledged by the Royal College of Psychiatrists. As mentioned in an earlier chapter, these drugs may also cause symptoms that inappropriately get diagnosed as part of a functional neurological disorder.

The explanation that we have offered also explains why any form of counselling or psychotherapy that *reduces* the amount of worrying a person is doing will help them. And any therapy that encourages and *increases* the amount of emotional introspection they do will harm them. Unfortunately, innumerable people around the world have had depression maintained or more deeply entrenched by well-meaning therapists working from psychodynamic, gestalt, hypnoanalytical and person-centred-type models, which focus patients' attention inwards. It was even the case some decades ago that American hospitals employing therapists using these models had been successfully sued for large sums of money by the relatives of depressed people, with evidence that these approaches were ineffective and harmful so strong that it stood up in court.[78]

The human givens approach to therapy incorporates therapeutic techniques that have been shown to work effectively. Indeed, in one study for depression already cited, human givens therapy, when compared with a control group receiving standard mental health services in primary care, was found to be of up to three times shorter duration.[79] Anything that works does so because it is in tune with the real needs of a person, and makes use of their own resources – in other words, is aligned with the givens of human nature. We know, for example, that behavioural therapies work because they guide people back into enjoyable physical activities that take the emotional focus off themselves and re-engage them with the environment, thus pulling them away from their negative introspection. As they take up challenging and interesting activities again, mental and/or physical, this, in turn, stimulates an increase in serotonin levels that helps to regulate onset of REM sleep.

One of the most important elements of the human givens approach is the stress on psycho-education of patients. As researchers from Staffordshire University found, a properly trained human givens therapist "is less likely to inappropriately emphasize the cognitive or emotional aspects of a disorder over important social factors, which may be of greater significance to the client's welfare. As well as psychological insight and emotional support, the client is helped to maintain their sense of social integration."[80] It is when people's needs are not being met that they are likely to feel stuck and then emotionally introspect about it. When people feel that they are losing control over their lives, it is usually because of money problems, unsatisfactory housing, deteriorating health, difficulties at work or school (including bullying), or problems around status, relationships and intimacy. One of the most common reasons for someone sinking into clinical depression is that they are in a deteriorating relationship at home or work, which they endlessly introspect about. The resulting depression itself adds to their problems, further destroying relationships because, when family and friends of a depressed person find that they too are beginning to feel depressed, they may pull away and emotionally disengage to protect themselves. This further isolates the individual, who succumbs to even deeper levels of misery.

Human givens therapists incorporate many interpersonal therapy techniques into their work to improve the quality of people's relationships (by teaching social skills, such as how to ask questions, how to take an interest in other people, how to converse and think about other people's needs, etc.). All this helps reduce introspection and normalize sleep patterns. The cycle of depression that is caused by prolonged grieving after bereavement can be broken by guiding the bereaved person to re-engage with life. Depression, of course, is also common among people who have highly disabling phobias or who suffer from post-traumatic stress disorder. Any treatment that successfully detraumatizes such people will invariably help lift their depression.

Bipolar disorder

Bipolar disorder gets its name because a sufferer swings between two poles – highs and lows, which are periods of mania followed by periods of deep depression. (It used to be called manic depression.) It is thought that there can be a significant genetic element and occurs with equal frequency in men and women. The current edition of the American Psychiatric Association's *Diagnostic and Statistical Manual of Mental Disorders (DSM-5)* now states that there are two versions of bipolar disorder: bipolar I and bipolar II, the latter being a less severe form of the former. Also in this stable is cyclothymic disorder, a so-called cyclic disorder that causes brief episodes of hypomania (excitable behaviour) and depression. So it has become quite a catch-all diagnosis which may, from a more cynical point of view, allow wider prescription of corrective medication.

Bipolar is usually treated with mood stabilizers such as sodium valproate or lithium, which can help regulate the emotional seesaw that propels the sufferer from mania (extreme excitement and sometimes even violence) to depression (pure inertia and lassitude).

Bipolar disorder occurs in a variety of profiles with some people visiting the depressed pole more frequently, and others spending more time in the manic state. Some may cycle through both poles with dizzying rapidity; others can spend years at the depressed end before experiencing mania, which is why it can take many years to diagnose accurately. Whilst in the depression phase people, as we have seen, are overusing the REM state, dreaming excessively. In mania, by contrast, people typically do not dream enough – working or playing hard, day and night, with minimal time set aside for sleep and rest because they feel they don't need it. By staying up all night every night they become starved of the vital REM sleep that would reduce the arousal (mania). So arousal levels build and build, till the inevitable point when there is a crash down into excessive REM sleep to make up for the lack ... and the consequent depression.

It is increasingly recognized that self-management of the disorder, is a crucial aspect of effective treatment for the majority of patients.[81] In the depression phase, the psychotherapeutic skills needed to treat depression are apposite. When the manic pole is threatening, it is important for a person to reduce stimulation – cut down on caffeine for example – and apply relaxation techniques. What is especially vital is getting a good night's sleep. However exciting life may seem to an individual during the manic phase, unless they get enough REM sleep they will heighten their arousal levels, accelerating the onset of mania. It is important, therefore, to help people recognise their trigger symptoms and danger signals (one woman realized that the first thing that signaled that she was going high was the urge to message everyone in her address book), so that they can calm themselves down before they spiral out of control.

Bipolar disorder in many ways highlights the role of black-and-white thinking in the genesis of depression. In the depressive phase the world is seen from a very black, pessimistic perspective indeed, whilst the opposite is true in the manic phase. Optimism and pessimism are two sides of the same coin. Just as runaway inflation is followed by recession in the world of economics, unbridled optimism is likely to trigger a pessimistic, depressive fallout when the unrealistic dreams turn into the ashes of disappointment.

For whatever reason it arises (as mentioned, there may be a genetic contribution to the condition), the extremes of black-and-white thinking can be more starkly observed in bipolar disorder. Black-and-white thinking is, as we have seen, associated with high emotional arousal. The pre-condition for the ability to see and understand the complexity of life and to navigate our way safely through it is, almost always, *less emotional arousal*.

From this understanding we can see that the therapeutic techniques deriving from an understanding of the human givens will be useful in the treatment of bipolar disorder. We have ourselves encountered a number of clients who are now successfully managing their condition using such techniques, without needing drug treatment, and very many benefit from a combination of drugs and human givens therapy.

Effective psychotherapy for depression

With a clearer understanding of what depression is, and what causes it, we can lift it more rapidly. The main focus in treating depression is to lower the emotional arousal and stop the patient worrying as quickly as possible – by any psychological means at our disposal. This is done by using whatever methods enable us to best address the unmet needs of the sufferer by making the most use of their life resources and by helping them to use their imagination positively instead of misusing it to worry. We routinely find that using *all* available approaches in one session makes progress much faster. That is why human givens therapy has been found to be so quickly effective for depression,[67] as well as all other emotional disorders.

As outlined in the previous chapter, the human givens therapist, as well as integrating behavioural, cognitive and interpersonal approaches, also uses relaxation to calm the emotions before attempting other interventions, and guided imagery, which stimulates the imaginative faculty to motivate people and help them change, solve problems and get back in control of their lives. We may also use humour to reframe situations and demonstrate that life is not a black-and-white affair. We encourage people and acknowledge their achievements; inform them; get them to exercise; raise their curiosity and so on. In this way we have a truly organic mind/body approach – which is what human givens therapy is – and can bring about the remission of depression in a fraction of the time that cognitive-behavioural or interpersonal therapy can. Human givens therapists routinely find that they can lift people out of a depressed state in just a handful of sessions, sometimes in one.[83,84] Clients quickly work to reduce negative introspections when it is explained to them that this is the mechanism that is generating their depression.

Sometimes it can be difficult for counsellors, GPs or social workers to see how to apply the approach we are advocating when they have a large case load of clinically depressed patients with huge social problems in their lives – debts, redundancy, no work, illness, disability, family break-up, single parenthood, etc. In fact, there is still much that can be achieved, by using our methods, to help people better manage a range of disabling conditions and circumstances and increase their joy in life.[85] A key point to remember, when a depressed person's problems seem to be rooted firmly in the environment, is that there is no life situation so dire that others haven't experienced it – and very many manage to cope without getting clinically depressed.[86] Clinical depression is an additional layer of suffering for a person in an already difficult situation. (As reported in *The Times*[87] we have demonstrated on film how much can be done in one session for people suffering from multiple problems. Filmed follow-up sessions often show them looking physically transformed for the better, as well as transformed in motivation and mood.)

We can see the negative impact of depression clearly in the case of people who know that they are dying from cancer. Not all patients who know that they are terminally ill become depressed. Very many remain actively engaged with life, perhaps participating in the decisions required in day-to-day family life, looking forward to visits from relatives, organizing the disposal of their estate, designing their funeral service, planning special trips and generally setting short-term goals that can be accomplished in the time they have left.

A terminally ill person who becomes depressed, however, will withdraw from the support of others and frighten themselves with emotional introspections about death and dying and, as a consequence, hasten the process. Negative introspection reduces serotonin levels in the brain. As one of the functions of serotonin is to modulate pain responses, the depressed patient may, as a consequence, experience not only more fear but also more pain. Thus depression is an additional problem to, not a consequence of, highly challenging life circumstances. When counselling depressed people in difficult life circumstances, it is essential to focus their attention outwards into problem-solving. Problems need to be broken down into manageable chunks, and practical ways sought to solve them. This may, for example, involve a counsellor in helping people renegotiate debt repayments or coordinate social services, or in showing them how to avail themselves of care relief services. This way, not only do people gain a degree of control over their environmental problems but also the emphasis on problem-solving stops them introspecting negatively about their circumstances and thus lowers their arousal levels.

Postnatal depression is often viewed as a special subcategory of depression. But it is caused, just like all other kinds of depression, by emotionally arousing worrying – concerns about coping and about the huge nature of the life change having a baby brings, coupled with inevitably disturbed sleep. As such, it too is best treated in the way we recommend.[88] As very many new mothers feel isolated and inadequate, connecting them with others in the community and building their confidence is vitally important.

Once depression is lifted, some additional psychological repair work may still need to be done. People are often lonely because they don't have the skills for making small talk and have not learned how to make natural, easy contact with other human beings. They may need to practise other social skills or learn how to job hunt, or prepare for a change of career, all of which are possible once the depression is lifted and the person can think again. We should never forget that emotional arousal hijacks our ability to think clearly and drastically limits our options, not only for thought, but also for action. Once arousal levels are lowered most people can get on with their lives.

But some people seem to get more than their fair share of bad things happening to them. This often happens not only because they have the pessimistic, emotional, black-and-white view but because they also have some additional vulnerability. Depression is often accompanied by other conditions, which may range from anxiety disorders, such as panic attacks and obsessive-compulsive disorders, to medical conditions and personality problems. Addictive behaviour is found in some depressed people because, having become depressed, they turn to drugs or alcohol as a way of trying to lift their mood. They then, of course, end up with two problems. All addicts, whether initially depressed or not, are likely eventually to become depressed because so many of their needs are unfulfilled.

Panic attacks often present with depression. Counsellors must know how to reassure a sufferer that there is nothing organically wrong and that their symptoms are in fact those of a fear reaction – inappropriate firing of the fight-or-flight response. Normalizing the event and taking the fear out of it will result in their introspecting about it less. Then they can be shown how to bring the anxiety under control by, for example, learning how to stop panic breathing.

The experience of sexual or physical abuse, a serious road accident, or extreme violence, may result in post-traumatic stress disorder. It will inevitably lead to depression if untreated. This is because traumatized people endlessly introspect about the traumatic event and their subsequent uncontrolled responses to it. This can usually be easily treated, as described in the next chapter.

Blueprint for an effective therapy session

All human givens practitioners are taught to follow the RIGAAR model, which we described in the previous chapter: building rapport; information gathering; setting goals; accessing resources; agreeing a strategy with the client; and rehearsing success (most usually using guided imagery). This is a summary of the steps involved when using it to help with depression.

We start building rapport from the moment we first set eyes on a new client. After greeting them warmly, we set about lowering arousal. It is important to calm a depressed person down sufficiently to be able to think more clearly again. (Someone who remains in a high state of emotional arousal is not going to take in any information we give them.) This is most effectively done, after clients have unloaded their story, by asking them about their sleep and how they feel when they wake up. In almost all cases depressed clients will express strong dissatisfaction with their sleep, and giving them the chance to talk about this helps build rapport.

We can then ask if they have been worrying about anything and, when they have told us what has been worrying them, explain what excessive worrying does to the sleep/dream cycle. This captures their attention, distracts them from their worries and makes them feel that what they are experiencing is not abnormal. At the same time as finding out which emotional needs are not being met in their lives, which their worries should tell us, we also find out about their good qualities, life achievements, abilities, etc (information gathering and accessing resources). No human givens practitioner will ever just history-take about the bad things that have happened to their client. Sometimes it can be difficult to get depressed clients to remember anything good about themselves or their lives, as they are locked in the trance of depression. We have to be persistent and creative in finding ways to draw this information from them.

Our job is to help our client create new positive expectations to replace the old negative ones and thereby stop the worry cycle. So we must find out what they would like to change about their life and what concrete steps they could take to bring this about (goal setting). We also need to identify and address what they think is stopping them.

We must now refocus their attention away from their negative expectations towards getting their needs met by encouraging physical activity, getting pleasure back into their life, improving relationships, solving the problems that cause them to worry and challenging negative thinking, agreeing the strategies to do so. Sometimes a depression is held in place because of psychological trauma that has not been dealt with. In this case, we may need to detraumatize them straight away. In such circumstances, when this is done, people can come out of depression in the first session of therapy.

We want to enable the client to *experience* a sense of acting differently to meet their goals and to feel that this is achievable and that they can cope with any setbacks. So it is essential that we help the depressed person to use their imagination positively – we use guided imagery to help them appreciate their resources, see how things can be different, build hope and rehearse the new behaviours (rehearsing success). At the same time, we create and offer them relevant helpful metaphors and stories, to embed new more empowering patterns.

All the above must be attempted in the first session, if at all possible. We want to bring about sufficient improvement to give clients hope that things can change for the better, and to make them want to continue to raise their mood and improve their state. Clients suffering from ante- or postnatal depression can be treated in exactly the same way. Indeed, many women who are fearful about pregnancy or giving birth feel frightened because of a complicated, traumatizing previous experience, and this can be quickly dealt with. Our detraumatization method is so effective that the Royal College of Midwives accredits a postgraduate training for midwives, obstetricians, nurses, health visitors and other birth professionals, which is based on our approach.[89]

Taking the wrong road

The adverse effects of too much emotionally arousing introspection explain why psychodynamic, 'insight' therapy may often be harmful. A restaurateur in her early 40s once came to see Joe. She had been attending various 'insight' therapists for counselling over the past two years and was referred to him by a body therapist whom she had started to consult, in some desperation, to relieve her misery. She said her confidence had completely collapsed to the degree that, were she to meet a good friend in the street, she would worry about what kind of an impression she was making and get into a high state of agitation. At her restaurant, if she were talking to a customer, she found herself becoming acutely self-conscious, getting tongue-tied and befuddled with them.

As she was quite clear that this problem had been getting worse over the past two years, Joe pointed out that it might not be a coincidence that the more counselling she had had the worse her problems seemed to have become. She agreed.

She told Joe that she and her husband had worked hard together and made a great success of their restaurant business. When she had accrued enough money and spare time she decided to "work" on herself and enter counselling to "develop my potential". At that point she was not depressed at all but, she said, the counselling made her realize that she had had problems all her life. These went back to her childhood and her relationship with her alcoholic father. She felt she had been "in denial" of those painful feelings until the therapy helped her to get in touch with the suppressed pain that was now coming out. This a pattern we come across time and time again in clinical practice. Clients attending well-meaning counsellors become emotionally dysfunctional. With the best of intentions, the counsellors help their clients to re-experience more and more emotional pain from the past. The more emotionally aroused the clients become, of course the less they are able to bring rational thought to bear, until they will even accept the twisted logic that *you have to become more dysfunctional before you can get better!*

Such twisted logic would be rejected in any other area of life. Imagine someone going to the doctor with a stomach pain for which they are given treatment, but the pain worsens. On re-examination the doctor says, "I can see what's happening. The treatment is really working. Before you came to see me your immune system was repressing a cancerous growth. It is now no longer repressing it. And as a result of my treatment, we are making progress – the painful cancer is growing!"

Clearly, that would be utterly absurd. And yet such reasoning is followed, in all innocence, by many counsellors and psychotherapists, who tell their clients in advance that they must expect the therapy to be emotionally painful! They then proceed to work in such ways as to fulfil their prophecy, damaging their patients in the process.

By contrast, for a human givens therapist, it is axiomatic that, if the client is emotionally distressed and disturbed, the reason is that their needs are not being met *now*, or that they are misusing the tools that nature gave them to get those needs met, or both. They usually need calming down first, so that they can access rational thinking, and then some practical coaching in how to improve their life.

Joe immediately directed the therapy towards finding out what needs were not being fulfilled in this woman's life. He asked her about her children – they seemed to be growing up normally with no more than the usual problems that parents encounter with a young family. She had no money worries. But, when he asked about her relationship with her husband, she readily admitted that this was deteriorating at an alarming rate. Sexual intimacy had stopped. In fact, they had arranged to meet a solicitor the following week to negotiate a separation.

Curiously, this was a subject she didn't even bring up until Joe questioned her. Instead she had been asking whether she could be helped to "get in touch with her past" because there *must* be something there, perhaps in her relationship with her father, and she felt if she could uncover this it would release her from her lack of confidence. In other words, she was asking for more of the same kind of emotionally arousing therapy that had exacerbated her problems.

Perhaps one of the most worrying aspects of this, and similar cases, is that this woman wasn't psychologically troubled prior to going to counselling. In fact, as she and her husband had built their very successful business together, it turned out they didn't have any significant marriage problems either. It was only when someone persuaded her to do some personal development work, as she now had spare time, and explore her "issues" that the marital problems seemed to magnify and she began to become emotionally dysfunctional. To be of use to this woman, Joe had to lower her emotional arousal so that her perspective widened, and taught her stress control techniques. Then he helped her rebuild her relationship with her husband, so that she could get her needs met within what was basically a good and productive marriage.

An avoidable death

Another woman told Joe about the circumstances of her depressed husband's death. She had been deeply worried about his depressed state and felt that he was at risk of suicide. She finally managed to persuade her husband to see his GP, although the husband felt it was pointless to do so. But, having got him to the surgery, all the GP did was change his antidepressant medication. This meant that any benefit he might have been getting from his previous antidepressant would diminish while the new antidepressant would take some weeks to start working.

Had the GP worked from a human givens perspective (and many have trained with us so that they can make most efficient use of their brief primary care consultations with patients) he would have known how to challenge the man's attributional style, curb his introspections, create a positive expectancy and buy crucial time by making him promise not to kill himself until he had given the doctor's methods a go.

The man was obviously highly emotionally aroused, so the GP could usefully have shown him how to calm himself down and relax, so that he could see his situation more clearly. The GP could have made positive true statements, such as, "Depression is not a permanent state and remits naturally in the majority of cases". He could have made him laugh, to break the trance of depression, or helped him decide on a course of action. He could have reminded him about things that he had achieved in his life and of his proven ability to make changes happen, thus raising his self-esteem. The man would then have left that GP's surgery believing that change was possible, having had it actually demonstrated to him. He could have been calmed, reassured and given hope. This is the kind of thing that GPs trained in the human givens do routinely.[90] But this GP's failure to realize the seriousness of the situation, and the importance of creating hope in his patient, meant that the man went out and hanged himself – the woman lost her husband, and his children lost their father.

Unfortunately, this is happening over and over again because of the mistreatment of depression. Although women are more likely to suffer depression than men are, men are more likely to kill themselves. This, again, is due to emotional arousal and the way strong emotion inhibits perceptions and thinking. Women tend to dwell more on their emotions while men tend to go into 'problem-solving' mode to deal with difficulties. A man engaged in black-and-white thinking will tend to see suicide as a solution to a problem. And, because males tend to be more action-oriented than females, they are more likely to carry their 'solution' out.

As we have seen, depression is an emotion that stimulates black-and-white thinking and introspection, creating exhaustion because of the excessive dreaming this causes. Techniques for lifting it quickly, working from the human givens perspective, include calming a depressed person down quickly; finding out what needs are not being fulfilled in their life; raising their self-esteem, by drawing their attention vividly to their competencies; identifying and challenging their attributional thinking style; and demonstrating, from the very first session, that change is possible – thus creating a sense of positive expectancy and a belief in, and will to, change. The following case histories are typical of this approach and show how the use of such skills can be incorporated into counselling sessions.

More casebook examples

The widow: Mary, in her late 60s, was physically robust but her face was etched with grief and despair. Her husband Tom, who had been the mainstay of her life, had died six months earlier. Mary was still tortured by images of his final suffering. She couldn't sleep at night and yet stayed in bed until lunch time because she saw no point in getting up. She was also scared to leave the house because of the panic attacks she had been suffering since Tom's death.

After listening to her story, Joe explained the importance of relaxation and how to control her panic attacks. With guided imagery and progressive muscle relaxation she slowed down her breathing, lines of tension easing from her face, and, with eyes closed, she gratefully sank back into the comfort of the armchair. Joe then quietly suggested that she could let go of the image of her husband's final suffering and recall instead happy images of their time together. He gave her time to do this and she clearly enjoyed it. He then reminded her of the many strengths and skills she had developed in raising her large family, now scattered around the world. He also told her that her husband would want her to call upon that strength, and the strength of her relationship with him, to face the new challenges in her life.

When she opened her eyes she and Joe worked out a plan together for what she would do each day, starting with what time she would get up. She said she would like to start baking again, so they built that into the plan. Joe explained the importance of aerobic exercise for keeping down her stress levels and lifting depressed feelings. She agreed to resume walking with her neighbour in the evenings, which she had stopped doing since Tom had died. To ensure that her need for human company would be met Joe also persuaded her to join a social craft group in the town.

Over the next few weeks, her mood lifted dramatically. As she became physically active again she took on more jobs around the house, including some decorating and gardening. Very soon after this, her son in America sent her a ticket to join him for a holiday. When she had stayed depressed so long, he had withdrawn from her and had been reluctant to invite her over. But now that she was focused outward again he was happy to see her, which lifted her spirits still further.

The effect of the human givens approach in this case was rapid and straightforward, as it so often is.

Mary was first helped to bring down her emotional arousal in order to free her to see reality in a more empowering way. Then the meaning of Tom's death and love was reframed into a challenge to her to move on in her life. She was given back a sense of control over her panic attacks. Pleasure and challenge were brought back into her life by resuming walking with friends, baking and decorating. The satisfaction of her need for attention was shifted from her therapist to her local community, by getting her to join a local craft group. Finally, the lifting of her depression brought her into closer contact with her family again.

The suicide attempt: Judith, a woman in her late 20s, was married with no children and living in rural England. She came to see Joe following her discharge from hospital after treatment for a 20-inch diagonal stab wound across her chest, inflicted in her attempted suicide. The stabbing had been so severe that she had been kept in hospital for a week. She had made this attempt on her life because her problems seemed so large and numerous that she could see no other way out.

Judith showed the very common risk factor for depression already referred to: black-and-white, global thinking – the tendency to see the forest but not the individual trees nor the various paths in it. To use another metaphor, if we hold a stone up to our eyes all we can see is the stone. The rest of the world is blotted out as surely as if the stone were as large as a mountain. For a global thinker, the little stone becomes the universe.

The global thinker tends to focus so much on their problems that they can see no way around or through them. All that exists are their problems. They inevitably lose a sense of proportion about their situation. Difficulties become catastrophes. Their imagination piles up the problems one on top of another so that a mountain of misery completely blocks out the wider view. This is exactly the process that led Judith to her desperate act of attempted self-annihilation.

This was her story. She had been unemployed for three years since injuring her back in an accident at work. She was currently waiting for a claim for legal damages to be heard by the courts. Shortly before her attempted suicide, she read in the paper about a person who had lost their injuries claim against their employer and was forced to sell the family home to pay their employer's legal costs. Judith was terrified that if she lost her legal action she and her husband might become homeless too. They were just, in fact, in the process of having a new house built and that was one more thing that troubled Judith; it had fallen behind schedule. "The builders are taking us to the cleaners," she said. "The house will *never* be finished. The site is a *complete* mess." Again we see pessimism and black-and-white thinking.

Judith also had a phobia about dogs. Her neighbours had a dog and, unless her husband was with her, she was scared to pass their house. This meant that, for much of her time, she was effectively trapped in her own home.

Judith was additionally much troubled by the fact that her sister, whom she was close to, had recently announced, as a result of counselling, that, as a child, their father had sexually abused her. Her sister expected and wanted her support. But Judith also had a very close relationship with her father, who vehemently denied the abuse. Naturally, her father wanted and expected Judith's support too. She didn't know what to do.

Here we again see black-and-white thinking at work. Black-and-white thinking creates a low tolerance for the inevitable ambiguities of life. So much of life is full of unknowns; certainty is the exception. We can't know for sure, for example, that we are choosing the right career, the right partner, the right house, or even the best holiday. In life, we can't always know for sure why what happens, happens. There are too many contributing factors. Someone might say, for example, "Why is my son a drug addict? Is it because I wasn't sufficiently firm with him? Maybe I didn't show him enough love. But, why then isn't my other son a drug addict? I didn't show favouritism to either of them. Maybe it's his genes? Or is it the company he keeps? Perhaps it was his disappointment in a love affair that made him vulnerable!" Maybe it was all or none of these reasons.

Black-and-white thinking demands a definite answer to every ambiguous life situation. Judith's thinking style demanded that she unambiguously support either her father or her sister. But she loved them both, so she was paralysed by her continual analytical introspections about the situation.

In the first session with Judith, Joe spent about 25 minutes getting her to relax, using guided imagery. He then dealt with her dog phobia (the method will be described in the next chapter) and, whilst she was still relaxed, discussed and reframed the other three main problems she was worrying about. Joe asked her what evidence she had that she was going to lose her court case. She repeated the story in the newspaper.

"That could be a completely different case from yours," he told her. "We must concentrate on the specific evidence. What does your barrister say is the likely outcome of your case?"

"Well, he says that I am certain to win since I was injured at work and there are sworn statements from other workers who were witnesses. All that remains to be decided, according to him, is how much in damages I receive."

Joe helped her to see that she was misusing her imagination by creating an improbable negative outcome to her court case. The idea that she was facing the loss of her family home was entirely unreasonable and, because she was relaxed and could think straight, she agreed this was so.

Next, the problem of the alleged sexual abuse of her sister by their father was looked at. It was clear that there was no external, validating evidence that abuse had taken place. Judith herself had never seen or experienced such abuse. In such circumstances, the only reasonable course of action was to tolerate the ambiguity of not knowing what, if anything, had actually happened. Her sister's memories might be true, or yet again they might be an artefact – illusory memories – created by the type of counselling that she was receiving. Joe explained that, at present, there was no way of knowing for sure. In any case, it wasn't her problem. Her father and sister were going to have to find a way of dealing with it themselves. Judith gave a huge sigh of relief when she realized she didn't have to solve the problem. She could offer her love and support to both family members – at least until more objective evidence became available.

Finally they considered her problem about her new home. What did the architect supervising the building programme have to say? "Well, according to him," she said, "we are only six months behind schedule." Joe joked with her that six months behind schedule was equivalent to 12 months ahead of schedule as far as the average builder was concerned!

When Judith came back the following week she was no longer depressed. Indeed, she had been out on her own and cycled past the house with the dog without experiencing a panic attack. She declared herself baffled by how she could ever have got things so much out of proportion. But we know why. It was due to her attributional style. Her global thinking style, combined with black-and-white thinking and endless worrying, formed the toxic brew that maintained the emotion of clinical depression and created her suicidal impulses.

The crying woman: Ivan saw Susan some years ago when her husband brought her into his clinic at her GP's suggestion. Her heavy figure oozed misery and seemed to suck the energy out of everyone around her. Speaking with reluctance – it was all such an effort – she described the history of her situation whilst tears slowly ran down her face: 11 years of severe depression, three serious suicide attempts, hospitalization, psychiatrists, antidepressants that hadn't worked, psychotherapy that made her feel even worse, "if that was possible". And now she was talking again about ending it all. "What is the point of living?"

Following the golden rule of not taking too much history with depressed people but showing the client instead that things can be different *in the first session*, after 30 minutes of listening Ivan set to work. She looked such a picture of despair that, on an impulse, he decided to use humour, an age-old and valuable way to help people see how they are exaggerating things. This need not mean telling jokes or being witty. He simply drew on her own resources and asked her what made her laugh?

Back came the inevitable slow monotone response, "Nothing makes me laugh".

"I don't believe you."

"I never laugh."

"*Everyone* has a sense of humour."

"I have *no* sense of humour. I *never* laugh."

So deep in her depression trance was Susan that he almost believed her, but he carried on anyway and asked her to do an experiment. "Just close your eyes and let your mind go back to the last time you had tears of laughter rolling down your face."

She obediently closed her eyes and Ivan sat back and waited, fingers crossed, while her brain went on a search. Within a few minutes she started to smile. The smiles turned to laughter. Then she started to cry, but this time with tears of laughter! She opened her eyes and splutteringly told of what she had remembered that was so funny. The laughter had dissipated her depression, puncturing a hole in the global blanket of misery she had held fast around her.

For a while, at least, her brain was working normally and they talked properly. Ivan then asked her what she most regretted about her depression and she said it was the fact that for 11 years, since her "illness", she and her husband had not been on a holiday and she felt this was so unfair on her husband because, when they were young, holidays had meant a lot to them and he still wanted to see more of the world. As it turned out, so did she. Ivan called the husband in. He was astonished and pleased to see her smiling and so changed. Whilst in this positive, lively state Ivan got them both to promise, as part of the treatment, to book a holiday straight away to somewhere they really wanted to go but where they had never been before.

Ivan had to see Susan 11 times in all before he was sure she was out of depression. (Coincidentally, once for every year she had been depressed.) At first she would come in and say she was just as bad as before – black-and-white thinking again – but, by getting her to scale her changing moods and achievements and teaching her how to change her attributional style, she got out of depression for good. Scaling the gradual remission of symptoms is a powerful tool of therapy precisely because it is *not* all or nothing. It is a technique drawn from solution-focused brief therapy in which, for instance, clients are asked to place themselves on a scale where 0 means no change in mood and 10 represents a completely positive and optimistic mood. It is a practical and motivating means of monitoring gradual upward changes.

The holiday, of course, gave Susan something outside of herself to focus on. They chose to go to Australia. It brought their relationship back to life: it brought planning, excitement and new experiences into their lives. Part of the reason people can't initiate such activity themselves when they are depressed is that they cannot easily make connections when they are emotionally aroused – the emotional arousal stops them thinking clearly. They just can't see the bigger picture. For some years, Ivan had postcards from Susan and her husband sent from various parts of the world, as they enjoyed their lives together again.

* * *

It has already been shown that antidepressants are much more dangerous than thought,[91] that the withdrawal effects can sometimes be long lasting,[92] and that the medical model ideology, which maintains that depression is caused by a chemical imbalance in the brain is just plain wrong.[93] As more and more research shows, the right type of psychotherapy is a much better treatment for sufferers. We hope that help for depressed patients will much improve as more health workers come to understand this and receive improved training in effective counselling techniques.

CHAPTER TEN

Terror in the brain: overcoming trauma

FEAR IS a natural reaction to danger, a survival signal that switches on the fight-or-flight response. Sooner or later everyone experiences it. Threatening events frighten all small children and unexpected attacks can temporarily terrify adults – but it is the experience of excessive, or inappropriate, fear of a kind that keeps people on permanent high alert that accounts for a whole range of common mental and behavioural problems. These we are going to explore now. Depression, low self-esteem, psychosis, and a great host of anxiety disorders, including post-traumatic stress disorder (PTSD), can result from an excessive firing of the fight-or-flight response. Neuroscience has revealed so much about this that we now understand why the brain's design makes it so vulnerable to extreme fright.

A traumatized creature lives a private hell: hyperalert, terrorized by an invisible mental wound, helplessly in thrall to a powerful emotional memory of a life-threatening event – or series of events – real or imagined. Horrific, violent events can clearly impact on the mind as well as the body to produce such a state, as vividly illustrated in the following description of a Vietnam War veteran's experience:

"I can't get the memories out of my mind! The images come flooding back in vivid detail, triggered by the most inconsequential things, like a door slamming or the smell of stir-fried pork. Last night I went to bed, was having a good sleep for a change. Then ... there was a bolt of crackling thunder. I awoke instantly, frozen in fear. I am right back in Vietnam. My hands are freezing, yet sweat pours from my entire body. I feel each hair on the back of my neck standing on end. I can't catch my breath and my heart is pounding ... The next clap of thunder makes me jump so much that I fall to the floor."[1]

Although originally PTSD was most commonly diagnosed among

soldiers, sailors and airmen returning from war zones, the most recent American estimates, at time of writing, were that prevalence of PTSD in one year ranged from 2.6–6 per cent of civilians and from 6.7–11.7 per cent among veterans. Lifetime prevalence ranged from 3.4–8 per cent among civilians and from 7.7–13.4 per cent among veterans; it was also acknowledged that prevalence might be higher among certain populations, such as women, emergency service workers, Native Americans, and refugees.[2]

It is estimated that 50–70 per cent of people will experience trauma in their lifetime and that, in 20 per cent of cases (10 per cent of a population), it may go on to become PTSD. After the covid-19 pandemic, prevalence figures were estimated at double or nearly triple previous figures. According to estimates, there were as many as 230,000 new PTSD referrals in the UK between 2020/21 and 2022/23 in England alone, a rise of about 77,000 cases.[3]

Traumatic experiences cover a huge range, including surviving terrifying natural disasters such as earthquakes, forest fires or avalanches, car, rail, boat or air accidents, heart attacks, complicated births, mugging, burning, rape or sexual assault. We now also realize that people can be vicariously traumatized. Some grandchildren of concentration camp survivors, for example, have subsequently become traumatized by hearing about their grandparents' memories.[4] A female client of Joe's, whose son and his fiancée were horribly burned to death in a tragic car accident, suffered terrifying traumatic flashbacks from her imagined fantasies about what it must have been like to be trapped in a car, burning to death in that terrible way. Even if an event didn't actually happen, if it is vividly imagined as life-threatening, it can be traumatizing. A colleague had a client who was traumatised by her imaginings of harm coming to her daughter, after reading of an attack on a little girl her own daughter's age.

Classic symptoms of PTSD include flashbacks of the traumatic events, as if they were happening right now, recurring nightmares, distressing, intrusive thoughts, physical sensations associated with extreme anxiety, panic attacks, avoidance behaviours or reckless behaviour, distorted thoughts and memory, irritability and anger outbursts. There are also now variants of PTSD recognized. For instance, complex PTSD (C-PTSD) is the diagnosis clinicians may make if, alongside classic PTSD symptoms, someone has severe difficulty in regulating their emotions, feelings of worthlessness, shame and guilt and/or struggles in relationships and has difficulties with trust.

A variety of treatments may be offered for PTSD, including drugs, trauma-based CBT, psychodynamic therapy, hypnotic techniques, such as eye movement desensitization and reprocessing (EMDR), the emotional freedom technique (EFT, often known as 'tapping'), critical incident debriefing, and various versions of exposure therapy, such as flooding or systematic desensitization. Not all treatments that are offered for PTSD are actually helpful and some may even be harmful. This is because, if someone suffering from PTSD is asked to recall the trauma, they go so fully back into the memory, into the trance state of the trauma, that they relive the trauma as if it were happening *now*. Clearly, this is likely to embed it even more deeply. Any process that has the potential to cure PTSD has to keep the person's awareness focused in the present so that the relevant networks of the brain can reframe the memory as a past event and put it in a realistic perspective.[5]

We can draw on the APET model to illustrate this more clearly.

The **A** in the APET model (the A standing for the activating stimulus from the environment) is, in this case, whatever event a person has experienced, witnessed or imagined that involved actual or threatened or imagined serious physical harm to them or others. The **P** for pattern matching in APET, in this context, is the process by which the amygdala, the brain's alarm system, seeks to ensure an organism's survival. It constantly scans the environment for potential threats, comparing all incoming stimulation, supplied by our various senses, with survival templates – fear memories – to see if they are life threatening or life enhancing. A crackle of twigs or a sudden silence in the forest may trigger the alarm system because previous experience of a crackle or silence has signalled a predator, setting in train an emotional reaction which leads to freezing, fight or flight. The sensory information is passed on to an adjacent organ in the brain called the hippocampus. Here, all of our most recent experiences are put in context and encoded before being stored in the form of specific patterns of neural activity throughout the brain. When we are asked about something that happened, that neural network is reactivated.

However, when stress is at a very high level, as in perceived life-threatening moments, the classic explanation is that the amygdala becomes hyper-reactive and also unresponsive to any input from certain areas of the prefrontal cortex. The hippocampus also becomes less able to function properly and so fails to lay down coherent memories in a way that puts them into context. Thereafter, whenever something in the environment 'recalls' the traumatic moment – a certain sound, smell, object or whatever – the amygdala becomes hyper-reactive again, triggering the alarm and again inhibiting the areas of the prefrontal cortex and hippocampus, which could have helped create a clearer picture of what is happening in the current context.[6] This is what occurs in post-traumatic stress. The most common findings in neuroimaging studies of trauma survivors who develop post-traumatic stress are reduced hippocampal volume and increased activation of the amygdala.[7]

However, this classic "hyper-reactive uncontrolled fear" model of PTSD has also been called into question. Some researchers suggest that, rather than understanding PTSD as exaggerated activation of fear circuitry, it might instead be that incoming information from the environment is experienced as more personally relevant than it should be by a hyper-aroused amygdala, an interpretation consistent with findings that the amygdala is part of an intrinsic brain network that helps to determine the personal or motivational significance to us of any given thing or event.[8] We will leave this to academics to wrangle over. For our purposes, the crucial element is that, in the highly stressed brain, the amygdala overreacts to certain stimuli and there is no corrective in place.

Susceptibility to PTSD depends upon a variety of factors, such as the degree of trauma and aspects of personality, such as trait anxiety and suggestibility.[9] The number of traumatic events experienced is also a factor – someone may withstand many highly stressful events and then succumb to PTSD after one stress too many, as a result of the cumulative effect. The final stressor may not even be the most severe but acts, in effect, as the straw that broke the camel's back.

The amygdala of someone who develops PTSD is imprinted with the pattern of the trauma, which contains all the information surrounding the event, and holds its emotional significance.[10] Thereafter, the templates contained in the amygdala, to which all new incoming stimuli are compared, also include a template for that traumatic event. Whenever, as explained, there is a match, *or a part-match*, the amygdala fires off the alarm reaction; the fight-or-flight response is activated and, because this all happens at an unconscious level, the person experiences an incomprehensible state of alarm – a strong emotional expectation (the E in APET).

It is because pattern matching is a metaphorical process – the amygdala is looking for something *like* something else – that people experience flashbacks and other severe alarm reactions when the amygdala spots anything with any similarity to some aspect of a traumatic event. This is why the origin of such reactions can at first seem mysterious. A graphic example of this is provided by the tale of a butcher in the 1920s who began to have 'strange spells': his heart would beat violently, and he would vomit and then lose consciounness. It emerged that these attacks usually followed exposure to certain odours from volatile oils – perfume, lemon oil, banana oil or ether. The butcher's shop he worked in was frequented by fashionable women, many of whom came heavily perfumed, and, as his doctor described it, "when they would enter the butcher shop ... the patient would become dizzy and lose consciousness". It turned out that, during the Great War of 1914–18, the butcher had had the horribly unpleasant experience of being gassed in the trenches whilst asleep. "The flushing, the rapid pulse, the dizziness and the vomiting," his doctor decided, were "a repetition of the original traumatic event which overtook him in sleep." The man's amygdala was simply pattern matching to *any* strange, strong smell.[11]

In the same way, people who have survived horrific car accidents can have exaggerated alarm reactions to the mere sight of a car, the smell of petrol or even just the sound of screeching brakes on a television programme. People who have experienced a violent, traumatizing sexual attack can later, in a loving relationship, become highly anxious at any form of sexual approach and withdraw from normal sexual intimacy. We can now see why counselling of a type that encourages a traumatized victim to relive their experience is not likely to be effective. As we have explained, the more emotionally aroused we are, the less able we are to think straight – as anyone who has ever fallen in love or lost their temper will know. If a counsellor invites the victim to talk about or recall the trauma, hoping to help them set it in context and put it behind them, an emotional charge is set off which inhibits the ability for any clear thinking. Each time an attempt is made to recall the trauma, off goes the alarm; mental processing is inhibited and the traumatic memory is further programmed into the amygdala.

Freeze, fight or flight

When we are exposed to a sudden and significant stress that we feel may endanger our life, our attention is intensely and instantly fully focused on the source of the threat. The amygdala instructs another structure in the brain, called the periaqueductal gray (we'll call it PAG for short) to freeze our movement. Specifically, it is the front (ventral) section of PAG that makes the freeze happen. Momentarily we are stuck to the ground like mesmerized rabbits, while the situation is risk assessed.[12,13] Then, once it is clear whether we need to defend ourselves or not, the front part of the PAG is instructed to stop the freezing, and either we relax or else the fight-or-flight response is set in motion[14,15] and we defend ourselves or run away.

But sometimes people can't flee, because all escape routes are blocked or a person is utterly powerless against the threat facing them. At that point, the back (dorsal) part of the PAG takes over from the amygdala and causes an immobilized, dissociated state, a state of shutdown, completely different from the freeze state.[16] The freeze state is associated with a slowed heartbeat, whereas, in the state of involuntary immobility, the heart rate speeds up. Although this state has been demonstrated in studies using rabbits, rodents and pigeons, biological evidence of it has also been identified in humans.[17] This is hugely important because some victims of sexual assault have been accused of 'not fighting back' when, in fact, they had gone into a state of shutdown.

In recent years, many therapists have adopted the understandings about the state of shutdown as explained by polyvagal theory, so it is important to mention this. The theory was developed by neuroscientist Stephen Porges, originally as a result of his work on heart-rate variability in prematurely born babies.[18] The vagus nerve is a major component of the parasympathetic nervous system, the part of the autonomic nervous system which regulates 'rest and digest' functions. Opposing this is the sympathetic nervous system, which prepares the body for physical activity and activates the fight-or-flight response when we are under threat. Porges claimed that the parasympathetic nervous system had two vagal branches, not one; alongside the element associated with repose, according to his explanation, was an older system inherited from our reptile ancestors, which led to shutdown in the face of threat. (Reptiles, which cannot scuttle away when threatened, instead rely on not drawing attention to themselves – they can survive several hours without breathing.)

Polyvagal theory proposes that the autonomic nervous system responds to stimuli, whether sensations within the body or something outside in the environment, through three pathways: the dorsal vagus, the oldest in evolutionary terms, which leads to immobilization (shutdown); the sympathetic nervous system, which leads to mobilization; and the ventral vagus, the 'newest' pathway, which Porges defines as concerned with social engagement and connection.

Therapist Deb Dana, who was the first to publish on putting these ideas to use clinically, has described the "autonomic ladder", which has the ventral vagal (safe and social) at the top; the sympathetic (mobilized) in the middle rungs; and the dorsal vagal (immobilized, collapsed) at the bottom. She describes it thus:

"When we are firmly grounded in our ventral vagal pathway, we feel safe, connected, calm and social. A sense (neuroception) of danger can trigger us out of this state and backwards on the evolutionary timeline into the sympathetic branch. Here we are mobilized to respond and take action. Taking action can help us return to the safe and social state. It is when we feel as though we are trapped and can't escape the danger that the dorsal vagal pathway pulls us all the way back to our evolutionary beginnings. In this state we are immobilized. We shut down to survive. From here it is a long way back to feeling safe and social and a painful path to follow."[19]

It follows that the therapist's task here is to identify the autonomic state the client is in and help them to return to, or achieve, the safe and social ventral state, where we are able to feel trust and connection with others.

However, the theory itself has drawn fierce criticism from biologists and neuroscientists on several counts,[20] most notably the idea that the vagal nerve pathways reflect different stages of our evolutionary development. Still, taken metaphorically, the understandings as articulated by Deb Dana may be helpful to some, especially as it is not controversial that therapists should want to enable traumatised clients to attain a sense of security, connection and fulfilment – indeed, vital human needs.

Let us take a look at other perspectives on the freeze, fight or fight response, which may shed more light on what is happening in the body, and ways of working with it. In evolutionary terms, freezing was – and is – actually beneficial for many animals. Although not engaged in voluntarily, if they suddenly stop moving they become invisible to those predators whose main focus is on movement, and so have a better chance of staying alive.[21] Naturalists watching animals being hunted have also noticed the freezing response occur an instant *before* the predator makes physical contact with its intended prey. Peter Levine, who holds doctorates in biophysics and psychology, and is now famous for his work with human stress and trauma, once vividly described what happened as a cheetah closed in on an impala. "It is almost as if the animal has surrendered to its impending demise. But the fallen impala is not dead. Although on the 'outside' it appears limp and motionless, on the 'inside' its nervous system is still activated from the 70 miles-an-hour chase. Though barely breathing, the impala's heart is pumping at extreme rates. Its brain and body are being flooded by the same chemicals (for example, adrenaline and cortisol) that helped fuel its attempted escape." This means that, should an escape route suddenly open up, the animal can take it.

"It is possible that the impala will not be devoured immediately. The mother cheetah may drag its fallen, and apparently dead, prey behind a bush and seek out its cubs who are hiding at a safe distance. Herein lies a short window of opportunity for the impala. The temporarily 'frozen' creature has a chance to awaken from its state of shock, shake and tremble in order to discharge the vast amount of energy stored in its nervous system, then, as if nothing had happened, bound away in search of the rest of its herd. Another benefit of the frozen (immobility) state is its analgesic nature. If the impala is killed, it will be spared the pain of its own demise."[22]

Although it appears that we have separated ourselves from animals like the impala and cheetah, our responses to threat are still biologically formed. They are human givens – innate and instinctive functions of our organism. For the impala, life-threatening situations are an everyday occurrence, so it makes sense that the ability to resolve and complete these episodes is built into their biological systems. Threat, albeit of a different kind, is a relatively common phenomenon for humans as well. Although we are rarely aware of it, we also possess the innate ability to complete and resolve these experiences. From our biology come our responses to threat, and it is also in our biology that the resolution of trauma dwells.

In order to remain healthy, all animals, including humans, must discharge the vast energies mobilized for survival. This discharge completes our activated responses to threat, and allows us to return to a more normal state. In biology, this process is called homoeostasis: the ability of an organism to respond appropriately to any given circumstance, and then return to a baseline of what could be called 'normal' functioning.

In a National Geographic video *Polar Bear Alert*, made decades ago, a frightened bear is shown being run down by a pursuing aeroplane, shot with a tranquillizer dart, surrounded by wildlife biologists, and then tagged. Later, as the massive animal comes out of its state of shock, it begins to quiver and ends up in almost convulsive shaking – its limbs flailing around seemingly out of control. The shaking subsides and the animal is seen to take three long spontaneous breaths that seem to spread through its entire body.

The biologist narrating the film comments that what the bear is doing is shaking off the stress accumulated during its capture. It is pointed out that, if the sequence is looked at again but slowed down in speed, it suddenly becomes clear that the seemingly uncontrolled leg movements are in effect coordinated running movements. The animal seems to be completing its 'flight' template, cut short when it was trapped, discharging frozen energy.[23]

Animals and most humans *don't* get traumatized when they can properly discharge their accumulated stress energy by activating the fight-or-flight response at the time of the event. So the question arises, what is happening in those who *do* develop PTSD, particularly those who experience the shutdown state?

The answer, we suggest, lies in that other everyday state in which mammals, including humans, become paralysed or frozen – the rapid eye movement (REM) state, the deep trance state we all slip into when we are asleep and dreaming. As we have seen, when we dream, the very same orientation response (the reaction which turns our attention to a sudden unexpected stimulus, such as a loud noise, and freezes our behaviour when awake) fires off while we are sleeping.[24] The orientation response has the same basic function when we are asleep but, as stimuli from the outside world are shut out, it is set off by undischarged emotional-arousal patterns from the day before, which arise in the brain in the REM state. The orientation response alerts the brain to these patterns, which are then discharged by being metaphorically acted out in a dream. The dream thus deactivates the emotional stress.[25] The very freezing or paralysis of movement that is triggered by the orientation response when something unexpected happens also occurs in the dream state (preventing us from physically acting out our dreams).

Our colleague Ezra Hewing has even made the case that dissociation, as activated in REM sleep, itself explains why trauma can result in shutdown.[26] He writes, "A paper by Ioannis Tsoukalas of Stockholm University proposes an evolutionary connection between immobilisation and REM sleep, based on the large number of features they share in common.[27] These include a similar pattern of brain waves, with some originating in the hippocampus. In both states there is a release of the neurotransmitter acetylcholine, involved in 'switching on' REM sleep in areas of the brainstem and forebrain, including the hippocampus and amygdala. In both states there is reduced serotonin activity in the area associated with 'switching off' REM sleep.

"There is also, in both cases, a surge in heart rate and respiration, albeit that this gradually declines during immobilisation, while fluctuating at elevated levels during REM sleep. Muscle tone and reflex signals between nerves decrease, while eye and face muscles and limbs jerk independently. Immobilisation in both states can last for up to 20 minutes, or in rare cases even longer. A form of immobilisation is experienced when people awake from REM sleep still in sleep paralysis.

"Tsoukalas observes that both immobilisation and dreaming are responses to emotional arousal: 'Dreaming during REM sleep is usually driven by a central emotion or emotional concern that is contextualised and elaborated in a series of loosely related scenarios. This concern can be a trauma that the person has suffered, a stressful situation, or some minor nuisance of everyday life ... which usually results in a therapeutic outcome.'[28]

"Research has also shown that, after a night where REM sleep is lost to insomnia, we dissociate more often the next day, whereas the better our sleep, the more able we are to remain focused, and the less often our attention drifts."[29]

Hewing further describes how accounts of dissociation and immobilisation resemble the experience of dreaming, illustrating this with one given by explorer David Livingstone in his journal of the dreamlike experience of dissociating when attacked by a lion:

"I heard a shout. Starting and looking half round, I saw the lion just in the act of springing upon me. I was on a little height; he caught my shoulder as he sprang and we both came to the ground below together. Growling horribly close to my ear he shook me as a terrier does a rat. The shock produced a stupor similar to that which seems to be felt by a mouse after the first shake of the cat. It caused a sort of dreaminess, in which there was no sense of pain nor feeling of terror, though quite conscious of all that was happening. It was like what patients partially under the influence of chloroform describe, who see all the operation, but feel not the knife. This singular condition was not the result of any mental process. The shake annihilated fear, and allowed no sense of horror in looking round at the beast. This peculiar state is probably produced in all animals killed by the carnivora; and if so, is a merciful provision by our benevolent Creator for lessening the pain of death."[30]

We mentioned earlier that it is during the REM state that the foetal and neonatal brain is programmed with its instinctive templates; and that hypnosis is a trance state with many features similar to that of the REM state, often including paralysis. It is when an individual is in this state that new learning can best be programmed. All forms of hypnotic induction work by duplicating part of the REM state programming: for example triggering rapid eye movements can induce a hypnotic state, as can firing the orientation response through shock, or relaxation (which triggers off the pathways to body paralysis in the

REM state). Hypnotic inductions are artificial ways of consciously accessing the REM state.[31] Similarly, in the paralysis of the immobilisation state during the traumatic event, the amygdala is programmed to retain fear. People 'paralysed' by fear who go on to develop post-traumatic stress disorder were in a profound trance during the event, long enough for the horrific experience to be deeply etched into the amygdala, where the survival templates are stored. From then on, whenever the amygdala finds a match or part-match for that experience in the environment, it sets off the alarm reaction. Even just a fleeting associated thought or memory can set it off because the amygdala is unable to distinguish between a thought and sensory information.

We would therefore expect to find that the people most prone to PTSD are those who are also most highly hypnotizable. And this has been shown to be so.[32]

When people have been badly frightened, talking about what happened can be a way of integrating the event and converting it into a normal memory. In such cases, 'talking it out' can be helpful. But for those people at highest risk of developing PTSD, their imaginations and emotions will be engaged in the re-telling, which, like a post-hypnotic suggestion, cues them to relive the trauma and further embed it. This is why any therapeutic intervention that encourages this is likely to harm more than help.

Creating calm

Effective treatment, by contrast, will involve recoding the traumatic memory as a low arousal memory. Research carried out in the laboratory by Joseph LeDoux and his colleagues shows that when we recall a memory it has to be recoded. That is to say, new proteins have to be synthesized in the amygdala to reconsolidate the memory.[33] If we can find a way, therefore, to get the memory recalled in a low-arousal state, it will be recoded as a low-arousal memory and the traumatic reaction pattern will be dissipated. We need to be in a relaxed state for the feedback mechanism to work. Once the information is processed in this way it becomes a normal memory. It will always remain an unpleasant one, but part of normal functioning – not something shadowy that keeps the brain continually on the alert while scanning the environment for danger, and thereby maintaining the person in a state of high arousal. Furthermore, when the trauma template is released, attention capacity is freed up. People literally become more intelligent again when the data-processing capability of the brain is no longer devoted to scanning input from the environment for a match to a threat.

The history of 20th century military psychiatry is full of examples of doctors and psychiatrists struggling to find ways to help traumatized individuals (the 'shell-shocked' as they were first called) and discover why some individuals seemed more prone to 'crack' under extreme pressure than others.[34] Some had great success, particularly those using hypnosis. This was a common treatment during the First World War when it was widely observed that 'hysterics', as they were called, were highly hypnotizable and open to suggestion (shown by the ease with which they copied one another's symptoms).[35] The following is a description of such work by Dr. William Brown, a mathematician and philosopher who took up academic psychology and graduated in medicine. At the outbreak of war he was reader in psychology at London University and a well-known academic expert on hypnosis. He gained practical experience with trauma victims in shell-shock hospitals in England and then went to work at front-line hospitals in France because he believed early treatment was important. About 15 per cent of the cases he dealt with concerned what we would call severe trauma symptoms and PTSD, and for these he used hypnosis.

"The patient would be brought into hospital lying on a stretcher, perhaps dumb, trembling violently, perspiring profusely, his face showing an expression of great terror, his eyes either with a fixed stare or rolling from side to side. When one questioned him and got him to answer in writing he would tell one that he was unable to remember what had happened to him. In some way or other he had been knocked out and had come to find that he was paralysed and unable to speak.

"I interview him alone in my office and tell him in a tone of conviction that I shall restore his speech to him in a few seconds if he will do exactly what I say. I then urge him to lie down upon a couch, close his eyes and think of sleep. I urge him to give himself up to sleep, to let sleep come to him, as it assuredly will. I tell him that he is getting drowsy, his limbs are getting heavy with sleep, all his muscles are relaxed, he is breathing more and more slowly, more and more deeply. Above all, that his eyelids are getting heavy, as heavy as lead, that he feels disinclined to open them however hard he tries. At this stage, which generally supervenes within two or three minutes, he really cannot open his eyes. This is a stage of very light hypnosis quite sufficient for my purposes.

"I now tell him that the moment I put my hand on his forehead he will seem to be back again in the trenches, in the firing line, in the fighting, as the case may be, and will live again through the experiences he had when the shock occurred. This I say in a tone of absolute conviction, as if there is not the slightest shadow of possibility of my words not coming true. I then place my hand on his forehead. He immediately begins to twist and turn on the couch and shouts out in a terror-stricken voice. He talks as he talked at the time when he received the shock. He really does live again through the experiences of that awful time. Sometimes he speaks as if in dialogue, punctuated with intervals of silence corresponding to the remarks of his interlocutor, like a person speaking at the telephone. At other times he indulges in imprecations [cursing and pleading] and soliloquy. In some cases he is able to reply to my questions and give an account of his experiences. In others he cannot do so, but continues to writhe and talk as if he were still in the throes of the actual experience. In every case he speaks and acts as if he were again under the influence of the terrifying emotion. It is as if this emotion had been originally repressed, and the power of speech with it, and is now being worked off and worked out."[36] After such sessions, the patients would collapse into a profound sleep.

British psychiatrist Dr. William Sargant described working with traumatized soldiers during the Second World War. His treatment, like that of many doctors before him, was to encourage an emotional abreaction because it was often found that sufferers aroused to extremes of terror by hypnosis, drama or drugs would collapse and, on waking, be fully recovered. In 1944, he began using ether to induce abreaction with traumatized soldiers because "ether released a far greater degree of explosive excitement, which made their recital of events extremely poignant or dramatic". Furthermore, "the sudden states of collapse, after emotional outbursts induced by ether, were far more frequent than after those induced by hypnosis or barbiturates.

"Under ether, certain patients could easily be persuaded to relive experiences of terror, anger, or other excitement. Some of them might then collapse from emotional exhaustion and lie motionless for a minute or so, unmoved by ordinary stimuli; and, on coming round, would often burst into a flood of tears and report that their outstanding symptoms had suddenly disappeared. Or they would describe their minds as now freed of the terror aroused by certain obsessive pictures; they could still think of these, if they wished, but without the former hysterical anxiety. When simple excitement at the recital of past experiences did not reach the phase of ... collapse, little or no change or mental improvement might be observed in the patient; if, however, the abreactive treatment was repeated, and drugs were used to increase the amount of emotional stimulation until collapse supervened, sudden improvement could occur."[37]

Sargant also found that, if he couldn't get a description of the traumatic event from his patients, he could invent horrific stories, of soldiers trapped in burning tanks for example, tell them to his patients and this would be sufficient to induce the necessary fear arousal prior to the abreactive collapse. In other words, by pattern matching to *any* terrifying aspect of an event – loud noises, fire, feelings of helplessness, etc. – the amygdala's alarm response would fire. As we would expect, an exact match was not required. The importance of this part of Sargant's work is that it showed that even if the surface details of a pattern or a template were different, as long as it was a frightening situation associated with war, it would trigger a state of terror. If this crude pattern match could be deactivated, the work was done.

Having earlier said that the emotional arousal created during certain types of counselling can cause harm to those at risk of PTSD, we now appear to be saying that, sometimes, getting people really worked up and emotionally aroused appears to help them to recover. The two statements are not, in fact, at odds because it is *not* the emotional arousal that heals the person. The real active ingredient, as Sargant observed, is the collapse into a totally calm state after exposure to the emotionally arousing stimuli (even if the stimuli are in an individual's imagination). The memory can then be put into proper context and encoded correctly. The active ingredient for effective therapy is *calmness*.

The reason, for instance, that exposure therapy, as sometimes used by clinical psychologists, can work for severe phobic reactions is that it requires a person to stay in a recreated fear situation until the emotional arousal (usually a terror of dying as a result of exposure to the feared object or circumstance) subsides and calmness follows. Once the person is calm in the face of the threat, executive networks within the prefrontal cortex are free to evaluate what has occurred. Having clear evidence that the fear is unwarranted (death didn't ensue), the brain can successfully recode its understanding of the stimulus.

It is only if the person stays in the situation *until the emotional arousal goes down*, however, that exposure therapy works. The danger with exposure therapy is that, if the person cannot handle the highly unpleasant arousal and leaves the situation before they are calm, the trauma will have been programmed in even deeper. This is also the problem, as already said, with any type of therapeutic intervention in which victims are required, in effect, to relive a traumatizing event – especially, as in some forms of critical incident debriefing, delivered soon after it has happened. Emotional reliving of the trauma is sufficient to create an emotional charge but not generally to achieve collapse and calm.

Clearly, it is highly painful to re-experience trauma to the point of collapse. The value of the technique that we are now going to describe is that such terrifying emotional arousal can be bypassed completely because the desired calm state can be created at the outset. It is, therefore, a faster, safer process and more easily tailored to each individual than many other techniques.

How to cure post-traumatic stress disorder

With the understanding of *why* people can suffer long-term traumatization – the imprint of a life-threatening event is embedded in the amygdala, which continually scans the environment, pattern matching to anything similar to elements of that event – we can solve the problem of *how* to remove the imprint and 'convince' the amygdala that the imprinted template is no longer necessary for survival. The technique we are about to describe is an effective and relatively painless way of doing just that.

The technique was first developed by Richard Bandler, one of the co-founders of Neurolinguistic Programming (NLP), after observing and studying films of Milton H. Erickson detraumatizing people after using hypnosis to put them in a trance.[38] The method is variously known as the 'fast phobia cure' (because it used to be most often used by hypnotherapists for curing phobias); the 'VK dissociation technique' (the V stands for visual and the K for kinaesthetic) by those who practise NLP; and the 'rewind technique' (which is the term introduced into the literature on PTSD in 1991 by medical practitioner David Muss[39]). This last is the term we prefer to use.

The version of the technique which is recommended by Human Givens College has been refined by us to emphasize those elements that we now know are essential in making it effective and to drop aspects we consider unnecessary. Clinical experience and research has long shown that it works reliably with almost all cases of post-traumatic stress disorder and phobia.[40,41] But, until the publication of our monograph on the subject in 2001, there was no satisfactory published explanation for why it works.[42]

Many medical, psychiatric and other health professionals have attended training workshops run by the Human Givens College to learn the technique and have subsequently been able to help severely traumatized people very quickly.[43]

The procedure involves relaxing a person deeply and asking them to imagine themselves in a comfortable and pleasant place of their own choosing. As the aim of the procedure is to separate the memory from the associated anxiety feelings, it is essential that the anxiety template connected with the trauma is activated before going any further. The individual may already be in touch with their anxiety, merely as a result of talking about the trauma. If not, he or she needs to be asked to concentrate for a moment on feeling the feelings. As soon as these are physically experienced, the person can be guided back into full relaxation (because, once the template is activated, it will 'stay live' at a deep level until deactivated.) We have always stressed how essential this step is. However, since the time when we started our teaching, it has also been scientifically demonstrated that activating the emotion of the memory is essential before it can be recoded as a non-traumatizing memory.[44]

This, in brief, is the rewind process. Once the person is deeply relaxed again, they are asked to imagine that, in their special relaxed place, they have access to a portable television, computer, tablet or a phone, on which a film can be viewed. When we started teaching, we had people imagine putting a DVD of the 'trauma film' in the DVD slot on the television or computer and take charge of a remote control switch. Those familiar only with more advanced technologies may feel more at ease imagining using the buttons on their devices. Clients are asked to imagine watching themselves watching a rerun of the traumatic event (termed doubly dissociation because they are being doubly distanced from the event). This keeps arousal low. Then they are guided to imagine 'floating back' into their bodies at the end of the memory, at a point when they knew they had survived the event, and then to imagine going quickly *backwards* – 'rewinding' – through the event as if they are actually in it, to a point before anything untoward had happened that day. Next, they are guided to 'fast forward' through the memory, as if seeing it on the screen, working from the point before the event occurred to the point after it had ended, when they had survived it. Then, as before, they rewind through it. This is repeated a number of times until the memories produce no trace of emotional arousal. Whilst people are in the process of doing this, rapid eye movements can usually be observed, as the brain is being reprogrammed. On completion, in most cases the event ceases to be an emotionally traumatic memory, just a highly unpleasant one.

When a competent practitioner employs this technique, it enables the patterns of traumatic memory to be released. In their relaxed state of low arousal, the person's observing self can be accessed and can reframe what happened as no longer an active threat to them. The hippocampus, also released from the traumatic stress, plays an important part in this, by putting the event into its proper context – something past, not present.

The three crucial elements are:

1. the trauma template must be activated to arouse the associated emotion
2. the emotional arousal must be lowered and kept low, even if this step takes several attempts or repetitions
3. the trauma template is replayed through consciousness at low arousal level.

This is an artificial way of achieving what nature does with all learning (another process that is a human given). All of us have memories of events that were emotionally arousing or even life threatening at the time, which we can now look back on and tell an amusing anecdote about. Those memories have moved out of the amygdala's traumatic store, so to speak, into ordinary functioning memory.

After the procedure has been carried out and while the person is still in trance, they will be encouraged to imagine themselves living their lives normally, without the terror. This might mean that someone traumatized by a car crash will be invited to visualize themselves driving safely again, taking the sensible precautions of any good driver and being alert and aware – and relaxed. Or a rape victim may be encouraged to visualize being close to their present partner and enjoying being touched and caressed by them, instead of pattern matching to the previous abusive partner. There is now plenty of research evidence to show that positive mental rehearsal of this kind has powerful effects.[45,46,47,48,49]

Only properly trained practitioners should ever use the rewind technique, and particularly great care must be taken in managing its use with people who tend to react to stress by going into a shutdown state (dissociating).

Why EMDR and EFT may also work

Any mechanism that enables a traumatic memory to be turned into an ordinary memory is going to cure phobias and post-traumatic stress. This is also how EMDR (eye movement desensitization reprocessing) and EFT (emotional freedom technique) work and these, too, can claim good numbers of successes.

The EMDR technique was 'discovered' in 1987 by the late Francine Shapiro, then a mature clinical psychology student in California, who refined it into a highly specific treatment.[50] It requires people to think of a scene that represents the traumatic event, and a positive and negative belief associated with the trauma. They are asked to focus on the traumatic event while following with their eyes the therapist's moving finger (or another form of bilateral stimulation involving rhythmic left-to-right eye movements, such as watching a moving light), paying attention to and rating the intensity of the emotions and beliefs that come up. After a number of repetitions, if successful, the emotions and negative beliefs subside and the therapist concentrates on strengthening the positive belief (eg "I am safe now"). It is included in the recommendations made by the National Institute for Health and Care Excellence (NICE) for treatment for PTSD, along with trauma-focused cognitive behavioural therapy,[51] largely because these are the only two treatments for trauma that have been subjected to a number of randomized controlled trials, albeit with results that are not overly impressive.

Shapiro originally proposed that the directed eye movements mimicked those that occur during rapid eye movement (REM) sleep and seemed to think this was key to the technique's success, supposedly enhancing hemispheric communication which somehow aided the correct recoding of the traumatic memories.[52] However, researchers Raymond Gunter and Glen Bodner found that the sideways eye movements, while definitely affecting the brain, are not what explains the success of EMDR when it works, because vertical eye movements are just as effective as horizontal ones, and so too is performing a simple hearing task instead of eye movements while focusing on the memory.[53]

EFT (also known as tapping) sprang initially from the work of American clinical psychologist Roger J. Callahan, who developed what he called "thought field therapy".[54] This involved tapping sequences of meridian points on the body, whilst recalling a traumatic event and experiencing the extreme discomfort associated with it. He thought that one needed to tap different meridian points to release different sorts of trauma. Engineer Gary Craig, who trained with Callahan, developed a simpler version, which he called the emotional freedom technique.[55] This again involved tapping a sequence of meridian points while recalling a highly stressful event, experiencing and identifying the feelings that came up, verbalizing and accepting or reframing them. For instance, tapping while saying, "Even though I am feeling guilty because I couldn't protect my child from danger, I still deeply and completely love and accept myself". Although the order of tapping is meant to be significant (and in alignment with acupressure points), various revisions have been made over the years and some therapists claim to have had success with the method, even when tapping randomly. Joe Griffin has experimented with just moving the fingers of one hand in and out, towards the palm and away, repeatedly, while saying the relevant words, and also found this successful.

Psychiatrist Farouk Okhai suggested that tapping works, when successful, through dissociation.[56] Focusing part of the attention mechanism on the tapping disengaes attention sufficiently to allow a different perspective to be taken regarding the trauma. The same effect is achieved with the rewind technique, when people view the trauma at a distance, mentally running very quickly forwards and backwards through it as if on a screen. When re-experiencing the trauma in a dissociated way, the hippocampus is no longer inhibited by high stress levels and can record the context as a safe one – the individual is aware of dealing with a highly unpleasant memory while safe in the therapist's room. Ezra Hewing, who has also made the case that dissociation is key, argues that treatments that focus on the body, such as the above, are taking into account the physiological features of REM sleep.[57]

Joe Griffin suggested well over a decade ago that EMDR, EFT and the rewind technique may all have the same underlying mechanism – the firing of the orientation response, already discussed, which is the electrical signal in the brain that alerts us to any surprising or unexpected stimulus that interrupts normal routine.[58] (The Russian scientist Ivan Pavlov gave this the rather nicer name of 'curiosity reflex'.) Research with animals as well as humans shows that the stimulus par excellence for firing the orientation response is movement. It grabs our attention at once. Movement, of course, is significantly involved in all three methods (for real, in EMDR and EFT, and in imagination in the rewind).

The dreaming state is signalled, and accompanied, by the repeated firing of the orientation response, which facilitates the processing of the day's unexpressed emotional arousals metaphorically in dreams – the expectations that didn't pan out or that we didn't act on. Dreaming clears them out and we actually forget them (see page 45). Thus the orientation response triggers us to forget intense emotional memories. The firing of the orientation response in waking life also causes us to forget temporarily whatever we are focused on, so that we can attend to a new stimulus (which, in evolutionary terms, might be life threatening and require responding to first). Joe suggests that, in PTSD, the orientation response (once fired by the movements made in the three techniques under discussion) enables attention to be temporarily withdrawn from the high levels of emotional arousal associated with the trauma, freeing up the blocked communication between the amygdala, hippocampus and cortex. This allows the cortex and hippocampus, in a low state of arousal, to provide a new context for understanding the trauma as something that is in the past, and to recode the memory accordingly.

Sleep researcher and professor of psychiatry at Harvard Medical School Robert Stickgold also arrived at a suggested explanation for EMDR's mode of action that involves REM sleep, proposing that "the repetitive redirecting of attention in EMDR induces a neurobiological state, similar to that of REM sleep, which is optimally configured to support the cortical integration of traumatic memories into general semantic networks".[59]

Raymond Gunter and Glen Bodner have suggested that the underlying mechanism in EMDR is the over-taxing of working memory through the splitting of attention which occurs when focusing on a traumatic memory and simultaneously focusing on eye movements or hearing sounds or some other such activity.[60] Further support for the 'working memory hypothesis', as it is called, was demonstrated most recently in an analysis of studies of EMDR, published in 2022. The researchers concluded, "Our results suggest that recalling a traumatic memory while performing a secondary task would shift the individual's attention away from the retrieval process and result in a reduction in vividness and emotionality, also associated with the reduction of symptoms."[61]

Whatever the precise mode of action, clearly the dissociation/distraction element is key. So, if therapy techniques that make use of such effects can *all* successfully detraumatize, are they interchangeable? We think not. In both EMDR and EFT, the methodology allows much emotionally disturbing material to come to mind in a relatively piecemeal fashion, with different upsetting memories arising one after another, as a result – we would say – of pattern matching to different emotionally arousing events. Although skilled therapists can successfully deal with these and reduce the high level of arousal each time (thus fulfilling the three elements crucial for success described earlier), there is the danger that a client could be left in an emotionally aroused state, if the work is not completed by the end of a session, in which case the process can not only fail but also be harmful. In reference specifically to EFT, some clients find the idea of tapping themselves odd, and being tapped as invasive, and this has to be respected. We prefer the rewind technique because it is carried out entirely in a state of calm and it is easier to guide a client back to a state of low arousal, should they become upset, by re-directing their imagination to the relaxing place they will have identified at the start of the procedure.

We do accept, though, that the rewind technique doesn't work for everyone, particularly those who have difficulty relaxing or who have difficulty getting in touch with feelings associated with the original trauma. This might particularly be the case for people on the autistic spectrum, whose brains may not store, or have access to, specific emotional memories in the way that a neurotypical brain does. However, not being able to visualize (the condition known as aphantasia) does *not* get in the way of the rewind technique working, as everyone imagines in their own way and not necessarily through visualizing. If the rewind technique does not work or seems inappropriate in a certain circumstance, it is certainly not unreasonable to try another method that has been shown to have a degree of success, as long as the client agrees and feels comfortable with it.

Fast, non-voyeuristic and safe treatment for trauma

There are three other advantages to the rewind technique. First, when delivered by a fully-qualified and experienced practitioner, who has taken steps to ensure that there are no contraindications to treatment, the technique is safe. Second, it is non-voyeuristic. A person who has been raped, for example, can undergo this treatment without, if they prefer, having to tell the counsellor about any of the intimate details of the experience. The counsellor doesn't watch the 'film'; the client does. A vivacious young woman came to see Ivan because she was having panic attacks, flashbacks, intrusive thoughts and exhibiting many other distressing symptoms of PTSD. She had been attacked and raped twice, a month apart, by two different men. Both men were caught and convicted. But she was now living in a state of high anxiety and hypervigilance, particularly when in the presence of men who were attracted to her and despite the fact that she hoped for a normal loving relationship. She had changed jobs several times because of her distress. And because of her psychological state she had also seen a clinical psychologist and a counsellor – encounters she had found disturbing, painful and unhelpful. She hated talking about exactly what had happened. Without knowing any more detail about the rapes than you have just read, Ivan detraumatized her in one session by using the rewind technique. When she returned a week later she confirmed that the anxiety had gone. She reported that she had gone straight home after the session, emptied her filing cabinet of all the papers relating to the court case and thrown them in the dustbin "with no emotion at all". Previously, just opening the door of the room where the cabinet was situated used to make her burst into tears.

Third, the technique is fast. One client traumatized by being in a rail crash, who as a consequence wouldn't use any form of public transport, and didn't even want to leave home, could use buses and trains again immediately after undergoing this process. This was the experience of a survivor of a major rail crash, who was treated by a colleague of ours at the request of the Metropolitan Police.

When traumas have been endured over a long period of time, although it may be possible to resolve them in a single session, some people will still need longer-term counselling. This is determined by how much damage was sustained to the personality while the traumatic events were ongoing. Two contrasting case histories illustrate this important point.

A young girl in her middle teens was brought to see Joe. She was suffering from acute anxiety, due to having been sexually abused over a number of years by a paedophile lodging in the family home. When she grew older, the perpetrator moved on into another family home in search of younger prey. Only then did the girl tell her mother what had been going on. The mother told the police and the police arrested the paedophile, who confessed to his crimes and was given a long prison sentence.

The mother then sent her daughter for 'conventional' counselling where she was encouraged to recall, in great detail, all the episodes of abuse to "get her anger out". Whilst she was in counselling, her parents noticed that the young girl was becoming more and more anxious, so they arranged for her to change to another counsellor. But the next counsellor's approach was much the same as the first and, over the next six months, the girl became progressively more anxious and dysfunctional. At this point, she was brought by her mother to see Joe. When the girl arrived it was immediately obvious that she didn't actually want to be treated because she felt that this would somehow be disloyal to her current counsellor, who she thought was her "best friend in the whole world". (It is interesting, as research has shown, that a person can be damaged by the counselling process and yet feel that the counselling has been positively helpful.[62] The reason for this response is that certain important emotional needs, such as those for attention or friendship, may often be met within a counselling relationship, particularly if the counselling is long term, as all too often it is.)

Joe explained to this young girl that, for his treatment for trauma, she did not have to give him any details whatsoever about the abuse. She smiled at once, highly relieved, and visibly relaxed. All she was asked to do was give different code words for her worst memories of the abuse.

She explained that she had been abused in almost every room in the house and that, consequently, she was terrified to be in any room other than her parents' bedroom, where she currently slept because that was the only room in which no abuse had occurred. She gave a code word, such as 'hairbrush', for her worst memory of abuse in her own bedroom, another word for her worst memory in her brother's, and so on for each room in the house. Then, in a single session, they detraumatized key traumatic memories relevant to each room in the house. The young lady went home tired, calm and changed.

When she came back a week later, her mother said that the girl's life had been transformed. She was now sleeping in her own bedroom for the first time since prior to the start of all her counselling. Her parents had placed their house on the market, thinking their daughter could never be happy there again, but she had now told them that she was perfectly comfortable about staying there and that they could take the house off the market. The parents themselves were also getting along better with each other (all the trauma and stress had put them at loggerheads), so the entire family had benefited from that single first session of counselling.

This is an example of a severe degree of trauma and a strong anxiety reaction that could be dealt with quickly. It was possible because the young girl's life had been working well, outside of the trauma itself. She had a good relationship with her parents; she was doing well in school, and her life had otherwise developed normally, so the trauma was something self-contained, which could be resolved quickly.

One case in which longer-term work was necessary was that of a 35-year-old man, who came to see Joe. He was suffering from the effects of long-term childhood emotional abuse at the hands of his alcoholic and violent father, who subsequently abandoned the family. This patient suffered from depression and low self-esteem and had made two suicide attempts. The rewind was very effective at eliminating his symptoms of PTSD. He needed 10 sessions in total to help him rebuild his confidence, enhance his work and relationship skills and to seek more challenging employment – i.e. get his needs met. The rewind technique was an essential part of the therapy, but so was the restructuring and training that took place alongside and after it.

Curing phobias

The rewind technique is highly effective for curing phobias, which are more common that you might think. It is estimated, at the time of writing, that about 10 million people in the UK have a phobia[63] and that 12 per cent of females and 6 per cent of men in the United States have a specific phobia at any one time.[64] Our admittedly anecdotal experience leads us to think that even more people report some degree of phobic response to certain stimuli – the most common of which are spiders, snakes, worms, flying, fear of enclosed spaces, fear of open spaces, fear of crowds and fear of heights. Indeed, as might be expected from what we have explained, people can develop a phobic response to *any* situation that is similar to one in which they previously experienced acute anxiety. People can be phobic about windows, if they witnessed something dreadful through a window; about birds, if they were ever suddenly frightened by a bird; about grass, if they had a panic attack whilst standing on grass; about a particular food, if they once almost choked to death whilst eating it; and so on.

The physiology of phobias is much the same as that of post-traumatic stress disorder – a pattern (memory template) is imprinted in the amygdala and is trapped there. The template may be embedded as the result of a trauma – for example, one woman developed a cat phobia as a child after having kittens thrown at her by other children, who thought it hilarious fun when the kittens' claws came out and dug into her chest. But, in many cases, children simply learn their phobias from their parents, because children are programmed by nature to learn the fear reactions of their primary carers. If a fearful mother hides in panic under the kitchen table every time there is lightning and a clap of thunder in the air, it is not surprising if her children develop a phobia about thunderstorms.

However, when treating a phobia with the rewind technique, we don't need to know whether the phobia was caused by a traumatic learning experience or whether it was caused by modelling. This is because the client's only need is to learn how not to be phobic in the presence of that stimulus. All that is important is the deconditioning of the response pattern. It really doesn't matter how the pattern got there.

To decondition the response pattern, we need the client to provide perhaps three or four examples – their most vivid memories – of when they felt fearful in the presence of the phobic stimulus. So, in the case of the phobia of cats, for example, the client was asked to recall three occasions when she felt very scared – a high degree of panic – in the presence of cats. She chose a time when, as a child, she visited her grandmother, whose cat suddenly jumped up onto a garden fence in front of her; when a cat rubbed itself against her legs; and when a cat unexpectedly wandered into her office at work. On all these three occasions, she would have felt extremely and unreasonably scared, with a strong urge to get away from the cat as fast as possible. So Ivan simply deconditioned each of those memories after relaxing her and using the rewind treatment as described. This is sufficient to detraumatize the response pattern completely.

Ivan then encouraged her to imagine, whilst still in the relaxed state, travelling into the future and seeing herself co-existing with cats in a normal manner: stroking cats, feeding them, picking them up, etc.

Often, at first, a client doesn't know for sure whether or not their phobic response has gone, so they might still retain a moderate degree of apprehension about their next encounter with the phobic object. To attenuate this reaction we try, if possible, to procure an example of the feared stimulus while clients are still with us, so that they can test out their reactions for certain. So, with a cat, one would arrange for a cat to be brought into the room after the technique had been carried out. For an arachnophobe, a spider would, if possible, be put in a glass jar and slowly brought towards the client, with the client always able to say, "Stop". Once the client becomes more and more comfortable with the proximity of the spider, we would suggest that, within a few minutes, the client will be able to hold the jar containing the spider, look at it closely, then take the jar outside and set the spider free. We have done this successfully countless times.

Similarly, if someone has a phobia of lifts, we would take them to any nearby building that has a lift and go into it with them. After accompanying the client the first time, we would then let them go up and down on their own to prove to themselves that the phobia is deconditioned. It is, of course, only after the client has encountered the spider, or gone up and down in the lift, that they know that their old reaction pattern has really gone.

The client finds this process exhilarating, not only because they are freed from the inconvenience of their symptoms but also because, thereafter, their brain literally has more spare capacity, once it is not using valuable energy to maintain the phobic template.

Panic attacks and agoraphobia

Therapists working from the human givens perspective use the rewind technique not only for PTSD or phobias but also in other ways.

Fear of panic attacks is common among people who have experienced one – an understandable reaction, since a panic attack is literally a 'dreadful' experience. This fear can easily develop into agoraphobia, where the person is so anxious and afraid of having a panic attack that they won't even leave home.

A panic attack occurs when the fight-or-flight response, the body's emergency reaction which prepares it to deal with physical danger, is inappropriately set off. Since people are rarely in the presence of life-threatening events, and yet still suffer from panic attacks, it is clear that the attacks are mostly triggered by a progressive rising in an individual's background stress levels. There comes a point when one more stress – and it can be quite a small one – becomes the straw that breaks the camel's back. Panic is the result. The person doesn't understand why their heart is pounding, why they are sweating, why their breathing rate is accelerating – all natural reactions to stress – and so jumps to the conclusion that something is seriously wrong (typically that they are having a heart attack), which causes even more alarm and more adrenaline to be released, magnifying the symptoms further.

During this extreme alarm arousal, the amygdala, naturally enough, is scanning the environment to find out what the source of this alarm could be, noting all kinds of accompanying details and coding them for future reference. Not surprisingly then, for many people, the association is with the environment where the panic attack happened. If it happened at the cinema, in future the person will tend to avoid cinemas. But because the panic attack was not caused by the cinema but by raised stress levels, the next time the person feels over stressed, perhaps whilst out shopping, they may experience another panic attack and so start avoiding shops as well – and so on. Progressively, the noose of agoraphobia develops, forming a stranglehold that restricts the person's ability to continue with any normal life.

A combination of relaxation, behavioural and cognitive therapy is a useful treatment method for this condition: in other words, teaching the person to deal with whatever is raising their stress levels, calm themselves down and progressively re-engage with life. However, this process is rapidly accelerated if the memories of their most frightening panic attacks are detraumatized first. Then the brain won't be pattern matching from the previous panic attack to whatever situation they are going into next. This greatly helps the recovery process.

It is much easier to work with panic attack cases once one understands that the memory templates of past panic attacks have become locked into the brain. Then it is possible to go ahead and do what is necessary to turn them into ordinary memories.

It greatly speeds up recovery for people who have developed agoraphobia if the pattern matches to environments that disturb them – typically, supermarkets, high streets, schools, tube trains, or any potentially crowded public situation – are defused in this way. They then need to be guided to rehearse imaginatively, in their relaxed REM trance state, entering those environments in a calm manner and going about their business normally. This rehearsal, by giving them a new mental template to match to, helps them more readily re-enter these situations in reality. The usual practice is to establish and agree with the client a hierarchical scale of feared situations and work through them, from least to most feared.

Obsessive compulsive disorder (OCD)

We discussed OCD in an earlier chapter. Obsessions are thoughts, images or impulses that cause marked degrees of anxiety or distress. Compulsions are repetitively carried out behaviours (such as hand washing) or thoughts (such as silently repeating certain phrases or counting things) that follow rigid rules and are performed in an attempt to reduce the distress brought on by the obsessions or as a way of making reparation for intrusive scary thoughts.

But OCD is a very unforgiving master, because the more rituals carried out to appease it, the more the frightening thoughts recur. As with agoraphobia, the noose gets pulled tighter and tighter and the person's area of effective functioning shrinks ever smaller. Every time sufferers carry out a ritual, they reinforce the OCD: just as every time an agoraphobic avoids going out they reinforce their particular fear pattern.

Two to three people in every hundred suffer from OCD.[65] We find that OCD responds well to the rewind technique during which the fear of not performing the obsessive behaviour is detraumatized (thus making it less frightening), followed by getting the sufferer to rehearse in a dissociated state what it will be like to live without performing the abnormal behaviour or having the compulsive thoughts. As with panic attacks, the triggering factor in OCD seems to be raised stress levels, which may be due to anything from physical illness to a fright, lack of sleep, business worries, relationship breakdown or exam worries. Some people have a propensity to develop this disorder when their stress levels are high.

Clients are clearly terrified of cutting out their rituals, whether they are washing their hands 50 times in case their son will be killed in an accident in school, or whether they are stacking all their clothes up in a particular order in their bedroom because they think that otherwise they will get a terrible disease. The strong emotion aroused locks them into a trance state. (OCD sufferers usually have no sense of time whilst carrying out their rituals, and often cannot remember whether they have carried out the ritual properly, resulting in the perceived need to perform it over and over. As we have seen, time distortion and amnesia are both hypnotic phenomena.)

In their trance the intrusive thought, like a powerful posthypnotic suggestion, instructs the individual that they must perform the behaviour to relieve the fear. This is clearly not rational thinking but just as when, in the REM state, we dream and believe in the reality of the dream, so do the entranced OCD sufferers believe in the reality of the OCD ritual and its consequences. They have no alternative, just as we cannot easily avoid dreaming. The thought of stopping the rituals genuinely frightens them.

One of the key steps in working with OCD – as in effective therapy for any symptomatology – is for the therapist to help the client to separate their core identity from their problem. In this process, by whatever means, the therapist or counsellor helps the sufferer to take a step back into their observing self and recognize that the OCD is not part of who they are (their core sense of self). It is outside them, separate but impinging in unwelcome ways.

Once the person can see themselves as separate from OCD they can recognize and separate out an OCD thought from a normal thought. This is vital: developing the ability to recognize when the OCD is in charge as distinct from when their brain is functioning normally.

Essentially, we want to keep the person in their observing self so that they can observe the OCD and keep their distance from it. Whenever they recognize the OCD thoughts intruding, they must have some form of distraction instantly available to them to pull their attention away from the OCD thought and calm them down.

A useful tactic is to replace the problematic behavioural rituals with less problematic ones and for people to have these harmless rituals prepared in advance so that they can switch into them when they need to distract themselves from the OCD thoughts. The harmless rituals can be anything such as aerobic activity, listening to music, calling a friend on the phone, reading a book of poetry or watching a film – anything that they can immediately engage with as a means of distraction so as to avoid carrying out the rituals that the OCD is commanding them to perform.

As the client learns to avoid, or minimize, carrying out the rituals, a feedback mechanism is set up from the environment, saying, in effect, to the part of the brain affected by the OCD, "Look, these thoughts aren't real ... those imagined bad consequences aren't happening". Once enough of this feedback is received, the OCD thoughts are switched off.

This is where, as mentioned above, the rewind technique can be so useful with OCD. While the client is in a calm, relaxed state, we detraumatize the experience of being terrified by the thoughts, then get them to visualize experiencing the frightening thought, but not carrying out the rituals. For instance, they experience, in a dissociated state, the OCD thought instructing them to wash their hands repeatedly, otherwise their son will die, and then watch themselves not washing their hands and, instead, doing something entirely different, such as knitting or doing a crossword, with no adverse consequences. Once they have that novel idea in their mind, associated with a relaxed state, they have created a new template that says, in effect, "My son will not die if I don't carry out the rituals – so I can stop doing them".

The following case history illustrates how OCD can be reduced in this way. A man worked in a garage in charge of the spare parts division. His father, at the age of 40, had died of a heart attack. When he himself reached that age he had a panic attack and made the common assumption that it was a heart attack. He went along to his GP who checked him out and told him his heart was absolutely fine. But the raised stress levels triggered off OCD in him. He started to get scary thoughts and developed rituals to appease the thoughts.

Two primary rituals caused him maximum distress. Every day, on his way home from work at the garage, the thought would occur to him that he had knocked somebody down, even though he had no awareness of doing so. He imagined someone lying unconscious on the road, bleeding to death as a result of his careless driving. This thought would become so powerful that, by the time he got home, he was in acute anxiety and would have to drive slowly back the whole 30 miles to the garage to check that there had been no accident. This ritual took up a large portion of each evening. The second ritual that distressed him was caused by the thought, which would occur to him as customers were leaving the garage after work had been done on their cars, that he might have supplied the wrong parts to be fitted. He would visualize the car catching fire and the occupants burning to death. He would experience extreme anxiety, rush out to retrieve the car from the customer and check the new part against the stock just to make sure it was the right one. This, of course, distressed customers and the management of the garage alike.

One useful aspect of working with people with OCD is that, if we give them something to do, they can become quite obsessive about carrying out our instructions, so we can use this compulsive tendency productively to facilitate the treatment. The first intervention with this man was to use guided imagery to help him achieve a deep state of relaxation. Joe got him to imagine himself somewhere really peaceful and safe. This part of the session was recorded on tape and included the message loud and clear: "Isn't it nice to know that your doctor has thoroughly checked you over and you have a sound, strong, healthy heart?" because that was the worry that had triggered off the OCD in the first place. During that first session Joe also gave the client the instruction that each evening, as soon as he got home, he was to go straight to his bedroom and sit down and listen to this relaxation tape, rather than drive back to the garage. He reinforced this by encouraging the man to visualize himself coming home from work and listening to his tape, with no adverse consequences.

The man did this for a couple of weeks and, as he found that there were no unidentified bodies being discovered on the road between his house and the garage, no hit-and-run stories appearing in the local newspapers, the feedback message from reality got into his brain and the obsessive thought faded away. He was then ready to deal with his next great fear, which centred around handing out spare car parts at the garage.

He was excellent at his job. He knew by heart every spare part the garage had in stock, but this problem of fearing he had supplied the wrong part was overwhelming him. One important counselling principle is that, if a problem is too big to solve in one go, the best thing to do is break it down into smaller chunks and deal with each one.

This is the approach that Joe took. When the thought occurred to the man that the wrong part had been fitted to a car, instead of rushing out and retrieving it to make sure it was the right part, he agreed to alter the ritual (not to check at all would have left him so anxious that he would have been dysfunctional for the rest of the day). In future, on handing out a spare part, he would write the number of the part in a notebook. Then, after the customer had left with the car, when he felt the anxiety about having given out the wrong part rising, he would go to the stockroom and check the number in his notebook against the stock to make sure the right part had been used. Doing this no longer disrupted the smooth running of the garage and started to moderate his anxiety, making it more tolerable. Again, after a few weeks, the obsessive thought just died away.

Joe saw him for about six sessions, using guided visualization on each occasion and showing him how to focus his attention outwards and think more positively and constructively, till the OCD was completely eliminated. Well, in truth, there was still one ritual left. He was still listening to the tape compulsively! So, the final step in the therapeutic procedure was to wean him off doing that.

In this case history we can see at work several principles of effective therapy which always work from the human givens: relaxation, enabling the person to go into their observing self; separation of the observing self from the problem; the principle of dissociation in order to facilitate a more realistic template being introduced to the amygdala and to accelerate the development of desired behaviour patterns; the use of imagination; drawing on clients' own resources; breaking down problems so that they can be solved, etc.

Social phobia, fear of job interviews and exams can be helped in much the same way.

The chair's problem

Erickson, who inspired the development of so many of the solution-focused approaches to therapy, used a method to cure phobias that was even shorter than the one which we have outlined. He found that it worked with good hypnotic subjects, although he seems not to have recognized that the phobic or traumatized state is always associated with good hypnotic subjects – such disorders are their vulnerability.

Once he had a phobic person sitting in a deeply relaxed trance in a comfortable chair he would ask them to recall what it felt like to be very frightened of whatever their phobia concerned. At the point when they were aroused to a high state of anxiety and very uncomfortable with that anxious feeling, he would ask them if they would like to lose their anxiety. When they nodded their heads, he would say something like, "In a moment ... I'm going to ask you to stand up and move to this chair over here ... and to leave your fear behind you in that chair". Because the subject was in a deeply hypnotic state – the

REM state, the programming part of the mind – the phobic's brain was receptive enough to take on board that instruction. They would move chairs and leave their phobia in the first chair.[66]

We now know that what Erickson was doing was taking the fear template in the amygdala, the pattern of feeling fear of flying or of cats or of thunder or whatever, and confining its reaction pattern to one stimulus only, namely the chair with which the brain now associated it. Indeed, when subjects came out of trance, Erickson would later ask them to sit down on the first chair again and their strong feeling of fear would instantly return because their amygdala would pattern match to the original template now associated with that specific chair in his office.

Erickson's rapid technique is as effective a cure as going through the rewind process we've described here. The difficulty, though, is that one does need great confidence in using hypnotic skills and a deeply hypnotic state in the client in order to effect the restriction of a phobic response pattern to a specific piece of furniture – preferably one that the person will never encounter again. However, his technique neatly illustrates the mechanics by which post-traumatic stress disorder and phobias are developed – a pattern is seeking its counterpart in the environment, seeking something to match up to.

For the sufferer from PTSD, phobias, panic or OCD, it doesn't matter how the result is achieved. Whether we remove this pattern from the amygdala with the rewind technique and get it processed as an ordinary memory, or change it by restricting the application of the pattern to an innocuous stimulus, as Erickson showed could be done, either way the distressing symptom is reliably disabled and dealt with, and the misery gone.

* * *

Effective counsellors and psychotherapists (there is no meaningful difference between the two titles – both need to be equally competent in relieving patients of psychological/behavioural distress as quickly as possible) require a range of skills that let them operate creatively, in a comprehensive, holistic way, treating each patient as an individual who has unique beliefs, resources and abilities. As we hope we have shown, human givens therapy is a package of skills that brings together all the knowledge and techniques from many different disciplines in the service of relieving distress. We believe that training counsellors and psychotherapists in this approach is the most practical and cost-effective way forward in this hitherto confusing field, for the treatment of all forms of emotional disorder.

However, the implications of our findings go much further than psychotherapy. Many professionals, as varied as heads of schools and other organizations, lawyers, teachers, social workers and business managers, have realized that the ideas set out in this book have enormous significance for their work.[67] And this has further important ramifications. The way we think about and plan for change in society, as we try to adapt, will benefit hugely if we all share a common perception about intrinsic human needs and work towards ensuring that we, our families families and the groups we belong to, are getting them met. Then we can concentrate on learning how to leave this place more easily, not grieving, not craving – but free.

References and notes

PART I – NEW DISCOVERIES ABOUT HUMAN NATURE

Chapter 1 – Seeking completion

1. Ayensu, E. S., Heywood, V. H., Lucas, G. L. and Defilipps, R. A. (1984) *Our Green and Living World*. Cambridge University Press.
2. Llinás, R. R. (2001) *I of the Vortex: from neurons to self*. The MIT Press.
3. Ratey, J. (2001) *A User's Guide to the Brain*. Pantheon Books.
4. Lewis-Williams, D. (2002) *The Mind in the Cave*. Thames & Hudson.
5. Shah, I. (1964) *The Sufis*. Doubleday & Co.
6. Shah, I. (1998) *Knowing How to Know*. The Octagon Press.
7. Deikman, A. J. (1993) *The Wrong Way Home*. Beacon Press.
8. Deikman, A.J. (2004) No Them, just Us. *Human Givens Journal*, 10, 4, 34–7.
9. Brayfield, C. (2001) What it feels like to be a child with no friends. *Sunday Times*, 8 July.
10. The Mental Health Foundation. (2001) I want to be your friend but I don't know how.
11. https://www.theguardian.com/society/2022/apr/04/pandemic-has-delayed-social-skills-of-young-children-says-ofsted-chief
12. Csikszentmihalyi, M. (1992) *Flow: the psychology of happiness*. Harper & Row.
13. Mehegan, L., Rainville, C. and Skufca, L. (2017) *AARP Cognitive Activity and Brain Health Survey*. Washington, DC. https://doi.org/10.26419/res.00044.001
14. Auty, G. (2000) *Postmodernism's Assault on Western Culture*. Quadrant.
15. Wengrow, A. and Graeber, S. (2022) *The Dawn of Everything: a new history of humanity*. Penguin.
16. Longrich, N. R. (2020) The Conversation. When did we become fully human? https://theconversation.com/when-did-we-become-fully-human-what-fossils-and-dna-tell-us-about-the-evolution-of-modern-intelligence-143717; Mithen, S. (1996) *The Prehistory of the Mind*. Thames & Hudson.
17. We would like to thank Peter Silvien for first suggesting to us that the caves were, in effect, schools.
18. Mind. (2020) Mental health facts and statistics. https://www.mind.org.uk/information-support/types-of-mental-health-problems/statistics-and-facts-about-mental-health/how-common-are-mental-health-problems/#References
19. Children's Commissioner (2021) The state of children's mental health services 2019/20. https://www.childrenscommissioner.gov.uk/report/mental-health-services-2019-20/
20. Cole, L. and Kingsley, M. (2022) *The Children's Enquiry: how the state and society failed the young during the Covid-19 pandemic*. Pinter & Martin.
21. World Health Organization (2022) *World Mental Health Report: transforming mental health for all*. WHO, Geneva.

Chapter 2 – Where does human nature come from?

1. Aserinsky, E. and Kleitman, N. (1953) Regularly occurring periods of eye mobility and concomitant phenomena during sleep. *Science*, 118, 273–274.
2. Jouvet, M. and Michel, F. (1959) Corrélations électromyographique du sommeil chez le chat décortiqué et mésencéphalique chronique. *Comptes Rendus de la Société de Biologie*, 154, 422–425.
3. Jouvet, M. (1978) Does a genetic programming of the brain occur during paradoxical sleep? In P. A. Buser and A. Rougel-Buser (Eds.), *Cerebral Correlates of Conscious Experience*. Elsevier, Amsterdam.
4. Karasov, W. H. and Diamond, J. (1985) Digestive adaptations for fuelling the cost of endothermy. *Science*, 228, 202–204.
5. Franklin T. B., Silva B. A. et al (2017) Prefrontal cortical control of a brainstem social behavior circuit. *Nature Neuroscience*, 2017 doi: 10.1038/nn.4470
6. Roffwarg, H. P., Muzio, J. and Dement, W. (1966) The ontogenetic development of the human sleep-dream cycle. *Science*, 152, 604–618.
7. Jouvet (1978), op. cit.
8. Jouvet, M. (1977) *Neuropharmacology of the sleep waking cycle*. In S. D. Iversen, L. L. Iversen and S. H. Snyder (Eds.), *Handbook of Psychopharmacology*, 8, 233–293. Plenum Publishing.
9. Roffwarg, Muzio and Dement, op. cit.
10. Hunt, T. H. (1989) *The Multiplicity of Dreams, Memory, Imagination and Consciousness*, 28–30. Yale University Press.
11. Hobson, J. A. (1989) *Sleep*. Scientific American Library, New York.
12. Reid, V. M., Dunn, K. et al. (2017) The human fetus preferentially engages with face-like visual stimuli. *Current Biology*, 27, 12, 1825–28.
13. Tyrrell, I. (1999) Talking to the man who listens to horses: an interview with Monty Roberts. *The Therapist*, 6, 1, 24–28.
14. Walker, S. (1983) *Animal Thought*. Routledge & Kegan Paul.
15. Tattersall, I. (1998) *Becoming Human*. Oxford University Press.
16. Gopnik, A., Meltzoff, A. and Kuhl, P. (1999) *How Babies Think*. Weidenfeld & Nicolson.
17. Lorenz, K. L. (1966) *On Aggression*. Methuen.
18. Manacéïne, M. de (1897) *Sleep*. Walter Scott.
19. Rechtschaffen, A. et al. (1983) Prolonged sleep deprivation in rats. *Science*, 221, 182–184.
20. Rechtschaffen, A. and Bergmann, B. M. (1995) Sleep deprivation in rats by the disk-over-water method. *Behavioural Brain Research*, 69, 55–63.
21. Hobson, J. A. (1994) *The Chemistry of Conscious States: how the brain changes its mind*. Little, Brown & Company, Canada.

Chapter 3 – The dreaming brain

1. De Becker, R. (1968) *The Understanding of Dreams and their Influence on the History of Man*. Hawthorne, New York.
2. Freud, S. (1953) *The Interpretation of Dreams*. In J. Strachey (Ed.), *The Complete Psychological Works of Sigmund Freud*. Hogarth Press.
3. Jung, C. (1965) *Memories, Dreams, Reflections*. Vintage.
4. Hall, C. S. (1953) A cognitive theory of dreams. *Journal of General Psychology*, 49, 277–282.
5. Aserinsky, E. and Kleitman, N. (1953) Regularly occurring periods of eye mobility and concomitant phenomena during sleep. *Science*, 18, 273–274.
6. Dement, W. and Kleitman, N. (1957) Cyclic variations in EEG during sleep and their relation to eye movements, body motility and dreaming. *Electroencephalography and Clinical Neurophysiology*, 9, 673–690.
7. Foulkes, D. (1985) *Dreaming: a cognitive psychological analysis*. Lawrence Erlbaum Associates.
8. Moruzzi, G. (1963) Active processes in the brainstem during sleep. *Harvey Lectures Series*, 58, 233–297.
9. Hartmann, E. (1967) *The Biology of Dreaming*. C. C. Thomas.
10. Jouvet, M. (1967) *Mechanisms of the states of sleep. A neuro-pharmacological approach*. Presented at the 45th annual meeting of, and published by, the Association for Research in Nervous and Mental Disease, 45, 86–126. New York.
11. Dement, W. (1968) The biological role of REM sleep. In A. Kales (Ed.) (1969), *Sleep: physiology and pathology*. Lippincott.
12. Foulkes, op. cit.
13. Dement, W. (1960) The effect of dream deprivation. *Science*, 131, 1705–1707.
14. Ferguson, J. and Dement, W. (1968) Changes in the intensity of REM sleep with deprivation. *Psychophysiology*, 4, 380–381.
15. Morrison, A. R. (1983) A window on the sleeping brain. *Scientific American*, 248, 86–94.
16. Morrison, A. R. and Reiner, P. (1985) *A Dissection of Paradoxical Sleep*. D. J. McGinty.
17. Griffin, J. and Tyrrell, I. (2014) *Why We Dream: the definitive answer*. HG Publishing, East Sussex.
18. Coran, S. (1996) *Sleep Thieves*. Free Press.
19. Siegel, J. M. et al. (1999) Sleep in the platypus. *Neuroscience*, 91, 1, 391–400.
20. Rowling, J. K. (2000) *Harry Potter and the Goblet of Fire*. Bloomsbury.
21. Schredl, M. (2010) Characteristics and contents of dreams. *International Review of Neurobiology*. Academic Press, 92, 135–154.
22. Blagrove, M. and Pace-Schott, E. F. (2010) Trait and neurobiological correlates of individual differences in dream recall and dream content. *International Review of Neurobiology*, 92, 155–180.

23. Ruby, P. M. (2011) Experimental research on dreaming: state of the art and neuropsychoanalytic perspectives. *Frontiers of Psychology*, 2, article 286.
24. Vallat, R., Chatard, B., Blagrove, M. and Ruby, P. M. (2017) Characteristics of the memory sources of dreams: a new version of the content-matching paradigm to take mundane and remote memories into account. *PLoS One*, 12, 10, e0185262
25. Hutchison, I. C., Pezzoli, S. et al. (2021) Targeted memory reaction in REM but not SWS selectively reduces arousal responses. *Communications Biology*, doi: 10.1038/s42003-021-01854-3
26. Eichenlaub, J. B., van Rijn, E. et al. (2018) Incorporation of recent waking-life experiences in dreams correlates with frontal theta activity in REM sleep. *Social Cognitive and Affective Neuroscience*, 13, 6, 637–47.
27. Walker, M. P. and van der Helm, E. (2009). Overnight therapy? The role of sleep in emotional brain processing. *Psychological Bulletin*, 135, 5, 731–48.
28. van der Helm, E. et al. (2011) REM sleep depotentiates amygdala activity to previous emotional experiences. *Current Biology*, 21, 2029–32.
29. Zohar, D., Tzischinsky, O., Epstein, R. and Lavie, P. (2005) The effects of sleep loss on medical residents' emotional reactions to work events: a cognitive-energy model. *Sleep*, 28, 47–54.
30. Yoo, S. S., Gujar, N., Hu, P., Jolesz, F. A. and Walker, M. P. (2007) The human emotional brain without sleep – a prefrontal amygdala disconnect. *Current Biology*, 17, R877–8.
31. McGilchrist, I. (2021) *The Matter with Things: our brains, our delusions, and the unmaking of the world.* Perspectiva Press; Ornstein, R. (1997) *The Right Mind: making sense of the hemispheres.* Harcourt Brace & Co.
32. Joseph, R. (1996) *Neuropsychiatry, Neuropsychology, and Clinical Neuroscience.* Williams & Wilkins.
33. Keeler, J. F., Pretsell, D. O. and Robbins, T. W. (2014) Functional implications of dopamine D1 vs D2 receptors: a 'prepare and select' model of the striatal direct vs. indirect pathways. *Neuroscience*, 282, 156–75.
34. Busáki, G. (1995) The hippocampo–neurocortical dialogue. *Cerebral Cortex*, 6, 81–92; Rasch, B. and Born, J. (2013) About sleep's role in memory. *Physiological Reviews*, 93, 2, 681–766.
35. Izawa, S., Chowdhury, S. et al. (2019) REM sleep-active MCH neurons are involved in forgetting hippocampus-dependent memories. *Science*, 365, 6459, pp 1308–13.
36. See for instance Friston, K. (2010) The free-energy principle: a unified brain theory? *Nature Reviews Neuroscience*, 11, 127–38; Clark, A. (2013) Whatever next? Predictive brains, situated agents and the future of cognitive science. *Behavioral and Brain Sciences*, 36, 3, 181–204; van den Heuvel, S., Evers, K. et al (2013) An anatomical substrate for integration among functional networks in human cortex. *Journal of Neuroscience*, 31, 44, 15775–86.
37. Feldman Barrett, L. (2017) *How Emotions Are Made: the secret life of the brain.* Macmillan.

38. Heilbron, M., Armeni, K. et al. (2022) A hierarchy of linguistic predictions during natural language comprehension. *Proceedings of the National Academy of Sciences*, 119, 32, doi: 10.1073/pnas.2201968119
39. Winson, J. (2002) The meaning of dreams. *Scientific American*, 12, 1, 54–61.
40. Ellman, S., Antrobus, J., Weinstein, L., Lewin, I. and Singer, J. (1991) *The Mind in Sleep*. John Wiley and Sons.
41. Moffit, A., Krammer, M., and Hoffmann, R. (Eds.) (1993) *The Function of Dreaming*. Albany State University of New York.
42. Ellman and Antrobus, op. cit.
43. Jouvet, M. (2001) The Paradox of Sleep. MIT Press.
44. Ibid.
45. Ibid.
46. Silveira, R. (1994) Children, television, fear and violence. *The Therapist*, 2, 1, 6–7.
47. Pendergrast, M. (1997) *Victims of Memory*. HarperCollins.

Chapter 4 – The mind entranced: sane and insane

1. Landry, M., Lifschitz, M. and Raz, A. (2017) Brain correlates of hypnosis: a systematic review and meta-analytic exploration. *Neuroscience & Biobehavioral Reviews*, 81, Part A, 75–98.
2. Wolf, T. G., Faerber, K. A. et al. (2022) Functional changes in brain activity using hypnosis: a systematic review. *Brain Sciences*, 12, 1, 108, doi: 10.3390/brainsci12010108
3. Rainville, P., Duncan, G. H., Price, D. D., Carrier, B. and Bushnell, M. C. (1997) Pain affect encoded in human anterior cingulate but not somatosensory cortex. *Science*, 277, 968–971.
4. Erickson, M. H. and Rossi, E. L. (1976) *Hypnotic Realities*, Irvington Publishers.
5. We are not referring here to animal hypnosis, which is well documented elsewhere, but to experiments that show that, when animals get overexcited and are in a life-threatening situation, they cannot see the obvious way out of their predicament in the same way that they can when they are not emotionally aroused. Spitz, R. (1965) *The First Year of Life*. International Universities Press.
6. Goleman, D. (1996) *Emotional Intelligence: why it can matter more than IQ*. Bloomsbury Publishing, London.
7. Jiang, H., White, M. P., Greicius, M. D., Waelde, L. C., and Spiegel, D. (2017) Brain activity and functional connectivity associated with hypnosis. *Cerebral Cortex*, 217, 8, 4083–93.
8. Griffin, J. and Tyrrell, I. (2014) *Why we dream: the definitive answer*. HG Publishing, East Sussex.
9. Hobson, J. A. (1989) *Sleep*. Scientific American Library, a division of HPHLP, New York.
10. Jouvet, M. (1978) Does a genetic programming of the brain occur during paradoxical sleep? In P.A. Buser and A. Rougel-Buser (Eds.), *Cerebral Correlates of Conscious Experience*. Elsevier, Amsterdam.

11. Yapko, M. (1990) *Trancework: an introduction to the practice of clinical hypnosis.* Brunner/Mazel.
12. Morrison, A. R. (1983) A window on the sleeping brain. *Scientific American,* 248, 86–94.
13. Rossi, E. L. (1993) *The Psychobiology of Mind-Body Healing.* W. W. Norton.
14. Rossi, E. L. and Nimmons, D. (1991) *The 20-Minute Break.* J. P. Tarcher Inc., Los Angeles.
15. Ibid.
16. Rossi, E. L. (ed) (1989). *Collected Papers of Milton H. Erickson.* Irvington Publishers, New York.
17. Waterfield, R. (2004) *Hidden Depths: the story of hypnosis.* Macmillan.
18. Hawkins, P. and Heap, M. (Eds.) (1998) *Hypnosis in Europe.* Whurr.
19. Chester, R. J. (1982) *Hypnotism in the East and West.* Octagon, London.
20. Morrison, op. cit.
21. Hobson, J. A. (1994) *The Chemistry of Conscious States.* Little Brown & Co, Canada.
22. Ibid.
23. Yapko, M. (1992) *Hypnosis and the Treatment of Depression.* Brunner/Mazel, New York.
24. McGill, O. (1996) *The New Encyclopedia of Stage Hypnotism.* Anglo American Book Company.
25. Griffin and Tyrrell, op. cit.
26. See, for instance, Zak, P. J. (2012) *The Moral Molecule: how trust works.* Penguin, New York.
27. Chester, op. cit.
28. Bhugra, D. (2005) The global prevalence of schizophrenia. *PLOS Medicine,* doi: 10.1371/journal.pmed.0020151
29. Padma, T. V. (2014) Developing countries: the outcomes paradox. *Nature,* 508, S14–S15.
30. Cohen, A., Patel, V., Thara, R. and Gureje, O. (2008) Questioning an axiom: better prognosis for schizophrenia in the developing world. *Schizophrenia Bulletin,* 34, 2, 229–44.
31. Read, J. (2023) Antidepressants and suicide: 7,829 inquests in England and Wales, 2003–2020. *Ethical Human Psychology and Psychiatry,* 25, 1, 8–28.
32. Moncrieff, J. (2013) *The Bitterest Pills: the troubling story of antipsychotic drugs.* Palgrave Macmillan.
33. Moncrieff, J. (2020) Misleading information about antipsychotics. *Psychological Medicine,* 50, 16, 2810–11.
34. Waddington, J. (1998) Mortality in schizophrenia. *British Journal of Psychiatry,* 173, 325–329.
35. Appleby, L. (2000) Sudden unexplained death in psychiatric in-patients. *British Journal of Psychiatry,* 176, 405–406.

36. Morrison, A. P., Hutton, H., Shiers, D. and Turkington, D. (2012) Antipsychotics: is it time to introduce patient choice? *British Journal of Psychiatry*, 201, 83–84.
37. Whitaker, R. (2002) *Mad in America: bad science, bad medicine, and the enduring mistreatment of the mentally ill.* Perseus Publishing.
38. Tyrrell, I. (2001) *The land of illusion: a filmed interview with a psychotic patient.* MindFields College.
39. Griffin, J. and Tyrrell, I. (2001) Trapped in the land of illusion. *Human Givens*, 8, 3, 2–3.
40. Abbot, E. (2001) Letter. *Human Givens*, 8, 4, 47–48.
41. Hewing, E. (2020) Psychosis: metaphorically speaking. *Human Givens*, 27, 1, 12–21.
42. Smith, D. M. (2000) *Moral Geographies.* Edinburgh University Press.
43. Shah, I. (1998) *Knowing How to Know.* Octagon Press.
44. Deikman, A. J. (1982). *The Observing Self.* Beacon Press.
45. Ibid. 95.

PART II – APPRECIATING OUR BIOLOGICAL INHERITANCE

Chapter 5 – The human givens

1. See, for instance, Maslow, A. H. (1943) A theory of human motivation. *Psychological Review*, 50, 370-96; Marmot, M. (1967-date) Whitehall Studies; Deci, E. L. and Ryan, R. M. (1985) *Intrinsic Motivation and Self-determination in Human Behaviour.* Plenum, New York.
2. Reis, H. T., Sheldon, K.M., Ryan, R. M., Gable, S. L. and Roscoe, J. (2000) Daily well-being: the role of autonomy, competence, and relatedness. *Personality and Social Psychology Bulletin*, 26, 419–443. Reis et al "have found that, across many eastern and western cultures, these needs are essential for psychological health in each country we have studied." The needs for autonomy, competence and relatedness form the basis for the internationally validated self-determination theory (SDT) proposed by Edward Deci and Richard Ryan (see below). The needs identified in the human givens approach have been validated against the SDT model. (See Culham, B. (2009) The Emotional Needs Scale. *Human Givens*, 16, 1, 36–40.)
3. Deci, E. L. and Ryan, R. M. (1985). *Intrinsic Motivation and Self-determination in Human Behaviour.* Plenum, New York. "[Knowing about needs allows] informed observers to understand whether people will flourish or wither. In other words, if observers know that people are experiencing satisfaction of the basic psychological needs, the observers can predict reliably that the individuals will likely experience healthy development and well-being, whereas if the people are experiencing thwarting of the needs the observers have a reliable predictor of some pathology or maladaptive functioning."
4. Morrice, A. (2022) The Mind-Body Connection: movement, emotion and calm; the Mind–Body Connection: food, mood and sleep. Prepared for Human Givens College.

5. See, for instance, Tsaroucha, A., Kingston, P., Corp, N., Stewart, T. and Walton, I. (2012) The Emotional Needs Audit (ENA): a report on its reliability and validity. *Mental Health Review,* 17, 2, 81–9.
6. Hagerty, S. L. and Williams, L. M. (2022) Moral injury, traumatic stress and threats to core human needs in healthcare workers: the covid-19 pandemic as a dehumanizing experience. *Clinical Psychological Science,* doi: 10.1177/21677026211057554
7. Hornstein, E. A., Haltom, K. E. B., Shirole, K. and Eisenberger, N. I. (2018) A unique safety signal: social-support figures enhance rather than protect from fear extinction. *Clinical Psychological Science,* 6, 3, 407–15.
8. Hornstein, E. A., Fanselow, M. S. and Eisenberger, N.I. (2021) Warm hands, warm heart; an investigation of physical warmth as a prepared safety stimulus. *Emotion,* 22, 7, doi 10.1037/emo0000925
9. Gopnik, A., Meltzoff, A. and Kuhl, P. (1999) *How Babies Think.* Weidenfeld & Nicolson.
10. Ibid.
11. Ibid.
12. Gualtieri, S. and Finn, A. S. (2022) The sweet spot: when children's developing abilities, brains and knowledge make them better learners than adults. *Perspectives on Psychological Science,* doi: 10.1177/174569162110459719
13. Kagan, J. (1983) Stress and coping in early development. In N. Garmezy and M. Rutter (Eds.), *Stress, Coping, and Development in Children.* McGraw-Hill.
14. See, for instance, Baumrind, D. (1966). Effects of authoritative parental control on child behavior. *Child Development,* 37, 4, 887–907; Darling, N. and Steinberg, L. (1993) Parenting style as context: an integrative model. *Psychological Bulletin,* 113, 3, 487–96.
15. Rizzolatti, G. and Craighero, L. (2004) The mirror-neuron system. *Annual Review of Neuroscience,* 27, 169–192.
16. Heyes, C and Catmur, C. (2021) What happened to mirror neurons? *Perspectives on Psychological Science,* doi: 10.1177/1745691621990638
17. Marmot, M. (1967) Whitehall Studies.
18. Ibid.
19. Cited in Robertson, I. (1999) *Mind Sculpture: unleashing your brain's potential.* Bantam Books, London.
20. Wall, P. (1999) *Pain: the science of suffering.* Weidenfeld & Nicolson, London.
21. Seligman, M. (1975) *Helplessness: on depression, development and death.* W. H. Freeman & Co., San Francisco.
22. Msetfi, R., Kornbrot, D., Halbrook, Y.J. and Senan, S. (2022) Sense of control and depression during public health restrictions and the covid-19 pandemic. *International Journal of Environmental Research and Public Health,* doi.org/10.3390/ijerph192114429
23. Egbert, L. D., Battit, G. E., Welch, C. E. and Bartlett, M. K. (1964) Reduction of postoperative pain by encouragement and instruction of patients. *New England Journal of Medicine,* 270, 825–827.

24. Rotter, J. (1954) *Social Learning and Clinical Psychology*. Englewood Cliffs, New York.
25. Gunter, B. (1999) *Pets and People: the psychology of pet ownership*. Whurr.
26. Langer, E. and Rodin, J. (1976) The effects of choice and enhanced personal responsibility for the aged: a field experiment in an institutional setting. *Journal of Personality and Social Psychology*, 34, 191–198.
27. See, for instance, Moilanen, T. Suhonen, R. and Kangasniemi, M. (2021) Nursing support for older people's autonomy in residential care: an integrative review. *International Journal of Older People Nursing*, doi: 10.1111/opn.12428; Hedman, M., Häggström, E. et al. (2017) Caring in nursing homes to promote autonomy and participation. *Nursing Ethics*, doi: 10.1177/09697330117703698
28. Biderman, A. and Zimmer, H. (1961) *The Manipulation of Human Behaviour*. John Wiley, New York.
29. Winn, D. (1983, 2000) *The Manipulated Mind: brainwashing, conditioning and indoctrination*. Octagon Press, London; Malor Books, Cambridge, Massachusetts.
30. James 4: 13–15. Holy Bible, New International Version. (1973, 1978, 1984, 2011)
31. Bordo, S. (1993) *Unbearable weight: feminism, Western culture and the body*. University of California Press, Berkeley.
32. Leichter, H. (1997) Lifestyle correctness and the new secular morality. In A. Brandt and P. Rozin (Eds.), *Morality and Health*. Routledge, London.
33. Mayo, E. (1933) *The Human Problems of an Industrial Civilisation*. Macmillan.
34. Daniel, N. (1979) *The Arabs and Medieval Europe*. Longmans.
35. Shah, I. (1978) *Learning How to Learn*. Octagon Press, London.
36. Ibid.
37. Ibid.
38. Seeman, T. E. and Syme, S. L. (1987) Social networks and coronary heart disease: a comparison of the structure and function of social relations as predictors of disease. *Psychosomatic Medicine*, 49, 4, 341–354.
39. Smith, T. W. (2022) Intimate relationships and coronary heart disease: implications for risk, prevention, and patient management. *Current Cardiology Reports*, 24, 6, 761–74; Bzdok, D. and Dunbar, R. M. M. (2022) Social isolation and the brain in the pandemic era. *Nature Human Behaviour*, doi: 10.1038/s41562-022-01453-0
40. Ainsworth, M. D. and Bell, S. M. (1970) Attachment, exploration, and separation: illustrated by the behavior of one-year-olds in a strange situation. *Child Development*, 41, 49-67.
41. Konner, M. (1991) Universals of behavioural development in relation to brain myelination. In K. R. Gibson and A. C. Petersen (Eds.) *Brain Maturation and Cognitive Development: comparative and cross-cultural perspectuves*. Aldine de Gruyter.
42. Bowlby, J. (1958) The nature of the child's tie to his mother. *International Journal of Psychoanalysis*, 39, 350–71; Bowlby J. (1969) *Attachment and Loss: vol. 1. Attachment*. New York, Basic Books.

43. E.g. Youngblade, L. M. and Belsky, J. (1992) Parent–child antecedents of 5-year-olds' close friendships. *Developmental Psychology*, 28, 700–713.
44. Santamaria, L., Noreika, V. et al. (2019) Emotional valence modulates the topology of the parent-infant inter-brain network. *NeuroImage*, doi: 10.1016/j.neuroimage.2019.116341
45. Murray, L. (1997) The effects of infants' behaviour on maternal mental health. *Health Visitor*, 70, 334–35.
46. Thomas, N. (2000) When love is not enough. *The New Therapist*, 7, 3, 16–23.
47. Goleman, D. (1996) *Emotional Intelligence: why it can matter more than IQ*. Bloomsbury Publishing, London.
48. See, for instance, Wade, T. J. and Mogilski, J. (2018) Emotional accessibility is more important than sexual accessibility in evaluating romantic relationships – especially for women: a conjoint analysis. *Frontiers in Psychology*, doi: 10.3389/fpsyg.2018.00632
49. Robertson, I. (1999) *Mind Sculpture: unleashing your brain's potential*. Bantam Books, London. Page 274.
50. Werner, E. and Smith, R. (1992) *Overcoming the Odds: high risk children from birth to adulthood*. Cornell University Press, Ithaca, New York.
51. Hammett, F. S. (1921) Studies in the thyroid apparatus. *American Journal of Physiology*, 56, 196–204.
52. Schanberg, S. M. and Field, T. M. (1987) Sensory deprivation stress and supple mental stimulation in the rat pup and preterm human neonate. *Child Development*, 58, 1431–1437.
53. Robertson, op. cit.
54. Gunter, op.cit.
55. Reite, M. (1984) Touch, attachment and health. Is there a relationship? In C. Brown (Ed.), *The Many Facets of Touch*. Skillman, New Jersey.
56. Maxwell-Hudson, C. (1999) *Massage*. Dorling Kindersley.
57. Egbert, Battit, Welch and Bartlett, op. cit.
58. Jakubiak, B. K., Fuentes, J. D. and Feeney, B. C. (2022) Affectionate touch promotes shared positive activities. *Personality and Social Psychology Bulletin*, doi: 10.1177/01461672221083764
59. Ratey, J. (2001) *A User's Guide to the Brain*. Pantheon Books.
60. Cacioppo, J. T. with Patrick, W. (2008). *Loneliness: human nature and the need for social connection*. Norton, New York.
61. Cole, S. W., Hawkley, L. C. et. al. (2007) Social regulation of gene expression in human leukocytes. *Genome Biology*, 8, R189.
62. Cacioppo, Wall, op.cit.
63. Goleman, op.cit.
64. Ibid.
65. Bzdok, D. and Dunbar, R. I. M. (2020) The neurobiology of social distance. *Trends in Cognitive Sciences*, doi: 10.1016/j.tics.2020.05.016

66. See, for instance, Hafen, B. Q., Karren, K. J., Frandsen, K. J. and Smith, N. L. (1996) *Mind/Body Health: the health effects of attitudes, emotions and relation ships*. Allyn & Bacon, Boston; Wolf, S. (1992) Predictors of myocardial infarction over a span of 30 years in Roseto, Pennsylvania. *Integrative Physiological and Behavioural Science*, 27, 3, 246–57.
67. Hammoud, R, Tognin, S, et al. (2021) Lonely in a crowd: investigating the association between overcrowding and loneliness, using smartphone technologies. *Scientific Reports*, doi: 10.1038/s41598-021-03398-2
68. Winn, D. (1991) *Please don't say that*. Sunday Times Magazine, 14 July.
69. Lynch, J. (1977) *The Broken Heart: the medical consequences of loneliness*. Basic Books.
70. Dawkins, R. (1978) *The Selfish Gene*. Oxford University Press, Oxford.
71. Margulis, L. and Sagan, D. (1997) *What is Sex?* Simon & Schuster.
72. Behe, M. J. (1996) *Darwin's Black Box*. Simon & Schuster.
73. Ward, A. (2022). *The Social Lives of Animals: how cooperation conquered the natural world*. Profile Books.
74. Lane, R. E. (2000) *The Loss of Happiness in Market Democracies*. Yale University Press.
75. Dunbar, R. I. M. (1992) Neocortex size as a constraint on group size in primates. *Journal of Human Evolution*, 20, 469–493.
76. Gladwell, M. (2000) *The Tipping Point: how little things can make a big difference*. Little, Brown & Company.
77. Hamel, G. and Zanini, M. (2020) *Humanocracy: creating organizations as amazing as the people inside them*. Harvard Business Review Press.
78. Hui, B. P. H., Ng, J. C. K. et al. (2020) Rewards of kindness? A meta-analysis of the link between prosociality and wellbeing. *Psychological Bulletin*, 146, 12, 1084–1116.
79. Ornstein, R. and Sobel, S. (1989) *Healthy Pleasures*. Addison-Wesley; Cregg, D. R. and Cheavens, J. S. (2022) Healing through helping: an experimental investigation of kindness, social activities and reappraisal as wellbeing interventions. *Journal of Positive Psychology*, doi: 10.1080/17439760.2022.2154695
80. For instance, as described in Eger, E. (2017) *The Choice*. Rider.
81. Zeig, J. and Munion, W. (1999) *Milton H. Erickson*. Sage.
82. Anderson, C., Hildreth, J. A. D. and Howland, L. (2015) Is the desire for status a fundamental human motive? A review of the empirical literature. *Psychological Bulletin*, 141, 3, 574–601.
83. Petit, N. C. and Sivanathan, N. (2012) The eyes and the ears of status: how status colours perceptual judgment. *Personality and Social Psychology Bulletin*, 38, 570–582.
84. Murphy. M. L. M., Slavich, G. M., Rohleder, N. and Miller, G. E. (2012) Targeted rejection triggers differential pro- and anti-inflammatory gene expression in adolescents as a function of social status. *Clinical Psychological Science*, doi: 10.1177/2167702612455743

85. Ferrie J. E. (ed.) (2004) *Work, Stress and Health: the Whitehall II study*. Cabinet Office.
86. Wilkinson, R. and Pickett, K. (2010). *The Spirit Level: why equality is better for everyone*. Penguin, London.
87. Oh, D., Shafir, E. and Todorov, A. (2020). Economic status cues from clothes affect perceived competence from faces. *Nature Human Behavior*, 4, 287–93.
88. Marsella, A. J., Escudero, M. et al. (1970) The effects of dwelling density on mental disorders in Filipino men. *Journal of Health and Social Behavior*, 11, 288–294.
89. Hassen, R. (1977) Social and psychological implication of high population density. *Civilisations*, 27, 230–36.
90. Gabe, J. and Williams, P. (1987) Women, housing and mental health. *International Journal of Health Sciences*, 17, 667–679.
91. Evans, G. W., Palsane, M. N. et al (1989) Residential density and psychological health: the mediating effects of social support. *Journal of Personality and Social Psychology*, 57, 994–999.
92. Wachs, T. D. and Gruen, G. (1982) *Early Experience and Human Development*. Plenum, New York.
93. Maxwell, L. (1996) Multiple effects of home and day care crowding. *Environment and Behavior*, 28, 494–512.
94. Baum, A., Aiello, J. and Calesnick, L. (1978) Crowding and personal control: social density and the development of learned helplessness. *Journal of Personality and Social Psychology*, 36, 1000–1011.
95. Baum, A. and Koman, S. (1976) Differential response to anticipated crowding: psychological effects of social and spatial density. *Journal of Personality and Social Psychology*, 34, 526–536.
96. Smith-Jackson, T. L. and Klein, K. W. (2009) *Journal of Environmental Psychology*, 29, 2, 279–289.
97. Hedge, A. (1982) The open-plan office: a systematic investigation of employee reactions to their work environment. *Environment and Behavior*, 14, 5, 519–542.
98. Cox, V. C., Paulus, P. B. and McCain, G. (1984) Prison crowding research: the relevance for prison housing standards and a general approach regarding crowding phenomena. *American Psychologist*, 39, 1448–1460.
99. Ng, B. and Kumar, S. et al. (2001) Ward crowding and incidents of violence on an acute psychiatric inpatient unit. *Psychiatric Services*, 52, 521–525.
100. Perry, J. (2004) The need for privacy: an overlooked human given. *Human Givens*, 11, 3, 46–47.
101. Bergefurt, L. et al. (2019) Loneliness and life satisfaction explained by public-space use and mobility patterns. *International Journal of Environmental Research and Public Health*, doi: 10.3390/ijerph16214282 (2019).
102. www.asurion.com/about/press-releases/americans-check-their-phones-96-times-a-day/
103. https//rootmetrics.com/en-US/content/rootmetrics-survey-results-are-in-mobile-consumer-lifestyles

104. https://www.pewresearch.org/internet/2020/02/21/concerns-about-democracy-in-the-digital-age/
105. Epstein, R. and Robertson, R. E. (2015) The search engine manipulation effect and its possible impact on the outcome of elections. *Proceedings of the National Academy of Sciences (PNAS)*, doi: 10.1073/pnas.1419828112
106. Reis, Sheldon et al, op.cit.
107. Jimerson, S. R., Anderson, G. E. and Whipple, A. D. (2002) Winning the battle and losing the war: examining the relation between grade retention and dropping out of high school. *Psychology in the Schools*, 39, 441–57.
108. Jimerson, S. R., Anderson, G. E. and Whipple, A. D. (2002) Children's ratings of stressful experiences at home and school: loss of a parent and grade retention as superlative stressors. Manuscript prepared for publication, available from authors at the University of California, Santa Barbara.
109. Jimerson, S. R. (2001) Meta-analysis of grade retention research: implications for practice in the 21st century. *School Psychology Review*, 30, 313–30.
110. See for instance: Gedikoglu, M. (2021) Social and emotional learning: an evidence review and synthesis of key issues. Education Policy Institute, UK; Public Health England (2014) The link between pupil health and wellbeing and attainment: a briefing for head teachers, governors and staff in educational settings. PHE publications gateway number 2014491; Durlak, J. A., Weissberg, R. P. et al. (2011) The impact of enhancing students' social and emotional learning: a meta-analysis of school-based universal interventions. *Child Development*, 82, 405–432; Zins, J. E., Weissberg, R. P., Wang, M. C. and Walberg, H. J. (Eds.) (2004) *Building academic success on social and emotional learning: what does the research say?* Teachers College Press, New York; Greenberg, M. T., Weissberg, R. P. et al. (2003) Enhancing school-based prevention and youth development through coordinated social, emotional and academic learning. *American Psychologist*, 58, 466–74.
111. Masten, A. S., Roisman, G. I. et al. (2005) Developmental cascades: linking academic achievement, externalizing and internalizing symptoms over 20 years. *Developmental Psychology*, 41, 733–746.
112. Henderson, H., Harvey, S. B. et al. (2011) Work and common psychiatric disorders. *Journal of the Royal Society of Medicine*, 104, 198–202.
113. Stansfeld, S. and Candy, B. (2006) Psychosocial work environment and mental health – a meta-analytic review. *Scandinavian Journal of Work and Environmental Health*, 32, 6, 443–462.
114. Ramirez, A. J., Graham, J. et al (1996). Mental health of hospital consultants: the effects of stress and satisfaction at work. *The Lancet*, 347, 9003, 724–8.
115. Almutairi, H., Alsubaiei, A. et al. (2022) Prevalence of burnout in medical students: a systematic review and meta-analysis. *International Journal of Social Psychiatry*, 68, 6, 1157–70.
116. Lambert, T. (2006) Creating meaning that works. *Human Givens*, 13, 1, 21–23.
117. Reker, G. T., Peacock, E. J. and Wong, P. T. P. (1987) Meaning and purpose in life and well-being: a life-span perspective. *Journal of Gerontology*, 42, 1, 44–49.

118. Headey, B., Muffels, R. and Wagner, G. (2010) Long-running German panel survey shows that personal and economic choices, not just genes, matter for happiness. *PNAS*, 107, 42 17922–6.

119. Brickman, P., Coates, D. and Janoff-Bulman, R. (1978) Lottery winners and accident victims: is happiness relative? *Journal of Personality and Social Psychology*, 36, 8, 917–927.

120. Koon P., Kooreman, P., Soetevent, A. and Kapteyn, A. (2008) The own and social effects of an unexpected income shock: evidence from the Dutch Postcode Lottery. Departmental Working Papers, Department of Economics, UCSB, UC Santa Barbara, http://escholarship.org/uc/item/07k895v4

121. Schaefer, S. M., Boylan, J. M., et al. (2013) Purpose in life predicts better emotional recovery from negative stimuli. *PLoS One*, 8, 11, e80329

122. Schnell, T., & Krampe, H. (2022) Meaningfulness protects from, and crisis of meaning exacerbates, general mental distress longitudinally. *BMC Psychiatry*, doi: 10.1186/s12888-022-03921-3

123. See, for instance: Lewis, N. A., Turiano, N. A. et al. (2017) Purpose in life and cognitive functioning in adults. *Aging, Neuropsychology and Cognition*, 24, 6, 662–71; Windsor, T. D., Curtis, R. G. and Luszcz, M. A. (2015) Sense of purpose as a psychological resource for aging well. *Developmental Psychology*, 51, 7, 975–86.

124. See for instance, Affleck, G. and Tennen, H. (1996) Construing benefits from adversity: adaptational significance and dispositional underpinnings. *Journal of Personality*, 64, 899–922; Ickovics, J. R and Park, C. I. (1998) Thriving [Special issue]. *Journal of Social Issues*, 54, 2.

125. Affleck, G. and Tennen, H. et al. (1987) Causal attribution, perceived benefits and morbidity after a heart attack: an eight-year study. *Journal of Consulting and Clinical Psychology*, 55, 29–35.

126. Janoff-Bulman, R. (1992) *Shattered Assumptions: towards a new psychology of trauma*. Free Press, New York.

127. Taylor, S. E., Kemeny, M. E. et al. (2000) Psychological resources, positive illusions and health. *American Psychologist*, 55, 1, 99–109.

128. Britton, A. and Shipley, M. (2010) Bored to death. *International Journal of Epidemiology*, 39, 370–371.

129. See, for instance, McClain, C. S., Rosenfeld, B. and Breithart, W. (2003) Effect of spiritual well-being on end-of-life despair in terminally-ill cancer patients. *The Lancet*, 361, 1603–1607; Nelson, C., Rosenfeld, B., Breithart, W. and Galietta, M. (2002) Spirituality, religion and depression in the terminally ill. *Psychosomatics*, 43, 213–20; Fehring, R., Miller J. and Shaw, C. (1997) Spiritual well-being, religiosity, hope, depression and other mood states in elderly people coping with cancer. *Oncology Nursing Forum*, 24, 663–671; Taylor, E. J. (1998) Spirituality and the cancer experience. In R. M. Carroll-Johnson, L. Gorman and N. J. Bush (Eds.) *Psychosocial Nursing: care along the cancer continuum*. Oncology Nursing Press, Pittsburgh.

130. Costanza, A., Prelati, M. and Pompili, M. (2019) The meaning in life of suicidal patients: the presence and the search for constructs: a systematic review. *Medicina*, doi: 10.3390/medicina55080465
131. Rogers, J. R. (2001) Theoretical grounding: the missing link in suicide research *Journal of Counselling & Development*, 79, 16–25.
132. See, for instance, Kinner, R. T., Metha, A. T. et al. (1994) Depression, meaningless ness, and substance abuse in "normal" and hospitalized adolescents. *Journal of Alcohol and Drug Education*, 39, 2, 101–111.
133. Lew, B., Chistopolskaya, K., Osman, A. et al. (2020) Meaning in life as a protective factor against suicidal tendencies in Chinese University students. *BMC Psychiatry* 20, doi: 10.1186/s12888-020-02485-4
134. Fischer, C.E., Churchill, N. et al. (2021) Long-known music exposure effects on brain imaging and cognition in early-stage cognitive decline: a pilot study. *Journal of Alzheimer's Disease*, doi: 10.3233/JAD-210610
135. Ponce de Leon, R., Rifkin, J. R. and Larrick, R. P. (2022) "They're everywhere!" Symbolically threatening groups seem more pervasive than non-threatening groups. *Psychological Science*, doi: 10.1177/09567976211060009
136. Romano., A, Sutter, M. et al. (2021) National parochialism is ubiquitous across 42 nations around the world. *Nature Communications*, doi: 10.1038/s41467-021-24787-1
137. Booker, C. (2020) *Groupthink: a study in self-delusion*. Bloomsbury Publishing.
138. Janis, I. C. (1972) *Victims of Groupthink*. Houghton, Mifflin.
139. Booth, J. (2022) *Have we all gone mad? Why group think is rising and how to stop it*. Biteback Publishing.
140. Dweck, C. (2015) https://www.edweek.org/leadership/opinion-carol-dweck-revisits-the-growth-mindset/2015/09
141. Yeager, D. S., Carroll, J. M. et al (2021) Teacher mindsets help explain where a growth-mindset intervention does and doesn't work. *Psychological Science*, doi:10.1177/09567976211028984
142. Hoyer, K., Zeelenberg, M. and Breugelmans, S. M. (2022) Greed: what is it good for? *Personality and Social Psychology Bulletin*, doi: 10.1177/01461672221140355
143. Russel, R. (1993) Report on Effective Psychotherapy: legislative testimony, Hilgarth Press. This report was later endorsed by the American Psychological Association. See also: Hogan, D. B. (1993 edition) *The Regulation of Psychotherapists*, 4 vols. Hillgarth Press.

Chapter 6 – Mind, brain, body

1. See, for instance, https://www.ucf.edu/pegasus/your-brain-on-music/; https://www.health.harvard.edu/blog/why-is-music-good-for-the-brain-2020100721062
2. Trimble, M. and Hesdorffer, D. (2017) Music and the brain: the neuroscience of music and music appreciation. *British Journal of Psychiatry International*, 14, 2, 28–31.

3. Christensen, J. F. and Chang, D-S. (2021) *Dancing is the Best Medicine: the science of how moving to a beat is good for body, brain and soul*. Greystone Books, Vancouver/Berkeley.
4. Morrice, A. (2022) Why sleep matters even more than we think. *Human Givens Journal*, 29, 2, 13–18.
5. Ibid.
6. Hewing, E. (2021) REM sleep: too little or too much explains many anxiety conditions. *Human Givens Journal*, 28, 2, 13–20.
7. See, for instance, Clapp, M., Aurora, N. et al (2017) Gut microbiota's effect on mental health: the gut-brain axis. *Clinical Practice*, doi: 10.4081/cp.2017.987
8. Järbrink-Sehgal, E. and Andreassohn, A. (2020) The gut microbiota and mental health in adults. *Current Opinion in Neurobiology*, 62, 102–14. Segerstrom, S. C. and Miller, G. E. (2004) Psychological stress and the human immune system: a meta-analytic study of 30 years of inquiry. *Psychological Bulletin*, 130, 4, 601–630.
9. Yaribeygi, H., Panahi, Y. et al. (2017) The impact of stress on body function: a review. *EXCLI Journal: Experimental and Clinical Sciences*, 16, 1057–72.
10. Ader, R. and Cohen, H. (1975) Behaviourally conditioned immunosuppression *Psychosomatic Medicine*, 37, 333–340.
11. Friedman, H. and Boothby-Kewley, S. (1987) The disease-prone personality: a meta-analytic view. *American Psychologist*, 42, 539–555.
12. See, for instance, McEwen, B. and Stellar, E. (1993) Stress and metastasis. *Archives of Internal Medicine*, 153, 18, 2093–2101; Martin, P. (1997) *The Sickening Mind: brain, behaviour, immunity and disease*. HarperCollins, London.
13. Cohen, S., Doyle, W. and Skoner, D. et al. (1997) Social ties and susceptibility to the common cold. *Journal of the American Medical Association*, 277, 24, 1940–44.
14. Kiecolt-Glaser, J. K. and Glaser, R. (1987) Psychosocial stress and human herpes virus infections. *In Viruses, Immunity, and Mental Disorders*. Plenum Medical Book Co, New York.
15. Kessler, R. (1991) Stressful life events and symptom onset in HIV-1 infection *American Journal of Psychiatry*, 148, 733.
16. Jones, F. (2000) Translating social support into health. *The Psychologist*, 13, 6, 296.
17. Bains, J. S. and Sharkey, K. A. (2022) Stress and immunity – the circuit makes the difference. *Nature Immunology*, 23, 1137–9.
18. Sklar, L. and Anisman, H. (1979) Stress and coping factors influence tumor growth. *Science*, 205, 513–515.
19. Sharot, T. (2017) *The Influential Mind: what the brain reveals about our power to change others*. Little, Brown.
20. Williams, R. B., Haney, T. L. et al. (1980) Type A behaviour, hostility and coronary atherosclerosis. *Psychosomatic Medicine*, 42, 539; Shekell, R. B., Gale, M. et al. (1983). Hostility, risk of coronary heart disease and mortality. *Psychosomatic Medicine*, 45, 109.

21. Wong, J. M., Na, B. at al. (2013) Hostility, health behaviors and risk of recurrent events in patients with stable coronary heart disease: findings from the Heart and Soul Study. *Journal of American Heart Association*, doi: 10.1161/JAHA.113.000052; Whooley, M. A. and Wong, J. (2011) Hostility and cardiovascular disease: Editorial comment. *Journal of American College of Cardiology*, 58, 12, 1229–30.
22. Ornstein, R. and Sobel, D. (1989) *Healthy Pleasures*. Addison-Wesley.
23. Cañas-González, B., Fernández-Nistal, F., et al. (2020) Influence of stress and depression on the immune system in patients evaluated in an anti-aging unit. *Frontiers in Psychology*, doi: 10.3389/fpsyg.2020.01844
24. Cited in Strain, J. (1991) Cost offset from a psychiatric consultation-liaison intervention with elderly hip fracture patients. *American Journal of Psychiatry*, 148, 8, 1044–1049.
25. Burton, H. et al. (1986) The relationship of depression to survival in chronic renal failure. *Psychosomatic Medicine*, 48, 261–269.
26. Bennett, P. (1999) Affective and social-cognitive predictors of behaviour change following first myocardial infarction. *British Journal of Health Psychology*, 4, 3, 247–256. Thornton, E. (1999) Affective status following myocardial infarction can predict long-term heart rate variability and blood pressure reactivity. *British Journal of Health Psychology*, 4, 3, 231–236.
27. Carney, R. et al. (1988) Major depressive disorder predicts cardiac events in patients with coronary artery disease. *Psychosomatic Medicine*, 50, 627–33.
28. Stewart, J. C., Perkins, A. J. and Callahan, C. M. (2014) Effect of collaborative care for depression on risk of cardiovascular events: data from the IMPACT randomized controlled trial. *Psychosomatic Medicine*, 76, 1, 29–37.
29. Musselman, D. L. et al. (1996) Exaggerated platelet reactivity in major depression. *American Journal of Psychiatry*, 153, 10, 1313–1317.
30. Sobel, D. and Ornstein, R. (1996) *Healthy Mind, Healthy Body Handbook*. DRx, Los Altos.
31. Ostell, A. and Oakland, S. (1999) Absolutist thinking and mental health. *British Journal of Medical Psychology*, 72, 2, 239–250.
32. Robins, L. N., Helzer, J. E., Hesselbrock, M. and Wish, E. (1980) Vietnam veterans three years after Vietnam: how our study changed our view of heroin. In L. Brill and C. Winick (Eds.), *The Yearbook of Substance Use and Abuse*, vol. 2. Human Sciences Press.
33. Peele, S. (1995 edition) *Diseasing of America*. Lexington Books.
34. Brown, G. and Winn, D. (2009) *How to Liberate Yourself from Pain*. HG Publishing.
35. Bennett, K., Diamond, C. et al. (2021) A practical review of functional neurological disorder (FND) for the general physician. *Clinical Medicine Journal*, 10.7861/clinmed.2020-0987
36. Stone, J., Carson, A., et al. (2010) Who is referred to neurology clinics? The diagnoses made in 3781 new patients. *Clinical Neurology and Neurosurgery*, 112, 747–51.

37. World Health Organization (2020) *ICD-11 for Mortality and Morbidity Statistics*. WHO.
38. O'Sullivan, S. (2015) *It's All in Your Head: true stories of imaginary illness*. Chatto & Windus.
39. Bennett, (2021) op.cit.
40. Ibid.
41. Grosset, K. A. and Grosset , D. G .(2004) Prescribed drugs and neurological complications. *Journal of Neurological and Neurosurgical Psychiatry*, doi: 10.1136/jnnp.2004.045757
42. Brown, M. (2021) https://www.bmj.com/content/371/bmj.m3745/rapid-responses
43. See https://www.neurosymptoms.org/en_GB/
44. Buchanan, T. W., Bagley, S., Stansfield, R. and Preston, S. (2011) The empathic, physiological resonance of stress. *Social Neuroscience*, 7, 2, 191–201.
45. Brandt, H. B. (2022) The social transmission of stress in animal collectives. *Proceedings of the Royal Society B*, doi: 10.1098/rspb.2021.2158)
46. O'Sullivan, S. (2021) *The Sleeping Beauties: and other stories of mystery illness*. Picador.
47. O'Sullivan, S. and Winn, D. (2021) The social elephant in the room. *Human Givens*, 28, 1, 28–33.

Chapter 7 – Understanding difference: gender, identity and neurodivergence

1. Cooke, C. (2022) *Bitch: a revolutionary guide to sex, evolution and the female animal*. Doubleday.
2. Rippon, G. (2019) *The Gendered Brain: the new neuroscience that shatters the myth of the female brain*. The Bodley Head, London.
3. Rippon, G. (2019). Not so gendered brain. *Human Givens Journal*, 26, 1, 28–33.
4. Eliot, L., Ahmed, A., Khan, H. and Patel, J. (2021) Dump the 'dimorphism': comprehensive synthesis of human brain studies reveals few male-female differences beyond size. *Neuroscience and Biobehavioral Reviews*, 125, 667–97.
5. Gottman, J. (1998) *Why Marriages Succeed or Fail*. Bloomsbury.
6. https://www.pewresearch.org/fact-tank/2014/05/05/millions-of-americans-changed-their-racial-or-ethnic-identity-from-one-census-to-the-next/
7. Barnes, H. (2023) *Time to Think: the inside story of the collapse of the Tavistock's gender service for children*. Swift.
8. https://www.eibscorp.com/neurodiversity-no-two-human-minds-are-exactly-alike/
9. https://neurodiversity2.blogspot.com/p/what.html
10. Zeman, A., Dewar, M. and Della Sala, S. (2015) Lives without imagery – congenital aphantasia. *Cortex*, 73, 378–80.
11. See, for instance, Moncrieff, J. and Tamimi, S. (2010) Is ADHD a valid diagnosis? *BMJ*, 340, c547; Müller, R. A. and Amaral, D. G. (2017). Editorial: Time to give up on autism spectrum disorder? *Autism Research*, 10, 1, 10–14; Waterhouse, L.,

London, E. and Gillberg, C. (2016). ASD validity. *Review Journal of Autism and Developmental Disorders,* 3, 4, 302–29.
12. Stark, E. (2021) Dropping my mask. *The Psychologist,* https://www.bps.org.uk/psychologist/dropping-my-mask
13. https://www.autism.org.uk/advice-and-guidance/what-is-autism/autistic-women-and-girls
14. Tunç, B., Yankowitz, L. D., Parker, D. et al. (2019) Deviation from normative brain development is associated with symptom severity in autism spectrum disorder. *Molecular Autism* 10, 46.
15. Arunachalam Chandran, V., Pliatsikas, C. et al. (2021). Brain structural correlates of autistic traits across the diagnostic divide: A grey matter and white matter microstructure study. *NeuroImage Clinical,* 32, 102897.
16. Blanken, L. M. E., Muetzel, R. L. et al. (2017). White matter microstructure in children with autistic traits. *Psychiatry Research Neuroimaging,* 263, 127–34.
17. Rolls, E. (2019) *The Orbitofrontal Cortex.* Oxford University Press.
18. Bachevalier, J. and Loveland, K. A. (2006) The orbitofrontal-amygdala circuit and self-regulation of social-emotional behavior in autism. *Neuroscience and Biobehavioral Reviews,* 30, 1, 97–117.
19. Liu, X., Bautista, J., Liu, E., and Zikopoulos, B. (2020) Imbalance of laminar-specific excitatory and inhibitory circuits of the orbitofrontal cortex in autism. *Molecular Autism,* 11, 1, 83.
20. Dobzhansky, T. (1962) *Mankind Evolving.* Yale University Press.
21. Thorpe, W. H. (1969) *Animal Nature and Human Nature.* Methuen & Co.
22. Tinbergen, E. A. and Tinbergen, N. (1972) Early childhood autism – an ethological approach. *Supplements to the Journal of Comparative Ethology.* Berlin and Hamburg.
23. Jouvet, M. (1978) Does a genetic programming of the brain occur during paradoical sleep? In P. A. Buser and A. Rougel-Buser (Eds.), *Cerebral Correlates of Conscious Experience.* Elsevier, Amsterdam.
24. Ornitz, E. M. and Ritvo, E. R. (1976) In B. J. Freeman, E. M. Ornitz and P. E. Tanguay (Eds.), *Autism.* Spectrum Books Incorporated, New York.
25. Sinclair, J. (1992) Bridging the gaps: an inside-out view of autism. In E. Schopler and G. B. Mesibov (Eds.) *High-functioning Individuals with Autism.* Plenum, New York.
26. Sacks, O. (1995) *An Anthropologist on Mars: seven paradoxical tales.* Knopf, New York.
27. Ornitz and Ritvo, op. cit.
28. Ibid.
29. Kaufman, D. N. (1970) *To Love Is To Be Happy With: the miracle of one autistic child.* Souvenir Press, London.
30. Claiborne Park, C. (1965). *The Seige.* Colin and Smythe Ltd, Gerrards Cross.
31. Ibid.

32. Ornitz and Ritvo, op. cit.
33. Ibid.
34. Wing, L. (1971) *Autistic Children: a guide for parents*. Constable, London.
35. Ibid.
36. Bond, J. E. (1979) *Biology of fishes*. W. B. Saunders & Co., Philadelphia, London and Toronto.
37. Furneaux, B. and Roberts, B. (1977) *Autistic Children: teaching, community and research approaches*. Routledge, London and Boston; https://www.autismspeaks.org/expert-opinion/parent-needs-help-4-year-old-autism-wont-eat-solid-foods
38. Kaufman, op. cit.
39. Moy-Thomas. J. A. (1971). (Revised by R. S. Miles) *Palaeozoic Fishes*. Constable.
40. Furneaux and Roberts, op. cit.
41. E.g. Jones, F. H., Simmonds, J. Q. and Frakel, F. (1974) An extinction procedure for eliminating self destructive behavior in a nine-year-old autistic girl. *Journal of Autism and Child Schizophrenia*, 4, 241–250.
42. Wing, op. cit.
43. Hermelin, B. and O'Connor, N. (1970) *Psychological Experiments with Autistic Children*. Pergamon Press, Oxford.
44. Wing, op. cit.
45. Schopler, E. (1965) Early infantile autism and receptor processes. *Archives of General Psychiatry*, 13, 323–335.
46. Hermelin and O'Connor, op. cit.
47. Ornitz and Ritvo, op. cit.
48. Bond, op. cit.
49. Thorpe, W. H. (1969) *Animal Nature and Human Nature*. Methuen and Co, London.
50. Bond, op. cit.
51. Kaufman, op. cit.
52. Laski, M. (1961) *Ecstasy: a study of some secular and religious experiences*. Cresset Press, London.
53. Shubin, N. (2009). *Your Inner Fish*. Random House.
54. Daeschler, E. B., Shubin, N. H. and Jenkins, F. A., Jr (2006) A Devonian tetrapod-like fish and the evolution of the tetrapod body plan. *Nature*, 440, 7085, 757–63.
55. Shubin, N. H., Daeschler, E. B, and Jenkins, F. A., Jr (2006). The pectoral fin of Tiktaalik roseae and the origin of the tetrapod limb. *Nature*, 440, 7085, 764–71.
56. Clack, J. A. (2002) *Gaining Ground: the origin and evolution of tetrapods*. Indiana University Press.
57. Forey, P. L., Gardiner, B. G. and Patterson, C. (1991) The lungfish, the coelacanth, and the cow revisited. In H.-P. Schultze and L. Trueb (Eds.), *Origins of the Higher Groups of Tetrapods: Controversy and Consensus* (pp. 145–172). Cornell University Press.

58. Greenspan, S. I. (1997) *The Growth of the Mind*. Addison Wesley.
59. Trevarthen, C., Aitken, K., Papoudi, D. and Robarts, J. (1998). *Children with Autism: diagnosis and interventions to meet their needs*. 2nd edition. Jessica Kingsley, Philadelphia.
60. Jordan, R., and Powell, S. D. (1993). Reflections of the option method as a treatment for autism. *Journal of Autism and Developmental Disorders*, 23, 4, 682–85.
61. https://www.autism.org.uk/advice-and-guidance/topics/strategies-and-interventions
62. See, for instance, Fitzgerald, M. (2014). *The Link between Asperger Syndrome and Scientific, Artistic, and Political Creativity: eleven case studies*. Edwin Mellen Press; Fitzgerald, M. (2015). *The Mind of the Artist: attention deficit hyperactivity disorder, autism, Asperger syndrome & depression*. Nova Science Publishers.
63. Jacobs, T. (2002) Inside a glass prison. *Human Givens*, 8, 4, 18–21.
64. Baron-Cohen, S. (2002) The extreme male brain theory of autism. *Trends in Cognitive Sciences*, 6, 6, 248–254.
65. See, for instance, Nash, A. and Grossi, G. (2007) Picking Barbie™'s brain: inherent sex differences in scientific ability? *Journal of Interdisciplinary Feminist Thought*, 2, 1, 5; Andrew, J., Cooke, M. and Muncer, S. J. (2008). The relationship between empathy and Machiavellianism: an alternative to empathizing–systemizing theory. *Personality and Individual Differences*, 44, 5, 1203–11.
66. Rose, K. D. (2006) *The Beginning of the Age of Mammals*. Johns Hopkins University Press.
67. Rescorla, R. (1973) Effect of US [unconditioned stimulus] habituation following conditioning. *Journal of Comparative and Physiological Psychology*, 82, 1, 137–143.
68. Hewing, E. (2020) Psychosis: metaphorically speaking. *Human Givens Journal*, 27, 1, 12–21.
69. Grillner, S. and Robertson, B. (2016) The basal ganglia over 500 million years. *Cell*, 26, 20, 1088-1100.
70. Lanciego, J. L., Luquin, N and Obeso, J. A. (2012) Functional neuroanatomy of the basal ganglia. *Cold Spring Harbor Perspectives in Medicine*, 2, 12, a009621.
71. Galvan, A., Kuwajima, M. and Smith, Y. (2006) Glutamate and GABA receptors and transporters in the basal ganglia: what does their subsynaptic localization reveal about their function? *Neuroscience*, 143, 2, 351–75.
72. Huot, P. and Parent, A. J. (2007) Dopaminergic neurons intrinsic to the striatum. *Neurochemistry*, 101, 6, 1441–7.
73. Bromberg-Martin, E. S., Matsumoto, M. and Hikosaka, O. (2010) Dopamine in motivational control: rewarding, aversive, and alerting, *Neuron*, 68, 5, 815–34.
74. Schultz, W., Dayan, P. and Montague, P. R.(1997) A neural substrate of prediction and reward. *Science*, 275, 5306, 1593–9.
75. Hewing, E (2022) Private communication.
76. Rolls, E. T., Deco, D. et al. (2022) The human orbitofrontal cortex, vmPFC, and anterior cingulate cortex effective connectome: emotion, memory and action. *Cerebral Cortex*, 20, 33, 2, 330–56.

77. Ratey, J. (2001) *A User's Guide to the Brain.* Pantheon Books. New York.
78. Frith, U. (2003) *Autism: explaining the enigma.* Blackwell, second edition.
79. Baron-Cohen, S., Leslie, A. M. and Frith, U. (1985). Does the autistic child have a "theory of mind"? *Cognition,* 21, 37–46.
80. Frith, op. cit.
81. Vermeulen, P. (2012) *Autism as Context Blindness.* Autism Asperger Publishing Co, US; Vermeulen, P. (2015) Context blindness in autism spectrum disorder: not using the forest to see the trees as trees. *Focus on Autism and Other Developmental Disabilities,* 30, 3, 182–92.
82. Vermeulen, P. (2011) Autism: from mind blindness to context blindness. *Autism Asperger's Digest* November/December issue.
83. Zeelenberg, M., Nelissen, R. M. A., Seger, M., Breugelmans, S. M. and Pieters, R. (2008) On emotion specificity in decision making: why feeling is for doing. *Judgment and Decision Making,* 3, 1, 18–27.
84. See, for example, Bromhall, C. (2003) *The Eternal Child.* Ebury Press.
85. See http://www.randomhouse.com/features/annerice/interview.html
86. Deikman, A. J. (1982) *The Observing Self: mysticism and psychotherapy.* Beacon Press, Boston.
87. Griffin, J. and Tyrrell, I. (2011) *Godhead, the brain's big bang: The explosive origin of creativity, mysticism and mental illness.* HG Publishing, East Sussex.
88. Ibid.
89. Hewing, E. (2011) Cannabis-induced caetextia: explaining the paradoxical effects of cannabis, *Human Givens,* 18, 4, 30–34.

PART III – EMOTIONAL HEALTH AND CLEAR THINKING

Chapter 8 – The APET model: the key to effective psychotherapy

1. See https://rxisk.org/ – website established by psychiatrist and psychopharmcologist David Healy, author of *Pharmageddon.* (2012) University of California Press.
2. Davies, J. and Read, J. (2018) A systematic review into the incidence, severity and duration of antidepressant withdrawal effects: are guidelines evidence based? *Journal of Addictive Behaviors,* doi: 10.1016/j.addbeh.2018.08.027
3. Nour, M. N., Liu, Y. and Dolan, R. J. (2022) Functional neuroimaging in psychiatry and the case for failing better. *Neuron,* 110, 16, 2524–44.
4. Taylor, J. J., Lin, C. et al. (2022) A transdiagnostic network for psychiatric illness derived from atrophy and lesions. *Nature Human Behavior,* doi: 10.1038/s41562-022-01501-9
5. See, for instance: Dalal, F. (2018) *CBT: the cognitive-behavioural tsunami.* Routledge; Moloney, P. (2013) *The Therapy Industry.* Pluto Press; Dineen, T. (1996) *Manufacturing Victims: what the psychology industry is doing to people.* Robert Davies; Dawe, R. M. (1994) *House of Cards: psychology and psychotherapy built on myth.* Simon & Schuster.

6. Rowland, N., Bower, P. et al. (2000) Counselling in primary care: a systematic review of the research evidence. *British Journal of Guidance and Counselling*, 28, 2, 215–31.
7. Haeffel, G. (2010) When self-help is no help: traditional cognitive skills training does not prevent depressive symptoms in people who ruminate. *Behaviour Research and Therapy*, 48, 2, 152–7. See also Alpert, J. (2012) In therapy forever? Enough already. *The New York Times, Sunday Review*. April 21.
8. https://en.wikipedia.org/wiki/List_of_psychotherapies
9. Dewdney, A. K. (1997) *Yes, We Have No Neutrons – an eye-opening tour through the twists and turns of bad science.* John Wiley & Sons.
10. Webster, R. (1995) *Why Freud was Wrong.* HarperCollins.
11. Jaynes, J. (1976) *The Origin of Consciousness in the Breakdown of the Bicameral Mind.* Houghton, Mifflin Co. Page 15.
12. "When I can sensitively understand the feelings which they are expressing, when I am able to accept them as separate persons in their own right, then I find that they tend to move in certain directions. And what are these directions in which they tend to move? The words which I believe are most truly descriptive are words such as positive, constructive, moving towards self-actualization, growing towards maturity, growing towards socialization ... to discover the strongly positive directional tendencies which exist in them, as in all of us, at the deepest levels." *The Carl Rogers Reader* (1990), Constable, London, page 28; "In Roger's view (1980) what psychologically troubled people most need is not to be analyzed, judged or advised, but simply to be heard – that is, to be truly understood and respected by another human being. Therefore the primary effort of client-centred therapists is to apply all their powers of attention, intuition and empathy to the task of grasping what the client is actually feeling." *Abnormal Psychology*. (1988) 5th edition. McGraw-Hill, page 193.
13. See, for instance, Arntz, A., Tiesema, M. and Kindt, M. (2007) Treatment of PTSD: A comparison of imaginal exposure with and without imagery rescripting. *Journal of Behavior Therapy and Experimental Psychiatry*, 38, 4, 345–370; Holmes, E. A., Arntz, A. and Smucker, M. (2007) Imagery rescripting in cognitive behaviour therapy: images, treatment techniques and outcomes. *Journal of Behavior Therapy and Experimental Psychiatry*, 38, 4, 297–305.
14. https://blogs.bmj.com/bmj/2019/10/21/improving-access-to-psychological-therapies-an-idea-thats-failed-to-deliver
15. Dalal, F. (2018) *CBT– The Cognitive Behavioural Tsunami: managerialism, politics and the corruption of science.* Routledge.
16. Cuijpers, P., Miguel, C. et al (2023) Cognitive behaviour therapy vs. control conditions, other psychotherapies, pharmacotherapies and combined treatment for depression: a comprehensive meta-analysis including 409 trials with 52,702 patients. *World Psychiatry*, 22, 105–15.
17. *Diagnosis, Vol. 2 Treatment Aspect*. United States Public Health Service Agency; Depression Guideline Panel. *Depression in Primary Care: Volume 2. Treatment of Major Depression* (1993). Clinical Practice Guideline, Number 5. Rockville, MD: US Department of Health and Human Services, Public Health Service, Agency for Health Care Policy and Research. AHCPR publication No. 93-0551.

18. Danton, W., Antonuccio, D. and DeNelsky, G. (1995) Depression: psychotherapy is the best medicine. *Professional Psychology Research and Practice*, 26, 574–85.
19. Danton, W., Antonuccio, D. and Rosenthal, Z. (1997). No need to panic. *The Therapist*, 4, 4, 38–41.
20. Ellis, A. (1971) *Growth through reason: verbatim cases in rational-emotive therapy*. Wiltshire Books.
21. Zajonc, A. (1995) *Catching the Light*. Oxford University Press.
22. LeDoux, J. E. (1996) *The Emotional Brain*. Simon & Schuster, New York.
23. LeDoux, J. E. (1884) Cognition and emotion: processing functions and brain systems. In *Handbook of Cognitive Neuroscience*, (Eds.) M. S Gazzaniga, Plenum Publishing, New York, 357–68.
24. LeDoux, J. E. (2015) Anxious: the modern mind in the age of anxiety. One World.
25. See, for instance, Panksepp, J. (2005) Affective consciousness: Core emotional feelings in animals and humans. *Consciousness and Cognition*, 14, 30–80.
26. Barrett, L. F. (2006a) Are emotions natural kinds? *Perspectives on Psychological Science*, 1, 28–58; Barrett, L. F. (2006b) Solving the emotion paradox: categorization and the experience of emotion. *Personality and Social Psychology Review*, 10, 20–46; Barrett, L. F., Lindquist, K. A., Bliss-Moreau, E., Duncan, S., Gendron, M., Mize, J., and Brennan, L. (2007) Of mice and men: natural kinds of emotions in the mammalian brain? A response to Panksepp and Izard. *Perspectives on Psychological Science*, 2, 297–311.
27. LeDoux, J. (2016) Rethinking the emotional brain. *Neuron*, doi: 10.1016/j.neuron.2012.02.004
28. For a very readable explanation of this, see Feldman Barrett, L. (2020) *Seven and a Half Lessons about the Brain*. Picador.
29. Johnson, R. (1997) This is not my beautiful wife ... *New Scientist*, 22 March.
30. Ramachandran, V. S. (1998) *Phantoms in the Brain*. Fourth Estate.
31. Mlodinow, L. (2022.) *Emotion: the new thinking about feelings*. Allen Lane.
32. Ibid.
33. Robertson, I. (1999) *Mind Sculpture*. Bantam Press. Professor Robertson beautifully described our brains as "vast, trembling webs of neurones ... in flux, continually remoulded, sculpted by the restless energy of the world".
34. McGilchrist, I. (2009) *The Master and his Emissary: the divided brain and the making of the Western World*. Yale University Press.
35. McGilchrist, I. (2021) *The Matter with Things: our brains, our delusions and the unmaking of the world*. Perspectiva Press.
36. As described in McGilchrist, I. and Cheshire, S (2019) Two ways of seeing. *Human Givens*, 26, 2, 28–32.
37. McGilchrist, I. (2021) Op. cit.
38. Danziger, S., Levav, J. and Avnaim-Pesso, L. (2011) Extraneous factors in judicial decisions. *Proceedings of the National Academy of Sciences*, 108, 17, 6889–92.
39. Dyas, C. (2023) The heart of the matter. *Human Givens Journal*, 30, 1 32–5.

40. Grinder, J. and Bandler, R. (1979) *Frogs into Princes*. Real People Press.
41. Battino, R. and South, T. L. (1999) *Ericksonian Approaches*. Crown House Publishing.
42. NICE (2005) *Obsessive-compulsive Disorder and Body Dysmorphic Disorder: treatment*. Clinical guideline [CG31]. National Institute for Health and Care Excellence.
43. Yaryura-Tobias, J. A. and and Neziroglu, F. (1997) *Biobehavioural Treatment of Obsessive-Compulsive Spectrum Disorders*. Norton.
44. Teasdale, J. D. (1988) Cognitive vulnerability to persistent depression. *Cognition and Emotion,* 2, 247–274.
45. Mathews, A. and MacLeod, C. (2005) Cognitive vulnerability to emotional disorders. *Annual Review of Clinical Psychology,* 1, 167–95.
46. Joormann, J., Teachman, B. A. and Gotlib, I. H (2009) Sadder and less accurate? False memory for negative material in depression. *Journal of Abnormal Psychology,* 118, 2, 41217.
47. Tavris, C. (1982) *Anger the Misunderstood Emotion*. Simon & Schuster.
48. Griffin, J. (2004) Great expectations. *Human Givens,* 11, 1, 12–19.
49. Griffin, J. and Tyrrell, I. (2005) *Freedom from Addiction: the secret behind successful addiction busting*. HG Publishing, East Sussex.
50. Hewing, E. (2020). Psychosis: metaphorically speaking. *Human Givens Journal,* 27, 1, 12–21.
51. Huot, P. and Parent, A. J. (2007) Dopaminergic neurons intrinsic to the striatum. *Neurochemistry,* 101, 6, 1441–7.
52. Bromberg-Martin, E. S., Matsumoto, M. and Hikosaka, O. (2010). Dopamine in motivational control: rewarding, aversive, and alerting, *Neuron,* 68, 5, 815–34.
53. Schultz, W., Dayan, P. and Montague, P. R. (1997). A neural substrate of prediction and reward. *Science,* 275, 5306, 1593–9.
54. Griffin, J. (2006) Molar memories. *Human Givens,* 13, 3, 9–18.
55. Adams, S. (2009). Why molar memory treatment works. *Human Givens,* 17, 1, 37–41.
56. Dixon, M. and Sweeny, K. (2000) *The Human Effect in Medicine: theory, research and practice*. Radcliffe Medical Press, Abingdon, Oxfordshire.
57. Kirsch, I. (2014) Antidepressants and the placebo effect. *Zeitschrift fur Psychologie,* 222, 3, 128–34.
58. Jarrett, C. (2019). The placebo effect, digested – 10 amazing findings. *BPS Research Digest,* https://digest.bps.org.uk/2019/03/11/the-placebo-effect-digested-10-amazing-findings/
59. Kaptchuk, T. J, Friedlander, E, Kelley, J. M. et al (2010). Placebos without deception: a randomised controlled trial in irritable bowel syndrome. *PLoS One* 5, 12, e15591, do1:10.1371/journal.pone.0015591
60. Carvalho, C., Machado Caetano, J., Cunha, L., Rebouta., P, Kaptchuk, T. J. and Kirsch, I. (2016) Open-label placebo treatment in chronic low back pain: a randomized controlled trial. *Pain,* 157, 12, 2766–72.

61. Kaptchuk, T and Miller, F (2018). Open label placebo: can honestly prescribed placebos evoke meaningful therapeutic effects? *BMJ*, 363, k3889
62. Mills, L., Lee, J.C., Boakes, R. and Colagiuri, B. (2023) Reduction in caffeine withdrawal after open-label decaffeinated coffee. *Journal of Psychopharmacology*, doi:10.1177/02698811221147152
63. Carvalho (2016). Op. cit.
64. Martin, P. (1997) *The Sickening Mind: brain, behaviour, immunity and disease*. HarperCollins.
65. Ibid.
66. Jarrett, C. (2019) Op. cit.
67. Williams, P. (1998) *Stories that Heal*. (MP3) HG Publishing. An account of this case history is given on this MP3, along with many others.
68. Rosen, S. (Ed.) (1982) *My Voice Will Go With You: The teaching tales of Milton H. Erickson*. W. W. Norton.
69. Griffin, J. and Tyrrell, I. (2014) *Why we dream: the definitive answer*. HG Publishing, East Sussex.
70. Griffin, J. and Tyrrell, I. (2001) *Hypnosis and Trance States: a new psychobiological explanation*. Human Givens Publishing Ltd for European Therapy Studies Institute.
71. McGilchrist, I. (2021) *The Matter with Things: our brains, our delusions and the unmaking of the world*. Perspectiva Press; Ornstein, R. (1993) *The Roots of the Self*. HarperCollins.
72. Shah, I. (1979) *World Tales*. Allen Lane
73. Harari, Y. N. (2015) *Sapiens: a brief history of mankind*. Vintage.
74. Behe, M. J. (1996) *Darwin's Black Box*. Simon & Schuster.
75. Taylor, S. (2020) Humans aren't inherently selfish – we're actually hardwired to work together. *The Conversation*. https://theconversation.com/humans-arent-inherently-selfish-were-actually-hardwired-to-work-together-144145
76. Rogers, C. (1951) *Client-centered Therapy: its current practice, implications and theory*. Constable, London.
77. Shah, I. (2000) *Knowing How to Know*. The Octagon Press.
78. Andrews, W., Twigg, E., Minami, T., and Johnson, G. (2011) Piloting a practice research network: a 12-month evaluation of the human givens approach in primary care at a general medical practice. *Psychology and Psychotherapy: Theory, Research and Practice*, 84, 4, 389–405.
79. Yates, Y. and Atkinson, C. (2011) Using human givens therapy to support the well-being of adolescents: a case example. *Pastoral Care in Education*, 29, 1, 35–50.
80. Tsaroucha, A., Kingston, P., Stewart, T., Walton, I. and Corp, N. (2012) Assessing the effectiveness of the "human givens" approach in treating depression: a study in primary care. *Mental Health Review*, 17, 2, 90–103.
81. Ibid.

82. Tsaroucha, A., Kingston, P., Corp, N., Stewart, T. and Walton, I. (2012) The Emotional Needs Audit (ENA): a report on its reliability and validity. *Mental Health Review*, 17, 2, 81–89.
83. Ibid.
84. Burdett, H. and Greenberg, N. (2016) *A Service Evaluation of PTSD Resolution Outcome Data*. King's College London.

Chapter 9 – A very human vulnerability: depression (and how to lift it)

1. World Health Organization. (2021) *World Mental Health Report: transforming mental health for all*. World Health Organization, Geneva.
2. Ibid.
3. Ibid.
4. Ibid.
5. Ibid.
6. https://www.mentalhealth.org.uk/explore-mental-health/mental-health-statistics/
7. https://www.nimh.nih.gov/health/statistics/major-depression#part_2565
8. https://www.mentalhealth.org.uk/explore-mental-health/mental-health-statistics/older-people-statistics
9. Office for National Statistics. *Census 2021: Suicides in England And Wales: 2021 registrations.*
10. McManus, S., Bebbington, P., Jenkins, R. and Brugha, T. (eds.) (2016). *Mental health and wellbeing in England: Adult psychiatric morbidity survey 2014*.
11. https://www.hopkinsmedicine.org/health/conditions-and-diseases/depression-his-versus-hers
12. McGrath, E. et al. (1990) *Women and Depression*. American Psychological Association.
13. Nemeroff, C. B. (1998) The neurobiology of depression. *Scientific American*, 278, 6, 28–35.
14. Feldman Barrett, L. (2020) Op.cit.
15. Feldman Barrett, L. and Simmons, W. K. (2015) Interoceptive predictions in the brain. *Nature Reviews/Neuroscience*, 16, 7, 419–29.
16. Seligman in J. Buie, op. cit. "On the whole, you do not find much in the way of depression as we know it – suicide, hopelessness, giving up, low self-esteem, passivity and the like – in nonwestern cultures ..."
17. Kleinman, A. (1995) *World Mental Health: problems and priorities in low-income countries*. Oxford University Press, New York (for the United Nations).
18. Curtis, A. and Tyrrell, I. (2002) A seething mass of desires: Freud's hold over history. Interview in *Human Givens*, 9, 3, 24–31.
19. Shah, I. (1998) *Knowing How to Know*. The Octagon Press. (p158)
20. Lloyd, D. and Rossi, E. (1992) *High Frequency Biological Rhythms: function of the ultradians*. Springer-Verlag, New York.

21. Rossi, E. and Nimmons, D. (1991) *The 20 Minute Break*. J. P. Tarcher Inc., Los Angeles.
22. Kubey, R. and Csikszentmihalyi, M. (2002) Television addiction is no mere metaphor. *Scientific American*, 286, 62–68.
23. Wei, H-T., Chen, M-H., Huang, P-C. and Bai, Y-M. (2012) The association between online gaming, social phobia, and depression: an internet survey. *BMC Psychiatry*, doi:10.1186/1471-244X-12-92; Thomée, S., Härenstam, A. and Hagberg, M. (2012) Computer use and stress, sleep disturbances, and symptoms of depression among young adults – a prospective cohort study. *BMC Psychiatry* 2012, doi:10.1186/1471-244X-12-176
24. Kubey and Csikszentmihalyi, op.cit.
25. Zada, J. (2021) *Veils of Distortion: how the news media warps our minds*. Terra Incognita Press.
26. Ferrie, J. E. (Ed.) (2004) *Work, Stress and Health: the Whitehall II study*. Cabinet Office.
27. Rutter, M. (1971) Parent-child separation: psychological effects on the children. *Journal of Child Psychology and Psychiatry*, 12, 233–60.
28. Richards, M. et al. (1997) The effects of divorce and separation on mental health in a national UK birth cohort. *Psychological Medicine*, 27, 1121–1128.
29. D'Onofrio, B., Emery, R. (2019) Parental divorce or separation and children's mental health. *World Psychiatry*. 18, 1, 100–01.
30. Musick, K. and Meier, A. (2010) Are both parents always better than one? Parental conflict and young adult wellbeing. *Social Science Research*, 39, 5, 814–30.
31. Border, R., Johnson, E. C. et al. (2019) No support for historical candidate gene or candidate gene-by-interaction hypotheses for major depression across multiple large samples. *American Journal of Psychiatry*, doi: 10.1176/appi.ajp.2018.18070881
32. See, for instance: Shadrina, M., Bondarenko, E, A. and Slominsaky, P.A. (2018) Genetic factors in Major Depression. *Frontiers in Psychiatry*, doi: 10.3389/fpsyt.2018.00334
33. Yapko, M. D. (1997) *Breaking the Patterns of Depression*. Doubleday.
34. Seo, E. , Lee, H. et al. (2021) Trait attributions and threat appraisals explain why an entity theory of personality predicts greater internalizing symptoms during adolescence. *Development and Psychopathology*, 34, 3, 1104–14.
35. Danton, W., Antonuccio, D. and DeNelsky, G. (1995) Depression: psychotherapy is the best medicine. *Professional Psychology Research and Practice*, 26, 574–585.
36. Moncrieff, J., Cooper, R. E., Stockmann, T. et al. (2022) The serotonin theory of depression: a systematic umbrella review of the evidence. *Molecular Psychiatry*, doi: 10.1038/s41380-022-01661-0
37. As reported in the editorial "What it takes to update thinking". *Human Givens Journal*, 29, 2, 1.
38. Hewing, E. (2021) Shattered dreams: how REM sleep, not 'chemical imbalance', explains depression. *Human Givens Journal*, 28, 1, 13–19.

39. Delgado, P. L. (2000) Depression: the case for a monoamine deficiency. *Journal of Clinical Psychiatry*, 61, S6, 7–11.
40. Delgado, P. L. and Moreno, F. A. (2000) Role of norepinephrine in depression. *Journal of Clinical Psychiatry*, 61, S1, 5–12.
41. *Diagnosis, Vol. 2 Treatment Aspect.* United States Public Health Service Agency; Depression Guideline Panel. *Depression in Primary Care: Volume 2. Treatment of Major Depression* (1993). Clinical Practice Guideline, Number 5. Rockville, MD: US Department of Health and Human Services, Public Health Service, Agency for Health Care Policy and Research. AHCPR publication No. 93-0551.
42. Of course psychodynamic therapy can, in its early stages, be helpful to some people. We all experience being troubled and worried about things and finding it helpful to talk about our problem with a friend. And, provided the friend is sympathetic, it can create a space wherein we can review what we are worried about and maybe get new perspectives on our problems. And that can be very helpful as long as the conversations are focusing on current problems. It is part of the way we deal with difficulties. But it is when the counselling relationship turns to resurrecting everything that has gone wrong in clients' lives – encouraging them to get emotional about it – that it promotes emotionally arousing introspection and will make people more dysfunctional. This seems likely to be the reason that psychodynamic counsellors have such problems around what they call 'countertransference' where the therapist gets emotionally involved with the client and finds that 'issues' from *their* own past keep coming up all the time. Then they have to go for supervision to talk this through to try and 'understand' it.
43. Mitchell, A. (2006) Two-week delay in onset of action of antidepressants: new evidence. *British Journal of Psychiatry*, 188, 105–106.
44. Dubovsky, S. L. (1997) *Mind-Body Deceptions: the psychosomatics of everyday life.* W. W. Norton & Co.
45. Fournier, J. C, DeRubeis, R. J., Hollon, S. D. et al. (2010) Antidepressant drug effects and depression severity: a patient-level meta-analysis. *Journal of the American Medical Association*, 303, 1, 47–53.
46. Glenmullen, J. (2000) *Prozac Backlash: overcoming the dangers of Prozac, Zoloft, Paxil, and other antidepressants with safe, effective alternatives.* Simon & Schuster.
47. Hengartner, M. P. and Ploderl, M. (2019) Newer-generation antidepressants and suicide risk in RCTs: a reanalysis of the FDA database. *Psychotherapy and Psychosomatics*, 88, 247–8.
48. Schaefer, A., Burmann, I. et al. (2014) Serotonergic modulation of intrinsic functional connectivity. *Current Biology*, 24, 19, 2314–18.
49. Kirsch, I., Huedo-Medina, T. B., Pigott, H. E. and Johnson, B. T. (2018) Do outcomes of clinical trials resemble those "real world" patients? A reanalysis of the STAR*D antidepressant data set. *Psychology of Consciousness: Theory, Research, and Practice*, 10.1037/cns0000164; Kirsh, I. (2008) *The Emperor's New Drugs: exploding the antidepressant myth.* The Bodley Head.
50. Cui, Y. and Zheng, Y. (2016) A meta-analysis on the efficacy and safety of St John's wort extract in depression therapy in comparison with selective serotonin reuptake inhibitors in adults. *Neuropsychiatric Disease and Treatment*, 12, 1715–23.

51. Rapaport, M. H., Nierenberg, A.A., Howland, R. et al. (2011) The treatment of minor depression with St. John's wort or citalopram: failure to show benefit over placebo. *Journal of Psychiatric Research*. 45, 7, 931–41.
52. Sarris, J., Fava, M., Schweitzer, I., et al. (2012) St. John's wort (Hypericum per foratum) versus sertraline and placebo in major depressive disorder: continuation data from a 26-week RCT. *Pharmacopsychiatry*, 45, 7, 275–78.
53. Linde, K., Berner, M. M. and Kriston, L. (2009) St. John's wort for major depression. *Cochrane Database of Systematic Reviews*, 4:CD000448.
54. See, for instance, Andrews, W., Twigg, E., Minami, T. and Johnson, G. (2011) Piloting a practice research network: a 12-month evaluation of the human givens approach in primary care at a general medical practice. *Psychology and Psychotherapy: Theory, Research and Practice*, 84, 4, 389–405; Tsaroucha, A., Kingston, P., Stewart, T., Walton, I. and Corp, N. (2012) Assessing the effectiveness of the "human givens" approach in treating depression: a quasi experimental study in primary care. *Mental Health Review*, 17, 2, 90–103.
55. Griffin, J. and Tyrrell, I. (2002) *Psychotherapy, Counselling and the Human Givens*. HG Publishing Ltd for the European Therapy Studies Institute.
56. Berger, M., van Calker, D. and Riemann, D. (2003) Sleep and manipulations of the sleep–wake rhythm in depression. *Acta Psychiatrica Scandinavica*, 108, s418, 83–91.
57. Palagini, L., Baglioni, C., Ciapparelli, A., Gemignani, A. and Riemann, D. (2013) REM sleep dysregulation in depression: state of the art. *Sleep Medicine Reviews*, 17, 5, 377–90.
58. Wang, Y. Q., Li, R. et al (2015). The neurobiological mechanisms and treatments of REM sleep disturbances in depression. *Current Neuropharmacology*, 13, 4, 543–53.
59. Vogel, G. W. (1979) *The Function of Sleep*. In Drucker-Collins et al. (Eds.), Academic Press, New York, 233–50.
60. Steiger A, Pawlowski, M and Kimura M (2015). Sleep electroencephalography as a biomarker in depression. *ChronoPhysiology and Therapy*, 5, 15–25.
61. Steiger, A. and Pawlowski, M. (2019) Depression and Sleep. *International Journal of Molecular Sciences*, 20, 3, 607.
62. Pflug, B and Tolle, R. (1971) Disturbance of the 24-hour rhythm in endogenous depression and the treatment of endogenous depression by sleep deprivation. *International Pharmacopsychiatry*, 6, 187.
63. "The efficacy of antidepressant activity, across drugs, is directly related to the capacity of drugs to produce large and sustained reductions of REM sleep." In S. J. Ellman and J. S. Antrobus (Eds.), (1991 2nd edition) *The Mind in Sleep*. John Wiley.
64. Tricklebank, M. D. (2019) Serotonin and sleep in M. Tricklebank and E. Daly (Eds.) *The Serotonin System*. Academic Press, pp 181–92.
65. Nemeroff, C. B. (1998) The neurobiology of depression. *Scientific American*, 278, 6, 28–35.

66. Danton, Antonuccio and DeNelsky, op. cit.
67. Morrice, A. (2022). Why sleep matters even more than we think. *Human Givens Journal*, 29, 2, 13–18.
68. Palagini, L. et al (2013). REM sleep dysregulation in depression: state of the art. *Sleep Medicine Reviews*, 17, 5, 377–90.
69. Lotrich, F. E. and Germain, A. (2015) Decreased delta sleep ratio and elevated alpha power predict vulnerability to depression during interferon-alpha treatment. *Acta Neuropsychiatrica*, 27, 1, 14–24.
70. Feng, X. and Wang, J. (2022) Presleep ruminating on intrusive thoughts increased the possibility of dreaming of threatening events. *Frontiers in Psychology*, 13, 809131; Galbiati, A. et al (2017) Worry and rumination traits are associated with polysomnographic indices of disrupted sleep in insomnia disorder. *Sleep Medicine*, 40, e105.
71. Peterson, C. and Seligman, M. E. P. (1984) Causal explanations as a factor for depression: theory and evidence. *Psychological Review*, 91, 341–74.
72. Yapko, M. D. (1999) *Hand-Me-Down Blues: how to stop depression spreading in families*. Doubleday.
73. Pänkäläinen, M., Kerola, T. et al. (2016) Pessimism and risk of death from coronary heart disease among middle-aged and older Finns: an eleven-year follow-up study. *BMC Public Health*, doi: 10.1186/s12889-016-3764-8.
74. Whitfield, J.B., Zhu, G., Landers, J.G. et al. (2020) Pessimism is associated with greater all-cause and cardiovascular mortality, but optimism is not protective. *Scientific Reports*, doi: 10.1038/s41598-020-69388-y
75. Nabi, H. et al. (2010) Low pessimism protects against stroke: the health and social support (HESSUP) prospective cohort study. *Stroke*, 41, 187–90.
76. Martin, P. (1997) *The Sickening Mind: brain, behaviour, immunity and disease*. Harper Collins.
77. See https://www.bmj.com/content/371/bmj.m3745/rapid-responses; https://www.bmj.com/content/376/bmj.064/rapid-responses
78. Dolnick, E. (1998) *Madness on the Couch*. Simon & Schuster.
79. The most important finding from this study is that although both HG and C group interventions were shown to be similarly effective as well as reasonably stable over time, "HG as a therapy is short, lasting only 1 or 2 sessions in total compared with 4-6 in the control group. This might suggest that if HG were integrated in the NHS as a standard treatment and offered as a choice to the patients, it could bring a dual benefit. Firstly, it could prove cost-effective for the NHS, as the introduction of the HG alongside other treatments could substantially reduce treatment waiting lists, which tend to be quite long at present for many patients who are in need for immediate therapy and support. Secondly, it would offer patients a greater choice of treatments; due to the high potential of reducing the waiting lists, they would not have to wait for so long to start their therapy and they may improve in a shorter time period compared to standard treatments where patients normally have to wait for minimum 6-8 weeks before onset of treatment. This might result in the patient's deteriorating or even having to resort to other alternatives (e.g. medication, private counselling, etc.)." Tsaroucha, A., Kingston,

P., Stewart, T., Walton, I. and Corp, N. (2012). Assessing the effectiveness of the "human givens" approach in treating depression: a study in primary care. *Mental Health Review,* 17, 2, 90–103.

80. The same researchers concluded that, "The effectiveness of HG over a shorter time scale may also be a result of its form of psycho-education. It has long been established that a cogent rationale for treatment, accepted by both therapist and client, plays a vital role in treatment. It may be that the manner in which the HG model takes the most viable aspects of existing models (as well as findings from updated neuroscience) provides the patient with a superior understanding of their condition and ways to deal with it independently of the therapy session. Another factor may be the way in which HG regards itself as a bio-psycho-social approach to mental healthcare. Therefore, an HG trained therapist is less likely to inappropriately emphasise the cognitive or emotional aspects of a disorder over important social factors, which may be of greater significance to the client's welfare. As well as psychological insight and emotional support, the client is helped to maintain their sense of social integration. This has benefits to other providers of social care." Tsaroucha, A., Kingston, P., Stewart, T., Walton, I. and Corp, N (2012). Assessing the effectiveness of the "human givens" approach in treating depression: a study in primary care. *Mental Health Review,* 17, 2, 90–103.
81. Thase, M. E. (2000) Psychopharmacology in conjunction with psychotherapy. In C. R Snyder and R. E. Ingram (Eds.), *Handbook of Psychological Change.* John Wiley & Sons.
82. Tsaroucha, Kingston, Stewart, Walton and Corp, op.cit.
83. Woodham, A. (2002) Depressed? Look on the bright side. *The Times,* 6 August.
84. Tsaroucha, Kingston, Stewart, Walton and Corp, op. cit.
85. Weeks, M. (2007) How to live a full life – despite a disabling condition. *Human Givens Journal,* 14, 4, 18–21.
86. Elwick, L. (1999) A headache to end all headaches. *The Therapist,* 6, 3, 28–34. This is a poignant description by a woman who, from being healthy and fit, suffered a transpontine infarction resulting in sudden total paralysis and locked-in syndrome. Over several years she found ways to communicate again, during which her sense of awareness and intelligence remained undimmed. Throughout this ordeal, doctors said that she did not suffer from clinical depression.
87. Woodham, A. op. cit.
88. For one mother's account, see Shoesmith, S. (2016) Postnatal depression – through an HG lens. *Human Givens Journal,* 23, 2, 24–7.
89. See https://www.birthtraumaresolution.com/find-a-therapist/jenny-mullan/
90. See, for instance, Lake, A. (2019) Ten-minute therapy. *Human Givens, Journal,* 26, 1, 34–39; Mahfouz, M. (2007) A much-changed practice. *Human Givens, Journal,* 14, 4, 11–17.
91. See rxisk.org
92. https://www.rcpsych.ac.uk/mental-health/treatments-and-wellbeing/stopping-antidepressants
93. Hewing, E. (2021) op.cit; Moncrieff et al. (2020) op. cit.

Chapter 10 – Terror in the brain: overcoming trauma

1. Charney, D. S., Deutch, A. V., Krystal, J. H., Southwick, A. M. and Davis, M. (1993) Psychobiologic mechanisms of post traumatic stress disorder. *Archives of General Psychiatry*, 50, 295–305.
2. Schein, J., Houle, C. et al (2021) Prevalence of post-traumatic stress disorder in the United States: a systematic literature review. *Current Medical Research and Opinion*, 37, 12, 2151–61.
3. See https://www.ptsduk.org/ptsd-stats/
4. Danieli, Y. (1985) The treatment and prevention of long-term effects and inter generational transmission of victimization. A lesson from Holocaust survivors and their children. In C. R. Figley (Ed.), *Trauma and its Wake*. Brunner/Mazel. 278–294.
5. Wolinsky, S. (1991) *Trances People Live By*. The Bramble Co. Wolinsky gives a clear description of how a person slips into an age-regressed hypnotic trance when they relive a trauma. He developed a technique very similar to Shapiro's EMDR, which keeps the patient's awareness focused on the therapist whilst recalling the trauma, thus stopping them from regressing completely into the traumatic memory. His technique also keeps emotional arousal from rising too high, facilitating the reframing and a recoding of the memory within the cerebral cortex.
6. Etkin, A. and Wager, T. D. (2007) Functional neuroimaging of anxiety: a meta-analysis of emotional processing in PTSD, social anxiety disorder and specific phobia. *American Journal of Psychiatry*, 164, 1476–1488.
7. Hull, A. M .(2002) Neuroimaging findings in post-traumatic stress disorder. Systematic review. *British Journal of Psychiatry*, 181, 102–10.
8. Suvak, M. K. and Barrett, L. F. (2011) Considering PTSD from the perspective of brain processes: a psychological construction approach. *Journal of Traumatic Stress*, 24, 1, 3–24.
9. Yehuda R. and LeDoux, J. (2007) Response variation following trauma: a translational neuroscience approach to understanding PTSD. *Neuron*, 56, 1932.
10. van der Kolk, B. A. (1996) In B. A. van der Kolk, A. C. McFarlane and L. Weisaeth (Eds.), *Traumatic Stress*. The Guilford Press.
11. Kardiner, A. (1941) *The Traumatic Neuroses of War*. Hoebe, New York.
12. Johansen, J P., Tarpley, J. W., LeDoux, J. E. and Blair, H. T. (2010) Neural substrates for expectation-modulated fear learning in the amygdala and periaqueductal gray. *Nature Neuroscience*, 13, 8, 979–86.
13. Roelofs, K. (2017). Freeze for action: neurobiological mechanisms in animal and human freezing. Philosophical Transactions of the Royal Society of London. Series B, *Biological Sciences*, 372, 1718, 20160206.
14. Johansen, J. P. (2010) Op. cit.
15. Brandão, M. L., Zanoveli, J. M. et al. (2008) Different patterns of freezing behavior organized in the periaqueductal gray of rats: association with different types of anxiety. *Behavioural Brain Research*, 188, 1, 1–13.
16. Ibid.

17. Norte, C. E., Volchan, E. et al (2019) Tonic immobility in PTSD: exacerbation of the emotional cardiac defense response. *Frontiers in Psychology*, doi: 10.3389/fpsyg.2019.01213; Volchan, E, Souza, G. G. et al. (2011) Is there tonic immobility in humans? Biological evidence from victims of traumatic stress. *Biological Psychology*, 88, 13–19.
18. Porges, S. W. (1995) Orienting in a defensive world: mammalian modifications of our evolutionary heritage. A Polyvagal Theory. *Psychopathology*, 32, 4, 301–308.
19. Dana, D. (2018) *The Polyvagal Theory in Therapy: engaging the rhythm of regulation*. Norton.
20. See for instance: Grossman, P. (2023) Fundamental challenges and likely refutations of the five basic premises of polyvagal theory. *Biological Psychology*, doi: 10.1016/j.biopsycho.2023.108589; Pearl, M. (2021) The problem with the polyvagal theory. https://medium.com/@maxwellbpearl/the-problem-with-the-poly vagal-theory-c70f55ca6b2e
21. Dixon, A. K. (1998) Ethological strategies for defence in animals and humans: their role in some psychiatric disorders. *British Journal of Medical Psychology*, 71, 417–445.
22. Levine, P. (1998) *Waking the Tiger*. North Atlantic Books.
23. Levine, P. (1998) Blowing off stress. *The Therapist*, 5, 2, 15–20.
24. Morrison, A. R. and Reiner, P. B. (1985) A dissection of paradoxical sleep. In D. J. McGinty, C. Drucken, A. R. Morrison and P. Parmeggiani (Eds.), *Brain Mechanisms of Sleep*. Raven Press, New York, 97–110.
25. Griffin, J. and Tyrrell, I. (2014) *Why we dream: the definitive answer*. HG Publishing, East Sussex.
26. Hewing, E. (2022) Taking leave of our senses. *Human Givens Journal*, 29, 2, 33–39.
27. Tsoukalas, I. (2012). The origin of REM sleep: a hypothesis. *Dreaming*, 22, 253–83
28. Ibid.
29. van Heugten-van der Kloet, D. and Lynn, S. J. (2020) Dreams and dissociation commonalities as a basis for future research and clinical innovations. *Frontiers in Psychology*, 11, 745.
30. Hirst, J. C. (1899) *Is nature cruel? A partial answer to the question: experiences of big game hunters and others while under the attack of wild beasts*. James Clarke & Co.
31. Griffin, J. and Tyrrell, I. (2001) *Hypnosis and Trance States: a new psychobiological explanation*. Human Givens Publishing Ltd for the European Therapy Studies Institute.
32. Spiegel, D., Detrick, D. and Frischholz, E. J. (1982) Hypnotizability and psychopathology. *American Journal of Psychiatry*, 139, 431–437.
33. LeDoux, J. (2002) *Synaptic Self*. Macmillan.
34. Shephard, B. (2000) *A War of Nerves: soldiers and psychiatrists 1914–1994*. Jonathan Cape.
35. Ibid.

36. Brown. W. (1934) *Psychology and Psychotherapy*. London.
37. Sargant, W. (1957) *Battle for the Mind*. Heinemann.
38. Bandler, R. (1985) *Using Your Brain for a Change*. Real People Press.
39. Muss, D. (1991) A new technique for treating post-traumatic stress disorder. *British Journal of Clinical Psyhology*, 30, 91–2.
40. Guy, K. and Guy, N. (2003) The fast cure for phobia and trauma: evidence that it works. *Human Givens*, 9, 4, 31–35.
41. Murphy, M. (2007) Testing treatment for trauma. *Human Givens*, 14, 4, 37–42.
42. Griffin, J. and Tyrrell, I. (2001) *The Shackled Brain: how to release locked-in patterns of trauma*. Human Givens Publishing Ltd for the European Therapy Studies Institute.
43. To find out more information about trainings delivered through Human Givens College please visit www.humangivenscollege.com
44. Schiller, D., Monfils, M-H., Raio, C. M., Johnson, D. C., LeDoux, J. E. and Phelps, E. A. (2009) Preventing the return of fear in humans using reconsolidation update mechanism. *Nature*, 463, 49–53.
45. Benoit, R. G., Paulus, P. C. and Schacter, D. L. (2019) Forming attitudes via neural activity supporting affective episodic simulations. *Nature Communications*, 2019, doi: 10.1038/s41467-019-09961-w
46. Datta, S. and Bryant, R. A. (2019) Reconsolidating intrusive distressing memories by thinking of attachment figures. *Clinical Psychological Science*, doi: 10.1177/2167702619866387
47. Arntz, A., Tiesema, M. and Kindt, M. (2007) *Treatment of PTSD: A comparison of imaginal exposure with and without imagery rescripting*. Journal of Behavior Therapy and Experimental Psychiatry, 38, 4, 345–370.
48. Holmes, E.A., Arntz, A. and Smucker, M. (2007) Imagery rescripting in cognitive behaviour therapy: images, treatment techniques and outcomes. *Journal of Behavior Therapy and Experimental Psychiatry* 38, 4, 297–305.
49. Smucker, M. and Dancu, C. (2000) *Cognitive-Behavioral Treatment for Adult Survivors of Childhood Trauma: imagery rescripting and reprocessing*. Jason Aronson, Northvale, New Jersey.
50. Shapiro, F. (2001) *Eye Movement Desensitization and Reprocessing: basic principles, protocols and procedures*. Guilford Press, New York.
51. National Institute for Health and Care Excellence (2018) *Guideline 116. Post-traumatic stress disorder*. https://www.nice.org.uk/guidance/ng116
52. Gunter, R. W. and Bodner, G. E. (2008) How eye movements affect unpleasant memories: support for a working-memory account. *Behaviour Research and Therapy*, 46, 8, 913–31.
53. Ibid.
54. Callahan, R. (2001) *Tapping the Healer Within*. Contemporary Books, New York.
55. Craig, G. (2011) *The EFT Manual*. Energy Psychology Press.
56. Okhai, F. (2005) Tapping versus rewind. *Human Givens*, 12, 2, 45–6.

57. Hewing, E. (2022). Taking leave of our senses. *Human Givens Journal*, 29, 2, 33–39.
58. Griffin, J. (2005) PTSD: why some techniques for treating it work so fast. *Human Givens*, 12, 3, 12–17.
59. Stickgold, R. (2002) EMDR: a putative neurobiological mechanism of action. *Journal of Clinical Psychology*, 58, 61–75.
60. Gunter and Bodner (2008) Op. cit.
61. Wadji, D. L., Martin-Soelch, C. and Camos, V. (2022) Can working memory account for EMDR efficacy in PTSD? BMC Psychology, doi: 10.1186/s40359-022-00951-0.
62. Harrington, R. and Harrison, L. (1999) Unproven assumptions about the impact of bereavement on children. *Journal of the Royal Society of Medicine*, 92 (May), 230–32.
63. See, for instance: https://www.nhsinform.scot/illnesses-and-conditions/mental-health/phobias
64. See https://www.nimh.nih.gov/health/statistics/specific-phobia
65. See https://www.nimh.nih.gov/health/statistics/obsessive-compulsive-disorder-ocd
66. O'Hanlon, W. H. (1987) *Taproots – underlying principles of Milton Erickson's therapy and hypnosis.* W. W. Norton.
67. The journal, *Human Givens*, has frequently published such examples. Many were collected in *An Idea in Practice: using the human givens approach*, published in 2008. The Human Givens Blog also contains an archive of such material. http://blog.humangivens.com

If you've found the ideas in this book of interest, please review it on our website or Amazon. You might also like the following:

www.humangivens.com
Information about the approach and examples of how it's being used

www.humangivens.com/publications
Explore our full range of books, self-help titles, journals and audio CDs/MP3s

www.humangivens.com/college
Human Givens College is the official source of training in the human givens approach – it offers a wide range of courses, online and in-person, as well as the flexible 3-part Human Givens Diploma in Psychotherapy.

www.hgi.org.uk
The Human Givens Institute (HGI) is the professional body of human givens therapists – its website hosts the international register of human givens therapists and includes information about mental health, free resources, an archive of fascinating articles and interviews from the HG journal, research findings, details of conferences and more...

Podcast
The Good Mental Health Podcast features lively discussions with a wide range of people who share their expertise and explore how the human givens approach has benefited their lives and work – follow on Spotify and all other major podcast streaming services.

www.humangivens.com/foundation
The HG Foundation is a charity that promotes research and public education into the 'givens' of human nature and their application into the treatment and care of those suffering from mental illness. Their work has included a free online course on depression for GPs, a free Depression App and research project funding.

Stay in touch
Sign up to our newsletter: www.humangivens.com/newsletter/

Follow us
Facebook: facebook.com/humangivens
Twitter: twitter.com/humangivens
Instagram: instagram.com/thehumangivens

Index

A

ABC model, 233
abreaction, emotional 341
abstract language, 124, 106, 246–8, 249, 276
abuses of hypnosis, 79–81
abusive relationships, 157, 249
accessing life resources, 280
accessing innate resources, 281
achievement, ix, 98, 150–52, 159–61, 174, 255, 313, 316, 317
activating agent, 233
activating stimulus, vii–iii, 233, 241, 244–45, 281, 330
addiction, 3, 57–58, 98, 101, 173–75, 229, 240, 253, 255, 257–61, 273, 296
addictive behaviour, 174, 225, 231, 259, 261
   affect bridge technique, 262–3
   depression, 315
   expectation theory, 256
   molar memory theory, 261–64
   pattern matching, 260
   reprogramming, 259
   rituals, 260
   self-empowerment, 259
   vulnerability to, 257–8
ADHD (attention deficit hyperactivity disorder) 187–88
adolescents, 144, 155, 161, 166, 173, 179, 283, 287, 296
adverse childhood experiences, multiple, 232
African violet lady case study, 141–2
age regression, 62
aggression, 36, 65, 147, 196
agitation, 147, 308, 318
agoraphobia, 355–57
alarm reaction, 251, 332, 339, 342
   See also fight-or-flight response
Albus Dumbledore, 44
alcohol, 46, 72, 77, 102, 255, 257, 292, 315
alcohol abuse, 11, 102, 173
Aldous Huxley, 201
alpha waves, 166

altered state of consciousness, 7, 64, 73–74
altruism, 136, 140
Alzheimer's disease, 133, 152, 169
   early-onset, 152
American soldiers, 173, 329
Amish community, 290
amnesia, 62, 70, 73, 82, 94, 253, 357
amphibians, 190, 201
amygdala, 132, 236, 237, 241–42, 330–33, 337, 339, 342–43, 346, 349, 353, 356, 361–62
anaesthesia, 73–74, 80, 83, 113, 130
ancient ancestors, 6, 14, 144, 193, 196, 201, 334
anger, 42–43, 45, 65, 101, 123, 124, 131, 135, 170–71, 213, 215, 220, 222, 229, 235, 237, 240, 248–49, 255–57, 261, 263, 288, 307, 329, 342, 351
   abstract language, 248–49
   APET, 240
   attention, 123, 235
   autistic children, 195
   context blindness, 213, 215, 220, 222
   disorders, 123, 255–57
   dreaming, 44–45
   emotional arousal, 65, 235
   hostility and heart, 169–71
   inhibiting, 43
   management, 171, 229, 256
   molar memories, 261–63
   PTSD, 329
animal kingdom, 24, 91, 136, 182
animals, sleep-deprived, 26–27
   social, 19, 137, 178
   warm-blooded, 196
anterior cingulate gyrus, 208–9, 242
antidepressants, 53, 172, 178, 225, 264, 297–99, 303, 309, 320, 325, 327
   and placebo, 298
antipsychotics, 80
   drug company marketing, 82
anxiety, 65–66, 85–89, 109–13, 115, 123, 127, 130, 135, 140, 159, 164, 166, 168–69, 213–14, 222, 229–30, 238–40, 244–45, 287, 360–61

anger, 213
  context blindness, 213–15, 220
  chronic, 167, 180
  depression, 88–89, 166, 214, 245, 287
  emotional needs, 101, 225
  exercise, 180
  extreme, 85, 215, 329, 359
  fear, 113
  generalized, 252
  pain, 113
  trait, 331
anxiety disorders, 98, 109, 231, 296, 315, 328
APET model, vii–viii, 180, 225–85, 233–34, 240–41, 244, 246, 250–51, 253, 255, 257–58, 266, 271, 280–81, 330, 332
  addictive behaviour, 257–61
  anger management, 255–57
  molar memory theory, 261–64
  obsessive-compulsive disorder, 253–44
  perception, 234–55
  panic attacks, 251–52
  placebo/nocebo, 264–72
  in practice, 244–51
  RIGAAR, 278–81
  summary, 281–82
  trauma, 330
aphantasia, 187, 350
aquatic response patterns, 192
arachnophobe, 355
Ariadne's thread, 88
Aristotle, 31, 256
arousal, *see* emotional arousal
Artemidorus, 32
Asclepius, 30–31
ASD (autism spectrum disorders), 210–11
ASD validity, 383
Aserinsky, 18, 34
Asperger's syndrome, 187–88, 204–6, 209, 210–14, 216–18, 220
associative thinking and imagination, 215
attachment, 127
attention, viii–ix, 64–69, 71, 74–79, 91–94, 101, 116–27, 125, 149, 157, 159, 161–63, 207–9, 213, 236, 239–40, 245–46, 267–69, 274, 288–89, 291–92, 301

consciousness, 77
  exchange, 118, 123, 125
  mechanism, 93, 239, 260
  paying, 37, 52, 187, 200, 208
  receiving, 116, 124
  seeking, 161
  starvation, 117
  working memory, 242
attention deficit hyperactivity disorder. *See* ADHD
attributional style, 298
autism, 186–89, 192–97, 200, 202–6, 208–11, 216, 222, 350
  aquatic past theory, 188–204
  gender dysphoria, 186
  high-functioning, 205
autistic spectrum, 181, 186–88, 204, 205, 206, 208–9, 210, 215, 218, 221, 222, 350
autonomic nervous system, 279
autonomy, 97, 108–11, 143, 150, 156, 228

B

babies, 21, 23, 28, 104–6, 126–29, 131, 142, 263
bacteria, 135–6
Bandler, Richard, 343
barbiturates, 341
Baron-Cohen, Simon, 205, 208, 210
basal ganglia, 208, 259
behavioural research, 149
behaviour, 19, 21–24, 37, 67, 71–72, 106–7, 140–41, 158–59, 182, 188–89, 191–94, 196–97, 202–6, 216–17, 220, 227–29, 253–55, 260–61, 271–73
  compulsive, 254, 262
  conditioned, 102
  context-blind, 222
  fishlike, 190, 193
  hallucinatory, 36
  self-destructive, 174, 196
  selfish antisocial, 296
  sickness, 289
behaviour therapy, 227–8, 252
  cognitive, 283
  rational-emotive, 233

beliefs, 31, 90, 109, 112–13, 122–23, 232–33, 235, 260, 264, 267, 282, 287, 291, 294
  destructive post-modernist, 12
  disempowering, 135
  inculcated, 157
  magical, 221
  moral, 103
  psychotic, 124
  religious, 212
benzene, 272
bereavement, 155, 310
bicameral mind, 228
biodiversity, 187
biological clocks, internal, 292
biological inheritance, 95
biological pattern, ancient, 138
biological templates, 100, 182
biophysics, 335
bipolar disorder, 166, 225, 311–12
birds, nestbuilding 22
birth, 20, 28, 90, 104–5, 183, 192, 202, 232, 234, 250, 255
black-or-white thinking, 172, 216, 257 58, 306–307, 312, 321, 323–25, 327
blood pressure, 70, 80, 132, 164, 172, 184
body–mind connection, 168–189
body language, 106
body temperature, 26–27, 206
body tics, 299
Bosnian refugee, 58
bowel, irritable, 176, 265
Bowlby, John, 127
brain, 6, 17–18, 35–37, 40–46, 50–52, 62–64, 66–68, 82–84, 86–89, 130–32, 164–79, 219–21, 234–37, 241–43, 265–68, 274–76, 299–302, 326–31, 333–63
  developing, 20, 132
  empathizing, 206
  evolved, 6
  female, 181–82
  healthy, 10, 82
  human, 107, 129, 211, 237, 259
  left hemisphere, 46, 72–73, 79, 83, 215–16, 221, 243
  male, 183, 206
  neonatal, 338
  neurotypical, 350
  right hemisphere, 46, 70, 72, 79, 83–84, 88, 214–17, 241, 243, 275
  systemizing, 206
brain activity, 17–18, 25, 63, 74–75
brain and body, 164
brain and gut, 177
brain and nerve cord, 6
brain changes, premature, 189, 208
brain connectivity, 166
brain damage, 299
brain development, 19
brain differences, 181
brain grey/white-matter, 133
brain–mind states, 28
brain networks, 46, 65, 238
brain physiology, 210, 240
brain and learning, 150
brain sex differences, 183
brainstem, 19, 35, 54, 337
brain structures, interconnected, 181, 208, 236
brain thermostat, 26–27
brainwashing, 18
brain waves, 19, 179
Brayfield, Celia, 8–9
breathing techniques, 220, 257, 321, 355
British Psychological Society, 282
bullying, 45, 60, 102, 108, 254
burnout, 124, 151
Brown, William, 340
Bzdok, Danilo, 133

C

caffeine withdrawal, 266
Callahan, Roger, 347
Calvin Hall's dream theory, 38
cannabis, 222
cannabis-induced theory of context blindness, 222
capacity, spare, 355
Capgras syndrome, 241
care, primary, 105, 127, 131
carrot (and stick), 174–75
case studies 339–41, 344–45, 351, 353–54
  addiction, 273
  anxiety, 317–20

bereavement, 321–22
control, 109–11, 113–14
depression, 142, 270–1, 320–21, 322–25, 325–27
dreams, 38, 40–42, 48–50, 54, 55–59
obsessive compulsive-disorder, 359–61
phobias, 354–55
trauma, 340–42, 351–53
catastrophizing, 252, 304–05
cave art, 14
CBT (cognitive–behavioural therapy), 229–31, 233, 252, 283
trauma-based, 330
central coherence theory, 209–10
cerebral cortex, 19, 35, 43, 45, 47, 54, 138, 215, 238
chemical imbalance myth, 297
chemical signalling (prediction), 237
childhood, 20, 59, 144, 160–61, 254, 262, 318
children, 8–9, 14–15, 106–7, 115–17, 127–29, 146, 150, 159–62, 179, 188, 199–200, 202–3, 275–78, 290–92, 294–95, 319–20, 354
autism, 188–203
cataracts and perception, 234
rapport building, 106–7
story effects, 277
child-rearing, 126, 145
chimpanzees, 23
choices, making, 23, 50, 72–73, 78, 112, 153, 211–12
chronic inflammation, 173
civil servants, 108–9, 145
client-centred therapy, 228–29
clinical depression, 228, 240, 260, 290, 298, 307, 310, 314, 325
and addictions, 240
clinical use of hypnosis, 64
cognitive-behaviour therapy, see CBT
collective unconscious, 33
Common Cold Unit, 168
community, 98, 101–2, 109, 131–39, 142–44, 157–58, 163, 179–80, 286, 290, 292
breakdown, 290
close-knit, 81
cohesive, 290

connection, 156
human, 119, 142
international, 291
life, 135
local, 322
psychotherapeutic, 250
scientific, 17
self-sufficient agricultural, 138
support, 138
competence, 98, 150–53, 159
complex PTSD (C-PTSD), 329
conditioned responses, 25, 45, 281
conditioning, 90–92, 99, 101–2, 123, 125, 247, 303
consciousness, 28–29, 32–33 60–61, 64, 68, 70, 73–77, 91, 156, 164, 228, 254, 256
context, 152, 205–11, 213–20, 222, 232, 235, 237, 275, 330–31, 333, 342, 345, 348
bigger, 219, 238
multiple, 219
right-brain, 217
social, 208, 244
context blindness, 205, 208–9, 211, 213–17, 220–22
context-dependent meaning, 209
control, 42, 80–81, 97, 108–15, 146, 118, 157, 215, 294, 312–15, 321–22
freaks, 115, 157, 222
influence, 222
locus of, 112
cooperation, 131–32, 136, 139–40, 158, 189, 208
coping skills, 103, 181
corpus callosum, 215
cortex, 19, 37, 43–45, 47–48, 216, 236, 349
hippocampus, 349
occipital, 35
premotor, 6, 107
primary motor, 6
cortisol, 132, 178, 288, 335
counselling, 25, 148, 163, 226–29, 271, 274, 279, 283, 286, 307, 309, 314, 317–19, 323, 325, 351–52
medication, 283

psychotherapy, ix, 89, 226, 240
   conventional, 351
   effective, 209, 228, 251, 234, 286, 314, 327, 360
   ineffective, 25, 229, 271, 332
   insight, 298
   longer-term, 351
   person-centred, 229, 298
   sessions, 57, 59, 321
   skills, 57
   training, 163, 229
   versus psychotherapy, 226
couples therapy, 163
C-PTSD (complex PTSD), 329
creativity, 62, 67, 87, 94, 156, 180, 221–22, 249
Craig, Gary, 347
Crick, Francis, 17
cults, 7, 120, 122, 157, 159, 200
cyberbullying, 293
cycle of depression, 10, 271, 309–10

D

Dana, Deb, 335
Darwin, Charles, 204
Dawkins, Richard, 135
daydreaming, 14, 219, 222
deconditioning, 262, 354
deconstructionalism, 12
'deep unconscious', 227
defeatism, 294
defocusing, 219
Deikman, Arthur, 91, 218
delayed gratification, 290
delusions, 72, 83, 89
Dement, William, 20, 36–37
dementia, 133, 166, 255
depression, vii, 3, 10, 78, 85–86, 88–89, 98–99, 101, 111, 137–38, 140–42, 165–66, 171–73, 222, 229, 231–32, 254–55, 286–328
   acute, 110
   addiction, 101
   anxiety, 111
   chronic inflammation, 173
   cycle of, 10, 271, 309–10
   deprivation, 28, 277
   gene, 296

   heart disease, 172
   learned helplessness, 110
   low self-esteem, 353
   manic, 225, 311
   maternal risk, 128
   mild-to-moderate, 299
   obsessive-compulsive disorder, 226
   postnatal, 314, 317
   psychosis, 85
   REM sleep, 29, 53, 61, 80, 82, 88, 166, 287, 297, 300–1, 304, 310, 311, 312
   schizophrenia, 222
   suicide, 138
   traumatic childhood, 166
desensitization, systematic, 330
detraumatization, 80, 229, 311, 317, 349, 354, 359
developing countries, schizophrenia, 81–82, 88
diabetes, 164, 168
Diagnostic and Statistical Manual of Mental Disorders, 225–26, 311
dissociation, 70–71, 73–74, 82, 208, 219, 337–38, 344–45, 348–49, 361
distorted thoughts, 329
divorce, effects, 295
dopamine, 82, 150, 174, 259
dorsal vagus, 334
dreaming, 29–30, 32–34, 36, 38, 41–44, 46–48, 50–52, 54–55, 60–62, 66, 68–71, 74, 78–79, 81–83, 85, 87, 89, 214, 300–304, 337–38
   depression, *see* depression – REM sleep
   hypnosis, 68–70, 74, 79, 83, 89, 338
   lucid, 68
   metaphor, 31, 39, 41–2, 44–47, 50, 52–3, 57, 59, 60, 69, 79, 83, 84, 87, 88, 214, 301, 337–38
   pattern matches, 47, 50, 51–52, 55, 87
   trance, 66, 68–70
dreaming brain, ix, 13, 30–61, 82, 89, 99
dream interpretation, 30–32
dreams, 28, 30–35, 37–42, 44–50, 54–62, 68–70, 74, 78–79, 81, 83–85, 93–94, 213–14, 300–301, 337, 358
   content, 31, 38–39, 45, 48, 59, 70, 82
   false, 31
   non-REM, 35

remembered, 31
repetitive, 44
right hemisphere, 46
script, 80
sequence, 39, 46
excessive, 302
dream state, 53, 61, 66, 68–70, 73–74, 79, 82–84, 93, 219
psychosis, 84
drug use/abuse, 173, 257, 260, 315, 324
DSM *(Diagnostic and Statistical Manual of Mental Disorders)*, 225–26
DSM-5, 311
duck-billed platypus, 43
Dunbar, Robin, 133
Dumbledore, Albus, 44
dyscalculia, 187
dyslexia, 187

E

education, 13, 100, 131, 247, 273, 275, 282
  emotional, 293
effective counsellors, 234, 240, 246, 286, 362
effective psychotherapy, 89, 180, 225, 309, 313, 316
EFT (emotional freedom technique), 330, 346–50
Einstein, Albert, 204
EMDR, 274, 330, 346–49
emotional arousal, 50, 52, 54, 63, 65, 232–33, 238–40, 267–68, 301, 304, 312–13, 315, 321–22, 327, 342–43, 345
  continuous, 238
  enhanced, 239
  excessive, 240
  high, 238, 255, 278, 306, 312
  lowering, 130, 235
  undischarged, 44
emotional freedom technique, *see* EFT
emotional intelligence, 128
emotional introspection, 240, 298, 302, 309, 314
  excessive negative, 303
emotional needs, 1, 3, 97–180
Emotional Needs Audit. *See* ENA

emotional wellbeing, 150–51, 284
emotions, 68, 99, 166–67, 171, 184, 214–17, 232–33, 236–37, 239–41, 249–50, 254, 261, 266–67, 279, 288–89, 307–8, 321, 346
empathy, 14, 99, 106–7, 128, 216, 279
ENA (Emotional Needs Audit), 100–101, 284–85
endorphins, 174, 180, 268
endowment, genetic, 100
energy expenditure and intake, 19, 26, 87
enlightenment, 247
epilepsy, severe, 72
Epstein, Robert, 149
Erickson, Milton H, 64, 71–72, 75–76, 92–93, 141–43, 260, 272, 343, 361–62
evolution, 7, 132, 135–36, 174, 189–90, 206, 208, 211
  of consciousness, 64
exercise, 97, 99, 115, 119, 121–22, 126, 164, 175, 180, 308, 313
  aerobic, 220, 257, 322
  prescribed, 121
expectation fulfilment theory of dreaming, 38, 44, 46, 61
expectations, 46, 48, 52, 54, 74–75, 246, 248, 251–52, 259, 262, 266–67, 290–91, 293
expectation theory of addiction, 258
exposure therapy, 330, 342–43
external locus of control, 113
extreme male brain theory of autism, 206
eye movement desensitization reprocessing (EMDR), 274, 330
eye movements, 19, 347, 349
  directed, 347
  inducing rapid, 93, 274
  left-to-right, 346
  vertical, 347

F

false memory, 46, 254
  syndrome, 60
faith healing, 264
fear, 109–10, 113, 127, 157–58, 203, 237–38, 248–49, 262–63, 279, 314–15, 328, 339, 353, 355, 357–58, 361–62

circuitry, 331
crowds, 353
enclosed spaces, 353
failure, 177
heights, 353
job interviews and exams, 361
loss, 253
loss of control, 110
memories, 330
open spaces, 353
panic attacks, 113, 355
reactions, 21, 315, 354
response, 113
template, 362
fetishism, 25
fibromyalgia, 166
fight-or-flight response, 67, 77, 167–69, 236, 251–52, 301, 305, 315, 328, 330, 332–34, 336, 355
firefighters, 169
fish ancestors, 191, 193, 195, 199
fish behaviour, 195, 199
Fitzgerald, Michael, 204
fixed mindset, 160, 296
fixed traits, 160
flashbacks, 59, 85, 329, 350
'flooding', 203, 330
flushes, hot, 266
flushing, 165, 332
FND (functional neurological disorder), 177–78, 309
focused attention, 64–65, 74–75, 77–79, 94, 123, 142, 213, 219, 242, 268–9, 292, 322, 333, 338, 348, 361
food intolerance, 177
Frederick II, 117
freeze, 37, 333, 335, 337
Freud, Sigmund, 32–33, 42, 60, 227
friendship, 8–9, 98, 105, 133, 286, 352
Frith, Uta, 210
Fromm, Erich, 115
frontal lobes, 6, 99, 281
fun, 164
functional disorders, 176–77
functional magnetic resonance imaging, 63, 182
fundamentalism in science and religion, 13

G

gambling, 257, 264
Gate of Horn, 31
Gate of Ivory, 31
gender, 181, 183, 185–87, 295
gender dysphoria, 185–86
gendered brain, 181–82
Gender Identity Development Service (GIDS), 186
gene mapping, 296
genetic illness, 296
genetic traits, 306
geniculate body, 35
Genova, Lisa, 152
gestalt, 229, 309
GIDS (Gender Identity Development Service), 186
Gilgamesh, The Epic of, 30
gill arches, 190, 201
goals, 11, 152, 160, 183, 242, 259, 275, 280–81, 314–17
goal setting, 152, 280, 314, 316–7
Goleman, Daniel, 128
Gore Associates, 139
greed, 7, 15, 65, 136, 161–62, 235, 261–63, 288, 291
Greeks, dream interpretation, 30–31
Griffin, Joe, viii–ix, 38, 45, 67, 258, 261, 347–48
Grinder, John, 248
groups, 6, 10, 14, 131–32, 138–41, 144, 158–59, 161, 163, 173, 187, 189
  cohesive tribal, 289
  interconnected, 65
  social, 98, 138, 208
  social craft, 322
groupthink, 158–59
growth mindset, 160
guidance systems, internal, 99, 102–3
guided imagery, 76, 80, 219–20, 239, 250, 252, 254, 259, 274, 281, 300, 313, 316–17, 321, 324, 360
guided imagery techniques, 239
guilt, 127, 308, 330
gurus, 247, 249
gut microbiota, 166

H

Hall, Calvin, 33
hand flapping, 193–5
hangover, 267–68
happiness, 153–54, 247, 249
Hawaiian resilience study 129
Hawthorne Effect, 117–18
headaches, 167, 177, 267–68
head banging, 197
healing, 70, 80, 165, 167, 266, 268
health, 108–9, 113, 115, 132–33, 154–55, 168–69, 269, 271
  alternative, 221
  physical, 37, 79, 102, 140, 166–67, 172, 180, 294
heart attack, 108, 133, 154, 170, 172, 184, 251, 329, 356, 359
heart disease, 126, 130, 167, 170, 172
heart rate, 35, 169, 184, 245
heart-rate variability, 333
helplessness, learned, 25, 110, 112, 146
hemispheres, brain, 44, 72, 79, 215, 236
  left, 72–73, 79, 83, 84, 88, 215, 216, 221, 241, 243, 275
  right, 46, 70, 79, 83, 84, 88, 214, 215, 216, 217, 241, 243, 275
heroin, 173, 260, 268
Hewing, Ezra, 89, 166, 207–8, 222, 259, 297, 337–38, 348
herding instinct, 12
hippocampus, 47–48, 52, 168, 330–31, 337, 345, 348–49
Hippocrates, 31
HIV-positive partners, 154
Hobson, Allan, 27
homoeostasis, 336
hopelessness, 124, 155, 276, 307–8
hormonal changes, 245, 255
hormone replacement medications, 288
hostility, 120, 167, 170, 250
hot-desking, 109
human givens, viii, 3, 9, 75, 81, 82, 84, 87, 88, 89, 97–149, 151–63, 180, 181, 231–32, 255, 273, 281, 336, 361
human givens approach, 9, 181, 252, 261, 282–84, 299, 309–10, 322
Human Givens College, 100, 164, 219, 344
human givens perspective, 81, 87, 141, 156, 299, 320–21, 355
human givens therapists/practitioners, 232, 244, 246, 250, 257–58, 262–63, 285, 310, 313, 316, 319, 355
human givens therapy, 281–85, 309, 312–13, 361, 363
human nature, 7, 10, 13, 17–29, 89, 105, 109, 232
Humanocracy, 139
humiliation, 262–63
humour, 40, 124, 246, 280, 326
Hutterites, 137–39
Huxley, Aldous, 201
Hygieia, 30
hypervigilance, 86, 350
hypnosis, 63–65, 68–76, 79–81, 83, 89, 94, 246, 250, 269, 338, 340–41, 344
  abuses, 79–81
  altered state of consciousness, 64–65, 250
  dreaming, 68–70
  expectation, 74
  placebo, 269
  psychosis, 81
  REM state, programming, 89, 338
  trance, 66
hypnotherapists, 66, 73, 76, 344
hypnotic ability, 68, 76, 92
hypnotic inductions, 71, 74, 76, 339
hypnotic phenomena, 68, 81–82, 94, 253, 357
hypnotic suggestion, 72
hypothalamus, 48
'hysterics', 340

I

Iain McGilchrist, 243
IAPT (Improving Access to Psychological Therapies), 230, 283, 285
ICD (*International Classification of Diseases*), 225
identity, 181, 185–87, 218
  neurodivergence, 181
  sexual, 215, 222
ideologies, 7, 89, 151, 281
  medical model, 225, 327

ideomotor apraxia, 235
ignorance, collective, 163
IKEA, dream metaphor, 56
imagination, 7, 14–15, 17, 65–66, 69, 76, 99, 101, 103, 215–17, 221, 230, 280, 313, 317, 348, 350
imbalance, chemical, 297, 327
immobilisation and dreaming, 337
immobility,
    involuntary, 333
    muscle, 35
immune responses, 132, 167
immune system, 62, 70, 140, 165, 167 69, 171, 180, 268–69, 271, 297, 318
impala, 335–36
imperviousness to pain, 82–83
Improving Access to Psychological Therapies (IAPT), 230, 283, 285
impulsivity, 187
incident debriefing, critical, 330, 343
indoctrination, ix, 62, 121–22
infants, 106, 119, 127
infection, 11, 18, 167, 169, 176–7
inflammation, reducing, 164
    chronic and stress, 173
information processing, 211
ingroups, 157
injection, placebo effect, 268–69
innate resources, 99, 124, 242, 300, 304
instinctive templates, 22, 24, 28, 42, 44, 90, 92, 106, 192
instincts, 21–22, 28, 42–43, 60, 71, 99, 192, 197
    aggressive, 45
    emotional, 46, 216
    herding, 12
    impulsive, 19
    primitive, 281
internal locus of control, 113
International Classification of Diseases (ICD), 225
internal guidance system, 99, 102, 103
interpersonal therapy, 210, 313
introspection, vii, 59, 163, 180, 302, 304, 310, 314–16, 320–21, 324
    continual analytical, 324
    negative, 142, 296, 301, 303, 310, 313–14
    prolonged, 301
intrusive thoughts, 254, 329, 350, 357

J
Jacobs, Tim, 204
Jami, Hakim, 230
Jaynes, Julian, 228
Jung, Carl, 33

K
Kekulé's discovery, 272
kinaesthesia, 105
Kirsh, Irving, 264
Konrad Lorenz, 24

L
lamprey worm, 208
language, 22–23, 33, 46, 106, 117, 124, 192–93, 199, 237, 265, 269
    abstract, 247–48
    acquisition, 106, 200
    complex, 14, 217
    hypnotic, 62
    learning facility, 106
    metaphorical, 88
laughter, depression therapy, 325–27
law of 150, 138
LGBTQIA+, 185
learning, 10, 12–13, 52–54, 64, 67, 107, 122–23, 150, 152, 156, 160, 174, 176, 189–90, 261, 272, 274–75, 280–81, 338, 354
learning theory, 110
LeDoux, Joseph, 237, 339
left-brained context blindness, 215, 216
left hemisphere, 46, 72–73, 79, 83, 84, 215–16, 221, 241, 243, 275
Leslie, Alan, 210
Levine, Peter, 335
locus of control, 113
loneliness, 8, 103, 132–35
long-term psychoanalytic therapy, 231
loss
    privacy, 147
    sense of control, 111
    status, 143, 303
Lovaas technique, 202
Lorenz, Konrad, 24

low self-esteem, 98, 152, 249, 257, 306, 328, 353
Luther, Martin, 32
Lynch, James, 135

M

mammals, 18–19, 22–23, 34, 44–45, 103–4, 167, 189–90, 206–8, 301, 337
   context awareness, 206–8
   fishlike behaviour, 190–91
mania, 311–12
manic depression, 225, 311. *See also* bipolar disorder
marriage, 115, 134, 170, 320
   breakdown, 289
massage, 130
matching movements, 105
McGilchrist, Iain, 243
meaning and purpose/meaningful, 6, 10, 13, 78, 81, 98, 115, 125, 150, 153–56, 161, 163, 174, 228, 251, 258, 287, 290, 302, 308
mechanism
   adaptive, 174
   attention-directing, 94
   attention-switching, 302
   body's fight-or-flight, 169
   defence, 45
   feedback, 339, 358
media, social, 125, 148, 186
meditation practices, 200
memory, 6, 99, 242
   consolidation, 53–54
   depression, 254–55
   false, 60, 254
   hippocampus, 168
   illusory, 80, 325
   low arousal, 339
   molar, 256, 261–63
   music, 164
   negative, 254, 259
   phobia, 353
   PTSD, 329–30, 333, 339
   REM, 45–47, 52–4, 70, 83
   rewind, 345–49, 352, 356
   sleep, 165
   social isolation, 133
   suppressed, 262
   traumatic, 80, 219, 244, 328, 339, 342
memory loss, 299
memory templates, 353, 356
memory trace, 54
menopause, 255, 288
menstruation, 288
mental disorders, 92, 187, 222, 225–26, 230, 232, 287, 311
   common, 151, 287
   See also depression; obsessive-compulsive disorder; panic attacks; phobias, post-traumatic stress disorder; psychosis
mental health, 99, 114–15, 146–47, 150–51, 153, 163, 165–66, 168, 180–81, 232
metaphors, 24, 40–41, 45–46, 79, 83–84, 88, 220, 246, 248, 250, 269, 271–72, 274–76, 278, 281
   appropriate, 24, 79, 252
   calming, 88
   complex, 209
   crude, 269
   dreaming, 31, 39, 41–2, 44–47, 50, 52–3, 57, 59, 60, 69, 79, 83, 84, 87, 88, 214, 301, 337–38
   humour, 246
   pattern matching, 22, 24, 242
   patterns, 24, 40, 246
   physical, 268–69
   placebo, 269
   reframes, 281
   script, 83
   sensory, 84
   stories, 275, 317
mind, 33–34, 38, 58–59, 63–93, 114–15, 124, 164–80, 210–11, 219, 232–35, 239–40, 256–57, 259–60, 275–76, 281, 328
   conscious, 25, 32–33, 60, 236, 238, 254
   imaginative, 75, 221
   subconscious, 237
   unconscious, 25, 32, 33, 60, 77, 171, 179, 214, 236, 249, 254, 255, 275, 276
mind–body connections, 77, 164–180, 282
mindfulness technique, 230, 257

mindset, 172, 260
    fixed, 160, 296
mirror neurons, 107, 132
mitochondria, 136
Mlodinow, Leonard, 241–42
molar memory theory, 256, 261–62
Moncrieff, Joanna, 297
monoamine oxidase inhibitors, 53
mood stabilizers, 311
Morrice, Andrew, 100, 164–6, 303
Moruzzi, Giuseppe, 35
mother's touch, 130
mother tongue, 106
motivation, 117–18, 139, 180, 257, 259, 287, 314
motor control, 132
    baby's, 128
motor excitation, 193
motor inhibition, 193
movement and meaning, 6
muscle relaxation, 274
    progressive, 321
muscles, antigravity, 19, 21, 35
music, 14, 62, 65, 78, 87, 106, 155–56, 164–65, 198, 292
Musselman, Dominique, 172
mysticism, 67, 156
myth, 33, 165, 182
    ancient Greek, 273
    antidepressant, 393
    archetypal, 34. See also storytelling

N

naps, 27
National Autistic Society, 186, 188, 197, 204
National Institute for Health and Care Excellence (NICE), 347
National Society for Autistic Children, 197
natural ultradian rhythms, 292
nausea, 266, 299
Nazism, 159
near-infrared spectroscopy, 63
negative life experiences, 254, 271
negative ruminations, 254, 271
negative suggestions, 269
nerve cord, 6

nerves, cranial, 201
nervous system, 37, 334–35
    autonomic, 54, 301, 334
    central, 20, 166, 192, 235
    parasympathetic, 257, 333–34
    sympathetic, 334
nest-building, 22–23
networks
    emotional, 68
    emotional salience, 242
    executive, 343
    executive control, 242
    intrinsic brain, 331
    neural, 155, 330
    social, 133, 144, 178, 183
    strong support, 133
    traditional, 138–39
neurobiology, 8, 264
neuroception, 334
neurodivergence, 181, 187
Neurolinguistic Programming (NLP), 249, 343–44
neurologists, 177–78
neurons, 10, 19, 48, 51, 107, 132, 215, 237
    mirror, 107, 132
    motor, 237
neurophysiologists, 107
neuroplasticity, 155
neuroscience, ix, 89, 182, 281, 328
neuroses, 32, 163
neurotoxicity, 299
neurotransmitters, 99, 298
neurotypical, 187, 202, 211
newborns, 21, 104–5, 166, 192
NHS Talking Therapies, 230
NICE guidelines on depression, 283
nightmares, 33, 59, 70, 220, 286
NLP (Neurolinguistic Programming), 249, 343–44
nocebo effect, 264, 269, 271, 276
nominalization, 246, 248
non-REM awakenings, 34
noradrenaline, 298
norms, 112, 185, 293
    cultural, 65
    social, 182

nutriment, 104, 116, 122–23, 271
nutrition, essential, 98

O

observing self, 89, 91–92, 99, 123, 218–19, 256, 345, 358, 361
obsessions, 7, 222, 252–53, 357
obsessive compulsive disorder. *See* OCD
obsessive thoughts, 166, 253, 360–61
OCD (obsessive compulsive disorder), 187, 253–54, 357–62
OCD thoughts, 254, 358–59
Odysseus myth, 273
Ondine curse, 44
Oneirocritica, 30–31
open-label placebo treatment, 265
optimism, 275, 312, 327
orbitofrontal cortex, 189, 209
organisms, single-celled, 175
orientation response, 37, 50, 126, 274, 292, 301–2, 308, 337–38, 348
orientations, instinctive mammalian, 202
Origin of Consciousness, 228
Ornstein, Robert, 170, 275
Orwell, George, 158
O'Sullivan, Suzanne, 178
overcrowding, 134, 146–47
overgeneralizing, 231
overindulgence, counterweight, 257
overload, sensory, 215, 218

P

pacing, 107
PAG (periaqueductal gray), 333
pain, 62, 64, 69, 71, 80, 82–83, 109–10, 112–14, 130, 164, 175–77, 265–66, 268–70, 338
  acute, 255
  anxiety, 110
  chronic, 166
  control, 70, 83
  emotional, 225, 318
  hot flushes, 266
  memories, 262
  misery, 305
  joint, 177
  severe abdominal, 176, 318
  suppressed, 318

pain relief, 113, 269
  post-operative, 112, 130
Palaeozoic fish, 196
pandemic, covid-19, 104, 115
panic, 245, 354–56, 362
panic attacks, 113, 220, 244–45, 251–52, 286, 315, 321–22, 325, 329, 350, 353, 355–57, 359
  agoraphobia, 355
  nightmares, 220
  obsessive-compulsive disorders, 315
paralysis, 37, 69–70, 79, 177, 337–39
  mental, 240
  muscle, 19, 35, 82
paranoia, 83, 86, 227
paraphrasing technique, 278
parathyroid glands, 129
parents
  divorced, 295
  middle-class, 295
  new, 147
  over-demanding, 160
  supervising, 148
parkinsonism, 79, 299
Parkinson's disease, 299
pattern matching, 13, 22, 28, 47, 50, 241, 245, 247, 249, 252–54, 260, 262, 267–68, 356, 362
  abstractions, 124, 247, 249
  addiction, 253, 260–61
  agoraphobia, 356
  anger, 171
  APET, 232, 233–34, 240, 244
  babies, 104
  crude, 342
  depression, 305
  dreaming, 52, 55
  EFT/EMDR, 349
  faulty, 252
  goals, 280–81
  innate resource, 99
  language, 106, 192
  metaphorical, 24, 25, 99, 242, 246, 272, 250, 272
  molar memories, 261–62
  nocebo, 271
  non-conscious, 238
  OCD, 253

panic attacks, 356
placebo, 266–69
post-hypnotic, 67
predictions, 51
psychosis, 87
PTSD, 330, 332, 339, 342–3, 346
rapport, 106–7
storytelling, 272, 275
pattern perception, 106
pectoral fins, 195, 199
pensieve, 44
perception, viii, 7–8, 10, 12–13, 15, 69–70, 87, 125, 145–46, 193–94, 204–5, 234–36, 239–41, 248–49, 274–75
  autism, 192–97
  emotional arousal, 239–41, 321
  hypnosis, 74
  illusory, 84
  pattern matching, 171, 249
  reality, 69, 239
  REM, 74, 84,
  refined, 7, 11, 162, 274, 278
  sensory, 69, 83, 91
  shared, 125, 227, 248
  skewed social, 133
peptic ulcers, 167
perfectionism, 160–61, 305
periaqueductal gray, 333
perimenopause, 245
Perry, John, 147
personality, 7, 57, 98, 122, 143, 306
personality changes
  cats, 36
  hormonal, 245
personality research, 306
person-centred counselling, 229, 298
pessimism, 167, 276, 289, 303–4, 306–8, 312, 315, 323
Petronius, 31
PET scans, dreaming and hypnosis, 47, 63
Pew Research Center, 149
PGO spike activity, REM sleep, 35–37, 300–301
phobia cure, fast, 344
phobias, viii, 231, 240, 323–24, 353–55, 361–62
phones, mobile, 112, 147, 293

physical needs, 3, 5, 11, 97–100, 102, 164–65, 304, 310
placebo effect, ix, 172, 231, 264–69, 298–99
  open label, 265
  prescribed, 265–66
Plato, 31
platypus, duck-billed, 43
pleasure, 153, 174–75, 194, 197, 257 59, 262–63, 286, 302, 308, 317, 322
political correctness, 11
politics, 90, 159, 181, 183, 291
polyvagal theory, 333–35
Porges, Stephen 334
positive abstractions, 249
positive attitude, 255, 265, 280
positive emotions, excessive, 262
positron emission tomography, 63
posthypnotic suggestion, 66–68, 70–73, 80, 89, 253, 339
postmodernism, 11–12
post-traumatic stress, 59, 240, 255, 331, 346
post-traumatic stress disorder, 29, 58, 219, 240, 286, 311, 315, 328, 339, 343–6, 353, 362. *See also* PTSD
Potter, Harry, 44
prediction, 51, 237–8, 289
prefrontal cortex, 19, 42, 46–47, 155, 214, 242, 331, 343
  evolved, 42
  executive, 242
  medial, 19
pregnancy, 245, 288, 317
primates, 138, 189–90, 208
privacy, 86, 98, 101, 146–49, 159, 164
  needs, 146–9
problem solving, 173, 183, 272, 292, 298, 314, 321
programming, 19–20, 37, 67–68, 89–90, 192, 249, 254
  genetic, 75
  instinctive, 18, 23, 46
programming trance states, 66–67
Prozac, 298
psychiatrists/psychiatry, vii, ix, 58–59, 81, 91, 188, 225, 227, 244–45, 297, 309, 325, 340, 349

psychoanalysis, 60–61, 227, 256, 303
psychobabble, 248, 286
psychobiology, 300
psychodynamic, 229, 309, 317
psychodynamic 'insight', 229
psychodynamic schools of therapy, 298
psycho-education, 284, 310
psychological trauma, 102–3, 317
psychologists, ix, 80, 92, 97, 118, 188, 229, 232, 264, 342, 351
psychology, 89, 152, 281–82, 335, 340
  academic, 228, 340
  cognitive, 152
  eastern, 91, 118
  human, 18, 94
psychosis, 18, 29, 81–82, 84–85, 87–89, 166, 221, 225, 328
  creative thinking, 84
  developing, 89
  risk, 166
psychotherapy, 89–90, 159, 163, 219, 226–27, 231, 248, 279, 282, 298–99, 309, 313, 326–27
psychotherapy and counselling, difference, 226–27
PTSD (post traumatic stress disorder), viii, 29, 219, 222, 285, 328–31, 336, 339–40, 342, 344, 347–48, 350, 353, 355, 362
  complex, 329
  cure, 330
  developing, 339
PTSD Resolution, 285
puberty, 144, 255
puberty blockers, 187

R

randomized controlled trials of CBT, 230
rapid eye movements, 17–18, 34–35, 44, 83, 165, 192, 337–38, 345, 347.
  See also REM
  absorption, 69
  depression, viii
  hypnosis, 93, 338
  PGO spikes, 35
  programming state, 192
  psychosis, 83
  rewind, 345

sleep, 34–35, 165
trance, 274, 337
rapport building, 76, 105–6, 126, 202, 278, 281, 316
RIGAAR, 278–81, 316
rational-emotive behaviour therapy, 233
rats
  experimental, 26
  newborn, 20
  sleep-deprived, 26–27
  unstroked, 129–30
reality, 7, 11, 12, 28, 30–31, 46, 48, 50–51, 65–66, 68–69, 74–80, 82–84, 88, 90–91, 93, 124–25, 192, 219, 233–35, 281, 306, 358
  alternative, 66, 69
  alternative visionary, 68
  autistic child's, 200
  bizarre, 79
  conscious, 237
  escape, 77
  hallucinatory, 83
  imaginary, 80
  inward, 69
  metaphorical, 88
  REM, 48
reality generator, 13, 61, 66, 68–69, 75, 84
reasoning, universal, 217
Rechtschaffen, Allan, 26–7
reciprocal altruism, 136
recording dreams, 38
recording sleep phases, 19
recurrent thoughts, 308
recurring nightmares, 58, 166, 329
redundancy, 173, 289, 294, 303, 313
reflective listening, 278–89
rehearsal, positive mental, 37, 142, 281, 346, 356
reification, 246
relationship breakdown, 177, 253, 295, 305, 357
relationships, 6, 9, 23, 25, 105, 107, 109, 111, 183, 249, 256, 259, 306–7, 310, 318–19
  close, 125, 128, 168, 324
  cooperative, 282
  disintegrating, 257
  failed, 303

good, 353
homosexual, 185
improving, 317
intimate, 101, 157
loving, 98, 332, 351
supportive, 129
symbiotic, 276
therapeutic, 59
relationship skills, 298, 353
relaxation, 75, 77, 250, 252, 257, 259, 292, 338, 344, 356, 360–61
relaxation techniques, 312
religious groups, 7, 122, 138, 159, 161
REM (rapid eye movement), 17–18, 23, 27–28, 34–36, 67, 69, 82, 89, 192, 337–38, 345, 347
REM sleep, 18–22, 26–28, 30, 34–38, 43–46, 52–55, 166, 274, 300–301, 308–12, 337–38, 348–49
  amount of, 20, 36
  deprivation, 27
  disordered, 309
  dreaming, 35
  excessive, 53, 82, 303–4, 311
  extra compensatory, 300
  mechanism, 61
  prevented, 54
  rebound, 27
  switching off, 337
  switching on, 337
  terrestrial animals, 44
REM state, vii–viii, 17–18, 20–21, 27–29, 35–37, 44–45, 48, 61, 68–71, 74–75, 82–84, 93, 250, 274, 337–39
  definition, 17–18
reptiles, 19, 22, 190, 206, 334
resilience, 128–29, 133, 154, 160
resources, 99–100, 102, 247–49, 278, 281, 286, 309, 317, 361–62
  basic physical, 99
  brain's, 242
  human, 179
  innate, 124, 304
  internal, 274
  mental, 180
reward chemical, 150
reward processing, 209

rewind technique, 219, 250, 252, 254, 343–46, 348, 350–51, 353–55, 357, 359, 362
  agoraphobia, 252
  OCD, 254
  panic attacks, 252
  PTSD, 343–46
  stages of the process, 344–46
RIGAAR model, 278–81, 316
right- and left-brained context blindness, 215–16
right hemisphere, 46, 70, 79, 83, 84, 88, 214, 215, 216, 217, 241, 243, 275
  activation, 46
  function, 46
  properties, 241
  psychosis, 88
Rippon, Gina, 182–83
rituals, viii, 7, 31, 62, 137, 213, 218, 253, 260, 268, 357–61
Roberts, Monty, 22
Rogerian school, 229
Rogers, Carl, 278
Rossi, Ernest, 75
Rumi, 122
rumination, 304
  excessive, 154

S

Sacks, Oliver, 193
Saint Jerome, 31
salience network, emotional, 242
Sandwell Primary Care Trust, 283
Sapiens, 276
Sargant, William, 341–42
schizophrenia, ix, 80–83, 89, 166, 207, 222, 226, 232
  pain resistance, 83
  sleep, 166
  therapy, 88–89
  waking reality and dreaming brain, 82–88
science and spirituality, 13
SCoPEd, framework, 226
SDT (self-determination theory), 150
security, 97, 104–8, 108, 125, 157, 165, 184
  needs, 104–8

seizures, 164
  dissociative, 177
selective serotonin reuptake inhibitors (SSRIs), 225, 298, 299
self, 41, 91, 115, 170, 217–18, 358
  sense of, 217–18
self-blame, 304, 306–7
self-determination theory (SDT), 150
self-esteem, 160, 258–59, 294, 320–21
self-harm, 166, 288
self-healing, 266
self-identification, 185
self-interest, 208
self-involvement, 170
selfish gene theory, 135
self-mutilation, 196, 203
Seligman, Martin, 110
sensory patterns, incoming, 51
sensory processing difficulties, 203
serotonin, 36, 297–98, 310, 314
  levels, 297, 310, 314
sex, 25, 32, 44, 97, 126, 181, 183–85
  differences, 206
  opposite, 126, 185, 235
  wrong, 185
sexual abuse, 59, 80, 258, 325
sexual assault, trauma, 329
sexual identity, 185–86
sexual daydreaming, 289
sexual dysfunction, 299
sexual frustration, anger, 255
Shah, Idries, 118, 121–22, 275, 282
Shapiro, Francine, 347
shell-shock, *see* post-traumatic stress disorder
shutdown, 333–34, 337
Sigmund Freud, 32, 227
Sinclair, Jim, 193
single mothers, young, 134
Sir Lawrence Olivier, nerves, 239
sleep, 17–18, 20, 23–24, 26–28, 32, 34–39, 44–45, 85, 97, 99, 109, 165–66, 300–303, 311–12, 316, 340–41
  alpha-delta, 166
  apnoea, 166
  cycles, 165
  deficit, 303
  disturbed, 166
  enough, 165
  good, 166, 328
  hemisphere, 44
  non-REM, 27, 34
  patterns, 45, 302–3
  paradoxical, 17
  paralysis, 337
  problems, 172, 288
  quality, 165
  reduced slow-wave recuperative, 303
  slow-wave, 18–19, 34, 303
  See also rapid eye movements, REM and REM sleep
sleep deprivation, 26–27, 43, 109
sleep research, 17, 26, 34–35, 44, 48, 349
sleep temples, 30
Sobel, David, 170
social brain, 131
social isolation, 8, 132–33
social prescribers, 180
social skills, 8–9, 141, 143, 280, 286, 293, 310, 315
  training, 8, 229
social support, 104, 131–35, 141
sodium valproate, 311
soldiers
  narcotics, 173
  traumatized, 329, 341–42
solution-focused approaches to therapy, 231, 307, 327, 361
South Sea Bubble, 159
Spielman, Amanda, 8
spirituality, 7, 13, 162
sport, 10, 78, 116, 151–52, 156, 183
squeeze machine, 203
SSRIs (selective serotonin reuptake inhibitors), 225, 298, 299
Staffordshire University, research, 284
stage hypnotists, 67, 69, 80–81, 83, 94, 274
stages of sleep, 27, 34, 165
status, 98, 101, 143–45, 151–52, 159, 161, 183, 185, 303, 310
  needs, 143–45, 161
  social, 144
Still Alice, 152

stimulation, needs, 127–28, 133, 146, 162, 308, 312
  autistic children, 195, 197, 312
St John's wort, 299
stories, vii–viii, 16–17, 62, 209–10, 227–28, 252, 254–55, 268–79, 316–17, 321, 323–24
  apposite, 252
  classical, 275
  patterns, constructive 275
  reframing, 79, 246, 276, 317
storytelling, 272
straight-line thinking, 102, 204, 213, 243
streams of attention, separate, 207–28, 215–16
strengths, 42, 112, 161, 181, 187, 226, 240, 249, 259, 299, 322
stress, 144, 146–47, 167–69, 171–73, 178, 251, 253, 288–89, 293–94, 331, 355
  anxiety and depression, 130, 214, 293
  chronic, 167–68, 289, 303
  constant, 102
  emotional, 337
  extreme, 88, 169
  health impact, 167-8
  levels, 146, 203, 215, 275, 280, 322, 356–57
  overload, 88, 137, 168
  post-traumatic, 108, 220, 260, 331
  pregnancy-related, 166
  raised, 252–53, 356–57, 359
  reactions, 77, 115, 294
  symptoms, 101
stress hormones, 77, 168–69, 251, 256, 292
stretching, mental 10–11, 13, 97, 153, 175
substance abuse, 78, 222, 295
suggestibility, ix, 64, 66, 331
suicidal thoughts, 103, 125, 155, 166, 288
suicide, 138, 155, 288, 299, 307–8, 320–23, 325, 353
Sumeria, ancient, 30
survival of the fittest, 276
survival templates, 330, 339
survivors, concentration camp, 329
systematizers, 206

T

tapping technique, 330, 347–48, 350
Tavistock Clinic's Gender Identity Development Service, 186
techniques, breathing, 220, 257
technique, emotional freedom, 330
technology, 137–39, 149, 290–91
telepathic communication, 85
television, 57, 59, 85, 111, 175, 291–92, 332, 345
television soap operas, 275
temperature regulation, rats, 27
templates, 12, 28, 43, 46, 192, 201–2, 216–17, 234–35, 239–40, 277–78, 281, 332, 342, 344
  core, 43
  imprinted, 343
  innate genetic, 12
  inner, 11, 235, 305, 309
  learned, 233
  metaphorical, 235, 273
  parallel processing, 216
  refined, 12
Temple Grandin, animal behaviourist, 193, 203–4
temporal lobes, 241
tension headaches, 130
Thaut, Michael, 155
'them and us' mentality, 157
theory of mind, 208, 210
therapists, vii–ix, 24, 58–61, 76, 80, 88, 90, 92, 123–24, 143, 147, 220, 232–33, 240, 244, 246, 249–50, 278, 280, 283, 285, 300, 309, 347, 349, 358
  human givens, 88, 141, 180, 232, 244–63, 250, 257–58, 263, 282–86, 310, 335, 355
  hypno-, 73, 344
  insight, 317
  occupational, 88
  psychoanalytical, 60
  solution-focused, 307
therapy, 60, 124–26, 142–43, 180–81, 226–32, 250, 279–82, 285–86, 298–99, 309, 317–19, 327
  alternative, 77
  behaviour, 202, 252

client-centred, 228
cognitive, 233, 252, 254, 356
cognitive-behavioural, viii, 229, 252, 356
couples, 183
effective, 45, 225–234, 251, 342, 358, 361–62
exposure, 343
holding, 203
human givens, 181, 244–63, 282–86, 312, 313, 316, 363
hypno-, 78
insight, 317
interpersonal, 310, 313
nocebo, 271
placebo, 272
psychoanalytical, 60, 227, 298
psychodynamic, 330
rational-emotive, 233
scaling, 327
solution-focused, 231, 361
trauma-focused cognitive-behavioural, 347
thought field, 347
thinking
black-or-white, 239–40, 304, 307, 324
catastrophic, 308
contextual, 215
creative, 84
critical, 46
disturbed, 124
global, 323
logical, 209, 215
negative, 317
psychotic, 220
straight-line, 102, 204, 213, 243
suicidal, 103, 288
thinking styles, attributional, 321
Thomas, Nancy, 128
thought field therapy, 347
time distortion, 357
Tinbergen, Niko, 191
Tourette syndrome, 187
torture, use of, 43, 114, 236
touch, 28, 51, 62, 129, 30, 184, 198, 205, 346
traditional Eastern psychology, 91

traditional story, appropriate, 273
traditions, shamanistic, 7
trainee psychotherapists, 163
training (of therapists) 76, 100, 163, 226, 229, 273, 282–83, 317, 327, 344, 363
trance states, ix, 62–71, 73–78, 79, 91–94, 172, 200, 239, 267, 269–71, 274, 276, 288, 337–39, 344, 346
  behaviours, 62
  depression, vii, 78, 172, 229, 288, 316, 320, 326
  dreaming, 68
  emotional, 65, 91, 239, 267, 288, 357
  expectation, 74–75, 267
  focused attention, 64–66, 69, 77, 269, 288–89
  hypnosis, 63, 76, 338, 344
  induction, 62, 94, 200
  literalism, 212
  observing self, 91
  OCD, 357–58
  negative, 172
  phenomena, 76
  phobia, 361–62
  posthypnotic, 66–68, 71–73
  programming, 66–68
  psychosis, 93
  PTSD, 339
  REM state, 66–69, 71, 74–75, 93, 274, 337–39, 356
  stories, 269, 270–71, 276
  trauma, 330
transcendence, 91, 200–01
transgender, 185
transition, 185–86
trauma/traumatic, viii, 102, 110, 129, 328–63. *See also* post-traumatic stress disorder
  addictive behaviour, 231
  amygdala, 346
  childhood, 166
  event, 316, 329, 331–32, 339, 342, 345–47, 351
  experiences, 154, 221, 250, 329
  memory, 80, 219, 333, 339, 345–47, 349
  stress, 103, 352, 345

suicidal thoughts, 103
survivors, 331
treatment, 255, 347, 352. *See also*
rewind
victims, 340
template, 340, 345
trials, 85, 139, 226, 231, 264, 284,
   double-blind, 264
   randomized controlled, 230, 268, 298
tribes, 15, 123, 132, 136–37
   cohesive, 137
tribes problem, 136
tulip mania, 159
tyranny, 13, 162
Tyrrell, Ivan, viii–ix, 67, 85, 86

U

Ugly Duckling story, 277
ulcers, stress, 167
uncertainty, 112, 114–15, 290, 293, 297
unconscious mind, 25, 32, 33, 60, 77, 171, 179, 214, 236, 249, 254, 255, 275, 276
unemployment, 284, 290
Upper Palaeolithic period, 6
Uta Frith, 210
Uyghurs, 179

V

vagus nerve, 333–34
   dorsal vagus, 334
   ventral vagus, 334
validity, predictive, 284
Vermeulen, Peter, 210
verrucas, 270–71
vertebrates, 19, 201, 207–8, 259
veterans, 285, 329
Vietnam War, 173, 328
violence, 238, 311, 315
   domestic, 177, 232
   political, 290
virus, 168–69, 172, 307
   common cold, 168
   herpes, 168
vision, tunnel, 141, 172, 240
visual illusions, 83
VK dissociation technique, 344

Voice of Patients research group, 178
voice recognition technologies, 149
voices, hearing, 83, 86

W

Wagstaff, Graham, 71–73
Wall, Patrick, 109
warm-bloodedness, 23, 26, 27, 206
'water babies' theory of autism, 187–89, 197–99, 201
Watson, James, 17
Western Electric Company, 116
whirling dervishes, 200
white/gray matter ratio, 183
Whitehall studies, 109, 145
Whyte, William H, 158
Wikipedia, 227
Williams, Pat, 273
willpower, 108
Winn, Denise, 134
wisdom traditions, 13
withdrawal effects, drugs, 178, 225, 226, 299, 309, 327
withdrawal symptoms, 174–75, 259, 266, 299
Wogan, Terry, 40
working memory, 6, 242, 349
workplace, bullying, 108
World Health Organization, 225
World Tales, 275
worrying, 61, 101, 103, 115, 165, 168, 280, 304, 308, 313, 315–16, 319, 324–25
Worth, Harry, 55–56

Y

Yuval Noah Harari, 276

Z

Zajonc, Arthur, 234
zero-hours contract, 294